NELSON: BRITANNIA'S GOD OF WAR

by the same author

TRINCOMALEE: THE LAST OF NELSON'S FRIGATES
WAR AT SEA IN THE AGE OF SAIL
THE FOUNDATIONS OF NAVAL HISTORY
THE CRIMEAN WAR: GRAND STRATEGY AGAINST RUSSIA 1853–1856

NELSON
Britannia's God of War
ANDREW LAMBERT

ff

faber and faber

First published in 2004
by Faber and Faber Limited
3 Queen Square London WC1N 3AU

Typeset by Faber and Faber Limited
Printed in England by Mackays of Chatham plc, Chatham, Kent

The right of Andrew Lambert to be identified as author
of this work has been asserted in accordance with Section 77
of the Copyright, Designs and Patents Act 1988

A CIP record for this book
is available from the British Library

ISBN 0-571-21222-0

2 4 6 8 10 9 7 5 3 1

To my father David Lambert,
another Norfolk man of the sea

Contents

Illustrations

MAPS AND CHARTS

Preface

I began this book after two decades researching, writing and teaching naval history. It was the last task that persuaded me to make the attempt. Students possess a remarkable ability to question received wisdom, and always expect better answers. I had long believed that Nelson's was a story so often told as to defy re-interpretation, but such thoughts were soon changed by the experience of trying to teach from the extant literature. The questions that my students posed were not biographical: they wanted to know about his education, his approach to strategy, his relationship with other senior officers, and the longer view of his significance. Why was Trafalgar such a landmark? Without those questions this book would not have been written. It was in the Naval History classes of the past decade that much of this approach was developed.

With the bicentenary looming, promising a dramatic upsurge of interest in the greatest Admiral, there would be no better time to address these questions. The fortuitous combination of an idea for a book and a publisher with the courage to try another Nelson has left me eternally indebted to my editor at Faber, Julian Loose, whose merits will only be truly understood by those who have worked with him. His oversight of the project has been one of its principal pleasures. As the idea turned into a manuscript I was fortunate to find willing and able readers. Michael Budden spoke up for the opposition, Michael Tapper provided a view of Nelson from Burnham Thorpe and a long immersion in the subject, while Colin White shared the fruits of his immense labours in the field, labours which have done much to widen our view of the man, and to uncover more of his legacy. Because they asked such good questions their input was invaluable; by seeing the work through their eyes my judgements have been questioned, and refined.

Support for the project was equally forthcoming from the staffs of the various libraries, museums and archives in which it was researched: the British Library, the National Archives, the National Maritime Museum, the Nelson Museum at Monmouth, the libraries of the University of Michigan and Duke University, North Carolina. The library of King's College, London, holds a wealth of important literature on the subject. The cultural impact of Nelson was equally significant, with major collections at Greenwich, Portsmouth, Monmouth and Great Yarmouth, along with the enduring presence of HMS *Victory*. Yet for me, and I suspect many others, the true meaning of Nelson only becomes clear in the crypt of St Paul's. My debt to those scholars whose ideas and research have contributed to this book, from the eminent students of Nelson to art historians and strategists, is reflected, if not adequately repaid, in the footnotes and bibliography. What merit this book has is largely a reflection of the range and quality of work on which it is based.

A very different kind of research took me to sea on the replica of HMS *Endeavour* in 2001. I will be eternally grateful to the BBC for the opportunity to serve in an eighteenth-century square rigger and learn about time and motion, the camaraderie of the sea and the inner life of the ship. They were also kind enough to send me home. In 2003 another BBC project took me to a number of Nelson sites, widening my understanding of critical campaigns. The University of Copenhagen hosted a lecture on the posthumous reputation of the hero, and provided an opportunity to see the site of the battle and the passage of the Sound at Elsinore. Similarly the National Museums and Galleries on Merseyside hosted a lecture on the artistic response to Nelson's death at the Walker Gallery, alongside two of the major canvases.

My family has given more help than I have a right to ask. Fortunately for Zohra and Tama-Sophie Calvi was a great holiday destination, but on so many occasions when the needs of an author have clashed with other demands they have understood. My parents have provided constant support, emphasising one thing that I am proud to share with my subject. I am a Norfolk man. While writing this book I incurred another debt, to the surgical team and all the staff at the Papworth Hospital in Cambridgeshire. Their skill and care transformed my father's life.

My colleagues at King's College provided the encouragement and consideration that make the academic community such a positive working environment. The support of the Tubney Charitable Trust has enabled the College to increase the provision of Naval History, uncovering yet more excellent students anxious to pursue the subject. That support has been greatly appreciated by the staff and students of the Laughton Naval History Unit. The Navy Records Society has provided another focus for Nelson studies, and the support of the Officers and Council has made my term as Secretary a pleasure. Disinterested scholarship and polite discourse are still alive in the twenty-first century.

By some curious chance I finished the manuscript of this book at the end of January 2004, the day I surpassed Nelson. Turning off the computer I was profoundly struck by the fact that I had just exceeded his lifespan, by half an hour.

Although many people have helped to limit my ignorance, and reduce the errors that appear in this book, for which they have my sincere thanks, they cannot share responsibility for what appears in print. That, very properly, rests on my head.

ANDREW LAMBERT
Dereham
Norfolk

Nelson Today, Nelson in Context

There are events and individuals in history so far outside the ordinary that a mere record of facts, however detailed, cannot convey their meaning. We do not understand them literally, but at a heightened, spiritual level. Their magic attracts the attention of every generation: they continue to shape our views, mould our actions. Horatio Nelson was one such individual, and the purpose of this book is to ask what he means for us now – at the start of the twenty-first century, in a state increasingly integrated into a pan-European system and spared the horrors of major war for sixty years. Nelson is no longer the national hero celebrated by Churchill in 1940, or the scandalous figure so hotly debated by the Victorians, let alone the granite statue, twice life-size, that stands in Trafalgar Square. Yet all of these incarnations have played a part in the making of our Nelson, removing him from the events of his own life. In an age of cheap celebrity and instant fame it is important to understand the enduring centrality of Nelson. Whatever it means to be British in the twenty-first century, Nelson is part of that identity, as he has been since his first great triumph in 1798.

Nelson remains a national secular deity, the god of war for troubled times, the last resort against overwhelming odds, guardian against tyranny. In life Nelson met and defeated the greatest challenge to the

Nelson aged 22 in Captain's uniform, by J. F. Rigaud

independence and prosperity of his country, through his genius for war, moral and political courage, and willingness to make the ultimate sacrifice. He lived at a time when his country had need of heroes, and became the central figure in a new national identity. Around him coalesced the very concept of Britain, a state committed to God, King, parliament and liberty, relying on naval power to keep Bonaparte out and the trade routes open. Nelson died in the heroic mould, and was interred as an example to be emulated, at the core of a new national pantheon. His name became the talisman of victory, his ship a shrine.

He was placed on a pedestal at the centre of London to remind his countrymen and women from whence their 'Wealth, Safety and Strength'[1] came, and at what cost. Nelson arrived at a crucial moment in the history of human thought, bridging the gap between the Age of Reason, when man replaced God at the centre of the universe, and the Romantic Age, which challenged the rational, mechanical conception of events, the 'Newtonian Universe', with a search for meaning beyond the facts. The search for a higher sensibility led some back to God, or other forms of spirituality – found in art or the notion of a universal hero. The latter role fitted Nelson to perfection. Unlike the military heroes of the age, who destroyed their romantic credibility in government, Nelson's greatness was entwined with the sea, an alien element, at once threatening, but distant; a theatre for the sublime. With his death and transfiguration Nelson assumed divine status: he was, and is, in Lord Byron's words, 'Britannia's god of war'.

Consequently we all think we know about Nelson: born in a humble parsonage in Norfolk, blinded and mutilated in battle, destroyer of French fleets, conqueror of Copenhagen and lover of Lady Hamilton. Among the most famous men of all time, his image is universally recognised, as picture, statue, caricature or fancy dress, and he has been subjected to more biographies than every other admiral put together. Writers from Robert Southey and Byron onwards have constructed Nelsons to meet their very different political agendas, conservative and radical, and Nelson has been over-painted, well and badly, by every succeeding generation. Yet the modern Nelson remains a patchwork image, reflecting the concerns of different generations and ages: we still know very little of the man.

By separating the events of Nelson's life from the way in which his myth has been transmitted by subsequent generations, we may hope to distinguish the human core from the heroic legend. To this end, the chapters of this book that deal with Nelson's life are based on contemporary evidence, while the judgements of later commentators are dealt with in the context of their own era. By removing posthumous constructs from his life we can separate what we know about Nelson into matters of record and matters of interpretation. The real task of this book is to free Nelson of the distortions, errors and absurdities that have been heaped on his name – most notably, the critical judgement of his conduct at Naples in June and July 1799 – but it will also seek to make him more human, and more relevant. It will focus on the development of his professional skill and assess his debt to his mentors: the flowering of a unique talent is at the core of this book, and it does not diminish Nelson to understand why he was the finest naval commander of all.

Nelson's private life will be dealt with where relevant, but without either the romantic hyperbole or sanctimonious moral judgements that have characterised those biographies for which this has been the main point of interest. Such approaches are unhistorical. Nelson's private life was unconventional, but not unusual; it never threatened his employment, or stopped him answering the call of duty. It was also a small part of his life: his time ashore after the spring of 1793 comprised six months to recuperate from the loss of his arm, six weeks at the end of 1800, when his marriage broke up, seventeen months during the Peace of Amiens, and three weeks before Trafalgar. Once at sea his letters were almost always about his work, and his professional concerns. Consequently his private life should be seen as a minor part of the story: he lived for duty.

This is not to say that Nelson's personality is unimportant to the concerns of this book. On the contrary, his leadership was so much more effective than that of fellow officers because he understood the human condition, and based his command on love, not authority. To work with Nelson was to love him: even the most hard-bitten veterans were unable to resist his courage, commitment and charisma. His colleagues were his friends, and he expected their love and loyalty, not mere service. He did his duty where lesser men just followed their orders. This was why he earned the love of a nation. These were fine qualities on their own – when combined with an unequalled mastery of war, strategy and politics they changed the history of the world.

Nelson's abilities as a naval commander may justly be described in terms of genius, not merely greatness. To paraphrase a very wise passage by John Lukacs, great men make the best of the world, men of genius transform it to conform to their own ideas.[2] It is a central contention of this book that Nelson transformed the art of war at sea, to render it effective in the titanic struggle of the French Revolutionary and Napoleonic wars. He used the newly forged instrument to block every extra-European initiative by the French, and he did so in the context of a total British response to the revolutionary era that generated a national identity and a far more powerful state.

In order to grasp such issues we need to understand the context in which Nelson emerged: we need to know far more about his intellectual and professional origins, his education, and the impact of the wider world on his career and conduct. In the two hundred years that have passed since Nelson's death, the art of war at sea – the theatre of his genius – has been transformed out of all recognition. Before we consider his life, it is essential that we understand the nature of his profession, the opportunities and the limits that constrained his thinking. We must examine the age in which he lived, and the profession in which he functioned, with the same rigour that other studies have applied to his life.

Nelson's career coincided with the age of revolution: he saw the world turned upside down, as first the American and then the French Revolutions transformed the relationship between the people and their rulers and shifted war from a limited affair that modified boundaries into a mechanism that could destroy states and transform continents.[3] Monarchies were overthrown and republics set up while nation states emerged from the morass of dynastic ties and petty principalities. All of these things would influence Nelson, giving him a foundation for loyalty, a simple patriotism and the task of withstanding a nation seemingly rendered invincible by its transformation. Winning wars in the age of reason had been a matter of persuading the enemy that it was in their best interests to concede some limited loss. This system, which dated back to 1648, had been based on an agreement of mutual convenience among monarchs. It was destroyed by the French Revolution: after 1793 war was about destroying rival states, and imposing one-sided treaties – conquer or be conquered![4] The war aims of Republican and Imperial France were inconsistent with a stable European state system. Territorial seizures, plunder and ideological pressures made the country so powerful that ultimately the rest of Europe was forced to destroy the French state, rebuilding it in a new form as the only guarantee for peace. There could be no lasting peace with a regime that did not accept the rules of the state system. This required a new level of war: the limited, formal engagements of the eighteenth century would no longer suffice – the age of total war had dawned.

Having raised the people to fight for their country – one million Frenchmen were mobilised in 1794 – successive French governments found themselves incapable of controlling the Frankenstein's monster they had made. War would destroy its begetters, consume its origins and ultimately generate a military superman who could transform it back into a political instrument. France would be led by men who would only survive while they continued to succeed, while the French economy could only function by conquering and plundering other countries, and stationing much of their million-man army abroad. This 'Jacobin' system terrified all right-thinking, property-owning members of the British establishment. The French Revolutionary wars changed British society, for although the British did not revolutionise their society, they found ways to mobilise a far greater level of strength, and raise far more revenue to pay for the defence of their interests. The instruments that made this possible were patriotism and loyalty: fear of the French and their revolution made men British, and belligerent. The sense of vulnerability generated by the presence of French armies at Boulogne, and Antwerp, and Brest, made this a question of national survival: for the first time since the Spanish Armada the very idea of England was under threat. Britain mobilised a huge force of militia and volunteer groups that militarised society, but did not leave the country. This released the regular army itself, and the mercenary troops funded by the taxpayer, for service abroad.[5]

Nelson had the good fortune to serve in the most successful fighting service the world had ever seen, his years of glory illuminating its heroic age. Unlike other great powers, Britain relied on naval power for national security: as an island, her frontier was the shoreline, and her fortresses were floating castles. In truth, the Navy created the modern state, for the cost of maintaining the world's most powerful fleet forced the state to modernise, to develop the tax-raising, bureaucratic and political structures that define the modern liberal state. Having been persuaded to pay for this powerful instrument of policy to defend the country from invasion, the commercial classes were quick to use it for their own advantage. By the beginning of the eighteenth century, Parliament was ordering the Royal Navy to devote a fixed proportion of its strength to escort merchant shipping. The City of London – traders, investors and insurers – kept the Navy strong, in peace as well as war. Their support had been crucial to Britain's victory in the wars of Empire that culminated in 1763. The Royal Navy defeated the French and Spanish fleets, crippled their economies and seized control of India, North America and other key trading posts.

After the humiliation of 1763 France and Spain renewed their alliance, rebuilt their fleets, and waited for the chance to have their revenge. Nelson's entry into the Navy was occasioned by the first such opportunity, the Falklands Crisis, and although the strength of the Royal Navy on this occasion deterred the allies, they only redoubled their efforts. France backed the American rebels in 1778 because her ministers saw an opportunity to weaken Britain, while Spain wanted to recover Gibraltar. Although they had only limited success in the American war, the French and Spanish continued their naval build-up after 1783, and by 1793 their combined strength of large fighting ships was significantly greater than Britain's. The imperative need to reduce these massive forces lent a particular character to the naval campaigns of the Revolutionary war. A tactical success, taking a few prizes, was no longer adequate. The Nile becomes more significant when seen against the total naval balance of 1798, since it took the Royal Navy from outnumbered to dominant in one fell swoop.

Nelson's genius lay in linking the different streams of naval skill that he had mastered with the political imperatives of the age – but like Napoleon, who had a very similar impact on land warfare, he would be fortunate in his opponents. The French Revolution had a devastating impact on the French navy, in marked contrast to her army. The professional skills of the seaman could not be replaced by patriotic zeal and numbers. In twenty-two years of war the French rarely won an action between forces of equal strength, and often needed very heavy odds to defeat inferior forces. Merchant ship captains and over-promoted midshipmen made poor admirals, even if they became good seamen.[6] The other major fleet that Nelson fought, the Spanish, had many ships and some brave, capable leaders, but few sailors. For Spain Trafalgar would be the last hurrah of a once-great service, a glorious defeat. The Danes and Russians didn't even risk going to sea – the quality gap was so great. Against all these opponents, Nelson clearly had an edge, and he used it to the full.

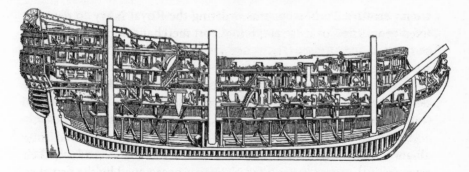

Cross-section of a ship of the line in Nelson's time

While war was transformed out of all recognition at the political and organisational level, the tools of the trade increased only in number. Muskets, cannon and ships of the line were unaltered, and Nelson's career witnessed no significant technical change. His flagship at Trafalgar was over forty years old, and still a first-rate, front-line warship. In consequence he could build on 150 years of naval experience fighting with ships, squadrons and fleets powered by the wind, armed with cast-iron cannon, dependent on the seamanship, dexterity and commitment of the crew to keep them functioning. The skills he had learnt as a boy and perfected as a young man were still central to the business of fighting at sea on the day he died.

When Nelson went to sea, the wooden sailing warship was nearing the end of a prolonged period of evolution. The combination of an effective three-masted sailing rig, durable wooden ships and muzzle-loading cannon had been established as the basic fighting system 250 years before, in the reign of Henry VIII. However, operating large square-rigged sailing ships remained a difficult and demanding art, acquired over many years of practical experience. As a system of propulsion it left much to be desired. It was inherently dangerous, since extremes of weather could leave a ship out of control. Sudden changes in wind strength could cripple a ship in an instant, notably the *Vanguard* in 1798, by breaking the delicate topmasts. Furthermore ships could only make progress when the wind was blowing: dead calm meant no movement, and their ability to make progress against the wind was limited. This precarious power source required a deep grasp of local and seasonal conditions, largely derived from hard-won experience. The ability to read the weather and to anticipate changes was vital for a sea officer. Nelson kept a weather log for most of his sea-going career, and was still filling it in on the day he died. This was more than meteorological curiosity: it was the building block of his system.

The mechanics of adjusting the ship's speed and course required the manual exertion of a significant part of the crew, including upwards of one hundred true seamen – men able to work up in the rigging, hauling in sail, mending rope and shifting masts and yards. The typical seaman was a young unattached man, between twenty and thirty, already experienced at sea. He would probably leave oceanic seafaring before reaching thirty to take up a shoreside job in the maritime industries, though a few stayed on to become masters, naval petty officers, or specialist ratings. Seamen were at the pinnacle of the working-class labour market, and vital to national security. Yet there were never enough of them in wartime, so much of the crew of a battleship would be composed of landsmen. Such men lacked the skill to work aloft, though they could haul on the ropes, run round the capstan and crew the guns; because they worked in the waist, the central section of the upper deck, they were often termed 'waisters'.

The basic fighting instrument, the muzzle-loading cast-iron cannon, came in several sizes, and two basic forms. Long guns could fire solid iron balls over a mile, but the most effective fighting range was 'point blank', about 200 yards, where they required no elevation to hit an enemy ship. On the upper deck the weapons were carronades, short-barrelled lightweight guns of large bore, which compensated for their shorter range by firing heavy-calibre balls. The largest cannon fired a 6.2-inch diameter thirty-two-pound solid iron shot that could punch a hole straight through two feet of oak, and on exiting sent a cloud of huge, jagged splinters scything across the deck. The lightly built bow and stern of a wooden warship were terribly vulnerable, once Nelson had destroyed the old tactical order of linear attritional combat.

British guns, being better cast, rarely exploded; French weapons were less reliable, which discouraged their crew from trying to fire fast, for the faster the guns were fired the hotter they became, and the more likely they were to explode. On a close, confined gun deck the explosion of a heavy gun would reduce the gun crew to a bloody shambles, along with those of the pieces on either side, shatter the deck above and below, and probably cause an ammunition fire. This was far more damage than was normally done by hours of enemy fire, and demoralised the rest of the crew. Little wonder the confident and experienced British gunners fired faster. One round every ninety seconds was possible in the opening stages of a battle. After the first broadside had been fired this rate of fire made British ships far more powerful fighting units than foreign ships of the same nominal rate.

Although they were built to the same basic design, major British warships were divided into six rates. The first three were strong enough to fight in the line of battle, the others were cruisers for scouting, trade protection and other detached roles. First-rates like HMS *Victory* had three complete covered decks armed with cannon, with further guns on the open upper deck. The total armament of a hundred or more guns gave each ship a broadside weight of fire superior to any contemporary army. Second-rates, like the *Temeraire*, were similar, but smaller, and carried fewer than a hundred guns. These two rates formed the backbone of the major fleets – Nelson reckoned a three-decker equal to two two-deckers. Third-rate ships were two-decked ships of between sixty-four and eighty guns: Nelson fought three of his four major engagements in seventy-fours. These ships were cheaper to build, usually sailed better than three-deckers, and could be used for a wider range of strategic tasks. They were the most numerous type of battleship. Fourth-rates were either very small two-decked fifty-gun ships, like the *Leander* at the Nile, or big frigates like the USS *Constitution*. Neither was common, being too expensive to build and operate for a type unable to fight in the battle line. By contrast, the fifth-rate frigate armed with thirty to forty eighteen-pounder guns was a standard warship built in huge numbers, while the twenty-gun sixth-rate, the smallest ship commanded by a captain, was equally numerous. Lesser ships were not rated, and were commanded by officers below the rank of captain.

The ships of other navies were built along similar lines, although those of France and Spain were often larger for the number of guns mounted. France favoured very big two-decked ships of eighty guns, like the *Bucentaure*, over three-deckers, because they sailed better. Spain created a unique four-decked ship, the *Santissima Trinidad,* which Nelson engaged twice, and a large force of powerful 112-gun three-deckers, but these ships were rarely handled with sufficient skill to exploit their strength. British officers and men were invariably better trained and more experienced than those of Spain, and after 1793 those of France as well. Nelson's tactics were founded on this unequal relationship between the Royal Navy and its rivals: he pushed his advantage to the limit in search of decision, speed and certainty.

Naval battles were rare, even for Nelson, but they provided the acid test of ships and men. The basic system of naval tactics was settled during Cromwell's regime, a close ordered line of battle to maximise firepower and strength. This remained the basis of fleet tactics until Nelson's day. Naval battles were usually lengthy affairs, taking many hours to resolve: at Trafalgar the fleets were in sight for six hours before they began to fight. Before 1793 fleets normally engaged in lines, broadside to broadside. The line of battle had been developed by the English as a defensive tactic to counter the more agile and aggressive Dutch fleets of the seventeenth century, relying on cohesion and firepower to smash the more lightly built Hollanders. It was used against the altogether less aggressive French and Spanish because it had become an article of faith, and the ultimate defence in the event of defeat. Failing to form a proper line was a serious offence, if the battle were lost. This regime bred admirals more frightened of losing than anxious to win. But the best admirals of the eighteenth century were quick to abandon the line, once the enemy had shown their weakness; Anson, Hawke and Rodney all used pursuit battle to destroy a fleeing enemy, and their approach culminated in that of Nelson, who began his plans with the annihilation of the enemy.

The tactics of war at sea in the age of sail have long fascinated armchair admirals, who have allowed the geometric precision of the printed page, and neat changes of course, to delude their senses.[7] Naval tactics were never as elegant as the theoretical drawings suggest. Any seaman knows that to keep a fleet of ships sailing in company, in close order, is a great achievement; to make them change course without losing all cohesion and order is even more difficult, particularly when under fire and smothered with smoke. To fight a fleet action both sides had to bring their forces into line, and keep close together, rather than allowing the enemy to cut the fleet into sections, and concentrate against a detachment. If both fleets were willing to fight, and kept a good line, the combat would be settled by firepower. As damaged ships fell out of line the fleets would begin to dissolve into individual combats, and after one side had given up and fled, the winner could clear up the crippled ships that were left behind.

Once a battle began it was almost impossible to signal any changes to the plan, as smoke made it impossible for all ships to see the flag-ship. Therefore the best tactics were the simplest: the line was ideal because it would be set before the fighting started, and no one would break it without sanction. Nelson was the master of simplicity. At Trafalgar he had prepared his captains before the event, by discussion, and also by transmitting a 'mission-analysis' memorandum. This told them what he hoped to achieve, but also to exercise their own skill and judgement in fulfilling those objectives. Nelson's predecessors – men such as Lord Hood and Earl St Vincent, from whom Nelson had learned much – also took their officers into their confidence, but because they faced more capable foes, they possessed less elevated ideas of the possible outcome. Nelson further refined the system such men had created, in pursuit of his goal of total annihilation of the enemy. His system removed the need to send any signals once the bat-tle had started, and even when he received Home Popham's new signal code,[8] he saw that it was best used to give his men a morale-boosting motto, relying for victory on the old system, prior discussion, and above all his own example. Collingwood, who knew the man and his ideas better than anyone, testified that 'he has the faculty of discover-ing advantages as they arise, and the good judgement to turn them to his use. An enemy that commits a false step in his view is ruined, and it comes on him with an impetuosity that allows him no time to recov-er.'[9] After Trafalgar Collingwood reflected that 'everything seemed, as if by enchantment, to prosper under his direction. But it was the effect of system, and nice combination, not of chance.'[10]

Once in combat, ships exchanged fire until one of them was unable to continue, either because her rigging was disabled, or her crew too demoralised by losses to continue.

The human face of such battles was terrible. Round shot smashed through the sides of the ships, scattering large, jagged fragments of timber, euphemistically referred to as splinters. These scythed down the gun crew, and men on the upper deck, inflicting a combination of cutting and crushing injuries that were hard to treat. Wounded men were taken below to the cockpit where, in the gloomy pallor of battle lanterns, the surgeon and his crew did their best. They could clean and stitch wounds, remove musket balls, amputate crushed or shattered limbs and comfort the dying. They knew nothing of antiseptic practice and anaesthetics, and had no treatment for shock. Even those who escaped obvious injury were not unscathed. The concussive detonation of so many guns left many men temporarily or permanently deafened; this, in combination with the horrors of the scene, may explain the unusually high number of insane veterans. These unfortunates had their own asylum (now the Imperial War Museum), where they provided post-war Londoners with a 'spectacle'.

For those who survived, the regular routine of loading and firing the gun became the main event, one that required their full attention. Discipline and training superseded human responses: any sane man would run away, but these men were conditioned to stay and fight. As a result those who fought on the gun decks rarely had any notion of the wider battle, and afterwards their concerns were local. How many of their mess had survived, where were their mates? For most it was the close comradeship of shared danger that got them through. No one wanted to let down their mess, gun crew, ship or admiral. Such concerns overrode private fears, gave them a focus that depersonalised the danger, and sustained them in a truly hellish world of noise, smoke, death and mutilation.

For all the horror and human cost, battle was not the object of war, only the means to an end. Nelson's real concern was the exploitation of sea power in the wider conflict with France. It was only by annihilating the enemy fleets that Britain could exploit the sea at the strategic level to sustain her own efforts, and crush those of France. Sea power would pressure French clients and puppets, ultimately prompting a pan-European uprising against the Bonapartist tyranny. Nelson was well aware of these issues, predicting the longer course of the war in June 1803. It would be national resistance in Portugal, Spain, Russia and parts of Italy and Germany that brought down Bonaparte, not the feeble policies and dynastic concerns of the old regimes.

The impact of sea power on the economic endurance of a large state like France was exceedingly slow – the grinding attrition of blockades contrasted starkly with Bonaparte's rapid, decisive land campaigns – but also terribly certain. Between 1689 and 1815 Britain and France fought seven major wars, and France was bankrupt at the end of every single one. The difference after 1793 was that France plundered her neighbours, and kept on plundering them until the rest of Europe finally acted as one. The Royal Navy stopped France from enjoying her conquests, and denied her the opportunity to rebuild her economy. Everywhere there was room to float a ship, the British were to be found, harassing the enemy, and trading with anyone who could pay.

The war between 1793 and 1815 was at root an economic struggle, and it was won by the stronger economy.

Britain had no desire to conquer territory on the European mainland. Her aims were restricted to removing the French from the Low Countries, especially the port city of Antwerp, and re-establishing a stable, peaceful European system, in which her role would be to balance the players, and press her commercial advantages. Five major coalitions and numerous alliances and subsidy treaties bear testimony to Britain's role as the linchpin of resistance to French aggression. The question facing the British government and its advisers was how to use its strengths – naval power, economic endurance and a balance of power policy – to defeat France. In reality, the only method was to exhaust every French offensive option against Britain – invasion, economic warfare, alliances and global strikes – while slowly crushing her resources. This strategy caused problems with resource allocation, for Britain had a limited fund of ships, men, soldiers and transports, and every theatre called out for more. From 1793 the offensive was split between Northern Europe, where every effort proved inadequate and futile, and the West Indies, where the French islands were largely secured by 1797. Only after the Nile did the British Government focus on the Mediterranean, because all other options had been exhausted and Austria called out for a fleet. The results were spectacular, because sea power could block the French once they tried to leave the western European theatre. However, the ministers were never wholehearted about Austria, and rightly so: Vienna was playing its own game. For much of this period the biggest problem was the endless compromises caused by the political needs of alliance warfare: British aims were blocked by allied concerns, and pure strategy was deflected by political problems.

The security of merchant shipping was another issue that had constantly to be borne in mind. In a theatre like the Mediterranean with endless harbours for small privateers and pirates, it was essential to convoy the most valuable merchant ships, and coerce the Barbary corsairs to ensure they did not attack British ships, or those supplying the British. Convoys heading for Britain were commonly escorted by ships heading for a home dockyard to refit. Although often short-handed and sluggish, their presence deterred all but the most powerful enemy forces. Protection was also needed for the valuable British sugar islands in the West Indies, since the wealth they generated was one of the economic foundations of the war effort. So valuable were they that Nelson left his station and chased the enemy to the West Indies in 1805: he went to save the country, not just a few islands.

Perhaps Nelson's greatest achievement was to render simple and direct everything that was, for lesser men, complex and imponderable. He removed uncertainty, doubt and fear from his subordinates. For Nelson's Prussian contemporary, Carl von Clausewitz, genius in war was largely a natural gift: it enabled one man to triumph over rules, or simply set them aside. It was an intellectual attainment: judgement, insight, comprehension leading to swift and correct decision.[11] Those who can do their duty in war are not uncommon: professionalism, teamwork, comradeship and shared danger can generate fighting men. Junior leaders, the petty officers and lieutenants who exercise tactical control, require more reflective attainments, to meet the uncertainties of battle with effective, predictable responses. This is the province of doctrine, the accepted methods of operating that have been the bedrock of fighting forces since the dawn of warfare. Yet genius requires a more open field of action. As soon as he was given an independent command, Nelson combined responsibility for his ship and crew with authority to act as he thought fit. From his first detached service, in Nicaragua in 1780, he demonstrated the confidence to act on his own judgement, accepting the awful responsibility of ordering men into battle and the possibility of criticism from higher authority.

Fleet command during Nelson's era required the integration of administrative tasks with strategic-level management, tactical command and high-level diplomatic and inter-service cooperation. While many men were given such commands, only a handful of them rose to the task. Most fell back on precedent, caution and fear. Among the handful who rose to the challenge, none has equalled the subject of this book. Nelson served the political leadership of the day, upheld his country and constitution, placed his trust in God, and did his duty. He cared deeply for his men, as human beings. He sought peace through victory in war. In an age when nations needed heroes who were larger than life and twice as impressive, Britain's hero was a slight, mutilated naval officer. Nelson saved his country, and in the process became 'Britannia's god of war'.

PART ONE

The Making of a Hero

CHAPTER I

The Student of War
1758–82

The testimonies of Nelson's mistress, wife and elder brother, not to mention his own brief and embellished accounts, sought to create an image of the young hero as a paragon of manly virtues: honest, brave, loyal and self-effacing. Even his petty larceny – for such is the reality of his orchard-raiding as a schoolboy – was dignified by pious sentiments. The truth of Nelson's all-too brief childhood was rather more prosaic.

Horatio Nelson was born at Burnham Thorpe in north Norfolk on 29 September 1758, the sixth of eleven children. His father, Reverend Edmund Nelson, was a Church of England cleric. Edmund's family background was firmly middle-class; though intelligent and well educated, he lacked ambition, seeming happy with a quiet life in the Rectory at Burnham. The connections that would provide his numerous family with opportunities for advancement came from his wife's family. Catherine Suckling was related to the powerful Walpole family, close neighbours of the Nelsons but far above them in wealth and social rank. She was the grand-neice of Sir Robert Walpole (later Lord Orford), the first British Prime Minister, who had built a dynastic power base in north Norfolk. It was the Walpole connection that secured Edmund the living at Burnham, and Horatio was named after Sir Robert's son, his godfather.

A Midshipman – sometimes claimed to be Nelson

Growing up in an isolated community, with few social equals, young Horace (as he was known in childhood) would have been well aware of his status. His family had servants and were on visiting terms with the minor Walpoles. But they did not visit Lord Orford's residence; though they were close to wealth, status and privilege, the Nelsons were still on the outside. For an ambitious young man, the family's connections would provide an opening, but individual effort in the service of the nation would be needed in order to convert this opportunity into social and economic promotion.

The vast skies and raw winds of north Norfolk have not changed since Nelson's day, but then agriculture and fishing rather than tourism dominated the region, and the sea played an important part in local trade. No great events marked his childhood, which passed in a constant cycle of seasonal changes. The war with France that raged from 1756 to 1763 gave Britain global power, but Nelson was too young to have appreciated 1759, the year of victories when the Church bells rang for Quebec, Quiberon, Lagos and Minden. These events would enter his consciousness later, as examples and precedents.

The real influences on young Horace's early years were closer to home: the sense of duty inculcated by his father's role in the community, and the awareness of death sharpened by the tragic events in his own family. Five of his siblings died in childhood or as young adults, and his mother died when he was only nine. The latter event left an aching emotional void, manifested most obviously in his violent mood swings, as well as in his compulsion as an adult to secure the unthinking worship of those in authority and private ease in the arms of a powerful woman. Yet he always kept his duty and his personal life separate, never allowing private desires to hinder the execution of his public functions.

Perhaps he learnt this lesson from Edmund, who never remarried and selflessly devoted himself to bringing up his children. He was a considerate, calm father who neither crushed his children's spirits nor expected too much of them: his amiable but chronically unambitious younger sons, Edmund and Suckling, were indulged with the same concern as Horace. Although Edmund was not a role model to Nelson, nor the spur that drove his ambition, the rector's personal charm and expressive use of language were important elements in the make-up of the admiral, while his sermons and moral authority helped

Nelson to find his own voice when he needed to justify his actions. A brief period in a boarding school provided a useful halfway house for the challenges of a naval career.

This career was influenced most strongly, however, by his Suckling uncles, Maurice and William. Maurice had made his name, and a worthwhile sum of money, after a successful battle in the West Indies on 21 October 1759. He lived in some style in South Norfolk, and as a childless widower he was an ideal patron for his sister's children. William Suckling took the eldest Nelson boy, also named Maurice, into public service in the Excise Office, then moved him to the Navy Board when Captain Suckling became the professional head of naval administration. Horace, meanwhile, took the initiative, as he was to do throughout his life. Reading that Captain Suckling was to command one of the ships being mobilised for a possible war with Spain over the Falkland Islands, he asked his elder brother William to write to their father, then taking the cure at Bath, to ask if he could go to sea – though it is probable that Suckling had already mentioned the subject to Edmund.

The opportunity that Suckling offered to Nelson was typical of eighteenth-century naval careers, which generally began through personal contact: the better the connection, the better the start a young

Captain Maurice Suckling, Nelson's uncle

officer could make. Successful senior officers could ensure that their protégés picked up their trade, and a wide circle of potential patrons. Careers began early, at twelve or thirteen, and required financial support. For the first four to six years the young man would not be a commissioned officer. He was a trainee, often rated as a midshipman, and would only be commissioned if he passed a professional examination, and possessed certificates for six years' service. Horace's path to a commission was smoothed by Suckling's connections. Captain Suckling found the boy the right ships, the right officers and the right stations, as well as taking charge of his education and paying his allowance.

In March 1771 Nelson joined the sixty-four-gun line-of-battle ship HMS *Raisonnable*, then lying in the River Medway off Chatham dockyard.[1] Within days the ship had moved down river to Sheerness, and Nelson witnessed his first flogging. When the armament was cancelled in May, Suckling shifted into the stationary guardship HMS *Triumph*. He felt that Nelson's interests would be best served by going to sea, however, so he sent him in a merchant ship that was trading with the West Indies, commanded by one of his old petty officers. By serving as a crew member for a year, the thirteen-year-old acquired a head for heights and a wide range of practical seafaring skills, maintaining the rigging, heavy hauling, anchoring and unmooring, as well as gaining an insight into the common seaman's far from favourable view of the Navy. In July 1772 Nelson rejoined Suckling on the *Triumph*, which had shifted back to Chatham while he was away. Already convinced by his uncle of the need to master practical seafaring arts, Nelson secured command of the only active vessel at the anchorage, the large boat that carried orders and officers from Chatham to London. Sailing in the shallow, tidal waters of the Thames and Medway, he developed the judgement necessary for inshore operations, a skill that would be vital to his later career.

Nor was this enough. The following year an expedition was in prospect. The Royal Society, patron of Captain Cook's celebrated voyage to the South Seas, which returned home in 1771, now proposed a voyage to the North Pole. When two warships were selected, Nelson, desperate to join, circumvented an order that no boys be taken by persuading Captain Skeffington Lutwidge to rate him coxswain on HMS *Carcass* – named for the explosive shells she was built to fire, not the more obvious meaning. Doubtless Suckling played a key role, as the ship was fitted out at nearby Sheerness.[2] Unfortunately for the young hero there was no glory to be had in the Arctic: they discovered nothing and the ships were nearly lost after becoming trapped in the ice.

Suckling clearly had no intention of keeping his nephew idle at home, since he next quickly secured him a midshipman's berth on the frigate HMS *Seahorse*, destined for the Indian Ocean. The ship's master, Surridge, was a talented navigator and teacher.[3] Unfortunately Captain George Farmer lacked leadership skills and his ship was far from happy: two first lieutenants were court-martialled inside a year. The voyage was an eventful one for Nelson: he saw his first gun fired in anger, at a Mysorean cruiser, and he met midshipman Thomas Troubridge, another name for the future. Finally he was struck down with malaria and invalided home in early 1776. He arrived at Woolwich dockyard just days before his eighteenth birthday.

In 1802 Nelson told how this voyage found him in the depths of despair about his career prospects: he felt that by being invalided, he had failed, letting down his ship and all who served in her. But his spirits soon revived, with the cooler climates and the abatement of the malarial symptoms, and he decided to seek the patronage of his king and country. He resolved to be a hero, trusting in providence that it was his destiny.[4]

The subtext of this outburst in 1802 was clear. Nelson was telling his audience that he had made it to the top without human help. This was not true: Suckling remained the architect of his career when he returned to England. He was now Controller of the Navy and MP for Portsmouth, a man of enormous influence. Any captain would be happy to help his nephew: Nelson completed his sea service on board HMS *Worcester*, supported by letters from his uncle to her captain. After six months at sea as an acting lieutenant Nelson was examined for his commission. On 9 April 1777 a board of three captains, chaired by his uncle, met at the Navy Board on Tower Hill. Needless to say he passed, although he lacked the full six years' sea service, and was a year too young. For the mature Nelson, however, Suckling's influence was an embarrassing fact that needed to be explained away. Many years later either he or William Nelson told John McArthur that Suckling had concealed their relationship from his two colleagues.[5] This is highly unlikely. There was no need to hold the examination in London other than to indulge Suckling, and Nelson's contemporary report of the matter makes no mention of the sub-terfuge.[6] He could expect Suckling to hold the Controller's post for many years, certainly long enough for him to secure the next two steps to captain. His career had been made: the next few years would demonstrate whether he would become the officer his uncle had worked so hard to educate.

Nelson was commissioned a lieutenant on 19 April, and appointed to the thirty-two-gun frigate HMS *Lowestoffe*, whose captain was William Locker. The selection was no accident. Locker was an excel-lent seaman and a sympathetic commander: he had served under Lord Hawke, the greatest fighting admiral of the previous generation, and shown great courage in boarding an enemy vessel, which left him with a crippled leg. Suckling considered him the ideal officer to direct the next stage of Nelson's education. Having mastered seamanship, the newly made lieutenant was anxious to learn about war. Characteristically, Nelson was soon on the closest possible terms with his captain. Long hours at sea and shared professionalism allowed the two officers to discuss naval tactics: the reflective Locker guided Nelson's development as a commander and leader of men, as well as his tactical judgement. The two men became firm friends, despite the older man being twice Nelson's age and his commanding officer. Locker became Nelson's naval 'father', providing example, guidance and confessional. Other officers would earn Nelson's esteem and affection, but none came close to Locker. The relationship remained close to the end of Locker's life. It was at Locker's request that Nelson sat for a portrait with John Francis Rigaud, RA.

Nelson and his new ship were soon off to the West Indies, escorting a convoy of merchant ships. Convoys were necessary because the American colonies were in open revolt, and their privateers were active. Furthermore there would be opportunities for prize-taking, and for glory. An active officer could make his name in war, and secure his place on the list of post captains. Once there he would become an admiral in the fullness of time, if he outlived those above him, and did not disgrace himself. Not that Nelson was going to let any opportuni-ty pass to push himself forward, to show himself in a heroic light. His opportunity came as 'captain' of the *Little Lucy*, named for Locker's daughter. Since the main targets were small colonial schooners bent on breaking the blockade it made sense to purse them in a similar vessel.

Captain William Locker

In her Nelson took his first prizes, and demonstrated his initiative. The newly-made lieutenant took particular pride in a very smart piece of boat handling in severe weather.

Plagued by ill health Locker had to invalid home, but he made sure that Nelson moved over to HMS *Bristol,* the flagship of Admiral Sir Peter Parker, in July 1778. At the same time, Suckling died suddenly, although the news took three months to reach Jamaica. The true significance of his uncle to his career prospects is painfully obvious from Nelson's response. He knew that among Suckling's last acts had been to write to Parker on his behalf.[7] Already Parker's first lieutenant, and thus marked for early promotion, he became master and commander of the brig HMS *Badger* in December. On 11 June 1779 he was appointed post captain, taking command of the small frigate HMS *Hinchinbrooke* when a death among the captains on station enabled Parker to promote his own son out of her into a better ship. Parker had the authority to fill such 'death vacancies' and with France now engaged in the war no one would question his action.

While waiting at Port Royal, Jamaica, for his new command, Nelson had time to extend his local contacts from the Admiral and Lady Parker, who treated him as a surrogate son, through Locker's friend the planter Hercules Ross, to the Governor, Major-General John Dalling. Dalling had served at the capture of Quebec with the immortal Wolfe, and regaled his friends with stories of combined

9

operations, matchless heroism and timely death that would inspire Nelson for the rest of his life.[8] With the French heading for Jamaica Nelson was given command of the main battery protecting Port Royal Harbour. When the danger passed the ambitious Dalling developed a plan to cut Spanish central America in half, opening a two-front campaign by ascending the San Juan River into Lake Nicaragua, and moving on to the Pacific coast. Parker was unenthusiastic, but after registering his concerns he detached Nelson to escort the expedition.

Striking a pose: Nelson volunteering to board a prize in a gale

With only sketchy maps, and little local knowledge, the troops soon ran into difficulties: even entering the river proved beyond their competence. Nelson offered his assistance without hesitation, bringing boats and seamen to get the troops moving. Although he had no authority to join the expedition, he could see that without his help the project was doomed. The river, in the dry season, proved to be shallow and rocky, enclosed by dank jungle harbouring clouds of mosquitoes. Unaware that these carried malaria, the men were more concerned by larger threats – snakes, crocodiles and jaguars. After ten days they overpowered a Spanish outpost, and moved up to Fort San Juan, a small hilltop work of masonry commanding the river. Nelson urged Colonel Polson to storm the place, despite the lack of ladders and artillery ammunition. Polson disagreed, and settled down to a regular siege. The logistics of bombarding a stone fort with tiny four-pounder cannon, far from the sea, were challenging. With the weather about to break time was of the essence, and only Nelson's skill and drive had got the soldiers this far. But the course he proposed was highly risky, and Nelson himself contracted tropical sprue, which soon led to severe dysentery, after drinking from a stagnant pool. His life was probably saved when Parker ordered him back to command a larger frigate. The *Hinchinbrooke* passed to Cuthbert Collingwood, although most of her crew died on the lethal coast. The Fort finally fell, but the expedition petered out as the rains came, leaving a terrible legacy of illness and death among all those who took part.[9]

Arriving at Port Royal in a litter, Nelson was lauded by Dalling, and brought to the attention of the Secretary of State. He was too sick to take command of his new ship. Captain William Cornwallis rescued him from the charnel house that was the naval hospital by placing him in the care of released slave women, who treated him with local remedies and kept him isolated.[10] Later, Lady Parker took him to the admiral's house. His health shattered, the doctors were convinced that he needed a change of climate, and in September he went home on Cornwallis's HMS *Lion*. The care of Cornwallis, and of Locker once he reached London, allowed him to join his hypochondriac father who was taking the waters at Bath. But his recovery took a long time, and his limbs were still partially paralysed months later.

By May 1781, however, he was well enough to apply for another ship, and in early August he was given the twenty-eight-gun frigate HMS *Albemarle*, recently converted from a French armed store-ship.

Nelson's biographers have accepted his claims that it was a merit appointment at face value.[11] But Nelson had done nothing to command favourable notice; he was very young and there were many officers waiting for employment. In reality this was another example of patronage at work, and once again his uncle had provided the necessary interest. This time it was William Suckling, now Deputy Collector of Customs, who contacted Charles Jenkinson, Secretary at War. Suckling also had the ear of the Prime Minister, Lord North, and his nephew looked to these connections for employment in peacetime.[12]

Jenkinson wrote to the First Lord of the Admiralty, Lord Sandwich, in February 1781, asking for Nelson to be employed – because he was Maurice Suckling's nephew, and he bore a good character.[13] While Sandwich claimed to make such appointments by seniority,[14] and did not interview Nelson for three months,[15] Jenkinson's support gave him the edge over his competitors. By the time Suckling followed up his initial approach to Jenkinson in April, he was told the job was already done.[16] Had Maurice Suckling lived, Nelson might have been given a better ship.

In the meantime, he had returned to Rigaud's studio to complete the portrait sittings. The fresh-faced youth of four years ago had gone, replaced by a confident post captain, with Fort San Juan in the background, representing his proudest achievement to date. The face had to be repainted; the subject was now thinner, and rather pale.[17]

Even so it is a remarkable image, portraying an assured master of his art, hardly past twenty, yet a veteran of war, competent to command the largest ships afloat.

Nelson took over his new ship in mid-August 1781 while she lay in dry dock at Woolwich. It would be another three months before she went to sea, in company with two other cruisers, to pick up a large convoy at Elsinore, where the Danish Crown secured the Sound Dues from ships passing the narrow waterway connecting the North Sea with the Baltic. (He would return with more serious intent twenty years later.) The convoy, some 260 ships, was highly important, carrying vital supplies of timber, rope, tar, turpentine and masts for the hard-pressed Navy. By late November the merchant ships were ready, and after a frustrating passage, with the *Albemarle* constantly chasing the laggards, the convoy reached Great Yarmouth. But a fortnight later, the *Albemarle* was run down and badly damaged by a large merchant ship.

Nelson was detained at Portsmouth for the next four months while she was repaired, before escorting a convoy to Quebec. Cruising in Boston Bay in mid-August 1782, he was pursued by four French battleships and a frigate, but avoided trouble by sailing into shoal water. By mid-September he was back in Quebec. The month-long stay there brought him better health, another lifelong friendship, and a love affair with a local beauty. Fortunately his new friend, the merchant and contractor Alexander Davison, persuaded him to follow his orders to escort troopships to New York, rather than chase a sixteen-year-old coquette.

Nelson's heart was set on battle and glory: the pinnacle of his ambition was to command a ship of the line on the West Indies station. For on 12 April, while Nelson lay at Spithead, patching up his makeshift frigate, the British and French fleets had clashed in the Saintes passage. Admiral Rodney's fleet smashed through the French line, taking six ships, including the flagship of their admiral the Comte de Grasse. In an afternoon the threat to Jamaica was removed and the reputation of the Royal Navy restored. Such glory earned two British admirals, Rodney and Hood, peerages and national adulation. For the young Captain Nelson, it fired his imagination and fuelled his dreams: commanding a line-of-battle ship was clearly the royal road to glory. When Nelson reached New York the hero of the hour, Sir Samuel, now Lord, Hood was there with his fleet, about to return south. Having been a friend of Maurice Suckling, Hood was predisposed to favour his nephew. According to Nelson's version, Hood was soon convinced that the charming young captain was a man after his own heart, dedicated to glory rather than profit. In truth Hood's rationale was more prosaic, and more obvious. Nelson was an experienced West Indian officer, from whom he obtained valuable information concerning the local navigation around Jamaica and Hispaniola.[18]

When Nelson went aboard Hood's flagship he met His Royal Highness Prince William, later Duke of Clarence and King William IV, who was serving as a midshipman. When the slightly built, incongruously youthful captain, dressed in old-fashioned clothes, came on board, the Prince wondered who he could be.

My doubts were however, removed when Lord Hood introduced me to him. There was something irresistibly pleasing in his address and conversation; and an enthusiasm when speaking on professional subjects, that showed he was no common being.[19]

Little wonder that Hood persuaded Admiral Digby to release Nelson's ship to accompany the fleet back to the West Indies. His confidence was repaid when the *Albemarle* picked up a French transport packed with masts, of which the fleet was desperately short. Overwhelmed by the flattery of a great man, and the admiration of a prince, Nelson was in rapture, telling his professional confidant Locker: 'He treats me as if I was his son . . . nor is my situation with Prince William less flattering.'[20] Such high expectations were bound to be disappointed: neither Hood nor the prince would live up to Nelson's hopes.

Desperate to gather some more glory before the war ended, Nelson, learning that the French had captured the tiny British possession of Turk's Island in the southern Bahamas, formed a small squadron from ships in the area and attacked. Despite a bombardment, the French were well prepared, and the landing on 7 March was beaten off. Fortunately Nelson was not ashore, and recognised the island was not worth the cost of recapture with peace imminent.

He was right. The Peace of Paris had been signed in January 1783 and he was recalled to England. On 25 June the *Albemarle* dropped anchor at Spithead, paying off nine days later. Nelson took great satisfaction from the impact of his leadership: the entire crew offered to follow him to another ship. With the war over, however, this was unlikely. King George had lost his American colonies, but he had kept the prize sugar islands, while France and Spain had once more been put in their proper place at sea.

Nelson's own position, nonetheless, had been immeasurably enhanced by the war. Not only had he risen from lieutenant to captain, he had acquired some useful patrons and was a welcome guest when Hood took him to a royal levee. He had a powerful circle of friends and contacts both in the Navy and among the merchants, traders and West Indian planters he had met on his travels. Equally important was the loyalty he commanded among junior officers and men from his ship. Their faith in him, expressed so forcibly at a time when other ships' companies were close to mutiny, showed that though Horatio Nelson might be 'the meerest boy of a captain', he was already an inspirational leader of men. His seamanship had been demonstrated, and his tactical judgement, guided by Locker, honed in combat. Aggressive, flexible and dynamic, his style was based on a broad comprehension of his profession. That he was still alive suggested his constitution was robust – he had survived the worst the East and West Indies could offer.

Yet despite the apparent strength of Nelson's position, he had no money. Although his well-placed uncle could help, his prospects were almost entirely dependent on further war service, and no one could guess when that opportunity would next arise. Several of his contemporaries would take their services to other navies – Russia, Sweden and Portugal all hired British captains – but Nelson's emotional engagement hardly suited him to mercenary service. The American war had paved the way for Nelson's greatness, but ultimately it proved to be only a preparatory stage. By 1782 Horatio Nelson had earned himself a footnote in history, but nothing more.

CHAPTER II

Nelson, the Americas and a Wife
1783–92

Numerous examinations of the period of Nelson's career between the American and the French revolutions have characterised it as a sequence of events in which he demonstrated the strands of greatness, browbeat his elders, obtained a wife and then wasted his time and talent ashore. Too little attention has been given to the motives that underlay Nelson's actions, and the potentially fatal damage he inflicted on his career prospects. It is more accurate to see this period as one in which Nelson desperately – if unsuccessfully – sought opportunities to further his career and his family interest.

Once he had paid off the *Albemarle*, Nelson made a brief visit to Norfolk, but the society of his family held little interest for a much-travelled young captain with a career to make, who fancied himself already at the elbow of the great. He soon moved on to France, where he and the fellow officer who accompanied him intended to learn the language of the enemy and profit from the lower cost of living. He had probably been advised by Suckling, Locker, Hood or another mentor that this skill would help his career – after all, the most advanced tactical and theoretical works on naval subjects were published in France. But Nelson wasted the opportunity: his hostility to the French was evident in every letter, a pair of pretty French girls distracted him from his study, and he soon fell in love with Elizabeth Andrews, an English cler-

Prince William Henry on board the *Prince George*

gyman's daughter. Hoping, without reason, that she might consent to become his wife, he sent a mean-spirited, unpleasant letter to his uncle, demanding an allowance, its tone veering between self-pity and moral blackmail. But the cause was hopeless, and Nelson quickly found an excuse to leave. After only two months, he was back in London, socialising with Hood and visiting Lord Howe at the Admiralty, where he was offered a ship. It is uncertain whether this followed an approach by Suckling or a recommendation from Hood – but it was not a question of pure merit. The political scene in Britain was complicated. After a series of government changes and reconstructions between March 1782 and December 1783, William Pitt the Younger had become Prime Minister, but few expected his ministry to last. Hood, one of Pitt's high-profile supporters and MP for Westminster, had real leverage, but it would not survive the return to government of his rival for the seat at Westminster, the Whig leader Charles James Fox.

Nelson's new ship, HMS *Boreas*, was another twenty-eight-gun frigate. A purpose-built British ship, now ten years old, she had seen considerably more service than her new captain, and was already in commission.[1] Nelson hoped to go to the East Indies, but soon found himself destined for the Leeward Islands station. Nor would this be his last disappointment. Brother William insisted on joining as the chaplain, then the pilot ran the ship aground in the Thames, and Admiral Hughes' wife and daughter joined an already crowded ship, an inconvenience made doubly trying by the added cost and the 'eternal clack' of the woman. Nonetheless, Nelson retained his infectious good humour: he occupied his time on the voyage educating and encouraging an unusually numerous crop of midshipmen, ensuring that all went aloft and took their navigation seriously.

After calling at Madeira for wine, water and fresh food, *Boreas* arrived in Carlisle Bay, Barbados in June 1784. As the senior captain on the station, and ranking second in command, Nelson would have much to do, especially as Admiral Hughes preferred a quiet life ashore. His orders were to protect the northern group of islands – Montserrat, Nevis, Anguilla, St Christopher and the Virgin Islands – and secure British commerce, which included preventing illegal trade. Though the duties seemed rather mundane for a thrusting young captain trying to make his name, Nelson would court controversy throughout the commission.

Soon after her arrival *Boreas* was tied up at Antigua, the other squadron base, to wait out the hurricane season. Here he fell under the spell of Mary Moutray, the charming and accomplished wife of the Dockyard Commissioner. Flirting with an older woman seemed to be almost the only relaxation for the squadron's captains – apart from alcohol, which the abstemious Nelson abhorred. Cruising through the Saintes passage, where so much glory had been won, Nelson must have been struck by the relaxed atmosphere of the station, especially in comparison with the discipline expected of Hood's fleet only two years before. He applied a harsh regime of punishment for this commission,[2] and he was quick to react to any oversight or inattention that appeared to slight his office, his dignity or the rights of the Crown. He was ill suited to peacetime service: his intense, analytical approach to his profession appeared out of place in the heavy, torpid atmosphere of the sugar islands, where life could be short and the temptation to pursue pleasure almost overwhelming.

Hughes commanded a powerful force – a fifty-gun ship, four frigates and two sloops – which reflected the proximity of the interlocking French islands of Martinique and Guadeloupe and the extensive commercial interests at stake. However, the French provided few problems, unlike the community the squadron was sent to protect. Only rarely did Nelson escape the routine of the station, surveying a Danish harbour, and very pointedly escorting a French warship that appeared to be intent on surveying the British islands. Whenever possible Nelson had his ship sail in company with others on the station, to conduct tactical exercises.[3] He wanted to retain the link with war service – the reason he had joined the Navy. Moreover, the exercises kept the ship busy, and gave the men a focus for their loyalties. The *Boreas* was a clean and well-ordered ship with a healthy crew.

The key to Nelson's tour of duty in the West Indies was the clash of economic and strategic interests that followed the separation of the American colonies from the British Empire. Until 1776 American shipping and commerce had been an important strategic and economic asset, playing a major role in the French wars and the growth of the British economy. Colonial status allowed the Americans to trade freely with the West Indian sugar islands, exchanging grain, timber, fish, tar, tobacco and other produce for sugar, rum, molasses and money. American independence brought an end to this thriving and mutually beneficial inter-colonial trade.

Post-war strategic considerations were complex: as Britain's fourth or fifth largest export market, and the source of the largest single import, the sugar islands were a major state concern. Moreover, the maintenance of naval mastery required a healthy merchant marine. But now the Americans had placed themselves outside the system, their sailors and shipbuilders should not be allowed to profit at the expense of loyal subjects of the crown, nor should the sugar islands keep their connection with the rebels, in case they too left the empire. Initial attempts to retain the old connection in a new form were quickly replaced by more hostile measures. The Navigation Acts, long regarded as the foundation of naval power, would be enforced against the Americans. The Order in Council of 2 July 1783 stated that American goods were only to enter the West Indies in British or colonial ships, which had to be British-built, and British-manned – a popular measure in London; American ships could only trade direct with Britain.

The West Indian lobby, a powerful group of MPs linked to the planters and merchants, attacked the Order in Council when it came up for renewal at the end of 1783, but they were soundly defeated by the argument that to open the trade to the Americans would undermine the commercial basis of British naval power, and on 31 May 1784 the Order in Council was upheld. In 1786 a measure to encourage British shipping was introduced by William Suckling's friend Charles Jenkinson, now Chairman of the Committee for Trade. British shipping recovered quickly after the end of the war, soon outstripping the pre-war levels. The rise of British commerce provided the maritime resources for the next war: many of the men whose jobs Nelson had been so anxious to secure in 1784–6 would serve in the Royal Navy after 1793. Both the policy and the application, in short, would be vindicated.[4]

Why did Nelson take this issue so seriously? This question is generally answered by emphasising his commitment to duty, regulation and honour. But these concepts, so necessary to the creation of a certain type of Nelson, hardly square with his sinecurist behaviour in continuing to pay his brother William for a further two years after he had left the ship.[5] Nelson's concern to advance his family was typical of the eighteenth century, and such family connections also provide the key to his remarkable conduct in the West Indies.

After Maurice Suckling's death, his brother William, Commissioner in the Excise Office, became the most important family member for the advancement of the young Nelson's naval career. William's links with powerful and ambitious ministers would prove invaluable, while his house in Kentish Town was a frequent destination for the young officer when in town. Nelson may well have encountered the debates over the Navigation Acts and the Order in Council while staying with Suckling in late March 1784, already knowing he was destined for the Leeward Islands.[6] The Excise Office raised revenue on a limited number of dutiable commodities, notably beer, cider, wine, malt, hops, salt, leather, soap, candles, wire, paper and silk. In the eighteenth century, excise – collected by the producers, and passed on unseen to the public – was the most attractive method of increasing state income. It provided around half of all revenue and was regularly raised to pay for wars. The nine Commissioners sitting in London supervised the office, acted as a court of appeal and attended the Lords of the Treasury once a week.[7] His role in the Excise gave Suckling access to the key players in Government, including the Prime Minister and Chancellor of the Exchequer.[8]

However, it was one thing to pass a popular measure in London, and quite another to uphold it in the West Indies, where the local commercial classes had long been in the habit of trading with the Americans. The trade proved impossible to eliminate, although it was restricted. Whatever the ministers had intended, the majority of West Indian officials, both Governors, and Crown Lawyers, connived in attempts to evade the statutes. Their early resort to financial power, through expensive legal threats, reflected the basic issue at stake: American ships could bring in goods cheaper than alternative suppliers.

By January 1785 Nelson had realised that Hughes was overlooking a trade made illegal under the recent Order in Council, and subverting the Navigation Acts that were essential to national security. He refused to join Hughes in his connivance with the local authorities, basing his stand on the law and his own dignity. This was hardly going to please Hughes who, when Nelson produced the relevant Act and Orders, claimed he had not seen them. Desperate to square the circle created by his own acts and Nelson's unwelcome zeal, Hughes ordered his officers to admit foreign ships if the local authorities gave them clearance. Nelson simply observed that this was illegal, and ran counter to the efforts being made back in Britain to suppress such trade. Not content with teaching the admiral his duty, Nelson copied the correspondence back to the Admiralty.[9] Hughes could not assert his authority, because he was so obviously in the wrong. Instead he quietly left Nelson and the Collingwood brothers Cuthbert and Wilfred to enforce government policy, and incur the animosity of the islanders. Nelson sought government backing through an extensive correspondence. The resulting argument with Governor Shirley of Antigua was only resolved by a response from London.[10]

Knowing his approach would be popular in London, Nelson wrote to the Home Secretary, Lord Sydney, who had also received a full report from Governor Shirley on Collingwood's initial actions. Meanwhile Nelson and Wilfred Collingwood had been stopping and searching suspicious trading vessels, many using false papers. The resulting seizures were entirely legal, but profoundly unpopular, provoking local merchants to issue a claim for damages. Just in case he had not caught the attention of the Ministers, Nelson then sent a statement of his services through Lord Howe to the King. Hughes merely reported proceedings and kept his head down. Nelson's correspondence with older and more experienced officers had the tone of a self-righteous, hectoring sermon. Little wonder it reduced Hughes and Shirley to splenetic rage, a condition exacerbated by the realisation that the arrogant puppy was perfectly correct.

Nelson's confidence was based on sound advice from London. He had been corresponding with Suckling on points of shared professional concern, debating the legal niceties of his position with him and seeking opinions from the Excise Board solicitor.[11] He doubtless sent his uncle copies of the official submissions, in case the originals went astray. By September he knew his stand had been backed in London, gaining Treasury approval and legal support. He was reconciled with Hughes, who must have been relieved that Nelson made no allegations against him. While Nelson affected to be outraged by the arrival of an Admiralty letter commending Hughes for his non-existent zeal in suppressing the illegal trade, his comments should not be taken too seriously.[12] They were, like much of his more vitriolic output, only meant for his friends. He knew that admirals always took the credit for the good work of their subordinates, along with a healthy share of the prize money and any other rewards on offer. However, he took the trouble to set out his case, including the evidence against Hughes, in a memorandum which was seen by a few key figures. Nelson had learnt a valuable lesson, and would not allow his merits to pass unnoticed in future. The seeds of his concern to manage his own publicity, so obvious after 1793, were sown in the Leeward Islands.

Nelson encountered another example of Hughes' lax approach to naval regulations when he arrived at Antigua for repairs in early February 1785. He found the *Latona* flying a Commodore's pendant: as her captain was Nelson's junior, he ordered that it be struck, but Hughes had directed Commissioner Moutray to act in a military capacity in his absence. This was clearly in breach of regulations, since Moutray's post was purely civil. Why Hughes chose to act in this way is unclear, but Nelson was correct. It did not help that the drunken and ailing Captain Sandys, for whom Nelson had already expressed his contempt, was at the centre of the affair.[13] But the Admiralty, while agreeing with him, considered he should have resolved the matter with Hughes. Taken together, the illegal trade and pendant issues showed Nelson to be a well-informed, confident young captain, who was prepared to take a stand on principle, with the moral courage and personal authority to make his case. Feeble, second-rate officers placed over him soon discovered that his loyalty was only given to those of superior merit, not superior rank.

When Moutray and his charming wife returned to England Nelson needed another female focus for his emotional dependence. Like many young officers, he found local society often resembled a marriage market, with eligible young women paraded before potential suitors. Nelson might be a master of his profession, but he had yet to show any talent in affairs of the heart, where his rather too obvious desperation and failure to empathise had already led him to make a fool of himself on at least two occasions. This time he was more reserved, suppressing his greatest asset, the charming conversation that appealed to all ages and both sexes.

One of his few friends and supporters among the planters was John Herbert, President of Nevis, who stood surety for him in a legal case arising from the American ship seizures. In the President's imposing mansion, Nelson met Frances Nisbet, Herbert's niece, a widow of about his own age with a five-year-old son. Unlike the girls he had hitherto taken to heart, Fanny needed Nelson at least as much as he needed her. It was a relationship of the desperate: a single mother and a penniless, almost friendless naval officer. Fanny was looking for a way out of her current situation, and Herbert encouraged the rela-

Frances Nelson, *née* Nisbet

tionship, flattering Nelson and promising him money that never appeared. However, Herbert was determined to keep Fanny, who was a useful part of his household, until it was time for him to move to England in 1787.

If Nelson's letters are to be trusted, there was little passion in the relationship.[14] As he explained: 'Duty is the great business of a sea officer. All private considerations must give way to it, however painful it is.'[15] At least he was honest. It would be duty that took him away from her, and duty that attracted him to other women. For Nelson duty was the drug, the spur, the key – it dominated his conscious life. He closed his life with the words: 'Thank God I have done my duty.'

It was on young Josiah Nisbet that the Nelson charm worked its effect most immediately, and through the boy Nelson secured a place in his mother's heart. It is revealing that Nelson saw much of Mary Moutray in Fanny, both in her looks and her manners. Such sentiments tell us what he was looking for in this relationship, and explain why the marriage lacked sparkle. Needing a maternal relationship he borrowed Josiah's mother. Only when he needed a mother to nurse him, after Tenerife, did he truly appreciate Fanny. She served many functions for Nelson, but there is no indication that she quickened his pulse, or occupied his thoughts when they were apart. His letters remained matter-of-fact, little different from those he sent to friends and relatives. Fanny, meanwhile, had no desire to live in society and never exerted herself to move in Nelson's world. She sought quiet and calm. The fact that she clung to old Edmund, an aged hypochondriac parson, has often been cited as evidence of her innate goodness, but it is also an indication of her wishes.

As Herbert would not provide adequately for his niece in his own lifetime, Nelson was left to beg Suckling for an allowance. Once again he found it awkward and embarrassing, and was upset when Suckling did not respond with enthusiasm. As ever with Nelson, astonishing ambition and prudent foresight collided. He could have managed without the money, even as a married man.

However, all that was in the future. Before the marriage could be concluded, two years after the initial meeting, Nelson would face further challenges. The greatest of these concerned a young prince, and exposed the flaw in his hitherto stiff and correct application of service protocol. The relaxed regime of Admiral Hughes came to an end in August 1786, leaving Nelson as senior officer on the station. In December the frigate *Pegasus* arrived, commanded by a newly made twenty-one-year-old captain, His Royal Highness Prince William Henry. The Prince's rapid promotion from midshipman to captain without any service in the intervening grades, allied to his limited capacity for reflection, did not promise well. William needed to spend time, as Nelson had, serving under a first-rate sea-officer like Locker. As First Lord of the Admiralty Lord Howe knew this, urging the King not to promote him out of turn. When the King insisted, Howe appointed one of Hood's protégés, the thirty-four-year-old Lieutenant Isaac Schomberg, as first lieutenant of his ship. Nelson knew and respected Schomberg, but William was only too well aware that the older man had been sent to ensure that he did not lose his ship, or his life, through inexperience.

William was on something of a royal tour of the North American station: part public-relations exercise, part opportunity to further his education. On the surface, he was doing well: he had brought his ship to the pitch of perfection, striking all who saw her as neat, tidy and smoothly efficient. But he did not command the enthusiasm of his officers, or his rigidly controlled crew. William was in the habit of publicly dressing down the vastly more experienced Schomberg in the presence of the other officers and high-ranking visitors. A more experienced officer would have realised that the regulations on which William insisted needed to be tempered by common sense. An explosion was inevitable, and in the closely confined wooden world of an eighteenth-century frigate the tension at the top would affect the morale of the crew. Someone needed to take William aside and advise him to cool down.

Unfortunately Nelson had no intention of taking this vital role. Instead he saw a golden career opportunity: 'It is in my interest to be well with the Prince.'[16] If William was to be a professional sea-officer, then he would need someone at his right hand to supply his deficiencies. The self-confident Nelson's charm and professional knowledge evidently made a powerful impact on the impressionable young prince, who derived 'vast pleasure from his instructive conversations about our Service in general, and concerning the illicit commerce carried on in these islands'.[17]

William's petty tyranny, which seems to have been exacerbated by Nelson, led Schomberg to demand a court-martial. Nelson responded by placing him under arrest for a frivolous complaint – a feeble, non-committal gesture. He must have known that taking action against Schomberg would risk his own relationship with Hood, on whose advice the lieutenant had been appointed. Nelson had backed the wrong horse. William, as Nelson might have realised had his veneration for royalty and vaulting ambition not clouded his judgement, could hardly rise to the top of the national arm. When Howe rebuked William, and by extension Nelson, for their petty and preposterous conduct, the two men responded in typical fashion: Nelson wished he could undo his actions, and asked William to forgive Schomberg; the bull-headed William was having none of that, and proceeded to pick a quarrel with Hood as well.[18] Unlike his friend, William had family and position to fall back on, and could sacrifice his career to his pride. By transferring his hopes to William, Nelson had lost the confidence of Hood and Howe.[19] He would have the opportunity to reflect on the real balance of power in the service over the next five years.

Nelson's connection with William did have one positive result, when the Prince used his authority and rank to force the procrastinating Herbert to hasten his marriage to Frances. The ceremony took place on 11 March 1787 at Montpelier, Herbert's palatial residence, and William insisted on taking the starring role by giving away the bride.

William also found Nelson a useful occupation to fill his last months on station, when he passed on a complaint about frauds in the local purchasing of government stores: a cartel of merchants was colluding to keep up prices and spread the rewards. This offered Nelson another opportunity to gain credit with Maurice Suckling's successor at the Navy Board, Captain Charles Middleton: if his response was successful it could mark him out as a suitable man for a dockyard or Board appointment. Whatever his mistakes over the Prince, Nelson was still William Suckling's nephew, in tune with the economic reform agenda of the age, and he would show the same determination and moral courage in assailing corruption and illegality as he had against the Spanish works on the San Juan river. But the affair brought Nelson no glory, and in any case his future did not lie in shipbuilding or administration. However, it did secure him an important friendship with George Rose, Secretary to the Treasury: a key confidant of Pitt and a name for the future.[20]

Nelson left the West Indies in June 1787, low in spirits, though this was probably more the result of boredom than real ill-health: he needed to be busy, active and at the forefront of events. A month later he anchored at Spithead, remained there for six weeks and then cruised round to the Nore. While the Dutch crisis remained unresolved the Admiralty was unwilling to pay off any ships, but Nelson found the wait demoralising. He was entitled to a spell ashore, he was newly married and if there was not going to be a war he might as well go home.

The *Boreas* was ventually paid off in late November 1787 and after various official and personal journeys the Nelsons arrived at Burnham in mid-1788. Initially they planned a brief visit before travelling to France to complete the linguistic studies interrupted four years earlier. Instead they ended up settling at the Rectory, where old Edmund found his naval son a source of great comfort as young Edmund slowly died. Fanny, however, as a child of the tropics, did not flourish in the biting cold winds of the open coast, often keeping to her bed for days on end.

Nelson's complaints about being ignored should not be taken too seriously. Six years ashore for a young captain was hardly unusual in peacetime, especially after a four-year commission. In any case, these years, as well as allowing Nelson to indulge in a little 'Capability'

Brown-style gardening and resume his place in local society, gave him the leisure to reflect on his career, and develop his professional understanding. He read the periodicals and the limited literature available; he studied charts, wrote and took in the wider political scene. His analysis of the link between local conditions and political unrest demonstrated a mastery of the labour market, the political claims of the radicals, and the most effective methods of securing the loyalty of lower orders. The people, while naturally loyal, required higher wages to remove the attraction of the radicals.[21] It was an analysis that the Navy would have to adopt five years later.

Nelson's evident mastery of the Navigation Acts and other legislation related to his profession stands in marked contrast to the failure of his efforts to master French. His acute intelligence was practical, not abstract. Nelson was not a deep or original thinker – such traits were ill-suited to the dynamic aggressive methods of junior leaders in 18th century naval warfare. His great strength was a quick and clear grasp of issues, the ability to acquire, assimilate and assess large amounts of information, which then formed the basis of his decisions. Nelson's detailed analysis also shows that he remained determined to play his part in current political events, rather than being the isolated, lonely figure implied by his correspondence

The one thing Nelson did not analyse with sufficient honesty was the value of his connection with the Prince. Unlike Nelson, William had been given another ship, more as a sop to the King, who wanted to keep him out of the way, than as a sign of approval of his conduct in the Schomberg affair. Yet Howe and Hood had already settled their views on William's career prospects. He was a liability, and could not be given fleet command either in peace or war.[22] William was created Duke of Clarence in 1789 and given a ship of the line in the Nootka Sound armament of 1790, unlike Nelson, but his quarrel with the King and increasing espousal of reform and the Whig cause in the House of Lords did nothing to endear him to Pitt's ministry. With Lord Chatham, Pitt's elder brother, at the Admiralty, and Hood as his principal professional adviser, William's chances of employment were not good. Unlike his equally outspoken and wrong-headed brothers, William had the misfortune to serve in a professional force, where rank could not replace ability. After war broke out William was quickly booted upstairs to flag rank, where his lack of experience precluded any active service. Even so he remained optimistic, considering himself an ideal First Lord of the Admiralty and promising to reward Nelson once in high office.[23] While making himself a thorough nuisance, William also ruined any hopes Nelson had of rising on his coat-tails.

Though Nelson had gone to the West Indies with the backing of the two most important men in the service, his privileged access to Howe and relationship with Hood did not translate into close personal contact. Hood, the closer of the two, did not correspond with him while in the West Indies, and made his views on the Prince William affair clear by distancing himself from Nelson and bringing Schomberg into his own ship. Nelson banked on William becoming admiral, so that he could command one of the ships in his line of battle. His letters to the Prince were both prescient and shameless in their flattery: 'It is only by commanding a Fleet which will establish your fame, make you the darling of the Nation, and hand down your Name with honour and glory to posterity.' The same letter even requested a household appointment for Fanny.[24]

In 1790 a fleet was mobilised for a possible war with Spain. Despite William's intervention with Chatham Nelson was ignored.[25] It was obvious to everyone but Nelson that the Prince had no influence. Nor did Hood do anything for Nelson in 1790, or in 1791 when he commanded the mobilisation aimed at Russia. Even in 1793 he remained distant. Nelson had abandoned Hood's school for William's entourage, exchanging duty and honour for the coat-tails of a loose-living, hard-drinking lightweight. Had William gone on to better things – and Nelson beleived he could have been a useful flag officer – his move would have seemed astute. In the event, though, it was another royal who rescued Nelson from the unemployed list: his name was Louis, and he had recently lost his head.

CHAPTER III

The Chance for Glory

1793

In late 1792, as the European situation deteriorated and war with France came closer, the Navy began to mobilise. Once again, Nelson reminded the Board that he was anxious to serve. This time he did not rely on Hood, whom he had not spoken to since 1790. Within the month, however, he had seen Lord Chatham at the Admiralty, and had been promised a sixty-four as soon as it was ready, or a seventy-four if he was prepared to wait. Characteristically – and fortunately, as it would turn out – Nelson went for the more immediate prospect, although he was anxious to commission the ship at Chatham, rather than Portsmouth or Plymouth. He got his way, and his exuberance at the prospect was clear from his report of the interview to Fanny: duty called, and in his mind he was already off to sea. By late January he knew the name of his ship: the *Agamemnon*, then refitting at Chatham.[1] The symbolism of a ship named for the king of men might have been lost on the crew, who referred to her as 'Eggs and bacon', but it would be appropriate: over the next three years, the *Agamemnon* would make Nelson a prince among captains.

To man his new ship, Nelson called back many old *Albemarle* and *Boreas* officers and petty officers, recruited in Norfolk, and asked Locker, then commanding at the Nore, to find a clerk and extra men. There was a personal and parochial strain to his selections: his new-

The burning of the French fleet at Toulon

entry midshipmen included Josiah Nisbet, a Suckling cousin, and William Hoste, son of another Norfolk parson. He would make them all captains, although only Hoste became a naval hero.

As he rushed back and forth between Burnham, London and Chatham, Nelson was still Hood's man. Only slowly would he come to rely on his own judgement, and he never dreamt of refusing Hood's orders as he had those of Hughes a decade earlier. While Hood held command Nelson deferred to him, although unlike most of his fellow captains he never ceased learning from the master. His period under Hood's orders would be the penultimate stage of his education in leadership and command.

War was finally declared on 11 February 1793. Initially, the British government had not been unduly concerned by the outbreak of war between Austria and revolutionary France in 1792. The Prime Minister, Pitt, had convinced himself and his colleagues that the internal condition of France was a force for peace, leaving the Ministry profoundly unprepared later in the year when the French extended their war into the Austrian Netherlands (modern Belgium), an area of fundamental concern to Britain.

The French occupation of Antwerp undermined the basis of British security: a hostile fleet at Antwerp was ideally placed to attempt an invasion, far better than at any French base. Preventing the city from falling into the hands of a major rival had been the basic tenet of British policy since the Tudor period. The threat from the north-east would be a major issue throughout the next twenty-two years of war.

In 1793 Britain lacked the troops to take on France in the Low Countries, her old ally Holland was no longer a major power, and the military resources of the three eastern monarchies – Austria, Prussia and Russia – were largely occupied by the partition of Poland. In addition all three were close to bankruptcy. The minor powers and petty principalities of Europe were no better placed. The only assets that Britain could use to secure her strategic interests were her fleet, and her credit.[2] Pitt, committed as he was to fiscal stability, was convinced the French would be defeated by the collapse of their economy. To this end, Britain applied her major military effort to the French West Indian islands, the motor of their economy and source of key maritime resources, ships and seamen. The islands would also be useful assets for any peace negotiations, and end the threat to the immensely valuable West India shipping from locally based warships or privateers.

To address the European dimension of the French problem, Pitt needed to build coalitions based on mutual interest, money and sea power. Mediterranean strategy was driven by the need to secure a friendly base within the Straits. Gibraltar was unable to handle a large fleet, and without a major base, like Minorca, Naples or Malta, the fleet would be hard-pressed to protect British merchant ships, let alone exert any influence over France. As Hood's fleet was assembling, British diplomacy was building a useful coalition. Piedmont-Sardinia signed a treaty in April, promising to keep fifty thousand troops in the field, in return for an annual subvention of £200,000 and the presence of a major fleet. The King of Sardinia was anxious to recover Nice and Savoy, which the French had seized in 1792. In July, Naples promised to provide six thousand troops and a naval squadron at no expense, although the British would have to transport the soldiers.[3] Further treaties with Spain and Portugal completed a Mediterranean system that encircled France, while providing bases and troops. Keeping the French fleet inside the Straits would greatly simplify the defence of oceanic trade, while providing distant cover for the West Indian campaign.[4] With a fleet in place, and allied armies to hand, France could be invaded on all fronts, her resources stretched along her frontier from Dunkirk to the Pyrenees.

As Commander in Chief in the Mediterranean, Hood was taking on the most complex task that fell to a British officer in wartime. While his primary task, like that of Howe off Brest, was to watch the French fleet and give battle if it came out, he was also responsible for theatre strategy, alliance-building and coalition warfare. Naval dominance, by battle or blockade, would enable Britain to use the Mediterranean for trade, diplomacy and strategy. He was to use any opportunity of 'impressing upon the States bordering on the Mediterranean an Idea of the strength and Power of Great Britain'. This would require the fleet to be spread across the theatre.

By staying in port the French would force Hood to keep his battle-fleet concentrated, while trying to protect trade from Gibraltar to the Dardanelles, cooperate with allies and clients and exert diplomatic leverage over the Barbary states. In conducting these multifarious tasks he would have to rely on his own judgement, forming his plans on the basis of local information supplied by British diplomatic representatives, and any intelligence that could be gleaned from passing ships, local newspapers, and chance occasions. Furthermore he would have to operate without a major base, or dry-dock. It was a task that called for a range of skills above and beyond fleet command – it needed a self-sufficient, confident personality, with the political courage to take responsibility for major initiatives without being able to consult London. Only Hood and Nelson truly rose to the challenge of commanding the Mediterranean theatre.

In March the *Agamemnon* went down the Medway to Sheerness: Hood hinted that Nelson should prepare for a cruise and then join the fleet at Gibraltar. The combination of getting to sea and a letter from Hood put Nelson in fine spirits; he told Fanny that 'I was never in better health'.5 While the ship completed for sea Nelson's personal possessions arrived on coasters from Wells. A short stretch down to the Nore in mid-April demonstrated a key feature of his command: 'we appear to sail very fast'.6 Desperate to join Hood, and fearful that his orders might change, he found every delay for bad weather a terrible trial. The vigour with which he drove two French frigates and a corvette into La Hougue, while cruising off the Normandy coast, spoke volumes about his anxiety to prove himself.

Nelson was anxious to get on with the war, and found another Channel cruise with Admiral Hotham's division between Guernsey and Land's End doubly annoying as neutral ships reported that the French Atlantic ports were full of captured British merchant ships.7 Not content to do as he was told, Nelson needed to know the purpose of his orders, spending much mental effort trying to understand their rationale. This was an important lesson in command: as a result of his frustration, he himself would always take junior commanders into his confidence, ensuring they understood the broader mission so they could exercise their judgement rather than relying on orders.

The purpose of the cruise only became clear to Nelson later on: because the Channel fleet would take some time to mobilise, detachments preparing for the Mediterranean were being used to cover the western approaches before proceeding to their proper station. On 25 May Hood brought his division out to join Hotham, and took command of the fleet. The master quickly took his charges in hand, conducting tactical exercises as they waited off the Scilly Isles to cover the incoming Mediterranean convoy against a French fleet sortie. An outbound East India convoy also passed through this dangerous choke point. The next day the fleet headed for Gibraltar, and Nelson called

on Hood on board his flagship, HMS *Victory*. He was relieved to find
Hood very civil, and told Fanny 'I dare say we shall be good friends
again.' This personal warmth was vital, since without Hood's
approval Nelson would have cut a very sorry figure. Had he joined the
Channel fleet, under the austere, uncommunicative Howe, his ardour
for the service may have cooled.

As the fleet passed Cape Trafalgar heading for the Mediterranean,
Hood detached ships to water at the Spanish naval base of Cadiz. For
the first time in a century the British were welcome – inspecting the
fleet, dining on the flagship and taking in the obligatory bullfight. A
week in Spain left Nelson with mixed emotions: admiration for the
large, well-built Spanish three-deckers, and confidence that as Spain
lacked the sailors to man them they would be worth very little in battle. The failure of the Cartagena division to form a line of battle a
week later only confirmed his estimate. Nor was he pleased by the savage spectacle of the bullring. For a man who would spend the critical
hours of his life amidst the bloody shambles of the quarterdeck in
close-quarters battle, he was remarkably sensitive about the maltreat-
ment of animals.

Back at sea Nelson, already picked to lead one of the three divisions
of the fleet, continued to ponder the purpose that led Hood to hasten
the fleet out of Gibraltar Bay, confident the French ships would remain
safely tucked up in Toulon. He started to keep a sea journal, a daily
record of activity with reflections on his favourite subjects: men, measures and the weather. The journal was also used to produce letters
home, appropriate segments being assembled with a more personal
introduction for Fanny, Clarence, Locker, Edmund, William and uncle
Suckling, among others.[8] These were usually replies to letters received;
he did not have the leisure to pursue a polite correspondence.

Nelson's active and enquiring mind was soon hard at work processing the intelligence gathered from neutrals, much of it unreliable 'in
my judgement'. Rumours that the French would fit their ships with
furnaces to produce red-hot shot should, he believed, have been kept
from the fleet. Ever the optimist, he hoped the blockade of Toulon and
Marseilles would force the French fleet to come out.[9] Nor did he spare
his colleagues, readily adopting Hood's opinion that the first
encounter between British and French warships had been mishan-
dled.[10] Once off Toulon he could see the enemy: rumour had it that
their flagship, *Commerce de Marseilles*, a vast ship of 136 guns, had

impenetrable sides. Nelson shared Hood's hope that the blockade would force a battle, and picked up many more opinions from the flagship. The fast and handy *Agamemnon* and her dedicated young captain were constantly on the move. Consequently Hood's offer of a seventy-four was refused – 'I cannot give up my officers,' he told Fanny. As the fleet was ready for battle and the war could not last long, it was the wrong time to leave a proven ship.[11]

Cruising off Toulon, Nelson realised that Provence wanted a separate republic from Paris, but had no interest in restoring the monarchy, and that as Marseilles and Toulon were desperately short of food they might be handed over to the fleet. This might bring him home for the winter. Clearly in Hood's confidence, Nelson told his father:

> In the winter we are to reduce Ville France and Nice for the King of Sardinia, and drive the French from Corsica. It seems no use to send a great fleet here without troops to act with them.[12]

Three days later, on 23 August, Hood signed a convention at Toulon that placed the fortress, fleet, town and arsenal in British hands in trust for a restored monarchy. Hood displayed remarkable political courage in seizing the opportunity, although his declaration was at variance with the views of the government, which was not committed to work for any specific regime in France. The example was not lost on Nelson, who would take more than one high-risk political decision in pursuit of strategic aims. Hood had taken twenty-two sail of the line, a fortress and a major arsenal from the enemy – by a stroke of the pen.

The government had considered a range of Mediterranean options, including attacking Toulon to destroy the French fleet, and securing Corsica as a fleet base. When Hood occupied Toulon in late August some in London saw it as a potentially war-winning stroke, opening the prospect of a counter-revolution. Yet the ministers had not anticipated this opening, and had no spare troops to exploit the opportunity, while Austria showed no interest in the project. After landing the troops on board the fleet as marines, Hood had to rely on Spain, Naples and Sardinia for most of his troops: Spain limited her involvement to a thousand men, yet still restricted Hood's freedom of action, anxious that the French fleet should not pass to the British or be destroyed.[13] Although Hood worked well with the Spanish Admiral Gravina, he found the pessimistic British Generals O'Hara and Dundas a trial, and relied on his own officers for many key posts ashore.

On 25 August Nelson was sent to Turin and Naples to inform the British ministers. Along the way he fell in with HMS *Tartar*, and learned that Hood needed troops as a republican army was approaching Toulon, fresh from the sack of Marseilles. Nelson's charm, determination and professionalism helped him to obtain Neapolitan troops under the recent alliance: with Sir William Hamilton's support, he secured four thousand men before Hood's official request reached Naples. Royal flattery compensated him for missing the entry of the fleet into Toulon, and the chance of a role ashore.

Nelson was soon off again, however, to deal with a French frigate off Sardinia.[14] The frigate was nowhere to be found, and he returned to Toulon on 5 October, to find the anchorage under fire, and more significantly, that:

> The Lord is very much pleased with my conduct about the troops at Naples, which I undertook without any authority whatever from him, and they arrived at Toulon before his requisition reached Naples.

Little wonder: two thousand Neapolitan troops reached Toulon on 27 September, and another two thousand followed on 5 October, timely reinforcements as the republicans were already firing on the town.[15] Only now did Nelson feel himself fully restored to the light of Hood's favour; he relished the opportunity to follow an officer of great ability and decisive character, declaring that 'Was any accident to happen to [Hood], I am sure no person in our fleet could supply his place.'[16] It is not clear whether he included himself among those lesser mortals: perhaps while Hood remained in command he chose not to reflect on the subject.

Hood recognised the abilities of his zealous subordinate, detaching him to Cagliari by way of Corsica to join Commodore Linzee. However, Nelson's concerns were more personal. Other officers had become public figures by capturing enemy vessels of equal or greater force, earning knighthoods, prize money and promotion for their followers. He had yet to fire a gun in anger. On 22 October, he had a chance to join the heroes, encountering three French frigates, a corvette and a brig off the coast of Sardinia at 2 a.m. The *Agamemnon* was short-handed, having left many men ashore at Toulon, and alone, having lost contact with an accompanying frigate. Moreover, the officers on the *Agamemnon* believed that one of the French vessels was a battleship. Once it was light enough to ascertain that they were enemy ships, however, Nelson pursued the nearest, the *Melpomene*, and engaged her for four hours, leaving her badly damaged. But just as he closed for the kill the wind failed. He concluded that it would be unwise to continue the action – though revealingly, he asked his officers whether they approved this decision, demonstrating that he was still honing his leadership, fighting methods and command style. The officers agreed to repair the damaged rigging in case the French chose to resume the action. *Agamemnon* had lost only one man killed and six wounded, while her opponent was shattered. Nelson's sea journal quoted a famous passage from Addison's *Spectator* of 1711, concerning death, resignation and the comfort he took from the support of God.[17] This simple faith was the bedrock of his world, giving meaning to his actions and a conviction that if God was on his side the enemy would not prevail.

Arriving at Cagliari, Nelson found Linzee far from helpful, and a belated pursuit proved fruitless: the enemy had, as Nelson guessed, run into a Corsican harbour. The squadron then headed for Tunis, where a French battleship and frigate lay, protected by the neutrality of the port. Nelson ran the *Agamemnon* between the two French ships, prepared for a fight and resigned his life to God. Linzee's instructions were to persuade the Dey to allow the ships to be taken, but the Dey was too clever for Linzee, who cautiously sent back to Toulon for further orders. Nelson thought it would be best to take the French ships, pay the Dey a suitable bribe to salve his wounded pride and have done with the business. He instinctively preferred action, and was convinced that 'the people of England will never blame an officer for taking a French line of battle ship'.[18] This was the course for personal glory, but it was hardly worth annoying a useful neutral in order to seize the last French battleship in republican hands.

After a fruitless cruise along the North African coast Nelson received orders from Hood to take the frigate *Lowestoffe* under his command to look out for the frigates he had engaged the previous month around Corsica and on the adjacent Italian coast. They were a threat to British trade and allied interests, but he found them anchored close under the batteries at San Fiorenzo. Nelson was buoyed up by this further mark of Hood's confidence and the 'very handsome letter' that accompanied it. However, far away from Toulon, he had completely misread the state of the war. With an optimism that reflected Hood's opinions, he told Locker that the naval conflict was over, Toulon was in no danger and that even if it had to be evacuated the fleet and arsenal could be destroyed. December would prove the error of this judgement.

Arriving at Leghorn on 22 December, Nelson heard about the evacuation of Toulon, of Hood's heroic conduct, the knavish behaviour of the Spanish, and the horrors of the republican entrance into the city. These events did not feature in his sea journal, so the letters sent to Edmund, Fanny and Clarence were fresh compositions. Although Hood's autocratic leadership style and adversarial approach to inter-service cooperation had created difficulties at Toulon, Nelson was correct in his judgement that no one else could have carried out the task. Hood had the experience, prestige and confidence to take on such a vast politico-military mission. He kept the Republican armies at bay until mid-December with a polyglot mixture of British, Spanish, Neapolitan, Sardinian and French troops, backed by naval gunfire and sustained by his optimism. Caught between the potential for an early and decisive blow through Toulon, and the pressing but limited objectives of securing Mediterranean trade, alliances and influence, Hood waited for the troops that would secure Toulon, and used the time to spread his fleet. On 16 December Civil Commissioner Sir Gilbert Elliot heard that two British regiments were coming, causing the gloom that had descended over the beleaguered fortress to lift. Within twenty-four hours the key position at Fort Mulgrave had fallen to a French assault, forcing Hood to order the city evacuated.[19] He had little more than a third of his fleet at Toulon when the crisis came. Little wonder the evacuation was unsatisfactory.

British Mediterranean policy collapsed because the major players – Britain, Austria and Spain – had divergent, often irreconcilable aims, while the minor powers were ineffective in the new conditions of mass mobilisation and total war. France, operating under new rules, and on home soil, could raise far more men than the *ancien regime* allies, and was prepared to use them with a speed and ruthlessness that smashed the ill-coordinated multi-national forces and overwhelmed the arthritic and disjointed command system of the allies. At Toulon numbers and ruthless political leadership had driven the allies out. France's fast-moving mass armies and her young generals such as Napoleon Bonaparte, pressed on by the financial needs of the Republic and the frailty of the anti-French coalition, had deprived Britain of a mainland resting place for her fleet.

Nelson, like Hood, was quick to make the best of the situation, declaring that the cost of occupation would have ruined the country. Hood withdrew the fleet to Hieres Bay, with three French battleships and smaller craft, to wait on developments. Though disappointed on the mainland, he continued to seek a secure base: the best option was the rebellious, newly French island of Corsica, which was under inspection before Toulon fell. The island would dominate the 1794 campaign.

CHAPTER IV

Corsica and the Passing of Hood

1794

The loss of Toulon ended a period of slow and inadequate attempts by the British government to reinforce their unexpected bridgehead in France. It gave the initiative back to the French, who quickly shifted their troops onto the Alpine front to attack the Sardinians and Austrians. Following the withdrawal, Hood had resumed his core role covering British shipping, supporting the allies on land, blockading a rapidly reconstituted French fleet in Toulon and attacking any French shipping.

There was still an overriding need for a secure base. Minorca, lost to Spain in 1782, could not be considered while she was an ally. However, Corsica was a recent acquisition of France. British planners had already considered the idea of retaining the island as a war indemnity when the short, successful war they anticipated ended. After Toulon, Hood and Sir Gilbert Elliot decided to seize the island as a base from which to continue the campaign on the coasts of Provence and Piedmont. Corsica was a prime source of naval stores, which could be used to support the British fleet, and there were several good anchorages – especially San Fiorenzo Bay on the north-west coast, only three hundred miles from Toulon and close to the Franco-Italian coast where naval support for the allies would be critical. Moreover, the political situation on Corsica encouraged the British: the islanders

The greatest man in the Navy: Admiral Lord Hood

were in revolt under the veteran nationalist leader Pasquale Paoli, confining the French to a handful of coastal towns. The British exploited this, supplying Paoli with money, weapons and ammunition; in return he was willing to place the island under British protection.[1] Once again Hood exceeded his political authority by accepting this offer.

In mid-December Hood had detached Nelson from Linzee's squadron to check reports that a French squadron was in San Fiorenzo. There were three frigates there, with another at Bastia; Hood was confident they would soon fall into British hands.[2] From early January Nelson was on station, blockading San Fiorenzo and regretting that he had not taken the *Melpomene* in October, when he had the chance – he feared there would be few more opportunities to gain public glory.[3] He also reflected on the rapid, threatening reconstitution of the French fleet and the imminent arrival of Hood with a small military force to capture the island.[4]

The squadron reached San Fiorenzo on 26 January, only to be driven back to Elba by gales. Nelson's concern that the French might profit from this opportunity to get troops into Corsica was mixed with hopes that his brother Maurice would find a permanent post.[5] Clawing his way back to his station, Nelson was alarmed to find Linzee in charge of the army transports, noting in his journal, 'Beware of dilatoriness. Expedition ought to be the universal word and deed.'[6] As if to prove his point he landed to burn some ships carrying wine for the French two days later, and opened correspondence with Paoli.

Linzee continued to blunder, this time being too hasty. On 7 February, 1,400 British troops were landed, but the following day the famous Martello Tower beat off Linzee's squadron. The troops quickly worked round to the rear of the tower, built a battery and drove out the garrison, securing the San Fiorenzo anchorage. Hood then sent Nelson with a small squadron to blockade Bastia and report on the defences. In his absence the San Fiorenzo redoubt fell to a neat and well-executed assault on 17 February, and the town was evacuated the following day. Bastia was only eight miles away, but the mountain road was twice as long, and posed problems for an army without draught animals or wagons.[7]

As yet there were few indications that this war would be anything more than another round in the century-long Anglo-French contest. Nelson was not alone in thinking the war could not last: he saw the conflict petering out, 'not by the French having an absolute monarchy again, but by our leaving them alone, perhaps the wisest method we can follow'.[8] His natural optimism led him to place too much reliance on Corsican claims that the garrison was weak, although he could see they were hard at work building batteries. Speed was of the essence, and he did not hesitate to engage the defences of Bastia with his ships between 24 and 26 February. Buoyed up by Hood's commendation and entrusted with the aims of the campaign, he hoped Corsica would be a permanent addition to the Empire, becoming prosperous by replacing the Italian states as a trading partner.[9] Hood offered him the seventy-four *Courageux*, which he wisely refused. He also showed him his correspondence with General Dundas, a conventional and pessimistic Scotsman who had already clashed with the dynamic Hood: characteristically, Dundas would not advance on Bastia, arguing that it could not be taken with only 1,500 troops and disputing Hood's claim to be the overall British theatre commander. When Dundas requested proof of Hood's pre-eminence the admiral declared that his faculties must be 'palsied'. The obvious peacemaker, Gilbert Elliot, arrived too late to prevent an irrevocable breach. Dundas resigned.

Hood feared he might have to rely on starvation to take Bastia and Calvi, the last two towns in French hands; Nelson, still over-confident, believed a naval attack would suffice, even though there were twice as many French troops as he had reported to Hood. He put his trust in the 'invincible' British seamen.[10] This immature outburst ignored the lessons of Toulon. It was unwise to treat the French with contempt.

The pace to the campaign was tied to the political situation on the mainland. An early British success in Corsica would do much to counteract the adverse impression left by the evacuation of Toulon. Britain needed allies on the mainland, and a fleet based on Corsica would secure their seaward flanks. Elliot made this point,[11] and Hood acted.

Dundas's resignation did not help Hood, since his successor General D'Aubant was equally averse to attacking Bastia. Elliot considered D'Aubant a fool, others thought him a coward – whatever the truth, the military force was paralysed while he remained. As Nelson considered taking Bastia by blockade, Hood's remarkable fund of mental resource provided an unconventional solution to the command problem. The fleet had been given several regiments of troops in lieu of the Marines that were not ready when they left Britain. Hood recalled these men, some six hundred, telling D'Aubant he needed them for a fleet action.[12] In fact he planned to land them at Bastia with junior

41

artillery officers and a naval party under Nelson.[13] Suitably inspired, Nelson detached a frigate to Naples to borrow mortars, shells and stores. The covering letter to Sir William Hamilton reflected his disgust with the soldiers' caution – it was San Juan all over again.[14] While Nelson waited, he sounded the approaches to Bastia, harassed the garrison at night with his gunboats and prepared a captured frigate as a floating battery.

When a joint service Council of War did not endorse his plans Hood simply ignored it, landing a force of 1,000 soldiers and 250 sailors three miles north of Bastia. They quickly secured a strong position only 2,500 yards from the citadel, and prepared for a siege. He instructed Nelson to ensure the blockade of the town was complete, in case he had to rely on starvation, and waited until the batteries were ready.

By 11 April the sailors had installed seven heavy guns from the *Agamemnon* and four mortars from Naples with a good supply of shot and shell. Hood's demand that the garrison should surrender was rejected with customary insouciant Republican bravado. The attack commenced on Hood's signal. He directed operations from the anchorage, advising Nelson on new positions and engineering co-operation with Paoli's irregulars. The following day a small group of officers and men were in the battery to observe the effect of the bombardment when a French shot killed a servant, only inches from Nelson.

On 20 April Nelson learned that Corsica was to become a possession of the English crown. The following day Hood urged him to move quickly – Elliot had just reported the French were advancing against Sardinia:

> The situation of affairs in Piedmont and Italy makes the reduction of Bastia of the greatest importance as soon as possible, that it will be reduced I have not the slightest shadow of a doubt, but it is an object to happen soon.[15]

The driving intellect at Bastia was Hood; Elliot provided political context. While D'Aubant carped from San Fiorenzo, the force ashore got on with the job. Nelson, finally at the heart of proceedings, and under the watchful eye of his Lord since April, was full of enthusiasm and energy, pushing himself forward wherever possible, anxious to gain full credit for the triumph. However, the wily Hood did not give him sole command of the troops and seamen he sent ashore, and when Nelson asked Hood to confirm his authority over all the naval detachments Hood merely requested the junior officers to follow Nelson's directions, carefully avoiding the word 'order'.[16] Fortunately Nelson chose to read Hood's letter as a vote of confidence, and cheerfully reminded Fanny that:

> [A] brave man dies but once, a coward all his life long. We cannot escape death, and should it happen, recollect that it is the will of Him in whose hands are the issues of life and death. As to my health it was never better, seldom so well.[17]

Nelson's health, always a mirror of his soul, reflected the fact that he was busy from dawn to dusk, under fire and enjoying the confidence of his beloved chief. Most of his work was arduous rather than glorious, organising working parties to bring up cannon, shot, stores and fascines, building batteries and employing enough seamen to crew a frigate. To hasten the siege, Hood advised building a new battery on a commanding ridge; it opened fire on 1 May. Now that Elliot had returned, Lieutenant-Colonel John Moore, who had served under Dundas and shared his doubts about Hood's approach, finally began to understand that the wider political context was driving the pace of operations, not pure military logic.[18] By contrast Nelson immediately understood Elliot's argument that Corsica would give Britain command of the Mediterranean. However, that depended on taking the two towns.

Worried by the paucity of deserters, suggesting the French were not starving, Hood ordered more guns landed. Then the squadron captured a boat full of refugees, who indicated that the French were in desperate straits. As the siege drew to a close he was anxious to keep D'Aubant's name off the capitulation, keeping the military glory for the junior officers ashore, while personally controlling the surrender.[19] When Moore wrote to say that six hundred more soldiers had arrived, and D'Aubant was now prepared to cross the mountains from San Fiorenzo, Hood brusquely told him not to bother: the town was about to fall and he could save himself the trouble.[20] Moore argued that starvation alone had caused the town to fall. Even if he was correct, the honour still belonged to Hood, who had directed Nelson to blockade the town, while the army did nothing to aid the process.

Thoroughly disenchanted with his situation, and unable to influence the admiral, D'Aubant tried to hand over command, but Hood would not even provide a frigate to take him to the mainland. Instead D'Aubant brought his small force onto the ridge above Bastia just as the surrender negotiations were beginning. Bastia had cost seventeen

British lives, twenty thousand shot and shell, and forty-two precious days. A blockade would have been equally certain, but taken longer. In too much of a hurry to allow any prolonged discussion, Hood allowed the garrison of 3,500 – more than double the besieging force – the honours of war and a passage home. But though he found time to thank the officers and men, whose conduct and character he promised to remember 'to the end of my life', Nelson was given no time to celebrate: 'You will do well to prepare for the removal of *everything* from your present posts, as no time must be lost in going off Calvi.'[21]

Always anxious that his actions were appreciated at home, Nelson wrote to Locker, reminded brother William that the French ships taken at San Fiorenzo and Bastia were those he had engaged, and told Fanny that Hood's thanks in public and private were 'the handsomest that man can pen'.[22] Yet in the public dispatch on the capture of Bastia, a triumph in which Nelson fancied he had played a key role, he received slight praise. Hood had skilfully played on Nelson's anxiety to be noticed, employing him on missions where decision, energy and initiative were essential. He quickly assuaged Nelson's wounded pride, using private flattery to make up for a public oversight, not for the first time.

In early June the French tried to interfere in the Corsican campaign, sending their hurriedly refitted, scratch-manned fleet to sea. On 5 June Hood heard the French were at sea. Believing himself heavily outnumbered, Hotham had retreated from seven sail with six of his own. As Hotham withdrew to San Fiorenzo Hood beat round from Bastia, joined him off Calvi on 9 June and signalled for a general chase as soon as he saw the French. *Agamemnon* soon took the lead, but the French scuttled into Gourjean Bay, close by St Tropez, before the British could catch them. While he planned his next move, Hood detached Nelson back to Bastia to pick up the stores and move on Calvi. If the French had a fleet there was no time to lose. They would throw troops and supplies into Calvi if they had the chance, and upset all his calculations.

Nelson was now in command of the naval force at Calvi, while General Sir Charles Stuart, Dundas's replacement, commanded the troops. Nelson joined Stuart at Bastia, picked up 150 troops and their equipment, stopped for further supplies at San Fiorenzo, then set sail. They landed a few miles from Calvi on 17 June. After inspecting the defences Stuart decided to land the troops, sailors and guns for the siege. Calvi, with three outlying works and a town wall, posed some problems, and there was little time for finesse. No sooner had the forces got ashore, moreover, than a gale drove the ships out to sea, cutting off contact for three days.

Veterans from Bastia knew that another siege would require large supplies of shot, powder and cannon. There were few surpluses so far from home, so Nelson checked with Hood before landing guns. The batteries were armed with French twenty-six-pounders from the *Commerce de Marseilles*, twenty-four-pounders from *Agamemnon* and the Neapolitan mortars.[23]

Hood, meanwhile, had been given good reason to think the French fleet had been reinforced from Brest and so had joined Hotham. On 10 June, he had chased the French ships into Gourjean Bay, believing that a direct attack with nearly two-to-one superiority would overwhelm them. But the wind failed, giving the French two days to improvise shore batteries and gunboats. Hood reluctantly accepted the judgement of a Council of War that he could not get at the French in Gourjean Bay. Leaving Hotham to cover the French ships, he returned to Calvi.[24] There were problems at Calvi: General Stuart, who had initially shown more enthusiasm for joint operations than his predecessors, was now taking the same narrow-minded, wearyingly critical attitude, threatening to throw up his command if Hood did not explain his pursuit of the French fleet.[25]

On 27 June, after beating off a sortie by the garrison at Calvi, the British installed their guns and prepared to open fire. Nelson continued the practice he had adopted at Bastia, of sending Hood a daily journal of events, much to the annoyance of the army. On 4 July the first battery opened on the outlying fort of Monachique. Stuart immediately requested 250 sailors to move his shot and stores. An attempt to advance a new work against the Mozzello fort that night failed because the army officer in charge started too late. However, Stuart asked Nelson to build a work inside the Revallata Point to open on the seaward flank of the French defences, to draw fire from the main battery. He also managed to cover the construction of a new work against the Mozzello by feinting an attack on the advanced work Monteciesco. As the fifth of the six guns was being placed in the new work the French realised their error and opened a heavy fire of grapeshot. The naval officer placing the gun, Walter Serocold, was

45

killed.[26] For Nelson his death was glorious: 'He fell as an officer should, in the service of his country.'[27]

Nelson himself did not escape. The French abandoned the Monteciesco battery on 11 July, but opened a heavy fire on new British works at daylight the following morning. Nelson was hit in the face by a shower of sand and small stones thrown up from the breastwork by a French round shot. An inch or two higher and it would have taken off his head.[28] Nelson made light of the wound, treating it as a badge of honour. He remained ashore, reporting himself 'a little hurt'.[29] But the sight of his eye would not recover: in addition to rupturing a blood vessel he appears to have damaged the optic nerve.[30] The eye was not disfigured, although the pupil was unusually large. The disability was not fatal to his career, but it must have affected depth perception and the judgement of distance, valuable assets to a commander making critical decisions involving time and distance in battle. Nelson quickly adjusted, however, and came to rely on the eyes of his subordinates. It may be surmised that among his many qualities, Thomas Hardy had excellent vision.

Stuart, for all the skill with which he had out-thought the French commander, lacked the youth and optimism that underpinned Nelson's activity. The siege of Calvi had hardly begun before he was writing home for permission to retire once it was over.[31] Though Hood's decision to remain and good progress in the batteries temporarily improved his outlook a few days later, Stuart had protested vehemently when Hood suggested summoning the garrison. Taken aback, Hood unburdened himself in confidential letters to Nelson. He was concerned by the rapid progress made by the French fleet, which threatened to upset the strategy of the theatre, discouraging allies and crippling British operations. No sooner had this problem passed than Stuart was complaining that Nelson had revealed his plan to storm the key Mozzello outwork to Hood. The senior officers ashore were uncomfortably aware that Hood relied on Nelson for daily reports on operations, and that they depended on naval support. Hood advised Nelson and Captain Hallowell to keep their own counsel.

The capture of Fort Mozzello, the key defensive position in front of the town, and the Fountain battery on the night of 18 July cheered the soldiers, especially as they kept the sailors out of the action.[32] Although the squadron off Toulon reported that no more French ships had arrived, Hood had become obsessed by the idea that a detachment from Brest was coming, to outnumber his fleet. 'This makes the speedy reduction of Calvi of the utmost importance', he wrote.[33] Although Hood shared his concerns with Stuart, the General merely asked for more sailors to help ashore, as his troops were tired. Stuart's pessimism even affected Nelson, who redoubled his efforts to build fresh batteries and persuade Hood to spare more powder. Hood disagreed with the military prognosis, and wondered what the extra men were for.[34]

In reality the siege was going well: superior skill and resources favoured the British, even if the harsh terrain and lack of natural cover forced them to build their batteries from barrels packed with earth. Stuart's mood continued to be dark, however, and truce negotiations failed. After a galley broke through the blockade the artillery attack was redoubled, and on 1 August a flag of truce was hung out on the city wall. It was not a moment too soon for the British, who were sickening under the enervating Corsican 'Lion Sun'.[35] It mattered little how far the capitulation was secured by the bombardment, and how far by starvation: the British had no time to sit and wait for the French to run out of rations. With a large and complex theatre to command, Hood could not afford to have his fleet tied down by a prolonged blockade while the French were preparing for sea and active on the mainland. The balancing act had succeeded, however: Hood had kept the French fleet blocked up, taken Corsica and saved Italy. These prizes were secure while the British commanded the sea.[36]

The French marched out of Calvi on 10 August, to be shipped home. Nelson was already hard at work getting his guns and men back on board the *Agamemnon*, anxious not to miss the fleet action that he expected now Hood was 'at liberty to look at the French fleet'. First he had to organise transports for the enemy soldiers and take over the captured frigates in the bay,[37] yet he found time to compile a full report on the siege and the prospects of the new British territory for Clarence.[38] That done, he hastened away to Leghorn to overhaul his tired and neglected ship in the best refit facility this side of Plymouth. Hood and Stuart argued about how many troops should be sent to help man the fleet, while Moore carped that the removal of the sailors left all the work to his men. It was an unedifying conclusion to a successful siege, which had secured the island for the Anglo-Corsican partnership.

After the siege, Corsica became subject to the British crown, which took over responsibility for external policy, but the island retained the

legislative assembly that had voted for the union – a compromise consciously modelled on Britain's relationship with Ireland. Elliot was
appointed Viceroy, but the arrangements were loose, reflecting the
lack of opportunity for a thorough discussion of policy in London and
the impossibility of responding to local events from Westminster.
Once again Hood had triumphed, against astonishing odds, with a little help from the army.

Nelson's role in the capture was useful, though by no means as
important as most of his biographers have implied. Yet he had derived
great benefit from the Corsican campaign, which formed the last stage
in his education in strategy and leadership. It had earned him the
opportunity for an independent command, no small achievement
when there were seven admirals in the fleet. The two sieges were hard
and dangerous, but they made an impression in the right quarters.
Hood found that he could trust Nelson to act on his own, a marked
contrast to the older colleagues who had signally failed to meet his
standards off Gourjean Bay. Elliot, too, had formed a high opinion of
this dynamic young captain, and this relationship would play a major
role in Nelson's strategic education.

Nelson, in turn, had seen enough inter-service cooperation to convince him that the army was slow-moving, hidebound and negative.
The generals would not see that command of the sea was the key to
Britain's Mediterranean strategy: the army was too small, too inexperienced and too widely spread to be used for large operations. Stuart,
though an improvement on his predecessors, had no grander concept
of strategy, and failed to grasp the points about the wider theatre that
both Hood and Elliot were at pains to explain. As Nelson observed:

> General Stuart and Lord Hood are as far asunder as the other generals. They
> hate us sailors, we are too active for them. We accomplish our business sooner
> than they like, we throw them and I hope ever shall both at sea and on shore in
> the background.

Not that this rivalry was without potential penalties: 'I may perhaps
suffer by it.'[39]

The wider consequences of Corsica were complex. With the island
secure, the British fleet could act on the Italian coast, in support of
Sardinia and Austria. However, the British had very few disposable
troops, and most were being sent to Holland or the West Indies.
Instead the ministers were looking to their allies for Mediterranean
manpower. The failure to wipe out the French fleet when the opportu-

nity allowed would complicate the British position for the next four years. The presence of a powerful, if not particularly capable enemy fleet forced successive British commanders to keep their battle fleet concentrated, and close to Toulon, leaving precious few resources to exploit command of the sea or cooperate with allies.

British Mediterranean policy throughout the Revolutionary War period was crippled by the priority given to the West Indies, the Low Countries, French royalists on the Atlantic coast and the need to build new coalitions. Only when Austria requested a fleet did the subject attract serious Cabinet consideration. Otherwise the ministers were content to leave the theatre alone, and rarely troubled themselves to reply to despatches from the admiral, or the Viceroy of Corsica. This forced the local authorities to develop much of their programme alone, a task that suited imperious optimistic men like Hood, and able statesmen of Elliot's stamp, but destroyed lesser men.

By the autumn of 1795 Pitt had lost interest in Corsica, seeing it as a source of problems with Spain, rather than the key to the Mediterranean. No one in London accepted Elliot's analysis that the island gave the British control of the Franco-Italian coast, while the loss of Hood and the resignation of Stuart left the military commands in the hands of political cowards.[40]

For Nelson, Corsica had been crucial to the formation of his concept of theatre strategy, influenced by Hood and Elliot, who demonstrated how the wider patterns of war and politics combined to make strategy, and where the power of the fleet could be most effectively employed. For the rest of his career Nelson sought bases in the Mediterranean to replace the lost British province of Corsica. In his time he secured Sicily and Malta, watched Minorca return to British control, and later pressed for Sardinia to be occupied. The battery commander who served at Bastia and Calvi would mature to replace his beloved mentor. Hood, who had returned home in November after his Corsican triumph, could rest easy at Greenwich while Nelson held his old command. He had done well to pass the mantle of theatre command to an officer formed in his own image, and yet entirely his own man.

CHAPTER V

The Commander Emerges

1795

While his worn and short-handed ship refitted at Leghorn Nelson took the time to reflect on his following, and his prospects. His naval 'family' was fast disappearing: Mary Moutray's son, a universal favourite, had died on the eve of a promotion, young Hoste was ill. The broader picture was no more favourable: the French fleet at Gourjean bay was bound to escape, once the weather turned. If only Hotham had attacked them when he had the chance – it was better to fight than to make overly nice calculations.[1]

Nelson was still expecting to accompany Hood on his way home for the winter.[2] After his stay in England, he would return for the next campaign in a fresh seventy-four with the best of his crew.[3] Both men were clearly still operating to an eighteenth-century concept of war, when campaigning seasons reflected the weather, the ability of armies to operate and the age of the senior officers. Men of Hood's age, past seventy, simply could not sustain theatre command for years on end. When war was a matter of provinces and islands, such relaxed attitudes were acceptable – but this war would change the rules. Neither shortages of food nor harsh weather would stop the numerous and dynamic armies of the French Republic. The rest of Europe would have to match them or be overrun. Nelson had yet to see the enemy at full strength, and his education in this new reality over the next three

Fighting a gun in action, by Rowlandson

years would be painful, testing his reserves of optimism, enthusiasm and professionalism.

The high opinion Hood held of Nelson was shown by the fact that he detached him, rather than one of the surfeit of admirals, to reopen relations with Genoa. These had been poisoned by the seizure of a French frigate in the harbour back in 1793. The new Doge was friendly and civil, but inclined to favour the French: the city was ripe for French plunder and the old men who ran it were nervous. Closer contact with Italian politics made Nelson realise that the petty principalities, republics and kingdoms of the peninsula were feeble, frightened and incapable of collective action. Nor were the Austrians, the main ally in the theatre, much better: Nelson concluded that 'The Allied Powers seem jealous of each other and none but England is hearty in the cause.' He realised that the imminent French invasion would hinge on Vado Bay, a strategic inlet in Genoese territory. The only place on the Riviera where large ships could block the advance of an army, it was now in French hands.4 Nelson was destined to spend a long time in that bay, and to realise that his own country was by no means hearty in this particular cause.

On his return to the fleet, Nelson reminded Hood that he had lost the sight of his eye, attaching medical notes: the loss was pensionable and he was anxious to secure his entitlement. Hood carried the correspondence to the Admiralty,5 but the pension could only be awarded when Nelson had been inspected by the medical board, by which time he had added another claim. Hood handed over command to Vice Admiral Sir William Hotham at the beginning of October, leaving Nelson to hope that the change would not be to his disadvantage: he had seen little of Hotham, who had commanded the fleet at sea while Hood was off Corsica.6 When Hood departed, on 11 October, Nelson did not go with him: there were too few battleships on station to allow a ship that could float, and had half a crew, to go home. Instead he hoped for a big battle, or peace in the spring, when 'I shall return to the plough with redoubled glee'.7

After three weeks at sea he was bored by the prospect of yet more cruising with the fleet, and regretted that Hotham had not detached him to the Levant. He complained to Fanny that 'I wish we could make a peace on any fair terms, for poor England will be drained of her riches to maintain her allies, who will not fight for themselves.'8 These sentiments may have been expressed to console her, though, since Nelson provided Locker with a more professional view. They could not get at the French fleet and were only making a show at sea, being unfit for any prolonged cruising. He feared that once the French ships were reunited, they would overrun Italy in the spring if the Austrians did not send troops into Piedmont. If the French occupied La Spezia, then 'Italy is lost to us', as the vital base at Leghorn would fall in a week.[9]

The root cause of these reflections was Hotham's approach to the theatre. Where Hood had divided his forces, attempting to solve a myriad of political, commercial and strategic problems with naval force, the new admiral was only too aware that he was *locum tenens*, anxious to hand back his charge undamaged and dominated by the resurgent French fleet. His caution was in direct contrast to Nelson's growing confidence in strategic and political affairs. When Nelson rejoined the fleet off Gourjean it was to find that, as expected, the French had scuttled away in one of the recent gales. Hotham took the fleet back to San Fiorenzo, sending Nelson to look into Hieres Bay and Toulon.

Though he could not count the ships at Toulon, it appeared that they were all in port, while local sources provided a rich haul of gossip. He copied the report, quite improperly, to Elliot, now Viceroy of Corsica, with a covering note advising him to reinforce the defences of Ajaccio. If the French managed to get ashore there they would be safe from the fleet.[10] This was thoughtful precaution, not alarmism. He was confident the island could be held, and well informed about its strategic value under British rule as a replacement for Minorca and a source of naval stores.[11]

Intelligence gathering off Toulon revealed that neutral powers were flouting the British blockade to supply the French with shipbuilding timber. Genoese vessels were the worst offenders, but the Danes and Swedes were also involved. The feeble attitude of the British government, a hangover from the Armed Neutrality of 1780, had enabled the French to build seven new battleships at Toulon.[12] Nelson took matters into his own hands, with a little help from the local diplomatic representatives.

Hotham, meanwhile, elected to keep the fleet in San Fiorenzo Bay – there had been a run of foul weather and stores, ships and men were in desperately short supply. Nelson, sent to Leghorn to shift the masts of the *Agamemnon*, lamented that 'the laying in port is misery to me'.

At least he could contradict rumours that the *Agamemnon* had been captured off Toulon, and relay the latest flattering comments from Elliot.[13] He condemned Hotham's feeble response to a mutiny on Linzee's flagship, the *Windsor Castle*. When the crew demanded the removal of the captain and first lieutenant Hotham surrendered.[14] He was more severe with the officers who allowed the seventy-four *Berwick* to roll out her masts at San Fiorenzo while under repair. The captain, first lieutenant and master were all dismissed from the service.[15] The logic was clear enough: men and masts were too scarce to be wasted, but there were plenty of officers.

While the *Agamemnon* was under refit Nelson attended to his more personal needs. He took a French master for himself, Josiah and young Hoste, reporting to Fanny that he was much improved in the language. However, the only extant example of his new-found proficiency is a letter to local opera singer and courtesan Adelaide Correglia.[16] Although it was common for officers on distant stations to take a mistress, this appears to have been the first time Nelson had succumbed to temptation. Exhaustion and wounds from the Corsican campaign had weakened his resolve. He seems to have kept up the connection while Leghorn was open to the fleet: Adelaide's local knowledge may have played a part in Nelson's growing understanding of the frailties of Italian politics.

Completing the refit in mid-December, Nelson rejoined the fleet. Within days he was back in love: 'she is the finest ship I ever sailed in'.[17] But the prospect of further prolonged periods at anchor was unwelcome, 'for I hate lying idle', and he was angling to get a detached command, a frigate squadron or something similar.[18] Once again the puny *Agamemnon* would be his salvation. He was the most senior officer in a ship that could be spared. All the flag officers were in three-deckers, vital for the line of battle, and the other senior captains were in seventy-fours – but his sixty-four was a marginal fleet unit. Nelson had done well to stay in the lower-rated and lower-paid ship.

Nelson clearly had the experience, all-round understanding and political insight required for decision-making at the highest level, and his assessments were usually correct. He was also beginning to assert his authority in small ways, second-guessing his unimaginative admiral. Yet he lacked the confidence to stand alone: he was therefore alarmed by rumours that Hood might not return, and desperate to have the great man back to guide his actions. His future was thrown into doubt by the change of leadership at the Admiralty on 19 December, when Earl Spencer replaced Lord Chatham. The change removed the Admiralty from the political fiefdom of the Pitt family into a broad-based coalition. Inevitably, distance and slow communication generated rumours, one of which had Hood replacing Howe in command of the Channel fleet. Nelson immediately declared himself 'tired of this country' and anxious to rejoin his mentor.[19] However, he was revitalised by a letter from Hood, who spoke of returning with reinforcements. Fanny was told he could look forward to a pension for his eye, or a colonelcy in the marines: an extra salary awarded to distinguished senior captains, relinquished on promotion to flag rank.[20]

Despite such occasional contact, the Mediterranean fleet remained isolated and remote from events in London. Letters took at least four weeks to reach them, and Hotham annoyed his officers by repeatedly failing to give them adequate notice of a homebound departure, resulting in hurried or non-existent correspondence.[21] By late February there had been no mail for nine weeks, which added to the fleet's sense of abandonment. This increased when the Grand Duke of Tuscany left the war and declared his neutrality, although Leghorn was still open to the fleet. Nelson thought it was time for a change of policy, or strategy:

> Therefore, as all powers give up the contest, for what has England to fight? I wish most heartily we had peace or that all our troops were drawn from the continent, and only a naval war carried on, the only war where England can cut a figure.[22]

Just when the campaign seemed to be dying of inaction, Hotham suddenly ordered the fleet to sea to meet the enemy. Four days later Nelson found time to compile a letter for Fanny. He was in sight of the enemy, the signal for a general chase was flying, but the ships were hardly moving in the light airs and the French were inshore. Once again he placed his trust in God and promised to do his duty. He was looking for his Wolfe moment:

> Life with disgrace is dreadful. A glorious death is to be envied, and, if anything happens to me, recollect death is a debt we must all pay, and whether now or in a few years hence can be but of little consequence.[23]

He would write several versions of this letter over the next decade.

The tedious business of bringing a reluctant enemy to battle occupied the next two days, and brought news that the jury-rigged *Berwick* had been captured by the French. So short-handed was the fleet that Nelson wanted to borrow men from the frigates, which would not fight in the battle line. Fortunately there was not time, for Captain Fremantle's *Inconstant* played a significant role in the battle that followed. After a partial action on 13 March in which a crippled French eighty, the *Ça Ira*, had been harried by Fremantle, and then by Nelson, the two fleets engaged the following day as the French cripple and the seventy-four-gun *Censeur*, which was towing her, were taken. On the first day Nelson was in his element, leading the fleet and keeping his fast and handy little sixty-four on the stern of the much larger *Ça Ira*, pouring in broadside after broadside, inflicting heavy damage on the ship and her crew, stopping any attempt to repair her rigging, and forcing the enemy flagship to put about to her aid. He managed all this without losing a man, demonstrating seamanship of the highest quality.

The following day his first lieutenant, George Andrews, took the surrender of the two enemy prizes. Nelson and Admiral Goodall went on board Hotham's flagship to press for a thorough pursuit. Having broken the enemy formation, demoralised their crew and taken two ships it was time to take a risk. Nelson, like Hood, could see the time was ripe to 'take, sink, burn or destroy', to make the French pay dearly for their temerity and solve the problems of the theatre at a stroke. Hotham, by contrast, was unwilling to risk dividing his fleet in the presence of a powerful and coherent enemy, or risk his prizes. Nelson soon discovered that the *Ça Ira* had a siege train in her hold for the recapture of Corsica, while the French flagship was reported to have the old mayor of Bastia among her passengers. The shattered, dismasted prizes were towed back to San Fiorenzo and stripped of stores. To refit them for service would require a dockyard, stores and artificers that Hotham did not possess.

Safely anchored at La Spezia Nelson reflected on his achievement. His sixty-four, with only 344 men on board, had destroyed an eighty-gun ship with 1,300 men. He made haste to provide Clarence with a full report, including a telling detail: the French were firing red-hot shot, although they were useless on a ship. Later he discovered the French had been issued with combustible shells, but the officers had refused to use them, perhaps afraid so glaring a novelty might lead to reprisals.[24] The professional report sent to Locker a few days later was more measured about the battle, and less critical of an admiral who had secured Corsica and Italy while short of ships, men and stores.[25] At least the battle had re-established England as mistress of the seas, as she would remain if the government sent reinforcements and supplies.[26]

Once back at San Fiorenzo Nelson was bored, and took an altogether more negative view. The French might split their fleet into detachments, sending out battleships and frigates to cut up British trade while Hotham kept his fleet idle at anchor.

> In short I wish to be an Admiral and in command of the English Fleet. I should very soon either do much or be ruined. My disposition can't bear tame and slow measures.[27]

As the alliance began to unravel – Spain and Naples were about to leave the war – a victory of annihilation became all the more necessary. The fleet had no spare masts, was only manned by prisoner exchanges and lacked a suitable admiral. Hotham was in good health, 'but heartily tired of his temporary command, nor do I think he is intended by nature for a Commander in Chief, which requires a man of more active turn of mind'.[28]

After six months and a battle under Hotham Nelson could see no alternative: he was ready to stand in for Hood. His judgement had been vindicated by events, and Elliot, the most important British official in the theatre, was writing to him in the most flattering terms. In response Nelson offered to command any sailors landed to defend Corsica, should the French get ashore. This was now more likely as six battleships had reached Toulon from Brest, without any countervailing reinforcement from England. Yet even with only fourteen battleships to face twenty-two French vessels he thought Hotham's defensive posture was not the best option.[29] Suitable reinforcements – and he reckoned Hood's majestic nose was worth four ships[30] – would make a difference, especially if the French continued to prosper on land.[31]

As the fleet dropped down to Minorca to meet the reinforcements, and away from any possibility of action, Nelson became depressed. Although in good health he was suddenly tired of the *Agamemnon*. The second lieutenant, Allison, was a drunk and Nelson would give up the ship rather than serve with him as first lieutenant. Such a feeble response to a basic leadership issue was temporary, but revealing. Nelson's thoughts were elsewhere, anxious to support the Austrian counter-attack on the Sardinian coast that promised to open Vado Bay and facilitate inter-allied cooperation. However, 'our Admiral does not feel himself equal to show himself, much less to give assistance in their operations'.[32]

To make matters worse, Nelson learnt that Hood would not return. This left Hotham temporarily in command: while he was 'elated with his appointment . . . It is more than most of his fleet are for we have made a sad change.' Bored and disheartened, he mused on what the French might do while the British were 'skulking' off Minorca. He also penned a striking denunciation of the Admiralty for dismissing Hood, though this was for his brother William rather than a professional audience.[33] After three weeks the reinforcements arrived: six ships under Rear Admiral Man. Nelson was disgusted to find no letters. There was some consolation, though: at least his old *bête noire*, Linzee, was going home – there was no place for such a mediocrity once his patron was no longer in command.[34] The French proved to be far too busy with a factional struggle at Toulon to trouble Hotham.[35] And, fortunately for Nelson, the allied council of war at Milan on 22 June stressed the need for the armies ashore to secure Vado Bay, to link up with the fleet. Even Hotham could not ignore such a high-powered conference, where the British minister had taken a leading role.

Nelson's black mood soon passed, and he was delighted when two frigates captured a French ship of the same rate: 'Thank God the superiority of the British Fleet remains, and I hope ever will.' He was equally pleased that the alcoholic lieutenant Allison was invalided, although he doubted he would live to reach England.[36] Allison outlived his captain's expectations, but only just, dying in England in November.[37]

Once at San Fiorenzo Hotham detached Nelson to cooperate with the Austrian General De Vins, with four smaller ships. Before he had time to savour his freedom, Nelson ran into the French fleet off Cape Delle Melle. Skilfully drawing the French after him, he made for San Fiorenzo to warn Hotham. The fleet put to sea in pursuit as soon as the wind allowed. The clean-hulled ships of Man's division soon overhauled the enemy, who were 'neither seamen nor officers', but the victory that seemed to be in their grasp died with the wind, leaving a solitary seventy-four, the *Alcide*, to be battered into submission. The singular fruit of their endeavour then burnt to the waterline, after her 'combustibles' caught fire. Nelson saw an opportunity to win the campaign in an afternoon, but despite the French blunders Hotham still would not take any risks.[38]

Four days later the *Agamemnon*, which had not been heavily involved in the battle, was tied up alongside the mole at Genoa. While his orders were to work with the allies, Nelson's first concern was to deal with the markedly un-neutral conduct of the Genoese. He found an ally in the suitably named British minister, Francis Drake. Hotham's orders were 'useless to the common cause' because they prevented him from stopping Genoese vessels, which he knew were supplying the French armies with food. Nelson asked Drake to get the orders revoked, and was ready to act immediately, if Drake agreed. This was vital because the allied armies were relying on famine to force the French troops out of their positions.[39]

The latest promotion had left Nelson just seven places from the top of the list of captains. Instead of an admiral's flag and early return to England he had the 'honourable and pleasant' marine colonelcy and had been mentioned to the King.[40] While he told Hotham he would stay, and follow Admiralty orders, he promised Fanny he would only move into a fresh ship under orders, as he hoped the fleet would be reduced in the winter, when *Agamemnon* would go home.[41]

The urgency of the Riviera campaign increased with the signature of preliminaries of peace between France and Spain on 22 July. The Spaniards had done nothing positive for a long time, but the peace would release forty thousand French troops from the Pyrenees. Once in newly recovered Vado Bay with his eight-ship squadron, Nelson – basing his actions on the countenance of the British ministers at Genoa and Turin, and the conviction that he was right – set about stopping the Genoese trade with France, despite his orders from Hotham. He could see that the admiral 'has no political courage, which is in an officer abroad as highly necessary as battle courage'.[42] He also appealed to Elliot for support. Britain should not be worried by the protests of Genoa, Tuscany or the Barbary states when a six-week close blockade would see the Austrians advance to Nice. Hotham, though, remained cautious, content while nothing was lost. 'I almost, I assure you,' Nelson told his brother, 'wish myself an admiral, with the command of a Fleet. Probably, when I grow older, I shall not feel all that alacrity and anxiety for the service which I do at present.'[43]

Nelson's squadron at Vado cut the coasting traffic between France and Genoa, stopping any vessels with French cargoes. When the Genoese protested he reminded the minister that French warships and privateers operated out of Genoa harbour. He also encouraged the Austrians to consider an amphibious manoeuvre to outflank strong French defences on the coast.[44] The mere thought of four to five thousand Austrian troops boarding transports, let alone landing from them, should have shown him the futility of the offer. These central European soldiers would rather fight a battle than go by sea. In the event General De Vins procrastinated and Hotham would not come to headquarters to press the case: 'Hotham hates this cooperation and I cannot get him here. The Mediterranean command has ever so much business, compared to any other, that only a man of business ought to be here.' Hotham was no theatre commander, but Nelson believed that the new admiral, Sir John Jervis, was just such a 'man of business'.[45]

To keep his mind off the inactivity of his admiral Nelson captured a French convoy of eleven vessels and the escorting corvette off Alassio on 26 August, scrupulously respecting the Genoese fort. A week later his men secured a Turkish ship, but took heavy casualties and were beaten off by two more.[46] He believed the blockade had stopped any Genoese vessels sailing to France for over a month. Even Hotham was pleased, although this may have reflected Nelson's utility as a provider of material for his otherwise featureless dispatches. Gradually Nelson realised that the Austrians were not entirely honest partners in the war effort. While British ministers grappled with Viennese aims in Northern Italy, Nelson saw its effect on his campaign. They had no intention of advancing, seeming more concerned to secure another £4 million of British money. This impasse made him regret Hotham's refusal to come ashore. 'I hope the general will be left without an excuse,' he pleaded, but to no avail.[47] A little of the admiral's time, and a few transports, might have embarrassed the general into moving.

On 20 September the Austrians attacked, directing their effort at the strongest point in the French line – casualties, it seemed, were of no account, only money. Recognising that purely military issues were now subordinate to policy, Nelson saw that the Mediterranean command carried with it another task: 'I shall now become a politician almost fit to enter the diplomatic line.' While England tried to control the war with money, the impecunious continentals did not join the common cause with any enthusiasm. As he told Elliot, the excuses offered were frivolous.[48] The newly arrived Neapolitan flotilla was proving awkward, needing an endless supply of flattery and patience to direct. The effort was necessary, though, because the Neapolitan craft were the only ones that could keep the French oared gunboats off the Austrian flank.[49]

With Hotham's tenure of office coming to an end, and the Austrians slipping further and further into absolute apathy, Nelson was ready for peace. The conduct of the Court at Vienna and failure of the latest émigré landings in Brittany were the final straw. If the French wanted a Republic they should be allowed to make their own choice. He despised all Frenchmen, of whatever politics: they were all 'false and treacherous', while Continental alliances were futile.[50] A cruise along the French coast in late October threw up some useful intelligence. The French sailors had all deserted, leaving the fleet immobile, but half the army from the Pyrenees was en route to Italy, some twenty thousand men, while new barracks for another eighty thousand were being built at Avignon. In defiance of the dictates of sound finance France was funding the war by depreciating the paper currency, but food was plentiful.[51]

A theatre commander with such insights might have been able to act, but Nelson was still tied to his task. Vice Admiral Hyde Parker had taken over the fleet, to await Admiral Jervis. Nelson renewed his call for a commodore's pendant. He did not expect to remain when the new man took over, so the pendant would have been a positive conclusion to his Mediterranean service. Not that he was going to let anyone ignore his work. The Austrians requested his aid on their seaward flank, expecting an attack, but the holding ground was poor, and he could only promise to come when called. Instead he had to act at Genoa, where French vessels, protected by Genoese neutrality had captured an Austrian command post with a large pay chest and returned to the port. This was blatantly un-neutral behaviour by the Genoese: Nelson and Drake demanded that the ships be disarmed and that Genoa satisfy the Austrians for the outrage. This was quickly granted. Genoa's pro-French policy was not damaged by a concession to *force majeure*.

Making the excuse that Hyde Parker was at sea with the fleet, Nelson copied his report to the Admiralty.[52] He wanted to make a

name for himself before he got home, and cared little about the protocol. In part, his insubordinate behaviour reflected a promising political opportunity back in England. The offer of a seat in Parliament was
in the air, but Nelson would only accept it on certain conditions. He
wanted to come in on the Portland interest, the mainstream Whig faction that had come into coalition with Pitt in 1794. He wanted to sit
for the same borough as his friend Lord Hugh Seymour-Conway,
already a naval lord, 'where the same Admiralty interest will support
us both'.53

Already expecting to be recalled, and well aware that a seat in
Parliament was an excellent lever with which to secure a prime
appointment, Nelson may have overplayed his hand. He soon had
work enough on the Riviera. Just when he thought both armies were
going into winter quarters, the French assembled a flotilla of small
craft, appearing likely to withdraw. Nelson asked Hyde Parker to
come and lead, or at least support, an attack. Instead Parker withdrew
the squadron. The French attacked at Voltri on 23 November with
their usual vigour and speed; 'the French, half naked, were determined
to conquer or die'. Without his smaller craft, and forced to keep
Agamemnon in Genoa harbour to stop the French using the ships in
harbour to outflank the retreating Habsburg army, there was no effective naval support for De Vins. Well aware that he would be used as a
scapegoat for the defeat, Nelson was anxious to set out his version of
events.54 He blamed Hyde Parker for failing to come to the bay before
the attack, when a suitable force could have stopped the operation.

The Austrians retreated from the coast, allowing the French to re-
occupy Vado Bay. Into this unfortunate scene came Admiral Jervis, 'to
the great joy of some and sorrow of others in the fleet'.55 Knowing
how important first impressions can be, Nelson quickly provided his
new Commander in Chief with a resumé of the Vado Bay campaign,
and the politico-military position after the Austrian defeat.56 Still
expecting to go home, Agamemnon being too rotten to remain,
Nelson was looking for peace. He was pleased to hear that Sir Charles
Middleton had left the Admiralty over the supercession of an aged and
timorous admiral. This suggested that Earl Spencer's Admiralty was
looking for young, aggressive officers.57

Nelson understood that the new type of war would require aggression, insight and resolve, with high political courage and a good relationship with the ministers, both in theatre and at home. However, he

had not yet fully appreciated just how far those half-naked French soldiers had raised the stakes of war, and transformed its methods. Hotham's timid half-measures had failed; an entirely different approach would be needed if the fleet was to retain any influence in a theatre where land and sea power were evenly matched, by nature and topography. The extent to which the new admiral, Jervis, could replace his old Lord was uncertain.

The degree to which both Hood and Jervis influenced Nelson's career and thought can hardly be overstated.[58] Though Nelson admired many of his captains, fine seamen and brave warriors like William Locker and Peter Parker, it was the great fleet commanders who did most to shape his approach to war. He had consciously sought the patronage of Hood, the leading strategist and tactician in the service, in 1782, before relocating his admiration and ambition onto the more durable figure of 'Old Jarvie' in 1796. He thus stepped neatly from one stream of opportunity to the next, changing his methods and sensibilities to match the new mood. Between them, the two men provided him with the practical training and inspiring example necessary to complete his education.

Of the two admirals, Samuel, Viscount Hood[59] was the more obvious source of inspiration, and he remained the dominant intellectual influence on Nelson's professional career. Hood's patronage nourished his aspirations in 1782, and helped to keep his career afloat during the turbulent years that separated the American War of Independence from the French Revolution. He and Nelson had much in common. Both were the sons of country parsons, reliant on a good start and their own merits to transform a steady career into rank, reward and public fame.

Hood's perspective on war was invariably offensive, seeking battle through active operations, anxious to engage the enemy wherever encountered, and without hesitation. He understood that battle had many purposes: blocking a superior force, securing trade or possessions or, when the opportunity arose, annihilation. He also saw that any engagement was only part of a campaign, and that it should be exploited to the fullest extent. His greatest achievements at sea – off St Kitts, in Frigate Bay and the Saintes – only hinted at the rich vein of insight and acumen that informed his approach to battle. Whenever the enemy offered the chance he was anxious to attack, to concentrate force against part of their formation, crush it and move on. He believed in an open blockade, and preferred drawing the enemy out to sea for battle, so that they could be destroyed. Here his ideas were in complete contrast to those of Jervis, whose close blockade proved to be the key to the very different war that emerged after 1795. Hood was an eighteenth-century admiral, ideally suited to limited wars where a single battle could decide the outcome, or at least the terms.

While his tactical and fleet-command skills were outstanding, it was at the highest level of strategic and political direction that Hood proved his greatness. His analytical approach to war, weighing up the options open to the enemy, provided a solid base for a truly remarkable confidence in his own judgement. Offered the keys to Toulon in 1793, he immediately seized an opportunity that would have terrified his contemporaries: he read the situation clearly, weighed up the options and took a wise decision. Despite the ultimate failure of the operation, it was the right move: it broke the strength of the French fleet more severely than the actions of Howe and Bridport combined, because it ruined the arsenal and workforce[60] as well as the ships, destroying the essential bond of trust between the Toulonese and the government in Paris.[61] Throughout the 1793–4 Mediterranean campaign, he worked tirelessly to fulfil his instructions to impress upon the local states 'the strength and power of Great Britain',[62] promote the national interest, cripple the French fleet, and exploit opportunities. His capture of Corsica was a wonderful demonstration of talent at all levels of war.

Hood's leadership style was direct. His concern for drill, exercise and discussion with his subordinates was noteworthy, providing a model for his most famous protégé.[63] His plans were carefully explained, and he used frigates to convey his orders to the battle-line. Even in defeat, at Toulon, Hood never lost his optimism, or his ability to think through the problems. And he was equally effective in using intelligence and other assets to further his aims. Above all, he never wasted time, constantly trying to exploit the fleeting chance of victory, and to press on the campaign while the enemy was off balance. Nelson took this to heart, valuing time and timing among the greatest of all assets.

Nor were Hood's supreme talents unknown to the wider public. As an Irish peer, he was elected MP for Westminster alongside (though in opposition to) Charles James Fox; he held high office as First Naval

Lord at the Admiralty and was widely consulted on naval questions after his dismissal from the Mediterranean. When Hood joined Pitt's party in 1783 Nelson, too, became a Pitt partisan.[64]

When Nelson returned to sea in 1793, having been out of favour with Hood, and everyone else in high office, for half a decade, he was desperate to prove himself. Though Hood consistently ignored Nelson's deeds in his correspondence and dispatches, implying that he was not particularly impressed, his open, free and encouraging conversation brought the two men ever closer as the campaign in Corsica kept them ashore, fighting thick-skulled redcoats as well as the enemy. Nelson valued the praise of Lord Hood above all other currency, just as his followers would esteem his own generosity half a decade later. The confidence he derived from Hood's praise allowed him to relax and reflect on his profession, rather than desperately seeking some sterile glory in battle.

Nelson did not possess the supreme egotism of which he is often accused: rather, he consciously built his methods and style on the best models and consistently sought the approval of his seniors. His anxiety to have his deeds recorded was part of this process, reflecting his fundamental and recurring insecurity. This trait drove him to excel, to take risks, and publicise his successes. In the same vein every setback was, to his mind, a disaster – the end of his career. He needed to know that his actions were approved, and only then could he relax. He freely acknowledged his need for praise, public applause and the outward show of glory: he lived his life for public service, and public acclaim. To this end he risked his life, because the spirit of the age required him to be personally brave.

CHAPTER VI

Nelson and Jervis, Partners in War
1796

Admiral Sir John Jervis took command of the Mediterranean fleet in early 1796. He was a hard-bitten veteran, with an awesome reputation for upholding discipline. He was also a shrewd judge of men and methods with a passion for sound organisation. With his political patron Lord Shelburne unlikely to return to the front rank of political life, he would have to rely on merit to make his career.[1] A man of unbending principle, Jervis would defend his convictions against his King, the Prime Minister and the Admiralty with equal determination. Little wonder he was the last choice for the Mediterranean. Having secured a fortune in prize money during his recent West Indian command, and survived an attack on his handling of local prize courts, further brushes with avarice, never far from an eighteenth-century naval career, could be studiously avoided. His ruthless campaign against peculation and fraud created the Victorian naval morality that considered profit vulgar. However, this was not the morality of his own age.

Jervis was not enamoured of the chaos he inherited from Hotham: the majority of his senior officers, legacies from Hood's regime, struck him as irresolute and inadequate. His views hardened when Rear Admiral Robert Man made a serious error of judgement, which in a rare moment of generosity Jervis attributed to a nervous breakdown.

A champion of order: Admiral Sir John Jervis

He considered few admirals on the list fit for their rank, preferring to use his chosen captains, citing Nelson as the example.[2] The tendency for officers to go home alleging 'health' or private business, a tendency that the absentee Lord Hood could hardly condemn, struck him as amateurish weakness. His insistence on a proper medical report and attempts to close 'unofficial' channels of communication with the Admiralty forced every commissioned officer to chose between hard service and half-pay.[3] Nor were the seamen exempt from his iron will. In return for improved food and conditions Jervis demanded absolute obedience. He replaced officers who allowed their men to be 'incessantly drunk' and who generally relaxed discipline.[4] After he had replaced the captain of the *Marlborough*, no officer would dare contend that he could not discipline his crew, or hesitate to hang the mutinous. Nelson shared his abhorrence of drunkenness, both in the service and in his family, where young Suckling Nelson was hurrying his way to the grave by the bottleful.[5]

Within weeks Nelson, ever attuned to the mood of the day, realised that this was not a man he could ask for leave. Instead he expressed a desire to stay in the theatre after the next promotion, when he would become a junior admiral. Claiming he would not regret the loss of a lucrative marine colonelcy impressed the new admiral as much as his obvious talent and dedication. Nelson's views of other officers began to follow Jervis's dicta, notably on the feeble conduct of Hotham, whom Jervis termed a 'crapule'. These opinions were, in turn, largely based on discussions with Nelson.

Seeking resolute professional commanders for his detached ships and squadrons, Jervis condemned the great bulk of those on the list. He urged Lord Spencer to hasten the promotion of Nelson, whom he had elevated to Commodore *pro tem*, and lamented the lowly situation of Captain Troubridge. Later he demanded the removal of Rear Admiral Waldegrave.[6] Throughout this period Nelson continued to garner praise, and established his claim to command the detached squadron in 1798. Before then, he would also have occasion to demonstrate his unique tactical acumen under the stern gaze of 'Old Jarvie', who affected to be the hardest man in the service.

Beneath his grim public persona, however, Jervis hid a sensitive soul. Off duty, he liked nothing better than playing practical jokes on junior officers and gossiping with other men's wives, although that was as far as he thought such things should go. That others were less resolute was a matter to be regretted and countered. In 1796 he had to send several lieutenants home, their venereal complaints too far advanced for shipboard treatment, ruined by the dissolute habits of Leghorn. Whether this was the reason he asked Emma Hamilton to keep Nelson away from the local belles of Naples is not clear, but the value of keeping the fleet permanently at sea, away from such temptation, was clear.

Four years as Commander in Chief Mediterranean was a terrible burden to place on any man, particularly one as dedicated and courageous as Jervis. Under his leadership the easy-going fleet that Hood had created, and which only he could lead, was reformed. New ships and men, drilled into professional fighting machines by constant exercise, transformed his small fleet into the most effective fighting force on the planet. Jervis's fleet would set the world an example of 'skill, discipline, and subordination' – it had never lacked the first quality, but the two latter were entirely absent when he arrived.[7] Even before he had the chance to prove his point, he knew the Spanish would be 'cut to pieces' by his fleet making 'its way through them in every direction'.[8] When the chance for glory came he was heavily outnumbered. But he not only won the battle, but also, having destroyed the enemy's will to fight, imposed a crippling close blockade, a very public humiliation for the proud Spanish admirals to endure.

These were the methods of a new age, the age of total war. With the mass armies of revolutionary France rampaging across Europe, only a revitalised fleet could resist the threat of a pan-European fleet – French, Dutch, Spanish and more. This 'Mediterranean Fleet' discipline was the terror of the service, and its salvation. Nelson was at one with him, and was accordingly sent to restore order on that 'abomination', the newly arrived *Theseus*.[9] Nelson admired Jervis's concern to impose sound, thoughtful administration, to preserve the health and welfare of his men, select and reward the dedicated professional officers, and keep his ships efficient and prepared for long cruises at any moment. The system Jervis developed – basing his fleet at isolated anchorages, far from the temptations of port and the endless excuses for delay to be found in dockyards – would be vital between 1803 and 1805. The fact that they saw eye to eye on this point removed any lingering doubts Jervis may have harboured about Nelson's fitness for a fleet command.[10] The point would be proved during the brief Baltic command of 1801, when Nelson would employ the same administrative and organisational style as Jervis: even his standing orders were largely based on those Jervis had issued, copies of which he kept as a handy reference.[11]

The two men possessed a complementarity that is perhaps unique in naval history. Jervis moulded fleets, reorganised strategy, overhauled administration and imposed his will on the enemy at the highest level. His root-and-branch reform of the Navy broke the back of an eighteenth-century attitude that tolerated abuses, corruption and incompetence as an inevitable consequence of the political and economic system.[12] Yet for all his solid professional merit, strategic grasp and understanding, Jervis lacked the intuitive, creative spark that could transcend the routine, the insight and judgement to unhinge the enemy, the *coup d'oeil* to spot the flaw in their dispositions and the absolute self-confidence to disobey a direct order. He found the qualities that he lacked in Nelson, qualities brought to fruition by Hood's tutelage, and he had the courage to stand by this troubled genius when things went wrong either in battle or on shore. Moreover, he understood the type of role that Nelson was well-equipped to take, and also that he would have been ill-suited to the drudgery of the Grand Fleet's close blockade of Brest: the very success of the blockade, meaning that the enemy would never come out while he was there, would have gnawed at his soul. Instead Jervis sent Nelson's friend and saviour William Cornwallis to take up that thankless task: here was a man who would not be defeated by storm, or any number of Frenchmen.[13] It was on Cornwallis that Jervis anchored the strategy of the war.

The Mediterranean campaign of 1796 began with some cause for optimism: the Fleet now possessed a secure insular base on Corsica, a new Commander in Chief, and the usual protestations of commitment from Austria and various Italian allies. Unfortunately the British government was too busy with other, more pressing demands to accord the theatre the priority it demanded. British resources were overstretched, while those of the various allies were failing. Corsica, which could have been a source of real strength, was largely neglected. As Home Secretary the Duke of Portland was responsible for the island, but he was only concerned to reduce expense. The strategic advantages obvious to Nelson, Jervis and Elliot were the key to an effective Mediterranean policy. Yet Elliot was always short of money and troops. Rather than exploiting his island as the base for offensive strokes, he had to concede the initiative to the enemy.[14] The scale of the war was too great for his tiny force to act alone on the mainland, and the Austrians were no longer on the coast.

Nelson had not enjoyed the brief period when Vice Admiral Sir Hyde Parker held the command: Parker 'did not treat me very well . . . and I should be sorry to put it in his power again', he observed later that season.[15] His third year in the Mediterranean began with reflections on the subjects that would dominate the following twelve months. Personally, as he told Fanny, he was anxious to go home, and his worn-out ship was only fit to escort the next convoy. Yet he remained intellectually committed to the war, anticipating that the French must attack to plunder the 'gold mine' that was Italy, and he expected them to come by the coast road with transport shipping. Blocking such operations had been his mission in 1795. The only way he could reconcile these conflicting concerns for home and glory was to hope for an early peace.[16]

His future was settled by his first meeting with Jervis. He had declined a written offer of a larger, better-paid ship but he was not prepared for the personal touch of a man he had met but once, and then briefly many years before. Jervis understood the man, and won his loyalty by making him feel special:

> I found the Admiral anxious to know many things which, I was not a little surprised, had not been communicated to him from others in the fleet, and it would appear that he was so well satisfied with my opinions of what is likely to happen, of the means of prevention etc., that he had no reserves with me of his information, opinions and thoughts of what is likely to be done, and concluded by asking me if I should have any objection to serve under him with my flag.

Nelson hedged a little, promising to stay if his flag came before *Agamemnon* went home, declaring that he would be proud to hoist it under Jervis's command.

The object of this letter was to persuade Fanny that his decision to remain on station was inevitable, reflecting merit, possibilities and rewards rather than his own desire. Jervis had won his heart. Nelson would not abandon anyone who was prepared to invest so much charm, flattery and genuine esteem in retaining his services. Subconsciously he hoped that retailing Jervis's compliments would satisfy Fanny and enable him to remain on station until the peace. Desperate for glory, and fancying the chances improved by the new admiral, he concluded, 'my health was never better than at the moment of writing'.[17]

Jervis, too, was satisfied to have confirmed what he had heard of this remarkable officer and secured his services for the foreseeable future. He informed the First Lord that he would send Nelson back to the Gulf of Genoa 'where he has so eminently distinguished himself'.[18] He was anxious that Spencer should recognise the name when the time came to ask for something more. This was significant as Spencer had just refused Nelson's request for a commodore's pendant, arguing that there were already too many flag officers in the theatre.[19] Spencer had missed the point: there were indeed many flags, but few of them belonged to admirals capable of independent command.

Fresh detached service occasioned a little jealousy on the part of fellow captains, but Nelson, confident he had earned the compliment, gave them a straight answer. The mission remained unaltered, blocking any small-scale seaborne movements.[20] He continued to be impressed by Jervis, who refused to go ashore at Leghorn, where his predecessor had lingered too long and where, as Nelson knew, many an officer was indulging his vices. He was a 'man of business' who would make short work of the French fleet. Having read the King's speech at the opening of Parliament on 27 October Nelson could see little hope of a just peace – France had not been beaten enough to concede.[21]

From the outset, Jervis treated Nelson as a trusted confidant, a close colleague and a fellow flag officer. He sent him to report on the condition of the French fleet at Toulon: there were five new ships of the line, so Jervis could spare none to go home. To reconcile Fanny to this new delay, Nelson retailed further flattery. 'Sir John from his manner I plainly see does not wish me to leave this station. He seems at present to consider me as an assistant more than a subordinate, for I am acting without orders.' He also reported Jervis's response to a query about Nelson's promotion prospects: 'You must have a larger ship for we cannot spare you either as admiral or Captain.' The older man had won the heart of his brightest subordinate by treating him as an equal, by concurring in his own estimate of his worth.[22] Until his flag arrived Nelson was anxious to have a commodore's pendant as symbol of his authority over his squadron, a higher rank to help his discussions with the Austrians and a record of his achievements.

Back at Genoa Nelson resumed his military and political work, liaising with the British ministers, developing a strategic view and pressing for allied cooperation to recover the vital water barrier at Vado Bay. The threat was obvious: he saw the French fleet preparing for sea, the weakness of the various Italian governments, and the inevitable attack. After all Italy was 'a gold mine' and the French were short of funds. Although the Government of Tuscany was increasingly pro-French, he hoped the Neapolitans would provide a flotilla for coastal operations, as the British fleet lacked the spare manpower for any small craft. However, he was convinced the sea was the essential avenue for any major advance from France into Northern Italy. After two years of small-scale advances on the Riviera he expected the French would use their fleet to land behind the Sardinian and Austrian forces at Genoa or Leghorn.[23] General Bonaparte had other ideas, recognising the option of leaving the coast and avoiding the naval threat. He could not entirely ignore the coastal route for logistics and heavy equipment, but he did not base his campaign on the Riviera.

Bonaparte's Italian campaign of 1796 would take all the Italian states out of the war, destroy the logistical base of the British fleet and outflank the blockade of Toulon, already complicated by a French squadron at Cadiz. The most effective British response would have been to adopt a genuine maritime strategy, securing Corsica with a significant military force, developing the embryonic naval base at Ajaccio and controlling all offshore territory. Trade could be sustained, a blockade imposed and Spain may have been deterred. The British government was unable to follow this strategy because it had failed to deal with any of the naval threats that it faced – from the Dutch fleet in the Texel to the French at Toulon – before Spain entered the war in late 1796. The addition of Madrid to the list of hostile powers complicated the arithmetic of naval power. Although the British retained a working command of the sea, and were qualitatively superior to their foes, they had not imposed their dominance in battle, and could not risk large detachments to the Mediterranean when the British Isles were threatened with invasion from several quarters.

The problem only arose because the largely static war on the Franco-Italian frontier was suddenly transformed. The latest round of an age-old contest between land power and sea power for the Italian peninsula was won by Bonaparte's army. Hitherto, naval control of the Riviera had been enough to block the advance of an army from France into Italy, or to facilitate an attack from Italy into France. Even in 1795, Nelson's squadron at Vado had been enough. But 1796 would be different. The French changed their strategy, and their command, adopting methods that made naval control irrelevant. Bonaparte, a keen student of military history, may have been inspired by Hannibal, in addition to the more recent work of Bourcet. Whatever the origins of his ideas, his appointment to command the Army of Italy in March 1796 transformed the outlook in the Mediterranean. French strategy was directed by Lazare Carnot, the 'Organiser of Victory'. Carnot had created the mass-conscript armies and the offensive approach that exploited these human resources. Well aware that Austria was France's main military opponent, his plan for 1796 was for the army on the Rhine to attack Austria, while the Army of Italy launched a diversionary offensive. If successful, the latter would take Piedmont-Sardinia out of the war, defeat the Austrian armies and drive them across the Tyrolean Alps into Austria, where they would join their colleagues from the Rhine to impose peace.[24]

In effect Italy was a side-show, although plunder from northern Italy was a major attraction to the cash-strapped, economically chaotic Republic.[25] Unaware of the new French policy, the British continued to view the theatre in isolation. This may explain why they consistently misread the object of the French campaign.

Nelson expected the French to use their naval assets to outflank the Austrians, but despite his success in blocking this route, seizing a siege train and Bonaparte's library, the French had abandoned this route. Their fleet remained in harbour, locked up by Jervis while the coastal route was insecure. To avoid using the sea Bonaparte risked advancing through the narrow Alpine passes, in effect outflanking the fleet. This was successful because the lightly equipped French soldiers lived off the land and did not need magazines and depots. This radical new method allowed them to outmarch the supply-obsessed Austrians. Led by young, aggressive, battle-hardened generals, the French soon knocked Piedmont out of the war, before turning on the Austrians, who were unable to resist the onset. Yet French victory at Castiglione was by no means a foregone conclusion: the unique talents of General Buona Parti, as Nelson initially named him, were critical. Equally important, the Italian states made only feeble efforts to save themselves: Piedmont-Sardinia had a mere fifteen thousand troops in the field, instead of the fifty thousand that were funded by the subsidy treaty with Britain.[26] The 1796 campaign was a major lesson in higher strategy. It seemed to confirm Nelson's view that Britain would be well advised to operate without allies, and rely on the sea. It would be his life's work to ensure this approach was successful.

To persuade his star officer to remain in the difficult inshore post, Jervis kept up the praise – this time for his handling of diplomatic negotiations at Genoa – and promised to write to Spencer to secure him a commodore's pendant. Unlike Hood, Jervis did write, and acted before he had heard from Spencer.

> Captain Nelson, whose merits are well known to your lordship, is very ambitious of becoming a flag officer, which does him the greatest credit, because of his having the Marines. Should the event happen he is also very desirous to hoist his flag in the Mediterranean. As he will hold a very important trust during the ensuing campaign, I hope you will not disapprove my giving him an order to wear a distinguishing pendant.[27]

Jervis would command the main body of the fleet, keeping Toulon closely blockaded. He took a firm grip on his squadron, quickly sorting the professionals from the lightweights, the reliable from the inconsistent, and transformed Hotham's force into the best-disciplined fleet ever sent to war. A new navy was being built, one ready for the demands of the total war: it would be self-sufficient, healthy, well drilled in seamanship and gunnery, exercised in squadron tactics and the school of the service. Some officers were beyond hope and were sent home, others with potential could be trained. A few needed no further education. First among these was Nelson, who knew that Jervis was 'using every influence both public and private with Lord Spencer for my continuance on this station'.

Nelson had been told that he would command a division of the fleet in battle, the highest honour anyone could pay a captain.[28] He quickly used his pendant to browbeat the Genoese authorities. When they complained that he had fired on their territory, he dismissed their protest on the grounds that Genoa was an occupied country, and he had only engaged the occupying French forces after they had fired on his ships. He kept Jervis, Elliot and Spencer informed of his proceedings.[29] Spencer used these naval successes to keep up morale at home despite a succession of disasters on land.[30]

Once again Nelson's hopes were no sooner raised than they were dashed. After three days of battle in the hills the Austrians were beaten everywhere, losing ten thousand prisoners, and between four and five thousand killed and wounded. 'The French fight on shore like our

seamen', Nelson reported, 'they never stop and know not the word
halt.'³¹ This was grudging admiration, but it reflected the reality:
Bonaparte's half-starved troops had carried the day. Naval support
had been limited by the lack of flotilla craft, Jervis could not afford to
risk a battleship close inshore, as he was already inferior in strength to
the French. Nelson's squadron managed to cut out some French store
ships at Loano on 23 April, but it was not enough. The Austrians
retreated from the coast.³²

By the end of April Piedmont-Sardinia was making peace, and the
Austrian army was in full retreat.³³ The French now occupied Genoa.
A depressed Nelson asked Jervis if his squadron would not be of more
use elsewhere in the Mediterranean. Britain was running out of allies:
it appeared inevitable that Spain would declare war, ending any
chance of saving Italy. He hoped Corsica could be held, and asked for
leave to take the baths at Pisa.³⁴ His mood mirrored the state of his
beloved *Agamemnon*, now 'a mere tub' floating on the water, in desperate need of a major dockyard overhaul and without the stores to
keep her patched up.³⁵

From his blockade station off Toulon, Jervis recognised the impending collapse of Nelson's morale. He administered the necessary tonic:
a mixture of praise for the operation at Loano, news that there would
not be a third flag officer in the fleet and that Spencer had been asked
to give Nelson his pendant, or his flag. Little more than a week later
he asked Nelson to serve out the rest of the war and offered him leave
to go to Pisa.³⁶ This was the treatment he needed. Nelson was immediately restored, abandoning the trip to Pisa and turning his thoughts
to the political situation.³⁷ He was astonished by French demands that
Parma, Modena and the Papacy hand over art treasures as well as
money to secure peace: 'The Louvre is to be the finest art gallery of
pictures in the world.' Having promised to see out the war he
explained his choice to Fanny by stressing what a compliment it would
be to hoist his flag on this station. With that they would have to 'rest
contented'. Peace seemed to be coming closer: Italy was lost, Corsica
hardly worth holding, while the fleet would be more usefully
employed elsewhere. His views were imperial: he was anxious that
Britain keep her conquests in India and elsewhere.³⁸

However, there was a still a war to be fought, and Nelson was far
happier after capturing a French convoy off Oneglia on 30 May. His
squadron took two small warships and five store ships, the latter load-

ed with guns and stores for the siege of Mantua. Captain George Cockburn was specially noticed.[39] The mortars and guns were sent to Corsica, but there were more interesting items of cargo.

> I have got the charts of Italy, sent by the Directory to Buonaparte, also Maillebois' Wars in Italy, Vauban's Attack and Defence of Places, Prince Eugene's History; all sent for the General. If Buona Parti is ignorant the Directory, it would appear, wish to instruct him; pray God he may remain ignorant.[40]

Further inspection turned up Hannibal's March over the Alps, and lives of the Duke of Berwick, Marshal Vendôme and Marshal Catinat. All were good editions, with plates.[41] Bonaparte did not need the books, he knew them well enough, but the guns were a serious loss and the siege had to be abandoned. While Nelson could not save Italy, he could make the French work much harder for their conquests. The books might have been a useful education for Nelson, but he sent most of them to Jervis, keeping only the Vauban for his own edification.[42]

This might have been the final event of his Mediterranean command, since Jervis's plan to keep him when the *Agamemnon* went home had run into problems. Fortunately another captain wanted to go home, and on 11 June Nelson shifted his pendant to the seventy-four HMS *Captain*. He had been anxious to stay, suggesting his local knowledge might be cited as a reason to retain him; in private he was also anxious to exploit his local reputation, rather than join another fleet.[43] Now confirmed as a commodore, Nelson was entitled to have a junior captain command the ship, and he chose Ralph Miller, an American-born rising star who would be a key player in three major battles. He also transferred a number of his followers into the *Captain*, which was 'well-manned, although not active'.[44]

Nelson was immediately sent back to the service at Genoa, although he commanded the van division of the fleet, which was the post of honour for a junior flag officer. This required him to have an intimate understanding of his admiral's signals, plans and ideas. The war was going from bad to worse: now it was the turn of Naples to make peace with the ubiquitous French – 'these fellows multiply like locusts,' he lamented.[45] At least he was able to take a tough stand at Genoa, dismissing local protests as ridiculous, although he also produced a detailed refutation for Jervis to send back to the Foreign Office. Ordered to evacuate British merchants and stores from Leghorn, he arrived to find the French had taken control the previous day, but not before Thomas Fremantle had skilfully carried out the task.[46] Nelson was assembling a constellation of followers on whom he could rely, some from Hood's command, others brought on by Jervis.

He had also been ordered to ensure there were sufficient transports in hand to evacuate Corsica.[47] With Bonaparte at Leghorn with his fellow Corsican, the political agent Saliceti, the French threat to Corsica was greatly increased. Small bodies of men were landed to sow dissension among the populace. Nelson recognised the danger, advising Elliot to seize the island of Elba and the key harbour of Porto Ferraio from the Tuscans. Elliot agreed, urging Nelson to act without waiting for Jervis's sanction.[48] Meanwhile Jervis had ordered him to institute a close blockade of Leghorn, which could not be considered a neutral harbour while under French occupation. After spending so much time in the city he was distressed by the suffering of the evacuees, although it would appear that Adelaide Correglia was not among them.[49] Nelson and Elliot quickly concocted plans to seize Elba, writing to Jervis to report the bloodless seizure of the harbour on 10 July.[50]

Jervis was delighted – doubly so, since Spencer had confirmed Nelson as a commodore. He also advised Elliot to rely on Nelson's advice when handling troublesome Corsican privateers operating under British authority, because 'he is a reasonable and disinterested man in money matters'.[51] Elliot needed no prompting: after thanking Nelson for his action at Elba he asked him to handle complex financial transactions at Genoa.[52]

While Nelson hoped the Austrian and Neapolitan armies would recover Leghorn, and seized on any rumour of allied success,[53] the war was moving away from the coast. Bonaparte's rapid and ruthless advance drove the old-fashioned, slow-moving armies of the *ancien régime* from post to post. Amidst the confusion Nelson reflected that the King of Naples had been England's 'most faithful ally',[54] an opinion that would influence his actions three years later. The Austrians were 'too inactive. They look to us for impossibilities.'[55] Finding the constant diplomatic fencing with the government of the Genoese republic unrewarding, he advocated more extreme measures, and had to be restrained by Elliot and Jervis. The latter, though convinced of Nelson's zeal and determination, had no evidence of any higher talent for fleet action or politics: he called his commodore 'an excellent partisan' who did not 'sufficiently weigh consequences'.[56] It was perhaps fortunate that Jervis had no competent admirals and that Nelson was the senior captain.

The precarious situation of the small French garrison at Leghorn seemed open for exploitation. Nelson was running a very tight blockade, and local intelligence suggested that the populace might rise against the French, allowing a small British expedition to secure the town. After his experience on Corsica, he was anxious to find a 'suitable soldier' – meaning one young enough to be under his command. Elliot dashed his dreams, stressing that General De Burgh, the ranking officer on Corsica, would command.[57] The limited British force could only be used to follow up Austrian success in the main theatre, where rumours abounded that Bonaparte had died of his wounds.[58]

Such optimism soon dissolved. With Spain about to join the war, Jervis faced the prospect that a powerful Franco-Spanish fleet from Cadiz would attack while he blockaded Toulon. He was caught between two fleets, each numerically superior. To lessen the numerical disadvantage he recalled the two battleships off Leghorn, leaving Nelson with his pendant flying in a frigate to support Elliot with smaller craft.[59] With the picture darkening rapidly, Britain's Mediterranean strategy was on the point of dissolution, and the main players were preparing for the worst.

Nelson understood the significance of the Corsican presence in the French army, and although he kept a brave face in public, he realised the island must fall if the Austrians were defeated.[60] He advised Elliot that the best defence would be to attack the French at Leghorn.[61] He was not troubled by the threat of a Spanish fleet, having absolute faith that the tactical skill and seamanship of Jervis would secure a victory over any enemy.[62] By the end of August, however, the Leghorn operation had been abandoned, and the troops from Corsica were sent back to Gibraltar.[63]

A brief period with the fleet off Toulon convinced Nelson that Jervis had the French under control. He returned to Genoa to withdraw the British merchants, and found himself acting for the British minister. Although this was 'much against my inclination',[64] he exploited the opportunity to impose a more logical policy on Genoa. The Genoese would not allow him to load a cargo of bullocks bought for the fleet, fearing a French takeover. When the Genoese fired on his squadron he did not dignify the insult with a reply, but used it as a pretext to carry out more useful actions, seizing a French bomb vessel from under batteries at San Pietro d'Arena on 11 September, blockading the harbour and seizing the Genoese island of Capraja on 18 September with Elliot's concurrence.[65] Jervis could not resist sending Nelson's reports to Spencer: few men were so capable with either the sword or the pen, and none with both.[66]

Having played a useful role in the capture of Corsica Nelson was dismayed to find himself preparing to evacuate the British minister, government and troops. The Cabinet had decided to evacuate the Mediterranean in August, unable to spare the necessary naval forces to secure command of the sea when faced by French, Spanish and Dutch fleets, each of which might escort an invasion of the British Isles. Matters became critical when the loss of northern Italy to the French deprived the fleet of vital supplies. If the fleet withdrew, Corsica and Elba would have to be evacuated. Inevitably Jervis select-ed Nelson, his most dependable, resourceful and independent junior. This prompted a Shakespearian outburst from the Commodore, who quoted from *King John* on the subject of England meeting the world in arms.[67]

With Naples about to make peace, and Spain about to make war, the logistics of the fleet were under serious threat, since Sicily and Barcelona had been vital sources of food.[68] On 25 September, Jervis finally received the long-anticipated order to evacuate Corsica: the Mediterranean was to be abandoned. He kept his fleet concentrated to cover the operations while Nelson evacuated the island and Captain Cockburn in the frigate *Minerve* blockaded Leghorn.[69] Jervis planned to join the Viceroy at Bastia once Rear Admiral Man returned from Cadiz with his squadron.[70] Shifting his flag into the sixty-four-gun *Diadem*, Nelson left Leghorn, where a thousand Corsicans were assembling for a landing at Bastia.[71] He had to remove the garrison and administration from an island in uproar: the local populace were desperate to appease the returning French by turning on the British.

With a squadron of ten warships and thirty transports under his orders, Nelson was in his element. At last he had a major task, albeit a negative one, in which he could show his worth. The operation pro-ceeded better than anyone except he might have expected. The Corsicans at Bastia tried to stop the evacuation and seize the British stores, but when Nelson arrived on 14 October he took his ships close to the town, sent for the local Council and threatened to bombard. This enabled the army and British merchants to remove their stores, cannon and equipment unhindered, while the rest of the island was changing allegiance.[72] The moral courage Nelson displayed at Bastia secured his place in Elliot's affections, and marked him as the man for a crisis. Jervis already knew this; he relaxed once he knew Nelson had reached Bastia.[73]

Belated orders from London to reverse the evacuation could have thrown the situation into confusion, but Jervis had the wisdom to ignore them.[74] It was now too late: the strategic picture was so changed by the hostility of Spain that the island would be invaded as soon as the fleet was drawn out of position, and could not be defended once the enemy were established ashore.[75] Nelson took his convoy to Elba, where the troops landed. Always the optimist, he concluded that possession of the tiny island had saved the Smyrna convoy and his own fleet from attack. It promised to be a useful base.[76]

He left Bastia on 19 October, 'rich in the praise of my Admiral and the Viceroy', and all the more satisfied as others had declared that it could not be done. The timing was perfect: twenty-six Spanish battleships appeared off Cape Corse the following day, heading for Toulon. Now all that was required was to bring the Spanish to battle: he was confident the fleet was ready, with an admiral 'fit to lead them to glory'.[77] Jervis agreed that he could beat them 'with such stuff as I have in this fleet'.[78] He praised Nelson's contribution to the evacuation, but did so within the context of a wider effort by the fleet: Nelson did not evacuate the island single-handedly.[79]

In early November Nelson rejoined the fleet, finding the leisure to catch up with his correspondence. He told Locker that the Franco-Spanish combined fleet was large, but ill-manned and worse commanded, while the British were small, but of unequalled quality.[80] But he had reckoned without the incompetence of Man, whose squadron had rejoined the fleet without replenishing stores: Jervis had to send him back to Gibraltar to remedy the oversight. Once there, Man had a crisis of confidence, or perhaps a nervous breakdown, and headed back to England after consulting his captains – something Jervis had specifically ordered him not to do. Man was the only admiral sent on detached duty in 1796, and he had failed. Having lost a third of his fleet, Jervis had to abandon the Mediterranean in some haste. On 22 October the fleet set course for the Straits, taking ships of the Smyrna convoy in tow, in vile, tempestuous weather. This chain of events depressed Nelson, but his spirits were cheered by Jervis's very public demonstration of confidence, the presence of Elliot and a charming letter from Spencer praising his 'spirited, dignified and temperate conduct at Leghorn and Genoa'.[81] This was the elixir of his genius.

After a few days anchored off Gibraltar, Nelson was ordered on 'an arduous and most important mission'. He was to shift his flag from the *Captain* into the frigate *Minerve*, and recover the garrison of Elba.[82] This was a hazardous task, requiring him to cross a sea controlled by over forty enemy battleships to the only remaining post under British control, and remain there long enough to embark the naval and military establishment. While Nelson was honoured by the trust, it is unlikely Jervis would have sent anyone else. Jervis ended his instructions with a telling passage: 'Having experienced the most important effects from your enterprise and ability, upon various occasions since I have had the honour to command the Mediterranean, I leave entirely to your judgement, the time and manner of carrying this critical service into execution.'[83] He told Elliot, the operation 'cannot be in better hands'.[84] Jervis himself, meanwhile, retreated to Lisbon, the closest secure anchorage, to refit, replenish his stores and wait for reinforcements. While he waited for Nelson to return, he had to keep the enemy inside the Straits and defend Portugal, Britain's last ally.

Back in London the crisis was deepening. The naval threat had reached an unprecedented level, Britain's allies had collapsed and the French appeared irresistible. Only a victory at sea could break the ever-tightening circle of events that threatened to strangle Britain. Spencer emphasised the point to Jervis: 'a good hard blow struck now or soon will be worth twenty a little later'.[85]

Sailing from Gibraltar on 15 December, in company with the *Blanche*, Nelson encountered two Spanish frigates off Cartagena late on the 19th. Immediately *Minerve* engaged and took the *Santa Sabina*, after a skilful action of slightly over two hours. Unable to resist the chance to show off his seamanship and tactical acumen, last seen in Hotham's action, Nelson took over from Captain Cockburn, fought the ship and wrote up the log entry. The next morning two Spanish battleships appeared, forcing him to relinquish his prize and escape. Fortunately for Nelson the Spanish were distracted by the prize crew of the *Santa Sabina*, led by lieutenants Culverhouse and Hardy.[86] Both Cockburn and Hardy were notable additions to his school, and Nelson was quick to exchange Hardy for the captured Spanish captain, Don Jacobo Stuart, a great-grandson of James II.[87] On Christmas Eve, *Minerva* took a six-gun French privateer, looking for intelligence rather than fiscal reward. The squadron arrived at Porto Ferraio on the 26th, where Nelson was anxious to consult Elliot on the political situation, but unfortunately he was absent in Italy. General De Burgh had no orders to evacuate and lacked the political courage to act on those Jervis had sent, as Nelson observed. Now that Naples had made peace with the enemy England had no source of supplies and was therefore finished with Italy. He left De Burgh in no doubt that Jervis's command no longer extended inside the Straits.[88]

During the campaign of 1796 Jervis and Nelson built a strong mutual respect and understanding. This was remarkable, given that Nelson spent relatively little time under Jervis's direct command. The key to their relationship was trust, allied to the sheer professionalism that Jervis insisted on; the result, for Nelson, was an 'unequalled' fleet, drilled and disciplined beyond anything the Royal or indeed any other Navy had ever seen. It was the tool that Nelson's genius required if it was to unfold its full potential, to exploit those sublime qualities of vision, judgement and daring that he had developed under Hood's tutelage.

PART TWO

Towards Greatness

CHAPTER VII

Triumph and Disaster

1797

Lying at Porto Ferraio, far from his admiral, or any other source of support, General De Burgh's refusal to leave presented Nelson with a serious problem. He had no choice but to embark the naval stores and wait for the battered *Minerve* to refit. In communication terms he was closer to London than the fleet: he kept Spencer informed of his proceedings through William Wyndham, the diplomat and spymaster temporarily on the island.[1]

Elliot's return from Naples provided an opportunity to discuss the war with a man of real political ability, someone he admired. While he could not persuade De Burgh to leave, the ex-Viceroy remained convinced that a powerful fleet in the Mediterranean would keep the French out of Italy, as the basis of a successful British policy.[2] Much of his case was built on the advice of his friend the Commodore. Nelson's hopes for an early peace were dashed by Pitt's additional financial measures, and the obvious disinclination of the French Directory to end a war that was keeping the regime in power. The only way ahead was for the nation to accept the need for a 'rigorous prosecution of the war which now only can insure an honourable peace'. It seemed that Naples, the last independent state on the mainland, was doomed.[3]

After preparing sufficient transports to embark the entire garrison, which he left under Fremantle's command, Nelson embarked Elliot

HMS *Captain* driven against the *San Nicolas*, used as a bridge to board the *San Josef* beyond and left Elba at the end of January. Taking advantage of Jervis's permissive instructions, he elected to return past Toulon and Cartagena, to look for the Combined Fleet.4 Once again, Nelson had carried out a complex mission requiring independent judgement, with skill and intelligence. He could be certain of a positive response from the admiral – little wonder he left in high spirits.5

Both Toulon and Cartagena were empty: realising the enemy was at sea, Nelson hastened south to rejoin Jervis in the Straits. He reached Gibraltar on 9 February, recovered his two officers and headed through the Straits, where he was pursued by a Spanish battleship. Passing through their fleet on the night of the 12th, he was fortunate to escape attack, though wholly justified in taking risks to bring vital intelligence to Jervis.

The enemy fleets were meant to concentrate at Brest. The French squadron, under Rear Admiral Pierre Villeneuve, escaped to Brest, but the Spanish were delayed by the poor condition of their ships and two changes of command in six weeks. When Admiral Cordoba finally got his fleet to sea, under enormous political pressure, he was also charged with assisting the siege of Gibraltar and escorting four vital mercury ships to Cadiz. Attempting two tasks on one cruise was always going to be problematic; to set three for a fleet as inexperienced as Cordoba's was a recipe for indecision and disaster. It was a mistake the British would have been unlikely to make.

Cordoba encountered heavy weather off Cadiz, but the need to wait for the mercury ships prevented him sailing for Brest and avoiding Jervis altogether. Instead he rode out the storm in the Atlantic approaches. Jervis had problems of his own: between Gibraltar and Lisbon two seventy-fours had been lost, two had to go home and a second-rate was damaged. Having taken station off Cape St Vincent on 6 February he gleaned enough information to know the Spanish were still near Cadiz. He was rejoined early on the 13th by Nelson, who had passed through the Spanish fleet the previous night. Lieutenants Culverhouse and Hardy, recently prisoners on board Spanish ships, told Jervis about the condition of the enemy. By the end of the day Jervis knew the enemy's strength, and that they lay to the south-east, heading for Cadiz. All he had to do to force a battle was to place his fleet in their path. The mood that evening was infectious, and Elliot petitioned to stay and watch; Jervis agreed that his frigate could loiter until after the fighting.

Fortunately, Jervis had recently been reinforced from the Channel fleet. He had fifteen ships of line: six were powerful three-decked ships, eight were standard seventy-fours, and there was a single sixty-four. Cordoba had twenty-three: seven three-deckers, two eighty-fours, the rest seventy-fours. The four mercury transports – big, armed ships – could be mistaken for ships of the line at a distance; but four battleships had been detached, and took no part in the fighting. In all other respects, the forces were very unequal. The Spanish were short of sea-time, seamen, and fighting experience; the British were all experienced and combat-hardened, the five Channel fleet units performing as well as the veterans. Both sides were well aware of the quality gap, and it would play a key part in the battle.

Believing Jervis still had only nine ships, Cordoba decided to push through to Cadiz. The absolute failure of Spanish strategic reconnaissance condemned him to detach his heavy ships to report on sightings just when he needed to form a compact, coherent line of battle. This tactic, the basis for fighting an inconclusive linear action, was his only real hope in the face of a more skilful and resolute opponent. Once he realised the British were more numerous than he had anticipated, Cordoba reversed course to cover his merchant ships. In the process a gap opened between the main body and the escort force.

This was all the encouragement Jervis required. He signalled to form a line of battle in the shortest time on a bearing set by the flagship, and advised the fleet that he meant to pass through the gap in the Spanish fleet. For a man of Nelson's temperament, either signal would have been a delight; together they confirmed all the hopes he had placed in his admiral. Jervis had abandoned eighteenth-century formalism, and was doing what he thought should have been done on many other occasions. It is hard to believe that Jervis would not have discussed his plans with his most acute subordinate at some stage in the previous fourteen months.

Jervis's move speeded up the approach to battle, and his fleet demonstrated remarkable seamanship by rapidly forming a fighting line. Cordoba was clearly unsettled by the speed and precision with which the British shifted formation. Had they moved no faster than his own ships, the Spanish would have been able to reunite their line before the fleets came into contact. Instead Troubridge, leading the line in the *Culloden*, forced the headmost ship of the smaller Spanish force, the three-decker *Principe de Asturias*, to sheer off, with two

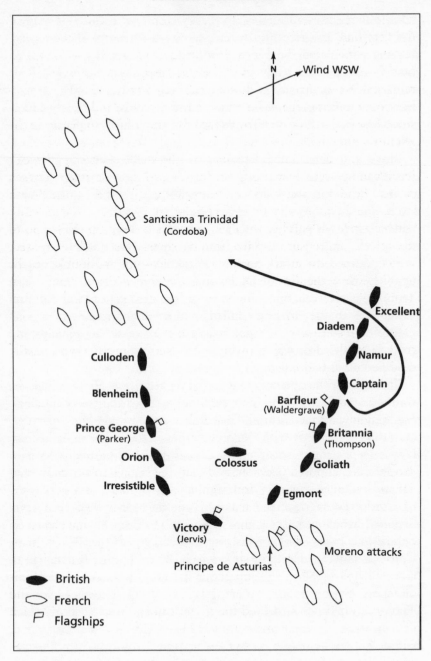

The battle of Cape St Vincent

double-shotted broadsides. With the Spanish now divided, Jervis had the fleet tack in succession to engage the main body of the enemy. Having anticipated the order, Troubridge had the answering signal already hoisted and ready to fly before Jervis's flags appeared. This remarkable concurrence of thinking reflected strong doctrine, excellent communication between admiral and captains, and clearly understood objectives. Nor was Troubridge the only officer to penetrate the admiral's intentions.

Brave and determined attempts by the detached force to block Jervis's move were beaten off, but this caused a gap to open between the five headmost ships led by Troubridge and the rest of the British force. Furthermore the wind had shifted, increasing the distance between the two parts of the fleet. Anxious to keep up the tempo of the attack, and ensure the five leading ships were not left exposed, Jervis planned an attack by his centre divisions to double on the Spanish while the *Britannia*, leading the rear division, would join Troubridge on the opposite side of the Spanish force. Admiral Thompson in the *Britannia* failed to take in the signal, to Jervis's mounting displeasure. The gap between the five advanced ships and the rest of the fleet was growing with every minute; Jervis's hastily modified plans had failed.

Throughout the opening phases of the battle, Nelson, on board the *Captain*, had been watching in admiration as Jervis's plans unfolded. His station near the rear of the British line gave him a good viewpoint, and as a commodore with a captain to command the ship he had the leisure to observe the big picture. He would have been conscious of Troubridge's exposed position, and read the signals to *Britannia* that Thompson failed to note. More significantly he had a very good view of Cordoba's flagship, the massive, unique four-decked *Santissima Trinidad*, which began to signal furiously. The fleets having passed on opposite courses, the Spanish now overlapped the British rear; Cordoba saw the chance to shift across the rear of the British line to reunite his fleet. When a group of Spanish ships began to move in this direction, Nelson decided to act. Jervis was too far away to see and Thompson had not answered the signal to tack in succession, which had now been overtaken by events. The situation called for action, and he did not hesitate to take it – his courage was born of confidence and a very good knowledge of his Commander in Chief.

He wore ship, rather than tacked – a quicker manoeuvre although less suitable for a squadron than a ship – then cut back through the British line and took station ahead of Troubridge's *Culloden*. The two ships quickly turned the Spanish fleet back onto their old course. The *Captain*'s approach had exposed her to Spanish fire, but it was here that Nelson's recent experience of Spanish gunnery and drill paid dividends. The risk was acceptable, but still costly. Nelson was hit in the side by part of a smashed rigging block, and would have fallen had Miller not caught him. The blow left him with a hernia, which would trouble him whenever he coughed. In the heat of the action, however, it did little to damp his enthusiasm, and as there was no open wound it required no treatment.

The Spanish fleet remained in a state of confusion – more a huddle than a line – throughout the fluid phases of the battle. Cordoba found his flagship under attack, with five other ships in company. Jervis had ordered the rear division into battle, and soon two lines of British ships were chasing the Spanish – one astern the other on the starboard quarter, both closing quickly. Collingwood in the *Excellent* led the main body, her finely honed gun crews shattering the rearmost Spanish ships as she passed on to attack new targets. Jervis ordered him to relieve the *Culloden* and the *Captain*, now closely engaged with several Spanish ships. *Captain* had been disabled by the loss of her wheel and foretopmast. Jervis flew the signal 'Engage the Enemy More Closely' – to Nelson's admiration, although it was hardly necessary. The speed and accuracy of British gunnery was far superior to the Spanish, enabling seventy-fours to master 112-gun three-deckers. After forcing two ships to surrender, Collingwood ran between Nelson and his opponents, pouring in rapid broadsides at pistol shot. The two Spanish ships collided, while *Excellent* set off after Cordoba in the *Santissima*, the ultimate prize.

Nelson, Troubridge and Collingwood had broken the back of the Spanish fleet, leaving four ships crippled, the rest fleeing in disorder. The eighty-four-gun *San Nicolas* and the 112-gun *San Josef* lay close by the *Captain*, stunned by Collingwood's fire, and still locked together. As the *Captain* could take no part in the rest of the battle, which would soon range ahead, Nelson ordered Miller to place her alongside the *San Nicolas* and prepared to board. He insisted on leading the attack personally, knowing the value of setting an example. Clambering over the cathead, Nelson entered the Spanish captain's cabin. His supporters quickly burst through onto the quarterdeck, wounding the commodore as they went. There they joined another group, which Berry had led over the bowsprit and across the spritsail yard. The Spaniards on the upper deck surrendered: with a quarter of the crew killed or wounded they had seen enough. Caught alongside, with a commanding view over the newly taken prize's upper deck, was the three-decker *San Josef*. She had suffered heavily: the admiral was dying below deck with both legs shot off, while a fifth of her crew were dead or wounded. Even so her crew opened fire with their muskets. Unable to defend themselves where they stood, the British had only two options. Nelson chose to attack. Summoning fresh men from the *Captain* to guard the hatchways on the *San Nicolas*, he scrambled up the side of the larger ship, getting a leg up from Berry into the main chains. Once on the Spaniards' deck, Nelson received her captain's sword as a token of surrender. He insisted on repeating the ritual with all the officers, passing their swords to William Fearney, one of his barge crew, who stowed them away under his arm like firewood.

This double success was unique. It was also highly risky, and fortunate. Both Spanish ships were badly battered, and the *San Josef* was taken while still fighting the *Prince George*, leaving the upper deck short of men and full of casualties. Both ships were ready to surrender: they had fought well for close on two hours, against far better trained ships, and were hastened in their decision by the sudden arrival of British boarders. Not that they gave up without a fight: a quarter of *Captain*'s eighty casualties came in this phase of the battle. Two more battleships were taken, and the *Santissima* probably hauled down her colours, but Jervis called off the attack just before James Saumarez in the *Orion* could take possession. The Spanish fleet crept away while Jervis's force secured their prizes and attended to their own damaged ships. This had been a hard fight: the most closely engaged units, revealed by their casualties, were all battered and in need of repair.

That evening Nelson left Miller to patch up his flagship, and went over to the *Victory*, where Jervis greeted his grimy and bruised commodore with exactly the sort of praise that he most liked to hear: a thoroughly professional appreciation of his merits. After a brief stand-off the following day, Cordoba withdrew. Jervis took his squadron into Lagos Bay, site of a great victory in 1759, to refit.

After this escapade, Nelson had earned the right to gather in his laurels, the praise of his peers and the admiration of amateurs like Elliot.

Jervis's brief formal public report did not single out anyone for special notice, but his private letter to the First Lord was a more honest reflection of his views, praising Troubridge, Collingwood and especially Nelson, 'who contributed very much to the fortune of the day'.[6] There were no complaints within the fleet, although Jervis was anxious to remove Admiral Thompson.

On 15 February Nelson wrote to thank Collingwood for his support the previous day, and visited his shattered flagship, where he gave Miller a ring. Elliot, meanwhile, was enraptured by what he had seen – 'Nothing in the world was ever more noble' – and he trusted Nelson would 'enjoy your honours and the gratitude and admiration of your country for many years'.[7] In reply Nelson let Elliot know he wanted the Order of the Bath, not a baronetcy.

Nelson's fame was further enhanced by printed accounts of the battle. While on HMS *Lively* in search of Elliot, he had given an impromptu interview to Colonel Drinkwater, already well known for a narrative of the siege of Gibraltar. The resulting account was published, as he had hoped, though it was later replaced in the popular press by Nelson's own article. A copy of this was sent to Locker at Greenwich, his naval 'father' and part-time press agent, with half-hearted instructions to replace the first-person narrative figure with a less personal device – but if Nelson had really wanted this done, surely he would have written it in the second person himself.[8] The report duly appeared in the *Sun* without editing. Fanny, Clarence and Admiral Waldegrave received copies; Nelson kept the original. As expected Fanny showed a copy to Hood, who was in raptures, while Clarence praised him at court.

The report did not pass unnoticed in the fleet, because it contained a factual error. Nelson claimed to have been in action for an hour without support, but Rear Admiral William Parker publicly challenged this – rightly so, since the time that passed in this perilous situation was only a matter of minutes, and Parker's flagship had been engaging the *San Josef* when Nelson boarded her.[9] Later editions are slightly amended to say that he thought it was an hour, but was unsure of the real time.

To cement his fame Nelson now made a typical gesture. Jervis had marked his personal estimation of the day by allowing him to keep the captured sword of Admiral Winthuysen. This was sent to the Mayor of Norwich, with a copy of his report on the battle. The City responded as he hoped, by giving him its Freedom, placing the sword in a special case in the Guildhall, and commissioning a portrait. The purpose of the gesture was to secure his place in Norfolk society, which he anticipated rejoining in later life.[10] In the event his fame soon outgrew the county: he never went back to Norwich or Burnham, and spent but a few hours in Yarmouth in 1800 and 1801. Although Nelson never forgot his home, and always gloried in being a Norfolk man, it quickly became obvious that he had outstripped his birthplace: Norfolk was too distant from the main centres of naval power.

On 1 April Nelson received his first English mail since the news of the battle had been known. It contained numerous letters of congratulation, newspaper reports and other signs of his hard-won, long-desired, and now very real public fame. He was the hero of the hour, and as he expressly desired, a Knight of the Bath, with a star and a red ribbon, rather than a Baronet with a title but no decoration. At the same time his promotion to Rear Admiral was confirmed, and he acquired a coat of arms which included the stern of the *San Josef*. These honours were gratefully given, for the success had been a tremendous fillip to domestic morale after years of dismal news. Now it was time to exploit the victory. The only jarring notes were Jervis's failure to praise him in the public dispatch, and Fanny's rather nervous plea that he give up boarding and other heroic actions.

As Jervis refitted his fleet, he reflected on the lessons of the battle. His heroes were Nelson, Troubridge, Hood and Foley, and the first among them needed a new flagship – preferably a large two-decker, should the anticipated flag promotion occur. Spencer agreed, and Nelson even turned down the brand-new 110-gun *Ville de Paris*, well aware that detached command, his forte, was not given to admirals in such powerful fleet units. Spencer passed on Cabinet thinking that a detachment should be sent into the Mediterranean, to re-establish contact with the Austrians and clear the Adriatic: 'I suppose you would naturally enough look to Admiral Nelson for this purpose, and possibly detach some [battleships] under him.'[11]

After the fleet was safely in the Tagus, Jervis detached Nelson with a small squadron to cover the approaches to Cadiz, hoping to intercept a rumoured treasure convoy, bring out the Spanish fleet, encourage the Portuguese court, and alarm the Spanish.[12] This was Nelson's reward for the battle that had helped to make Jervis Earl St Vincent. Although he found nothing, the impulse would ultimately lead to the attack on Tenerife.

Cadiz was officially blockaded on 11 April. Confident the Spanish would not come out, Nelson handed over the task to Saumarez the following day,[13] before heading back into the Mediterranean to attend to some unfinished business at Elba. His thoughts were turning to the 'rich ships from La Vera Cruz and Havana' that the Earl reported were on passage. Discussions with Troubridge led him to put forward a plan to capture the treasure galleons, although he added, 'I do not reckon myself equal to Blake'.[14] But success would 'ruin Spain, and has every prospect of raising our Country to a higher pitch of wealth than ever she yet attained'. Military cooperation would be very useful, but he was prepared to make the attempt with the limited force then embarked on the fleet. Ultimately he knew the 'risk and responsibility' rested with Jervis.[15]

The cruise to Elba was uneventful, because the ambush Nelson had anticipated was spotted off Minorca and avoided. The news from Italy was bad: the Austrians had been driven back to within 150 miles of Vienna by a vast French army under Bonaparte, seemingly unable to resist 'these extraordinary people'. This only emphasised the need to strike at Tenerife.[16] Although he hastened back to the fleet by early May, hearing rumours the Spanish would come out, the situation off Cadiz left little hope that the enemy would try their strength again. Jervis had been reinforced, and was now stronger than he had been on the famous 14 February.

After repairing battle damage at Lisbon and sending home his prizes, Jervis led his fleet south to blockade his beaten foes in Cadiz, Spain's southern naval base. The Spanish had changed their commander and begun to shake up the fleet. Initially Jervis expected they would offer battle, but by mid-June he accepted they were unlikely to move without a powerful inducement. He now faced the greatest challenge of the age: how to get an inferior fleet to leave the safety of a fortified arsenal and give battle at sea. On 19 May he made the blockade complete, including all commercial shipping. This would starve the local economy and the fleet, as both relied on sea transport. The stopper in the Spanish bottle would be a squadron of seventy-fours anchored in the harbour mouth, in sight of the town and only just out of gunshot from the walls. This tiresome command was given to

Nelson, who had done the same job at Leghorn the previous year. None of the senior flag officers protested at this appointment – that would only come later. Instead the fleet were annoyed to find a detachment of the Channel fleet cruising in the track of the treasure ships, which they believed were their due.[17]

Nelson was in signal distance of the fleet, sending Jervis any scraps of intelligence that he could glean from the shore, from conversation with local craft or observation of activity in the harbour. He even opened a polite correspondence with the Spanish admiral, warning him of a royal salute to be fired on the King's birthday, fearing that it might alarm the ladies. Admiral Mazzaredo's reply was both dignified and charming.[18] While the economic life of the port was devastated the Spanish fleet would not come out. Instead the biggest threat to Jervis's fleet was internal. While the Spithead mutiny was essentially a trade dispute about pay and conditions, it spread through the Navy and reached the Mediterranean fleet in a more politicised form. After a mutinous outbreak in June, four men from HMS *St George* were tried and hung the next day, a Sunday. Jervis blamed lax officers. He shifted Nelson and Miller into the worst-behaved ship in the squadron, with a leaven of his old followers in all ranks. Within a fortnight the men of the *Theseus* were devotees at the feet of their admiral, and a credit to the service.

Throughout June, Nelson and Jervis prepared for an attack on Tenerife, assembling scaling ladders, guns, stores and a few extra red coats to dazzle the Spanish. The target of the operation was money, and the situation at home gave it a particular significance. The war was making unprecedented demands on the British economy, enough to cause problems even for a fiscal expert such as Pitt. In the wake of failed peace negotiations in late 1796, the evacuation of the Mediterranean and the landing at Fishguard in February 1797, there was a run on the banks. Money was in short supply, and cash even more so. While the tax system needed reform, the coinage was in a ruinous condition with a limited stock of old and worn money, numerous tokens and other substitute and counterfeit items in circulation. To meet the problem Pitt suspended bank payments in gold and silver, introduced paper money and issued captured Spanish silver dollars as legal tender from March 1797. These were overstruck with the head of King George, leading one wit to rhyme:

The Bank to make their dollars pass
Stamped the head of a fool on the neck of an Ass.

Nelson's operation in Tenerife was intended to find treasure to meet the crisis. It would be difficult, but if successful, with 'six or seven million pounds sterling . . . thrown into circulation in England, it would ensure an honourable peace'.[19] It would also knock Spain out of the war. These were the stakes for which Nelson would gamble his life, and those of his men.

In the mean time, however, there was always a risk that the new Spanish admiral, Gravina, would give battle once Nelson had left, so he paid minute attention to local intelligence. On 13 June the non-appearance of his regular vegetable boat persuaded him they were coming out,[20] but still they did not come. Hoping to round off the season with the treasure ships, he retailed the latest congratulatory verses and seamen's messages to Fanny. She must have begun to tire of phrases such as 'The imperious call of honour to serve my country is the only thing which keeps me a moment from you', especially when combined with the news that Jervis would be unwilling to let him go even in the autumn. He hoped for riches, but advised her not to bank on them when buying the 'little cottage' somewhere in Norfolk to which he hoped to return.[21]

To keep the men occupied Jervis and Nelson agreed to bombard Cadiz, using their sole mortar vessel, the *Thunder*. After a sanguinary boat action on the night of 3 July, in which Nelson provided vital leadership when the British boats faltered, some damage was done. However, the means were altogether inadequate and with the Spanish fully alerted Jervis admitted defeat, withdrawing Nelson's squadron on 14 July.

As the bombardment had been abandoned it was time to seek out the Mexican treasure convoy. Nelson and Troubridge planned a combined operation with four thousand troops, similar in concept to the operation at Capraja. Their scheme was based on sound intelligence. Scouting and cutting-out operations around the Canary Islands encouraged Jervis to fall in with Nelson's plan. He was given three seventy-fours, three frigates, a cutter, and a small mortar boat, and their captains were among the best of Jervis's protégés – Troubridge, Hood, Bowen and Fremantle. Jervis didn't bother to tell Spencer about the operation until early August, when he stressed there was no idea of keeping Tenerife.[22]

Their target was a large merchant ship and her cargo, which Nelson thought might have been landed. Unfortunately the local defences were in good repair, and adequately manned by 800 professional soldiers, 110 French sailors and 700 local militia. The Commandant General of the Islands, Don Antonio Gutierrez, was an experienced officer, unlikely to collapse in face of British bravado.

En route for Tenerife, Nelson called his captains to conference four times; he remained Lord Hood's man at heart. His final plan, as at Capraja, was to land at a distance from the enemy, secure a commanding position and send in an ultimatum. Over nine hundred seamen and marines were to be put ashore in a carefully planned operation. The night landing on 22 July was hampered by heavy weather, and when the alarm was raised ashore Troubridge, in tactical command, hesitated and went back to consult Nelson just when he should have pushed on. It was a rare failure for so bold and enterprising a man. A second attempt to capture higher ground in broad daylight left the men roasted by the sun, and then dismayed to find they had climbed the wrong hill. They retreated in bad humour.

Now Nelson faced a hard decision: he could admit defeat and sail away, or try again. After a twenty-four-hour delay for bad weather and another Council of War, he elected to launch a frontal assault on a well-defended town at night, basing the decision on the report of a Prussian deserter and the local knowledge of Thomas Thompson, captain of the newly arrived *Leander*. All the officers knew this would be a desperate affair, and Nelson was not going to let anyone else lead it. Failure was possible, but not until he had tried himself. Knowing the risks were great, he deliberately burnt the letters from his wife.

In attempting an assault on well-prepared shore defences from the sea, at night and with only small arms, the British were relying on surprise to unsettle the defenders. If the Spaniards stood to their guns and defended their positions until daybreak, the attack must fail. Around midnight the boats went in, planning to land on the Mole and storm the central castle. Inevitably strong currents dispersed the boats and the men came ashore in a variety of locations. Once roused, the Spaniards produced a terrific volume of fire that stalled the attack in all areas. The operation had failed.

Nelson himself never reached the shore. As he was preparing to land from the *Seahorse*'s barge, a musket ball shattered his right arm just above the elbow. With a major artery cut through, he could have bled to death, but his stepson Josiah quickly staunched the flow and applied a tourniquet. This act, which Nelson acknowledged had saved his life, was heavily featured in Clarke and McArthur's official life. It distracted attention from the failed attack, and ensured Fanny could give her son some credit.

Although badly wounded Nelson remained perfectly calm, deliberately placing his uncle's fighting sword in his left hand. The sword was a talisman that he always carried into battle, until he forgot to buckle it on on the fateful anniversary of Suckling's triumph. The barge now carried Nelson back to the squadron. A small force that gathered on the Mole were pinned down by heavy fire. When the officers tried to lead them forward they were hit: Richard Bowen was killed, Fremantle and Thompson were wounded. The Spanish officers had placed their cannon well; at such short range, blasts of canister shot were devastatingly effective.

While the landing force had been large enough, it had not arrived together, nor had the whole force actually landed. Some boats sheered off when faced with a rocky shoreline and heavy fire. As a result the attacks were on a small scale and easily broken up. After sunrise on 25 July Hood and Troubridge managed to extricate the force ashore from a desperate situation, but only by admitting defeat and promising not to come back.

Josiah had taken Nelson back to the fleet, although the admiral insisted on stopping to rescue men from the cutter *Fox*, which sank suddenly. He also refused to board the *Seahorse* for treatment, as Fremantle's wife was on board and he had no news of her husband. Arriving alongside the *Theseus*, he refused to be carried aboard, using his left arm to climb up to the companion way. Once there he told the surgeon to prepare his instruments, as he knew the arm must be amputated. 'He underwent the operation with the same firmness and courage that have always marked his character', reported midshipman Hoste – although that did not prevent Nelson recalling the terrible sensation of cold steel cutting into living flesh. Within an hour he was back at work, signing, with his left hand, a demand for the Spaniards to capitulate and surrender the Manilla galleon. It was never sent. Instead, the *Theseus* came under fire from the shore batteries, cut her cable and stood out to sea.

Nelson's state of mind at this point can hardly be imagined. Mutilated and in agony, he was uncertain of the situation ashore, but well aware that the signs were not good. As the shore party marched away with their arms Gutierrez allowed them to think they had been defeated by eight thousand troops, a neat piece of disinformation that would reinforce Hood's promise not to return, and quickly became part of the Tenerife legend. Had the garrison been so large it must have been known before the attack, and condemned the operation as insane.

Until the men were safely back afloat Nelson's professional concern for duty masked his inner feelings, but once he had finished bolstering the morale of his juniors he gave way to the inevitable shock and depression. His first thoughts were to explain the failure to Jervis. Characteristically he made no mention of the Councils of War, or the advice of others, taking full responsibility while praising the heroism of his followers. This was greatness in adversity. It explains why so many men wanted to follow him. Under his guidance, they would be able to use their skill and contribute to the planning, without being held to blame, even in private, if things went wrong.

To his report, he attached an early example of his left hand at work. 'I am become a burthen to my friends and useless to my Country . . . When I leave your command I become dead to the world; I go hence and am no more seen.'[23] It was not surprising that he should close with a paraphrase of Psalm 39, which had just been read over the dead at the burial service; it was a familiar refrain from the life of a clergyman's son, and all the more affecting from the number of his closest friends who had been killed. Jervis's protégé Bowen was a terrible loss, while one of Nelson's own favourites, Lieutenant John Weatherhead, shot in the stomach, could not live.

It took nearly three weeks to get back to the fleet off Cadiz, time that hung heavy on his mind. Desperate for moral support he turned to Jervis, who rose to the challenge, opening his reply with the matchless phrase, 'Mortals cannot command success: you and your companions have certainly deserved it, by the greatest degree of heroism and perseverance that ever was exhibited.' He added the promise of a ship home, promotion for Josiah and further rumours of imminent peace to lessen the blow of leaving.[24] He took full responsibility for the attack in his public report, and wrote to Fanny to report that Nelson had added considerably to his laurels, while his wound was not dangerous.[25] This was at once great and considerate.

Four days later Nelson shifted across to join Fremantle and the

The last letter written by Nelson with his right hand, and (opposite)
the first letter written with his left hand

other invalids on the *Seahorse*. He was going home for the first time in five long years. This was not how he had envisaged his homecoming – hero of the battle and commander of detached squadrons. He should have come back in glory, with prizes and plunder, not mutilated and surrounded by reminders of his greatest failure.[26]

Having dealt with the professional consequences of defeat, Nelson wrote to Fanny, expressing the hope that she would be pleased by a left-handed letter, and a claim he was 'never better' – a phrase that hardly did justice to his physical or mental state. He praised Josiah's actions, and trusted his country would not leave him without pecuniary reward. On reaching the fleet, he added a few lines to report that he was 'perfectly well', and that Jervis had promoted Josiah to the rank of Master and Commander. In reality he was deeply depressed, and in great pain.

Nelson would have been comforted had he read Jervis's correspondence with Spencer. The two Earls were already taking a dangerous *y will be able to give me a[gate to convey the remains of my carcuse to England, God Bless you my Dear Sir & Believe me your most obliged & faithful*

Horatio Nelson

You will excuse my scrawl considering it is my first attempt

Sir John Jervis K B.

pleasure in discussing their remarkable new admiral. St Vincent was anxious that the First Lord did not think Nelson had been permanently crippled: he had returned from Tenerife 'in such health that nothing could prevent his coming on board the *Ville de Paris* . . . I have very good ground of hope that he will be restored to the service of his king and country.'[27]

Dark as the horizon must have seemed, Tenerife had not harmed Nelson's career: as long as he made a full recovery from his wound he could return to service. His days at the head of the boarding party were now past, but he would always find brave men to fill that role. It would be as a fleet commander and strategist that he would establish his reputation as Britain's greatest admiral.

Landing at Portsmouth on 1 September, Nelson was immediately back in contact with his admirers. Commander in Chief Sir Peter Parker had made him a captain, while the cheering crowds testified to his fame. Arriving in Bath, he found that this phenomenon was not confined to the dockyard towns: civic greetings competed for his attention with glowing letters from Hood and Clarence. Within a month he was anxious to return to sea, but still suffering from the slow healing of his amputation. In constant pain, he required opium to sleep. Consequently, when Locker persuaded him to sit for a portrait, to meet popular demand, the face that Lemuel Abbott captured was ravaged by pain. It was also focused and powerful. This was no boyish enthusiast, it was a man of war, a man who had tasted victory and defeat, loss and suffering.[28]

Although the amputation had been hurried, it was a silk ligature, tying off an artery, that caused the problem. These were meant to come away as the artery withered, and one of the two in Nelson's wound did so; the other hung on far longer, possibly attached to a sinew, but the only cure for the pain it caused was time. When the rogue ligature finally came away in early December, Nelson requested that his local church make reference to his thanksgiving. He rewarded the young surgeon who had dressed his wound by making him surgeon of his flagship the following year.

The months spent ashore between Tenerife and the Nile gave him the chance to learn how to operate with his new writing hand, to adjust his clothes and equipment, and to increase the strength and dexterity of his left arm. The mental adjustment was if anything less difficult than the physical. The powerful strain of religious resignation in Nelson's thought ensured that he saw the loss as God's will – a chance of battle, and only one of a catalogue of wounds he would continue to suffer.[29] Wounds were tokens of glory and honour, not defects to be hidden. He never tried to hide his empty sleeve, pinning it across his chest, frequently joking about his loss and naming the stump his 'fin'. The missing arm even featured at his investiture into the Order of the Bath, at St James's Palace on 27 September. When the King thoughtlessly blurted out that he had lost his arm, Nelson quickly introduced Edward Berry as his 'right hand'. This ancient ceremony, rich in imagery, pageant and theatre, was a key element in Nelson's recovery. The act of putting a star on his breast made Sir Horatio Nelson a real hero: his countrymen looked on him as a talisman, while the Freedom of the City of London testified to the commercial impact of his services. He was ready to make the next step.

While he waited for his recovery, Nelson was examined for his wounds pension; he also pressed his youngest brother's claims and commiserated with Weatherhead's father. By late November he was preparing to go back to sea, on the new eighty-gun second-rate, HMS

Foudroyant, a ship named for Jervis's last command as a captain. As she was not ready, he was moved into the seventy-four gun *Vanguard*, then fitting at Chatham, and directed Berry to take command. He was officially pronounced fit to serve on 13 December; five days later the *Vanguard* came out of dock.[30]

By the time Nelson returned to service, the very nature of the war had changed. The stakes had been raised, and the prospects of a negotiated settlement were much reduced. Intermittent attempts to secure peace with the French Directory had been under way at Lille since July, but Bonaparte's triumph in Italy encouraged the French to continue a struggle they were winning. In mid-September the British envoy, Lord Malmesbury, was told to leave. He had arrived home just in time to hand the King the sword with which he dubbed Nelson. The symbolism was powerful: new times need new men, and no one would rise to the challenge of total war like Nelson.

Nelson's return had coincided with a major change in the strategic situation. On 11 October Adam Duncan's North Sea fleet, recently the infamous Nore mutineers, encountered the Dutch fleet off Camperdown. Without waiting to form a line of battle, and in no particular order, Duncan launched a two-column attack on the enemy, who were desperately seeking the sanctuary of their shallow coastal waters. The lighter Dutch ships were shattered in the resulting close-quarters fighting; many surrendered, including their admiral. When the news reached London two days later it was greeted with rapture, although the revellers who called at Nelson's door to demand the windows be illuminated went away once they knew it was his house. Camperdown was the ideal riposte to the collapse of peace talks. It had been expected that the Dutch fleet would escort an invasion of Ireland, always a weak point in the British defence plan.[31] The destruction of the fleet ended this threat. On a broader canvas the victory decisively altered the balance of naval power in Britain's favour. While the captured Dutch ships were small and badly damaged, some were used on the North Sea station,[32] where the enemy now had far fewer ships. This released British units for service in the Channel and the Cadiz station. Without Camperdown it is unlikely the Admiralty could have found the ships for the reoccupation of the Mediterranean – the central event in Nelson's life.

The politicians were not slow to exploit the triumph for public consumption. Foreign Secretary Lord Grenville argued that Camperdown was the most important victory of the war in political terms. He advised Spencer:

> One of the great objects is the raising of people's spirits, and I wish to suggest to you with this view whether it would not be right . . . that the [Dutch Commander in Chief's] flag should be paraded through the streets with a proper detachment of sailors, and lodged in St. Paul's. You are too sensible of the effects of impressions of this nature to treat this idea lightly; for if we had done in this war half that our enemies have done to raise the courage and zeal of their people, we should not now be where we are.[33]

Clearly French propaganda was having an effect. The country needed a more national, British message, not the limited, conventional celebrations accorded to earlier victories. It was all very well for the King to honour Howe on his flagship after the First of June, but it was hardly a public event.[34] A better model was the Elizabethan pageant at St Paul's after the defeat of the Armada in 1588. Once Spencer had accepted the idea of a public event the Prime Minister broadened it into a truly national naval pageant:

> I trust your idea of the Te Deum at St. Paul's is not laid aside, though it may as well not take place till the first Sunday after the meeting of Parliament. Might it not include in the object of the thanksgiving all the great naval successes of the war?[35]

Two weeks later Pitt demonstrated the meaning of the new war. It was not, he declared, about trade, colonies or Empire, but about the very liberty and independence of the British people. The country had the wealth and power to fight for its survival, and it was a matter of honour to stand up to France, in the interests of Europe: every man should 'be ready to sacrifice his life in the same cause'.[36]

The age of total war had dawned and Pitt was creating the fiscal means to wage such conflicts. The income or 'war' tax would limit British borrowing, helping to keep the interest rates markedly lower than France ever managed, and ensuring the City of London was at one with the government. Linking naval victory and the commercial hub of the empire with the symbols of success, loyalty and the Church went a long way towards the creation of a new national identity – and this identity would find its ultimate symbol in Nelson.

The ceremonial laying-up of the captured flags went ahead as Pitt had suggested on 19 December, with a grand service of thanksgiving at St Paul's attended by the King and royal princes. The spacious cathedral adapted to its new role as the national pantheon with ease, while the City of London, for which much of the naval activity of war was undertaken, must have been delighted by the obvious connection of State, Navy and City. The King was the central figure, his procession being led up the nave by Spencer, carrying the sword of state. George pointedly stopped to speak with Duncan. During Holy Communion the organist and choir played Purcell's 'I will give thanks unto thee, O Lord', and naval officers marched through the choir screen carrying an impressive collection of captured enemy ensigns, each on a pole with a placard noting where it had been taken. There were French colours at the head and Dutch at the rear, but in the middle of the parade were those taken off Cape St Vincent. Two admirals escorted these trophies – Thompson and Waldegrave, supported by Nelson, who had been called to participate by Spencer. As the flags were passed to the Dean, Nelson stood on the very spot his coffin would occupy at the beginning of his funeral a mere eight years later. Both the event and the atmosphere met his idea of the heroic. This was how the state commemorated its greatest deeds and raised the spirit of the country in times of adversity. It was for just such a public demonstration of his fame that Nelson would lay his life on the line, over and over again. The pioneering event was not universally popular, of course – some saw the underlying French model, and did not enjoy the connection; others of a more radical stripe preferred outright condemnation of the minister who was raising taxes to pay for the war, and burnt effigies of Pitt across London.[37]

Nelson received the Freedom of the City of London on 28 December, rounding off a year in which he had reached flag rank and public fame, but lost an arm and a battle. He was already awaiting orders to go back to sea. The war was entering a new phase, one in which his unique abilities would be fully employed.

CHAPTER VIII

The Nile Campaign
1798

By the end of 1797, Rear Admiral Sir Horatio Nelson's fame was firmly established. Even the failure at Tenerife had not dented his reputation, because his earlier Mediterranean exploits had been so memorable, and his conduct in defeat was as stirring as his most daring moments at St Vincent. Yet he remained the hero of another man's battle – as he had told Clarence a decade earlier, he would not be the national hero until he had led the fleet to victory.

The war was changing rapidly from an eighteenth-century question of provinces, islands and indemnities into a struggle for survival. The collapse of the first coalition left Britain with little prospect of an ally capable of defeating the French and restoring the pre-war frontiers, let alone the pre-war regime. Britain's coalition partners generally failed to see the war in such absolute terms: they continued to run balance sheets of profit and loss, a trifling game that Britain was forced to play because she had no war-winning strategy of her own. The two core adversaries, Britain and France, remained in an uneasy stalemate, each side victorious in part, but unable to find a settlement of their differences that could bring long-term security. On the one hand French plans to invade Britain had been utterly defeated, by wind, weather and warships; yet on the other, Britain could not be secure while France occupied Belgium and controlled Holland, and would not

Nelson views the destruction of *L'Orient* from the quarter-deck of HMS *Vanguard* prosper while she controlled access to European markets. Nelson's solution to this impasse would be to take the art of war at sea to new levels, securing British naval dominance by annihilating any hostile fleet that put to sea. Only by securing an absolute command of the sea could Britain survive without allies, and impose a truly effective blockade on France.

Pitt's financial reforms and the naval successes of 1797 provided a platform to sustain the British war effort. British government borrowing was secured at a far lower rate of interest than that paid by her rivals, and further economic changes would develop Britain's capability to sustain her power over the long term. However, long wars make grave demands, and the government continued to look for powerful allies. The obvious focus for Britain's foreign policy was the Mediterranean: she needed to renew links with Austria, the only major power that appeared both ready and willing to fight, and to reopen the major markets that had been closed for the last year.[1]

Nelson, nursed back to health by his mother/wife, was ready for these new challenges. He had no thought of leave, or of settling down in the mythical 'cottage' that had occupied so many of his letters to Fanny. His soul did not take wing in a quiet cottage garden, but on the quarter-deck of a battleship, commanding squadrons and fleets, matching his insight, judgement and intellect against the best the enemy could do. For him the path seemed divinely pre-ordained, even if it was not revealed. Perhaps he was resigned to death as the ultimate price of immortal glory – certainly his fixation with the career and death of James Wolfe suggested as much.

After 1797 Nelson knew he had the ability to lead: the promise held out by his earlier minor triumphs had been fulfilled. This was not simply a matter of intellect and resolve. The Mediterranean campaigns from 1793 to 1797 had demonstrated that his remarkable, warm, human leadership, his care for those he led, inspired ships' companies, fleets and fellow officers. Even hard-bitten old professionals like Jervis succumbed to his zeal, charm and professionalism; and the envy of his peers and elders was almost always replaced by recognition that he was the better man.

Nelson's company was now sought by the leading men of the age; he divided his stay in England between Bath and London, not finding time to return to his native Norfolk and making only a flying visit to the house he had bought near Ipswich. His social popularity was delightful after the bitter years in the wilderness, and he recorded the kindness of the great with a naive pleasure. He mixed regularly with Cabinet ministers and his views influenced their strategic discussions. Secretary at War William Windham recorded a dinner on 28 November, for example, at which Nelson was among his guests, along with the Lord Chancellor, Foreign Secretary Lord Grenville, Elliot and Norfolk peer Lord Cholmondley.[2] At such dinners, the themes that occupied Nelson's every waking thought – Navy and Empire, trade and power – were the main topics of discussion, and the authority with which he spoke was soon recognised. Windham, for example, noticed that the letters he received from Earl St Vincent in the Mediterranean agreed entirely with the predictions made by Nelson at the dinner table.[3] The Nelson effect was almost universal: the formidable Lady Spencer was so taken with the 'wonderful mind' that 'broke forth' that she wanted to see Nelson whenever he came to the Admiralty, and noted his every action at a farewell dinner.[4]

Although Nelson took great pleasure in being the lion of the season, he was anxious to rejoin his Commander and resume his career. He hoped to rejoin the fleet off Cadiz in early March.[5] At the same time St Vincent and Spencer were discussing the entry of a squadron into the Mediterranean, prompted by the impending withdrawal of Portugal from the war, and consequent exclusion of the fleet from Lisbon. The loss of Portugal threatened Britain's economic lifeline: the Atlantic trade routes. French warships or privateers based at Lisbon could annihilate the trade on which Britain depended. The British had to act quickly: the only friendly ports inside the Straits were in Naples, but to use them would only encourage the French to take control of even more of the peninsula. There was an air of desperation in Spencer's idea, prompted by St Vincent, of sweeping round the sea to see what damage could be done before retiring to England.[6]

Everything depended on the movements of the French, and the Brest Squadron caused considerable alarm in January by preparing for sea. A convalescent Nelson was frustrated by being in Bath, far from the centre of action. He and Fanny returned to London in late February, and attended a Royal Levee on 28 February. He took leave of the King in mid-March, and prepared for sea; Fanny would go back to Bath, to rejoin old Edmund.[7] There was time to write his will, leaving almost everything to Fanny, before hoisting his flag on the *Vanguard* at

Portsmouth on 29 March.[8] Spencer, writing to St Vincent, was confident that he would be pleased by the news:

> I am very happy to send you Sir Horatio Nelson again, not only because I believe I cannot send you a more zealous officer, but because I have reason to believe that his being under your command will be agreeable to your wishes. If your lordship is as desirous to have him with you as he is to be with you, I am sure the arrangement must be perfectly satisfactory.[9]

The passage to Lisbon, escorting vital naval storeships, occupied a tedious fortnight. Nelson then set out for the fleet off Cadiz. The voyage south gave him time to think about the next stage of the campaign. He was hoping for a fleet action, but feared that the Spanish would not come out, while St Vincent had too few ships to detach a squadron 'up the Mediterranean, to endeavour to get hold of the French squadron, now masters of that sea'.[10]

Nelson reached the fleet on 30 April, and immediately went aboard the flagship, where his presence gave 'new life' to St Vincent. Nelson had been thinking about the bombardment of Cadiz with mortar and gunboats, but reports that Bonaparte's army was at sea made a strategic reconnaissance the most likely option. At this stage he accepted the usual analysis that it was destined for Sicily, Malta, Sardinia, Naples or Portugal.[11] Two days later St Vincent sent him inside the Straits with the seventy-fours, *Alexander* and *Orion*, and three frigates, to 'endeavour to ascertain the real object of the [French] preparations'. His senior companions were two of St Vincent's best men: James Saumarez, who had distinguished himself off Cape St Vincent in 1797 and would command the Baltic fleet between 1808 and 1812, and Alexander Ball, who would later become Governor of Malta.

Even as Nelson set off on his mission British policy, and his career, were about to change. The ministers in London were reviewing the policy. Elliot had called on Spencer to advance both his own Mediterranean opinions, and the merits of Nelson to command the necessary force. Following a cabinet meeting on 28 April Spencer directed St Vincent to send a more substantial force into the Mediterranean. Initially the object was to oppose the French armament thought to be destined for Naples. This rumour had so alarmed Austria that she was likely to rejoin the war, something the ministers were anxious to encourage. The British doubted the French would go to so much trouble for Naples, and fancied either Portugal or Ireland was the target, but they were happy to see the views of Vienna changing. A fleet in the Mediterranean would block the French, encourage the Austrians and perhaps bring the war to a speedy termination. St Vincent could have taken his entire force on a mission of this importance, but the minister preferred him to divide his command.

> If you determine to send a detachment into the Mediterranean, I think it is almost unnecessary to suggest to you the propriety of putting it under the command of Sir Horatio Nelson, whose acquaintance with that part of the world, as well as his activity and disposition, seem to qualify him in a peculiar manner for that service.

Reinforcements would be sent from the Channel fleet, but the advance notice would allow time to prepare the necessary ships from the fleet off Cadiz.[12] This was a momentous turn in the pattern of the war: the British were shifting from the defensive to the offensive, with a terrible swiftness that would outpace friend and foe alike. Nelson, who had long believed Hood's argument that it was necessary to destroy the enemy whenever the opportunity arose, was the perfect choice to lead this new type of mission. Nor would it be in vain, for the French were on the verge of making a major mistake, by trusting an entire army on an overseas expedition. Even the optimistic Nelson could never have dared to hope for so much.

Although the Austrians left the war in October 1797, bought off by territorial concessions, their defection followed the morale-boosting victory at Camperdown. Britain might be alone, but the threat of invasion had been removed: her policy-makers could fight alone, relying on maritime control. Such a strategy had been useful in the era of limited war, when economic exhaustion and a few islands could persuade the enemy to seek terms, but the new enemy was too ruthless and unreliable for such negotiation. Foreign Secretary Lord Grenville accepted that Britain would not be secure until France was stable, and Europe at peace. This in turn required the combined resources of the rest of the Continent to bring about a regime change in Paris. To fall back on the defensive would pass the initiative to France, allowing her to threaten invasion of Britain or Ireland, attacks on trade or further European conquests, all of which harmed British commercial interests. The loss of Portugal, the last ally, would be particularly serious.[13] Lisbon was the key to the defence of the East and West India convoys, and vital to the financial health of the nation.

Throughout 1798, then, Grenville sought a Great Power coalition, linking Britain with Austria, Prussia and Russia, with a single war aim and a coherent strategy. The hope was illusory: self-interest, mutual suspicion and the instability of the Russian Tsar made the coalition impossible, and the whole-hearted support of any one power highly unlikely. It would take another fourteen years of Napoleonic aggression to overcome such hurdles. However, the British realised that Austria was the most likely to rejoin the war, because the French were not keeping the terms of the 1797 treaty. Knowing the Austrians wanted a fleet in the Mediterranean to defend their interests, Grenville and Pitt overrode Spencer's objections. The naval officers at the Admiralty wanted to keep a reserve to secure Ireland, but the Cabinet insisted that it be sent to the Mediterranean, despite the danger. In addition the blockade of Brest was tightened, to reduce the possibility of the French using their main fleet, thereby improving the security of Ireland.[14]

News of a possible Franco-Austrian rupture, and the intervention of the King, resulted in eight ships being sent. To emphasise the speed with which Britain shifted from the defensive to the offensive, the reinforcements came from the Irish coast, where the French had only recently landed. The degree of risk involved became clear in August and September, when Nelson seemed to have failed.[15] Even so the force sent was a sortie squadron: it had no staff and no base, and the duration of the cruise could be no more than three months, unless the ports of Naples were opened.[16]

St Vincent rose to the challenge, detaching his elite inshore squadron. He intended that Saumarez should return, leaving his favourite Troubridge as the ranking second, and consequently did not send Collingwood, who was senior to both men, to his immense chagrin. Nor did he intend sending the *Audacious*, with her uninspiring captain Davidge Gould. George Murray in the *Colossus* would have gone, had he arrived in time.[17] Two days later St Vincent ordered Nelson with his reinforced squadron to pursue the enemy armament, and 'use your utmost endeavours to take, sink, burn, or destroy it', looking to Naples, Tuscany and the ex-Venetian territories for supplies.[18]

The loss of the Dutch fleet, coming on top of the defeat of the Spanish, left the French with few options for an offensive stroke against Britain. Making strategic combinations for a three- or four-pronged seaborne movement from the Texel, Brest, Cadiz and Toulon was no longer realistic. Bonaparte was sent to review the northern invasion plans in February 1798, and did not like what he saw of the cold, muddy coast, or the feeble forces to hand. With no prospect of success, he was unwilling to risk his own position, and recommended against the attempt. Instead he advocated turning to the Levant, to strike at the Indian base of British prosperity. He had already secured the Ionian Islands for France, and with France dominating the Mediterranean it made sense to continue the career of conquest by seizing Malta and Egypt. This would counter the recent British seizure of the Cape of Good Hope from the Dutch, opening a new route to the east.

The wholly unjustified illegal seizure of these two territories demonstrated the fundamental change in the international order. Small states were no longer safe. Malta was held by the Order of the Knights of St John of Jerusalem, an organisation left over from the Crusades, which conducted permanent, if rather desultory warfare against Muslim states. While the islands lacked agricultural riches, and had limited supplies of water, they were located at the choke point between the eastern and western basins of the Mediterranean, and Grand Harbour at Valletta, secure behind its massive fortifications, was the best naval base in the central Mediterranean. The Knights had long since lost their crusading zeal, living in faded and apparently rather dissolute splendour amidst a Maltese population who despised them. The order was dominated by French Knights, and funded by property in various European countries. France had expropriated many of these lands, leaving the Knights short of funds, and increasingly irrelevant. The new state system of nations and empires had no place for such anachronisms: why should not the French replace them?

Egypt was in no better condition. Under the nominal authority of the Ottoman Sultans, de facto control had long passed to the Mamelukes, a warrior elite recruited from Circassian slaves. Under their petty tyranny the country had become a backward, crumbling, plague-ridden desert, full of the ruins of past glory. Many of these were connected with the two greatest conquerors of antiquity, Alexander and Caesar, men who fascinated Bonaparte. From a distance, Egypt seemed ripe for redevelopment through French science and political reform.

Foreign Minister Talleyrand supported Bonaparte, arguing that Egypt would be a substitute for the lost colonies of the West Indies. A combination of greed, fear and persuasive advocacy won over the

Directory in early March, with the eventual object of linking up with the Mysorean ruler Tippoo Sultan against British India. On 12 April, Bonaparte was appointed to overall command of an expedition whose ultimate aim was to drive the English from their oriental possessions and open the Red Sea to French traffic. Within a week troops and shipping began to collect at Toulon, Marseilles, Genoa, Civita Vecchia and, appropriately enough, Ajaccio. An army of thirty-one thousand, half of them veterans of the 1796–7 Italian campaign, with 170 guns and 1,200 horses, would be accompanied by a remarkable collection of scientists, scholars and artists, Arabic printing presses and assorted paraphernalia. The scale of the movement made complete secrecy impossible, but the ultimate object was well concealed. Bonaparte arrived at Marseilles in early May and addressed the troops, with his usual mixture of bombast and extravagant promises.[19]

British agents around the Mediterranean were soon sending intelligence to London, and to the fleet off Cadiz. From early April it was evident that the French were preparing for a major move, and Naples and Sicily were the obvious targets. These reports had prompted St Vincent to plan a strategic reconnaissance, and led London to dispatch Nelson for the mission.

After calling at Gibraltar Nelson set off, promising St Vincent, 'I do not believe any person guesses where I am going. It shall go hard, but I will present you at least with some frigates, and I hope something better.' He would head along the Spanish coast past Cartagena and Barcelona, round Cape St Sebastian and look into Toulon, seeking information to guide his further movements.[20] The instructions for his battleship captains reflected the danger that so small a force faced when isolated in an enemy-controlled sea. They were to keep within sight of the flagship, even if they had to break off action. Two of the frigates were to head for Toulon, where they could cruise for up to ten days in search of intelligence, before rejoining at one of the pre-set rendezvous. In an attempt to preserve his secrets for a few more days he had the squadron sail from Gibraltar after dark on 8 May.[21] Unfortunately they were delayed by light airs and were fired on by Spanish batteries the next morning.[22]

On 17 May one of the frigates captured a French corvette off Cape Sicie, about seventy miles from Toulon. Interrogating the crew provided considerable information on Bonaparte and his armament,

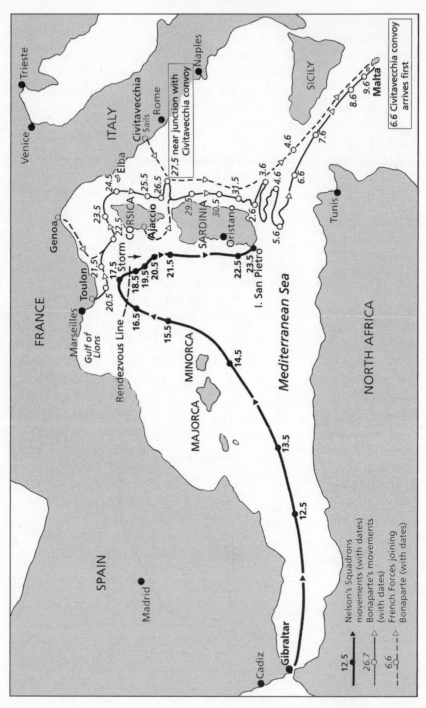

Nelson in the Mediterranean

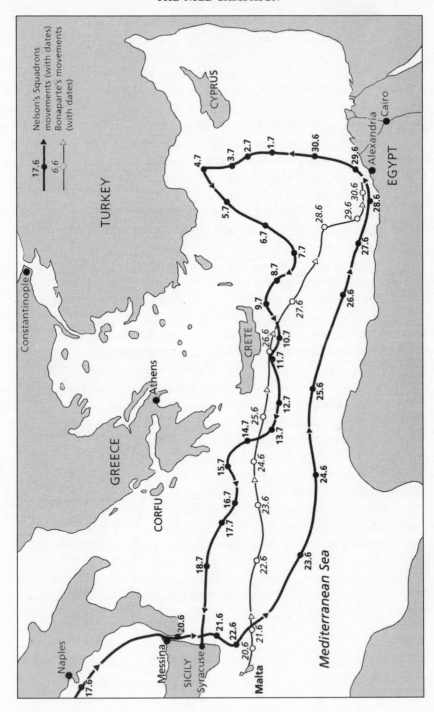

although none on his destination. Cruising about seventy-five miles south of Toulon, Nelson was ideally placed to pick up any ships heading for Italy, or the Straits. Intelligence gathered by Saumarez indicated the French had embarked cavalry. Whatever the object, however, Nelson had no doubt that his duty was to fight the enemy, if he found them at sea.[23] Although he had only three battleships, it is probable that he envisaged using them to break up the French fleet, leaving the frigates to attack the transport ships. With numerous French warships and transports running south along the Italian coast there was every chance of contact if Nelson hovered between Toulon and Sardinia. Instead he ran into a storm.

A furious gale from the north-north-west hit the squadron on 20 May. No significant damage was done to the other ships of the squadron, but Nelson's flagship, the *Vanguard*, was severely affected. Berry seems to have misread the weather, setting up the higher masts for light airs. Saumarez and Ball did the opposite. So while the other two seventy-fours had sails blown out, *Vanguard* lost all three topmasts, and then her foremast. Effectively crippled, with the foremast beating against the side of the ship, *Vanguard* was in serious danger. Nelson took command after the disaster, and managed to wear the ship off the rocky coast of Corsica. He now planned to anchor in a Sardinian bay to the south, and ordered the *Alexander* to take his flagship in tow. Despite exemplary seamanship, this apparently simple task occupied over eight hours. However, light airs and a strong current took them past the anchorage, and left the two ships drifting towards the coast, and unable to anchor. Unless the wind picked up the two ships were going to run aground. But for the audacious seamanship and determination of Ball, one or both of them would have been wrecked. In a passage of high drama, Nelson ordered Ball to save to his own ship, but he refused and kept calm. Finally a breeze picked up, and the ungainly partnership anchored safely between the island of San Pietro and the mainland at midday on 23 May.

Once anchored Nelson hastened to thank Ball, whom he had hitherto considered a conceited coxcomb. Typically, he took his new friend into his inner circle without hesitation, and came to trust his judgement on questions far beyond seamanship. Nelson also had to acknowledge another mistake: Berry was not up to the job, both his seamanship and his judgement left a great deal to be desired. For the next two months Nelson would take a far more active part in handling the ship than he might have hoped. However, he would not have dreamt of disgracing Berry, or even replacing him, at this critical juncture. Remarkably, Nelson showed no signs of hesitation: he would repair the ship and carry on with his mission. He did not consider the obvious options of returning to the fleet with his crippled flagship, nor shifting into another ship and sending his flagship back. Instead, the carpenters of the three battleships quickly created a temporary or jury rig for the *Vanguard*. Five days after anchoring with her rigging in ruins the *Vanguard* was back at sea: she sailed well and would not compromise the mission.

A fresh prize revealed the French were at sea, and on 5 June Hardy in the brig *Mutine* joined the squadron at the rendezvous off Toulon to inform him of Troubridge's reinforcement. The new ships linked up with Nelson on 7 June, and the entire force was together on Sunday 10th. He now commanded thirteen seventy-four-gun ships – all English-built, medium-sized units, with almost identical rigs, armament and crew. The fifty-gun *Leander* was an odd packet, too big to be a frigate, but too weakly armed and built for the line of battle and no faster under sail. St Vincent sent her because he had no more frigates. As Nelson's frigates, hearing of his accident, had returned to Gibraltar, scouting duties would be left to the tiny *Mutine*. St Vincent had intended that the *Orion* should rejoin his fleet, as Saumarez was anxious to go home, but the damage to the flagship persuaded Nelson to keep him.

Over the next seven weeks of almost constant cruising, chasing and refitting, the squadron would build on the very superior attainments it possessed, reaching the highest levels of proficiency in all aspects of its task. These ships were fit champions for England – none better existed – and they would be tested to the limit before their work was done. Nelson had no doubt he would beat the French, but in 1798 the Mediterranean was a vast expanse of water with very limited communications, surrounded by a host of potential destinations and harbours where a fleet might find shelter behind batteries. His hardest task would be to find the enemy, and the key to this would be the acquisition and processing of intelligence. British officials in neutral ports and cities could help, but only if Nelson could make contact with them; intelligence from London and even reports sent by St Vincent would be out of date. The best source would be other ships. Prizes and neutral vessels could reveal much. The French knew this and deliberately destroyed as many passing vessels as they could, but Nelson stopped and spoke to at least forty-one craft between May and August. As a result, he was never far from Bonaparte's armada, eventually overtaking the French at sea.[24]

The squadron orders reveal an admiral bent on battle. The day after Troubridge joined he divided the squadron into starboard and larboard squadrons of seven and eight ships, commanded by himself and Saumarez, with Troubridge leading the line as he had so memorably at Cape St Vincent.[25] Later a more conventional formation was adopted, with Nelson, Saumarez and Troubridge commanding distinct divisions. If he found the French at sea Nelson would use two units to engage their warships while the third cut up the transports.[26] Whatever tactical divisions he adopted Nelson insisted that they keep in visual contact. He wanted his force together, in supporting distance, ready to exploit any fleeting opportunity for battle.[27]

While Nelson had been close to disaster on the west coast of Sardinia, Bonaparte's force had found easier conditions to the east, as the various detachments linked up and headed for Malta. Arriving on 9 June, the French landed on the following day, securing the islands and the massive fortress of Valletta by a combination of force and treachery on the 12th. After installing a small garrison the main force left on the 18th. At this stage Nelson was less than a hundred miles astern, making far better time than the huge, unwieldy French force.

Nelson had arrived off Telamon Bay on the Italian coast on 12 June; though this was a potential rendezvous for the French force, he found nothing and pressed on south. He wrote to Hamilton for information on the French and an idea of what help he could expect from the Neapolitans. He also opened a running journal-letter for St Vincent, recording his daily proceedings and reflections, the whole dominated by his anxiety 'to prove myself worthy of your selection . . . for this highly honourable command'.[28] On 14 June he heard that the enemy had been off Sicily on the 4th – information which, when combined with recent winds, allowed him to rule out an attack on Portugal, Ireland or anywhere else to the west. If the French were landing on the Neapolitan coast he would attack them, even at anchor, as long as they were not in a fortified anchorage.[29]

On 15 June he wrote to Spencer, in anticipation of his next landfall. He had already decided what the French were doing:

If they pass Sicily, I shall believe they are going on their scheme of possessing Alexandria, and getting troops to India – a plan concerted with Tippoo Saib, by no means so difficult as might at first view be imagined.

He enclosed a letter for Fanny reporting the changed situation and, as he was busy, his normal good health.[30] Arriving off Naples on 17 June he sent Troubridge ashore to call on Hamilton and the Neapolitan ministers. He was desperate for frigates, without which he feared the French convoy would escape, and pressed the case for the Neapolitans to blockade Malta, and gain 'part of the glory in destroying these pests of the human race'.[31] Hamilton knew the French were at Malta, but in his concern for Sicily forgot to pass on useful evidence that Egypt was the ultimate destination. The Neapolitan people seemed well disposed, but the government was divided and paralysed, fearing a French attack if they assisted the British.

Nelson appealed to Hamilton to obtain flotilla craft, sending extracts from the official correspondence to show that his squadron would remain in the Mediterranean as long as it could, a time that would be determined by Naples. Expecting a battle off Malta, he called for a Neapolitan flotilla so he could attack the French anchored between Gozo and Comino without risking his battlefleet.[32] Discussing the political questions with Hamilton helped Nelson to refine his opinions; the minister offered a different sounding-board to the more narrowly professional approach of his captains.

With reliable intelligence that the French were at Malta, Nelson hurried south, taking the short cut through the historic, picturesque Straits of Messina. On 22 June a Ragusan merchant ship provided a mixed haul of intelligence. The French had left Malta, but the reported date was three days earlier than their actual departure. This information, combined with the westerly winds, led Nelson to conclude that they had not doubled back to Sicily and decided to press on for Egypt, but it misled him as to the head start the French had gained. He called his chosen captains – Saumarez, Troubridge, Darby and Ball – on board the flagship, where they were joined by Berry for a consultation. Nelson did not call a formal 'Council of War', which might have disagreed with him. Instead he set them a few heavily loaded questions, which they understood to mean he was bent on heading east. They did not disagree, although Saumarez was not convinced, thinking Nelson's arguments 'the merest conjecture'. As the opinion of the ranking second makes clear, this was not an easy decision: it was more a leap in the dark than a simple pursuit.³³ The Royal Navy had little experience of the Eastern Mediterranean, and no English charts. This makes it somewhat surprising that Nelson did not summon Samuel Hood, who had considerable recent experience of the eastern basin, to his conference.

Shortly after the decision had been made Nelson recalled ships that were pursuing French frigates. His decision was based on the erroneous departure date. If the French were six days ahead he would be wasting his time chasing these detached units. In fact they were the outer screen of the French armada, as a closer inspection would have revealed. The relentless pursuit driven on by Nelson had caught the French, and that night as their tracks crossed he overtook them. With a vast convoy of craft, many unable to navigate other than by coastal marks, the French admiral hugged the south coast of Crete. Nelson, anxious to make up distance took the direct route, passing further south.

Even before the squadron reached Alexandria, Nelson must have had his suspicions: there was no evidence of the French ahead – no rubbish, no stragglers and no ships. This only heightened the tension. Arriving off Alexandria late on 28 June, Nelson found no French ships. The following day Hardy went ashore: he could not find the British consul, and the Egyptians were perfectly at ease. Unable to contain his mounting fear that his decision might have been wrong, rather than correct but based on inaccurate dates, Nelson did not linger. On 30 June he sailed north, wondering where else the French might have gone. His darkest fear was that they had doubled back to seize Sicily and Naples. Twenty-five hours later the French arrived, and began to land the army. Although Nelson had openly discussed the possibility he might arrive ahead of the French, he still had not waited – an error for which he would later apologise profusely to St Vincent.

St Vincent was waiting anxiously for news. He had sent his best ships and his best men on a high-risk mission, and the little scraps of information that filtered back were far from reassuring. A dismasted flagship, retreating frigates and a leap in the dark made Nelson's reports grim reading, and not, he believed, suitable for the eyes of the Admiralty Board. Instead he sent them to Spencer in a private letter, that the First Lord might 'see the inmost recesses of such a soul as

Nelson's'.[34] It would be another ten weeks before he heard good news, but his faith and his anxiety to shield Nelson from the small-minded criticism of the naval officers on Spencer's Board showed him at his best.

After heading north for two days, in case the French had made for Turkey, Nelson surrendered to his fears and set a course for Sicily. Arriving on 20 July he found no news of the enemy, but confirmed that they had not returned to the west. Only now did he learn that both Hamilton and Neapolitan Prime Minister Sir John Acton also thought the armada had been bound for Egypt.[35] Four days at Syracuse provided fresh food, water, and even an opportunity for the bold to send their washing ashore. Contact with the shore and a few comforts helped to restore the morale of the squadron.[36] Nelson attributed the more accommodating attitude of the Sicilian authorities, who provided food and water, to the intervention of the Hamiltons. He set off on 24 July trusting to providence.[37]

The French admiral, François-Paul Comte de Brueys d'Aigallieri, a forty-five-year-old pre-Revolutionary officer and aristocrat, had learnt his craft in the West Indies under De Grasse and seen at first hand the great events of 1782. He had been in the West Indies after the war, at the same time as Nelson, commanding a small ship. Rejoining the navy after the Jacobin excesses of the Robespierre period, he had impressed Bonaparte.

The small French transport ships were soon safely moored in Alexandria harbour, but the much larger, deep-draught battleships posed a problem. They could only be brought into harbour very slowly, by taking out their guns. This would leave them trapped, easily blockaded by one or two British ships. Brueys would have preferred to head for the safe harbour at Corfu, but Bonaparte denied him that option. Instead he anchored just along the coast in Aboukir Bay on 7 July, taking up what he considered a strong defensive position similar to one Lord Hood had used to defeat De Grasse in 1782. He presumed that any attack would be against the rear of his formation, which was more exposed. Consequently his most powerful ships were in the rear and centre of the line, those at the head were the oldest and weakest. With more care he could have positioned the ships tight up to the shoals, and closed up the line by anchoring at the bow and stern. Instead the ships swung at a single anchor, leaving room for an attacker between each ship, and more significantly inshore of the line. The appearance of two British frigates off the Bay on 21 July increased French concerns, although they were not in contact with Nelson.

Meanwhile, as Nelson entered the Gulf of Coron, he finally picked up the final pieces of the intelligence jigsaw, and once more set course for Egypt. However, this only redoubled his anxiety. Surely he would be too late: the French would be ashore, and their fleet safely tied up in harbour, out of harm's way. He would be left to impose a temporary blockade, until his supplies ran low, and then limp back to Gibraltar – the man who missed Bonaparte, and exposed the Indian Empire to a French attack. Had he known that the cabinet was even then reaching such conclusions he would have been further depressed. It is significant that he wrote nothing in this period, too highly wrought to eat, sleep or think of anything but the chance of battle, the long-hoped-for chance to annihilate the enemy.

Arriving off Alexandria from the west early on 1 August, Nelson could see no battleships, only the French transports crowded inside the harbour, relatively safe from attack. It was mid-afternoon, shortly before 3 o'clock, when Foley and Hood, in *Goliath* and *Zealous*, spotted the masts of the French fleet further along the coast. Aboukir was the only suitable fleet anchorage on the coast, and as the news was received Nelson sat down to a hearty dinner, while Saumarez and his officers paused only to drink to the battle before rushing on deck to see the enemy. The men cheered, from anticipation of glory and prize, or sheer relief at finding the target.

The moment that made Nelson immortal beckoned. He had four more hours of daylight, but his ships were still scattered: two had been looking into Alexandria, while Troubridge's *Culloden* was seven miles astern, with a prize in tow. It would be two hours before he could reach the enemy, leaving a mere two hours to fight before darkness fell with equatorial haste. With Brueys at anchor the initiative lay with him: he could attack, or haul off and wait for the following day. The risk of running aground in an unknown bay, which the French had chosen, or of friendly fire after dark were among the factors that would have given him cause for concern. However, Nelson was confident his squadron could deal with the enemy, and saw no reason to give Brueys the chance to improve his position, or sail out of the bay and try to escape. Brueys had made a fatal error, and as Collingwood stressed, any admiral who made a mistake in Nelson's presence was doomed.

Nelson's command system relied on clear, simple concepts, communicated in plain English at the outset of the cruise, reinforced by discussion. This was a style he had inherited from Hood and St Vincent, and modified with his own unique human insight and warmth. He left his subordinates ample opportunity to develop on his plans, but made sure they had a safety net. His captains knew what was expected. Those who were present at Cape St Vincent needed little reminding that initiative, aggression and skill would be rewarded while the admiral would take responsibility for a bold failure. During the four days at Syracuse there were opportunities for discussion, but no formal conference. That Nelson trusted his captains was evident in every move, yet he knew that while all were competent, they were not equal. Troubridge, Ball, Saumarez and Hallowell were potential fleet commanders; Miller and Foley were fine captains; Hood was relatively unknown, but his very name was a guarantee of talent.

Just before three o'clock Nelson signalled the squadron to head for the French, recalled the detached ships and ordered Troubridge to cast off his prize. He would not wait to form a line of battle, relying on his ships to get into action as quickly as possible. The *Vanguard* was among the leading ships as they passed the western shoal, some three miles from the enemy, Nelson called across to Hood asking if it was safe to proceed. Hood promised to lead in with the leadsman, a skilled hand with a weighted line to measure the depth of water. He was making for the head or van of the French line. Nelson then shortened sail and called up Miller in the *Theseus* to act as his support, allowing *Orion* and *Audacious* to pass. At 5.30, with contact imminent, Nelson signalled to form a line as convenient, while Foley, who had a recent French chart, slipped ahead of Hood in the race for the post of honour, leading the line.

Brueys had been warned of the British squadron by 2 o'clock and had begun to prepare for battle. He had a large number of men ashore, foraging, many too far away to recall. As some of the ships were already two hundred short of complement he called on the four frigates to send over their best gun crews. But Nelson had seized the moment, and Brueys could not recover the time he had lost through faulty dispositions. Instead he was forced to wait as Nelson headed for the weakest part of his line, exploiting ideal wind direction and strength to attack three feeble, old and weakly manned ships. The fort on Bequieres island opened fire, but the range was too great. At least

Brueys' crews were disciplined: they held their fire until the British had come to point-blank range, about 250 yards. Even so, the opening French broadsides were inaccurate, and did not halt the attack: firing with a slow match, instead of the flintlocks used by the British, and aiming on the upward roll of the ship, most of their shot went high, or at worst through the British rigging and sails.

Nelson had anticipated a battle at anchor, adding a signal for cables and springs to be run out through the stern ports to his repertoire of flags at the outset of the cruise. He flew the necessary signal at 4.22, as the ships entered the bay. Unlike Brueys' force, which had more time to act and no sails to handle, the British ships were prepared by the time they joined the fight, although the failure of three ships to control their stern cables suggests the margin was close. The job was made that much easier by the process of beating to quarters, with marine drummers signalling the ship to 'clear for action' as the men removed partitions, bulkheads, spare gear, livestock, and even dinner, to ensure nothing interfered with the smooth steady operation of the guns. Elsewhere the surgeon and his team prepared the cockpit for service as a makeshift operating theatre, and warmed their instruments on Nelson's specific instruction – for him, the sensation of steel cutting into living flesh was all too recent a memory.

At 4.52 Nelson signalled for an attack on the van and centre, a concentration of force against part of the enemy line, which he selected because the wind was blowing directly down the French line, making it almost impossible for the rear ships to take part in the opening stages of the battle. He did not know that Brueys had put his weakest ships in the van. He also signalled for each ship to place four lanterns in a vertical alignment on the mizzen mast, to avoid friendly fire after dark.

Having won the race to lead the line, Foley was responsible for the opening move, and like his chief he did not flinch from exploiting the opportunities his practised eye discerned, satisfied his well-drilled crew would meet his expectations. As he closed the French line Foley could see that the ships were at single anchor, and he worked out that he could sail round the leading French ship, attacking on the inshore side where he expected they had not prepared for battle. At almost the same moment Nelson saw the opening, although it was too late for him to signal. This strongly suggests that Nelson, having foreseen a battle at anchor, let his captains know that he favoured doubling on

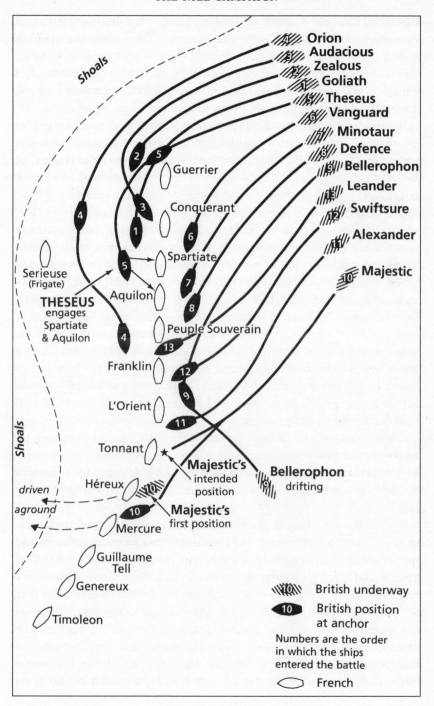

The battle of the Nile

the enemy line following the precedent set by Lord Hood off Gourjean Bay back in 1794. The only question left for Foley to settle was whether he could get inside the French ships.

As *Goliath* rounded the head of the French line Foley fired a first broadside into the bows of the feeble old *Guerrière*, causing serious damage and loss of life. He planned to anchor alongside, where he was delighted to see the French gunports still packed with stores and quite unprepared, but the anchor cable through the stern ports was allowed to run out to the full extent, and she brought up between the second and third ships in the French line. This left a space for Hood, who also poured his first broadside into the bows of the *Guerrière* before taking up a position off her port bow, which gave the *Zealous* a favourable angle of attack. Gould in the *Audacious* followed him round, fired into the *Guerrière* and then anchored between her and the next ship, the *Conquerant*. Saumarez swept further inshore to clear his squadron mates, planning to attack the third French ship, the *Spartiate*: however, the frigate *Sérieuse* rashly fired on the *Orion*. Saumarez waited for his puny opponent to close, before pouring in a single broadside that dismasted and sank the French vessel. In the process *Orion* missed her mark, and brought up on the bows of the fifth French ship, *Peuple Souverain*. Miller took the *Theseus* round the head of the line, her fire dismasting the unfortunate *Guerrière*, before picking his way between the *Zealous* and her target, to avoid the inshore shoals. He took position off the bow of the *Spartiate*.

Nelson had watched his captains open the battle in magnificent style; now he elected to change the angle of attack. The inshore berth, as Miller had found, was becoming crowded. It was time to double on the enemy, and he turned outside the line, placing *Vanguard* alongside the *Spartiate*. The next two ships astern, *Minotaur* and *Defence*, followed him, extending down the French line to engage *Aquilon* and *Peuple Souverain*. *Bellerophon* failed to bring up alongside the eighty-gun *Franklin*, a formidable opponent for a medium-sized seventy-four, ending up off the bow of the three-decker *L'Orient*, a ship with a tremendous advantage in weight of broadside and height out of the water. *Majestic*, the last of the ships in close order when the attack began, arrived off the French line little more than thirty minutes after *Goliath* had rounded the *Guerrière*. She also missed her mark. It was now dark, and gunsmoke was beginning to shroud the battlefield. *Majestic* ended up bow-on to the *Hereux*, the ninth ship in the French line, unable to fight her guns and under heavy musket fire from the French ship. Captain Westcott was killed before anything could be done. That these two ships both made serious errors of positioning reflected their inability to see the target. Both would pay heavily for their admiral's temerity in launching an attack under such difficult conditions.

Further out, Troubridge had cast off his prize at 3 o'clock and hastened to join the fight. He never arrived. As he rounded Aboukir Island he cut the corner and failed to clear the shoal, going hard aground at 6.40. Never one to dwell on a disaster, Troubridge immediately signalled that the *Culloden* was aground, to warn *Alexander* and *Swiftsure*, then coming up astern, and called Hardy over in the tiny *Mutine* to lay out his anchors in an attempt to get the ship off. Despite lightening ship, and using every exertion, the *Culloden* was stuck fast, pinned at the bow and stern, her fire-eating captain condemned to be a spectator at the greatest naval battle ever fought. Coming up astern Ball and Hallowell arrived at the French line around 8 o'clock. They entered a diabolical scene, the dark night and thick smoke repeatedly punctured by sharp, stabbing flames from guns, whose thunderous noise was counterpointed by high-pitched yells and screams. That excellent seaman Ball calmly took the *Alexander* into an ideal position, just off the after-quarter of the French flagship, where his broadside would tell on her weak stern galleries, without risking the response that had already dismasted and shattered *Bellerophon*. She had cut her cable and was drifting down wind, out of the action and without her recognition lights. She was nearly fired on by *Swiftsure*, but fortunately for all concerned Hallowell had decided to take up his position before opening fire. This meant that he could furl and secure his sails before releasing the men to serve the guns, thus avoiding the problems suffered by three of his predecessors. *Leander* was the only fighting ship not engaged, or aground. Thompson's first thoughts were to assist *Culloden*, but Troubridge advised him to join the battle. Thompson finally got into the fight after 9 o'clock, taking up a perfect position across the bow of *Franklin*.

Twelve of Nelson's thirteen fighting ships had now been in action: one had already been knocked out, and another heavily hit, but the attack had been a remarkable success. The van of Brueys' fleet was being overwhelmed, while his rear was unengaged. With the ships at or inside point-blank range the battle now settled into a steady

exchange of fire. The limited damage that any one shot, or even broadside, could inflict made naval battles in this era a question of hours,
not minutes. The faster and more accurate broadsides of the British
soon dominated the contest, gradually breaking the physical and mental resistance of the enemy. The French fought bravely, but they fought
like men resigned to defeat, their officers more anxious to show how
well they could die than to win the battle. Nelson and his captains
were also setting an example of bravery under fire, to inspire their
men, but they were looking for opportunities to secure victory. The
gun crews toiled away in an environment of stunning noise and parch-
ing smoke, knowing that any error in drill could be disastrous. They
had no concept of the battle, only of their immediate surroundings,
punctuated by occasional reports from the topsides. In the magazines
powder charges were packed and handed on to boys too small to haul
the gun tackles, while ready-use shot were stored on the deck, with the
main supply in the shot lockers down in the hold, which had to be
opened once the initial supply had been fired.

Casualties were an inevitable part of such battles: they were quickly removed, usually by their messmates. The dead were unceremoni-
ously heaved overboard, to maintain morale and keep the sanded
decks free of slippery gore. The living were taken down to the cockpit,
to wait their turn with the surgeon. At 8.30 Nelson joined them.
Standing with Berry, looking at a sketch of the bay taken from a
French prize, he was hit on the forehead by a scrap of iron from an
anti-personnel projectile. It was a nasty wound: the flesh was cut away
from the skull over an area an inch long and three inches wide. The
blow knocked him off-balance, but Berry caught him.

It was at this moment that Nelson demonstrated his underlying
Wolfe fixation. He was about to win the greatest naval battle of all
time so, in the manner of his hero, it was the perfect time to die. The
enemy had now obliged. He could go to meet his maker, and the architect of his destiny as one of the immortals. Stunned and blinded, his
only good eye covered by detached flesh and copious amounts of
blood, he began to 'perform' the Death of the Hero. There had to be
an affecting death scene, something for Benjamin West to capture in
oils, for posterity to record, for his countrymen to admire and lament.
This time he did not quite rise to the occasion: all he could offer was
'I am killed; remember me to my wife', before Berry applied a dressing
and had him helped below. Staggering down three companion ways

Nelson began to recover his composure. By the time he reached the cockpit he insisted on waiting his turn – there were far worse injuries to be dealt with. Surgeon Jefferson quickly cleaned up the wound, bringing the edges together with sticking plaster and a bandage. He sent the stunned admiral to the nearby bread room to rest, and to get out of his way. Determined to have his say Nelson called for his Secretary, who had been slightly wounded, and tried to dictate an official report. The Secretary, overcome by the situation, passed the task to the chaplain, but they soon gave up. There was not enough light and even Nelson needed to rest, if only to allow the first symptoms of shock to pass.

His battle was going well. *Majestic* escaped from her dangerous position when her jib-boom gave way, and brought up between *Hereux* and *Mercure*, able to fire on both with relative impunity. At the head of the line *Guerrière*, *Conquerant* and *Spartiate* were overwhelmed, surrendering after two to three hours of unequal combat, in which they lost hundreds of men. *Aquilon was* also doubled and lasted no longer, while *Peuple Souverain* put up a stout fight, hitting Saumarez and his ship quite hard, until her cables were cut and she drifted out of the line. The vacant position exposed *Franklin*'s bow, and Thompson exploited it to perfection. With her decks being repeatedly raked the big eighty-gun ship was soon reduced to a helpless wreck, but her surrender was delayed by more startling events.

L'Orient, Brueys' flagship, was a tougher nut. Her height out of the water, weight of fire and heavily built hull made her a difficult opponent. After dismantling *Bellerophon*, which suffered a quarter of the British casualties, she was attacked with more skill by Ball and Hallowell. *Alexander* fired into her stern, killing Brueys, and starting a fire in the great cabin. The fire quickly spread: some accounts suggest that oil-based paint had been left on deck, while Hallowell deliberately directed his guns into the blazing mizzen chains to stop any firefighting. An explosion was inevitable; Ball cut his cable and moved down the line, Saumarez ordered fire precautions, while Hallowell, confident that any explosion would be vented upward by the stout hull, wetted his sails and decks and sat tight close to the blazing threedecker. Astern of the flagship *Tonnant*, *Hereux* and *Mercure* cut their cables: the former was dismasted, the others went aground.

Nelson was sufficiently recovered to return to the deck to see the spectacle, and immediately sent his last remaining boat to save lives.

This instinctive, humane action disproves the silly notion that he was a bloodthirsty killer, a mere butcher of men, dominated by hatred and blood lust. Around 11 o'clock the two magazines on *L'Orient* exploded, a stunning *son et lumière* to mark the defeat of the French fleet. The concussion, noise and spectacular pall of smoke suspended the fighting for at least fifteen minutes; those further away in Alexandria saw before they heard. Debris rained down on the ships of both fleets, setting fire to sails and damaging rigging. Captain Casabianca and his ten-year-old son, the famous 'boy who stood on the burning deck', were drowned, but Chief of Staff Rear Admiral Ganteaume was saved.

The French had lost their flagship and their admiral, although the treasure of the Knights of Malta had been landed by Bonaparte to fund his campaign and occupation of Egypt. Plunder, rather than the island or the harbour, had drawn him to Valletta. Nelson had lost a tremendous prize, a prestige vessel which had defied him as the *Sans Culotte* back in 1795, and would have been a fitting trophy for his cabinet. Instead he made do with her lightning conductor, and a little later a smart example of carpenter's work, knocked up from her mainmast. He had also lost his share of the prize money for the ship. Unlike some of his contemporaries Nelson was unlucky with money.

Not that such thoughts would have troubled him. While ten French battleships and a frigate had been taken, destroyed or run ashore, there were still three undamaged battleships, and three frigates at the end of the line, commanded by Rear Admiral Pierre Villeneuve. Villeneuve spent the night paralysed by uncertainty: he had no orders to act and no standing instruction to reinforce the van. As Brueys made no signal, he sat still. To move against the wind would have been difficult, and dangerous under fire. The battle petered out around midnight, with only a few shots being exchanged before 4 a.m., when the sun came up. The men were so tired they simply slept where they fell, alongside their guns, or slumped over the capstan bars. Once he could see the situation Nelson ordered his least damaged ships down to continue the battle: as he had said when criticising Hotham's action, it was not enough to win, it was necessary to annihilate. The nearest of the French ships, the seventy-four *Timoleon*, was soon crippled by a well-directed fire at medium-range, and after further indecision Villeneuve elected to escape, getting away at midday with two battleship and two frigates. Hood in the *Zealous* was the only ship in a position to block his path, but after exchanging fire on opposing courses Nelson called her back, unwilling to risk a reverse at this stage. *Tonnant* and *Timoleon* covered the escape by remaining in action for the rest of the day, the latter being deliberately burnt after surrendering.

Having won the battle, and surpassed the standard of victory set by previous generations, Nelson now had to clear up the battlefield, bury the dead, attend to the living, patch up his ships, repair his prizes and as soon as possible turn the battle to strategic account. However, before attending to any of those concerns he ordered a public thanksgiving for the victory at 2 p.m., before the last of the French ships had surrendered. This was not mere form, but unusual and heartfelt: Nelson had no doubt his God had preordained the victory. It was equally characteristic of Nelson to share the credit even for his greatest victory with his subordinates; his captains responded, in turn, by assembling on the *Orion* and agreeing to buy a sword and a portrait of their commander, and to set up a Nile Club to remind them of the occasion. Nelson had won their hearts, as well as a battle.

Good discipline and the support of his captains remained critical: he had two fleets to repair, a large body of prisoners to control and no friendly base closer than Gibraltar. The repairs were aided by stripping some of the prizes, especially those already ashore, to supplement his stores. Two British ships, *Majestic* and *Bellerophon*, were totally dismasted, and most of the rest had been damaged aloft; the French ships were almost all bereft of masts. Until they could be repaired they were perfectly immobile on a hostile coast, controlled by the French. With little food, and many wounded prisoners, Nelson started sending the French sailors ashore, only keeping the senior officers and those unwounded officers who refused to give their parole. On 12 August he ordered Saumarez to take five of the best British ships, along with the two most badly damaged, and five prizes to Gibraltar. They sailed on 14 August, but made slow time. *Culloden* had finally floated free on the 5th after an epic struggle. Anyone other than Troubridge would have given up: she required urgent dockyard attention. Nelson decided to accompany her to Naples, hoping to repair the shattered rigging of his flagship at the same time.

A public dispatch announcing the victory was addressed to St Vincent and sent on 5 August on board the *Leander*, which was relatively undamaged. Berry – brave but inconsistent, and not the best man to run a flagship – was sent to gather the laurels of taking it to

Court, a knighthood being customary on such occasions, while Hardy was promoted into the flagship. The brief despatch opened: 'Almighty God has blessed His Majesty's arms in the late battle, by a Great Victory . . .' and set out the basic facts. The fleet had been 'absolutely irresistible' and no words could add to the glory of all concerned.[38]

Rewards were quickly given. Lieutenant Capel from the flagship took over the *Mutine*: he was a good officer and as Spencer's nominee particularly well connected. More significantly Lieutenant Cuthbert, who had fought the *Majestic* so well after Westcott was killed, retained the command to await St Vincent's decision. Every first lieutenant could expect to be promoted for the victory, while their captains would receive other distinctions. The men would get prize and head money for every ship taken and every man they contained at the outset of the fight.

Those who died of their wounds in the weeks that followed were buried ashore on Aboukir Island, secured to provide shore exercise for the men. It had not been an easy victory: casualties amounted to almost nine hundred officers and men, around a tenth of the force engaged, with 172 of them fatalities. The French fought hard, and at close quarters their determination made them dangerous opponents. Losses were very unevenly distributed. Hood's *Zealous* lost only one killed and seven wounded, *Bellerophon* 49 and 147 respectively, and *Majestic*'s list was almost identical.

Having easily penetrated the ultimate destination of the French force, Nelson wasted little time in sending an officer to India, via Alexandretta, Baghdad and Basra, arriving at Bombay on 21 October. The news arrived only two weeks after that of Bonaparte's landing in Egypt. From Calcutta the British Governor General Lord Mornington declared, 'I cannot doubt that this success must awaken Europe.'[39] India was safe, Tippoo was already dead, the Royal Navy had occupied the Red Sea – Indian forces would help to clear the French out of Egypt. Here Nelson had been in step with the Cabinet, which had accepted Henry Dundas's argument in early June, reinforcing the subcontinent with troops and money, placing a naval force in the Red Sea, and giving orders to attack Tippoo if he showed any sign of encouraging the French. While Mornington, and his younger brother Arthur Wellesley, the future Duke of Wellington, destroyed the threat posed by Tippoo's regime in Mysore, Nelson had shattered Bonaparte's dream of conquest.

The first fruits of the newly won British control of the Egyptian coast were a collection of French despatches and letters that revealed Bonaparte's ambition 'to be the Washington of his country'. These would be printed, as part of the propaganda offensive against the French, being both divisive and despondent.[40]

Though Nelson told Fanny, some ten days after the battle, that he was much better than might be expected,[41] professional correspondents heard a very different story. The head wound had left him sick and distracted, and he was considering handing over the command to Troubridge. The arrival of orders from St Vincent on 14 August changed the picture. The information that the British were already changing their focus to offensive operations, notably the seizure of Minorca, persuaded him to give up the hopeless struggle to refit the remaining French battleships. Two were hard aground, while the *Guerrière* was an old hulk that had been transformed into a picturesque ruin by close-range broadsides. They were not worth the time and trouble required to repair them, but to destroy them would deprive the men of their prize value. Nelson understood there were more important issues than money, and burnt them, along with the half-submerged *Sérieuse,* although he wrote to Spencer and the Admiralty asking that the men be given their share. He would have burnt two more of the prizes for the same reasons, but regarded the other four ships as 'a treasure to our navy'.[42] The *Franklin,* renamed HMS *Canopus,* became the model for a whole class of post-war ships, and remained in service until the late 1840s.

Nelson now divided his remaining six battleships, leaving the three in best condition, with three of the belatedly recovered frigates under Hood, to blockade the Egyptian coast, open links with the Turks and cut French communications. Leaving the newly historic bay on 19 August Nelson headed for Naples. These three ship squadrons were more than equal to anything the French could now muster, and demonstrated the value of annihilating the enemy. Naval power could be spread across the Mediterranean, to cut off the French, encourage the Neapolitans and reinforce the fleet off Cadiz.

On passage, Nelson turned his thoughts to the wider war: he had written off the French army, and hoped his success would encourage others to take up the struggle. A few bomb vessels would complete the destruction of the French transports in Alexandria, and he hoped that Naples or Turkey would provide them. The Turks declared war, but were less forthcoming with such specialist equipment. Naples was waiting on the Austrians, who were also waiting, although it was not entirely clear why.

The voyage to Naples was long, hampered by the slow sailing of the *Culloden* and the elements' continuing grudge against the *Vanguard*. Hit by a squall off Stromboli on 15 September she lost her foremast, part of the main topmast and the jib-boom. The crippled admiral arrived for his triumph at Naples in a suitably crippled flagship, towed into the harbour on 22 September.

CHAPTER IX

Naples and the Hamiltons
1798–9

In the months that followed the victory of the Nile, Nelson, battered and concussed, stood at the epicentre of a tidal wave of euphoria and enthusiasm that spread slowly but irresistibly from Aboukir Bay to the Admiralty. As more than one contemporary observed, as the victor in the most complete naval battle ever fought and the saviour of India, he had become an immortal. He could expect to be made a peer of the realm, and richly rewarded by a grateful King and country. Yet before he returned home to claim these rewards, accusations of reprehensible behaviour in both the private and public sphere would threaten to tarnish his name. Some biographers have been quick to convict Nelson of acting dishonestly, conniving in judicial murder, dishonouring his flag and his country, and abandoning his wife for another woman.[1] Yet only the last of these is a matter of fact. The other supposed offences – taking vengeance on defeated enemies in cold blood, dishonouring his service and his country, being a party, principal or associate in a crime – are so wholly and obviously out of character that Nelson's admirers have sought an excuse to explain his behaviour: the concussive blow to the head at the Nile, exhaustion, the enervating and corrupting atmosphere of the Neapolitan Court, or the blandishments of a designing woman. It is curious that such admirers did not pause to consider that the 'crimes' might be fictional.

Art and passion: Lady Hamilton

The scene of Nelson's 'disgrace' would be Naples, the largest city in Southern Italy. Renowned for its easy-going eighteenth-century morality, Naples had long been a favourite destination for pleasure-seekers. Located on a sweeping bay, tumbling down from the hills to the shore, Naples was a strikingly beautiful city – complete with an active volcano, Vesuvius, and the recently uncovered remains of Pompeii – but it was also densely populated and unstable. The local defences were primarily intended to guard against the city's inhabitants, not an external enemy: the key fortress of St Elmo commanded the city, not the approaches, while the sea forts were old and feeble.

For the past sixty years Naples had been capital of the Kingdom of the Two Sicilies, ruled by kings from the Spanish branch of the Bourbon dynasty. King Ferdinand I was an idle buffoon devoted to the pleasures of the chase and the table. He left the business of state to his wife, Maria Carolina, sister of the ill-fated Marie Antoinette, and his Minister Sir John Acton, an able administrator with a multi-national background. The French Revolution and the execution of the Queen's sister had shattered the easy-going calm of the Bourbon regime. The emergence of a Jacobin movement among the aristocracy and bourgeoisie threatened the old order of king and church, while the Queen had drawn her husband into an Austrian alignment, and away from the more obvious link with his royal brother, the King of Spain. Naples had fought in defence of Italy, but left the war in 1796 with the defeat of Austria. An uneasy peace persisted to the middle of 1798, though it was constantly threatened by French plundering. Naples was too weak to take on France alone – while the Emperor of Austria, the Queen's nephew and son-in-law, who did not share her unrelenting hatred of the French, was reluctant to intervene on Naples' behalf.

The longstanding British representative at the Bourbon court was Sir William Hamilton, an ageing connoisseur and serious vulcanologist. Hamilton's close relationship with Acton, his long years of service and elevated manners made him an effective peacetime envoy, but he was quite out of his depth in such an elemental conflict. The British victory at the Nile had transformed the Italian situation, encouraging Ferdinand and Maria Carolina once again to look to Austria for a lead in renewing the war with France. Hamilton and Nelson had met in 1793; now they developed a close personal and political rapport that would endure for the rest of their lives. This relationship would be the key to the political developments of the next eighteen months.

Without Hamilton's insight, advice and linguistic skills Nelson would have been politically impotent at Naples. Hamilton, meanwhile, would use Nelson's energy to push the soporific court into war.

Hamilton's position at court had been reinforced by the close friendship that developed between his wife and the Queen. After many years as a widower, Hamilton had been sent his nephew's cast-off mistress, whom he took in, educated and ultimately married. This caused no concern in permissive Naples, where Emma's charm and rapid mastery of Italian helped to open doors, and her artistic performances made her one of the 'sights' of the city. Emma had been an artist's model, and in Naples her 'attitudes' – performances in which she took up well-known classical poses, including some from wall-paintings at Pompeii and Herculaneum – had an astonishing impact. Sir William, friend of Garrick and an enthusiastic supporter of the theatre, provided artistic direction, but it was Emma's raw talent and striking presence that earned the admiration of major figures from Goethe to Madame de Stael. The attitudes evolved into pantomime shows, and the only setting that could do them justice was Naples.[2]

Although Emma was firmly established at the Neapolitan court by 1798, it is unlikely that she would have forgotten her impoverished and precarious origins. These explain her later behaviour, which some have inappropriately condemned as self-seeking and grasping.[3] Emma would always need a guardian and protector, someone of position, wealth and power. Her relationship with Sir William was based on mutual esteem, and there is no evidence that she was unfaithful to him before 1798–9, despite her public prominence and the lax morals of the city. Initially Sir William was amused and entertained by her, but as she developed into an effective political partner he conceded a large degree of equality. As long as they were in Naples the Hamiltons lived in polite society, and Sir William had no wish to go home. Emma was acceptable in Naples, where her common manners and speech, unusual background and notoriety were hardly unique. In London, despite Sir William's promises of a reception at court, it was unlikely that she would be accepted so easily.

The woman that Nelson met was tall and strikingly beautiful, if by now on the heavy side; she was also capable, persuasive and confident. She had earned his undying gratitude through her intervention, real or otherwise, to facilitate the watering of the fleet at Syracuse only weeks before, and he soon realised, if he had not known before, how close

Emma Hamilton posing in an 'attitude', sketched from life

she was to the Queen. This was no ordinary woman. Her obvious 'performance' after boarding the *Vanguard* was carefully contrived – it is important to know what you are doing if you want to be caught by a one-armed man – but there was also genuine emotion. Emma won Nelson over in much the same way that she had won over Hamilton: by joining in his world, and taking a role in his drama, as she had in Sir William's dramatics. Her political access, linguistic skills and fortitude in adversity, prominently displayed in the evacuation from Naples and the stormy passage to Palermo, gained her access to his inner life. Once there she provided him with an environment in which he could relax his exhausted mind and body. The home Emma provided was so attractive, in contrast with his own peripatetic, parochial domestic arrangements, that he could not bear to give it up, whatever the cost. After living among the great events of the Neapolitan court, Round Wood cannot have seemed very enticing; nor can Fanny's descriptions of dinners with the damp and depressing local worthies have competed with the chance the court offered for refined conversation on his favourite subjects – war, strategy and self.

Sir William was content to share his wife and his home with his friend, and seemed to take pleasure in Nelson's obvious affection for Emma, much as he had relished the attention her 'attitudes' had received in earlier days. We do not know when that sharing became something more than close friendship, or whether Sir William ever resented his demotion in her affections. The only time he ever protested about their actions was when they affected his comfort, spoilt his peace, or hampered his fishing. After all, Emma had been handed on to him, and at his age it would have been unbecoming to protest the loss of one aspect of her affection. She remained a devoted companion and comfort to the end: he died in her arms. In his will he left his favourite picture of Emma to Nelson, a remarkable testament to their friendship. The moral issues that have fixated biographers seem to have had no place in Sir William's world. Emma was free to act according to her own judgement, rather than being bound by social and religious convention.

Even as Nelson and his tiny squadron headed for Naples, his mission was changing. The French had been thrown onto the defensive, and it would no longer be enough simply to keep Bonaparte cut off in Egypt. Nelson was well aware that he had to exploit every opportunity to strike at the French, who were still reeling after Aboukir Bay, and that the best prospect lay in Italy. If British and Austrian interests could be reconciled, and the Neapolitans drawn into the alliance, the French could be driven back over the Alps. As the only friendly Mediterranean power with suitable ports from which the fleet could operate, Naples was the strategic key to the Anglo-Austrian partnership that Foreign Secretary Grenville had created.

Hamilton reported the rapturous response of the Neapolitan royal family and people to news of the battle, which had arrived on 4 September. 'You have now completely made yourself, my dear Nelson, *immortal.*' More significantly, he reported that King Ferdinand had thirty thousand troops, with another fifty thousand being raised.[4] Such a force, Hamilton believed, could clear the French out of Italy.[5] Prime Minister Acton told Nelson that Naples would join the war when Austria was ready.[6] Hamilton believed Austria would go to war on receiving news of the Nile, while the Neapolitans were talking of occupying Rome. In truth, he was indulging in a little wishful thinking, but it chimed in with the euphoria of the hour.

After the Nile, Nelson moved onto a new level of command. No longer did he have the luxury of a single target and no allies to satisfy; now he had a host of partners, each with their own political agenda, and had to negotiate the complexities of conducting coalition operations across large theatres. In an alliance, as Clausewitz wrote in 1805, 'it is endlessly difficult to satisfy all the interests at stake *without unduly violating sound strategic principles* and reducing the probability of success.'[7] Hitherto Nelson's missions had been restricted to the conduct of war at sea, or occasionally on land, and only dealt with allies and soldiers at the tactical level. Now he was responsible for the development and execution of British strategy and policy in the central and eastern Mediterranean. He had to balance the concerns and ambitions of the Turks, the Russians, the Neapolitans and the more distant Austrians with the requirements of British policy. Many senior naval officers – Hotham, most conspicuously and most recently – had found the change from fleet command to theatre command beyond them.

Nelson's trusted 'band of brothers' would be crucial to his success: Troubridge, Ball and Hood executed complex tasks under Nelson's overall direction. His furious response when Captain Sidney Smith was sent into 'his' theatre with quasi-independent powers was not a matter of personalities or vanity, but of command and responsibility. Nelson could not control the theatre when junior officers did not report directly to him.

The main danger came from a superior enemy fleet, intent on relieving Bonaparte or – although this was far less likely – on seeking battle to recover command. After St Vincent and the Nile, Nelson knew the quality of the French and Spanish fleets. This gave him the confidence to take the initiative. Though the French still had a useful naval force, the two battleships that escaped from the Nile, along with a half a dozen weak, old ex-Venetian and ex-Maltese sixty-fours and smaller craft, were spread from Alexandria to Toulon, via Corfu, Ancona and Malta. Without a concentrated enemy threat Nelson could disperse his own resources for maximum impact. The Two Sicilies provided the central position, combining location with resources – a dockyard, food and water. Controlling the Kingdom would also enable him to keep the two basins of the Mediterranean separate, to isolate the French army in Egypt, support the siege of Malta and bolster British influence in Italy. Moreover, Naples had a large army that might, with Austrian aid, clear all Italy of the French, to the inestimable benefit of British trade – it was certainly a prize worth fighting for.

Though Nelson's obsession with Naples has often been interpreted as a distraction that deflected him from the pursuit of the enemy,[8] in reality, without Naples and her ports, Nelson would not have reached the Nile, and would have been forced to abandon his cruise without a battle. Naples was the most important point in the Mediterranean to anyone thinking about the logistics of maintaining a fleet: the Neapolitan campaign was motivated by fleet logistics and grand strategy, not personal feelings or misguided admiration of the Bourbon court. In contrast to Naples, neither Malta, which did not fall for many a long month, nor Minorca, which fell easily but was indefensible without the fleet, could provide skilled manpower for repairs, supply the fleet with food, water or stores, or offer any troops. These small islands were the fruit of naval success, not the springboard to Continental victory. Those who have criticised Nelson for refusing to obey orders to shift his priority to the security of Minorca have failed to understand this crucial distinction.

Nelson could not have failed to be swayed by the reception he received in Naples – he admitted that the praises of the court and popular cries of 'Nostro Liberatore' were enough 'to make me vain'[9] – but he was concerned that the locals were wasting precious opportunities to follow up his success.[10] Anxious to patch up his ships he requested Hamilton to prepare the Castellamare dockyard to heave down the *Culloden*, find masts for his flagship and refit other ships. The campaign in the central Mediter-ranean was left in Nelson's hands. Instructions from London were invariably out of date, and rather general; as for St Vincent, once he had finally heard the glorious news of the Nile, he conceded that Nelson would 'do much better by following your own impulse'. St Vincent himself would hold the shield of the Mediterranean fleet in the straits, to meet the danger that the Brest fleet might try to relieve the army in Egypt, while Nelson acted as his sword arm, dispersing his force to attack on all fronts.[11] The close accord between Nelson's actions and the official instructions sent to St Vincent on 3 October reflected the growing importance of the theatre to the ministry, and the opportunity for a new coalition against France.[12] At this point, the politics of coalition warfare compromised Nelson's purely strategic aims. His own priority – to destroy the French transports at Alexandria, to ensure Bonaparte's army would never return to Europe – would never be pursued.[13]

After the grand theatre of his official welcome at Naples on 22 September – complete with royal greetings, huge crowds and fainting ambassadress – and a ball to mark his fortieth birthday, Nelson was quick to turn his attention to bigger issues. His ships were being repaired, if more slowly than he would have liked, and he was anxious to make the next move. He soon realised that Naples was a city of talk, rather than action: 'a country of fiddlers and poets, whores and scoundrels', he declared, somewhat ungratefully, the morning after the ball.[14] Furthermore, it was badly sited to support the wider campaign he was planning, striking north against the French while keeping control of the choke point around Malta. Syracuse was a far better location for a sailing fleet. In short, 'Naples is a dangerous place, and we must keep clear of it', as he observed in early October[15] – but he would not escape so easily.

On 4 October 1798 Nelson wrote directly to Pitt:[16]

> Sir, When I was in England I was an earnest Solicitor, that my Elder Brother who has faithfully served the King in the Navy Office for near 30 years with a character unimpeachable might have a better situation than a Clerk, I am now again a Solicitor that He may be a Commissioner of the Navy. If ought in my Character impresses you with esteem, this is the favor I request.
>
> I shall not attempt to say more of the State of this Country than that the Queen and every person from the highest to the lowest seem to see the propriety of an Immediate war to save the Kingdom. The Marquis Gallo seems to like the destructive system of procrastination , but as Gen'l Mack is hourly expected, I sincerely hope the army will move forward, nothing I can assure you shall be wanting on my part to destroy the French and to save Italy.
>
> Ever with the highest Respect Believe Me
>
> Your most obedient servant, Horatio Nelson

To days later he was gazetted Baron Nelson of the Nile and Burnham Thorpe. He was now Lord Nelson.

Nelson interpreted the signs in Naples to mean that the moment was opportune, an opinion largely based on that of Hamilton, the agent of British policy.[17] In their haste they misunderstood Austria's opportunistic Italian policy, and overrated the Neapolitans, who were putting on a show of strength without substance. Nelson's initial failure to see past the fine new uniforms and smart appearance of King Ferdinand's army was widely shared, especially by their Austrian commander, General Mack. While no one foretold just how feeble the army would be on the day of battle, Nelson soon recognised Mack's inadequacies.[18] Realising that Naples could not stand against France, he placed his hopes in an Austrian intervention.

Nelson left Naples on 15 October. He had not planned to return, but Ferdinand felt safer with him close by, and used his rank to secure this comfort. When Hamilton reported that Austrian Chancellor Thugut had promised support to Naples if she went to war, Nelson restricted his cruise to Malta.[19] Here news of the Nile and the plundering of churches had sparked a revolt on 2 September, driving the French garrison into Valletta.[20] Saumarez supplied the insurgents with a thousand French muskets from the captured ships when he passed on 25

September, and Nelson detached Ball to support them early in October. Arriving off the island on 24 October, Nelson realised that the three-thousand-man garrison was secure behind the stupendous fortifications, and had supplies for over a year. Tedious blockades were not part of Nelson's repertoire, so he left Ball to sustain the effort. Back at Naples on 5 November, the royal family exacted a 'promise' that Naples Bay would never be without a British man-of-war.[21] However, this was the cost of alliance, not a gesture of sycophancy.

In exchange for this naval presence Nelson expected action. The Anglo-Neapolitan war party, Hamilton and Nelson, allied with Acton and the Queen, received a powerful boost from a forged French plan to attack Naples,[22] and persuaded Ferdinand, against his better judgement, to take the initiative. An amphibious force would seize Leghorn, to disrupt French communications in the north, while the main army under Mack drove the enemy from Rome. At the last moment, news from Vienna changed the Bourbons' mood: Chancellor Thugut was refusing to honour the Austrian guarantee, insisting that it was a purely defensive arrangement, only invoked if France was the aggressor. In truth, Austria feared a Prussian stab in the back, and decided to wait until Russia guaranteed her security in turn. Vienna withdrew the guarantee of Naples on the very day Ferdinand decided to go to war, and subsequently accused Britain of trying to drag Austria into the conflict.

It was too late to pull back. An Anglo-Portuguese squadron with five thousand Neapolitan troops secured Leghorn without a fight on 29 November. Leaving Troubridge to blockade Toulon and Genoa, Nelson returned to Naples on 5 December. It was well that he did, for the main offensive had flattered only to deceive. Mack marched quickly to Rome, King Ferdinand entering the city in triumph on 29 November with a suspicious lack of resistance. The far smaller French force had withdrawn, regrouped, and a week later launched an audacious attack – in the face of which the undertrained and poorly led Neapolitan army panicked and ran away. Nelson evacuated the royals, the British community and a large amount of treasure from Naples to Palermo before the rampant French arrived. They left on 23 December, and the *Vanguard* soon ran into a terrible gale. Emma attended to the Bourbon exiles and nursed the youngest of the Princes, who died in her arms. It was her courage and resolve in a crisis that won Nelson's admiration and ultimately his heart.

After these terrible events, Nelson was closely bound to the interests of the Neapolitan court, partly by a sense of responsibility, partly by strategic motives: Ferdinand was a major ally and his ports on Sicily were essential to British command of the Mediterranean. Moreover, to abandon him with half his kingdom under French rule would annihilate Britain's reputation as an ally. The events of the past three months had shown Nelson at his best: repairing his fleet, developing a new strategy, exploiting the opportunities of the war and meeting the disasters of Mack's army by rescuing vital British allies and their resources from the French. He had saved Sicily, and the operational capability of his fleet. He had made mistakes, but they reflected the intelligence to hand rather than poor judgement.

The New Year did not open auspiciously for Nelson. Despite the consummate skill with which he had conducted the evacuation from Naples, such retreats brought no glory and little credit. Now anchored in Palermo harbour, he was honour-bound to support his royal allies. While Ferdinand didn't object to his exile, given Sicily's fine hunting and food, Maria Carolina had little reason to celebrate. Recent events had exposed the republican underside of Neapolitan life that she had long feared, reprising the fate of her less fortunate sister in Paris, but this time more as farce than tragedy. The base ingratitude of the aristocracy, the bourgeois and the clergy was simply monstrous. The traitors had destroyed the sacred bond that united monarch and subject, and could not be forgiven – on this point the British and their allies were as one. In the midst of a war for national survival, French-supported traitors threatened the very existence of the state, and Pitt's government felt this danger as keenly as Naples.

Nelson had no sooner disembarked his royal passengers and their retinue than he had to face further disagreeable news. The Foreign Secretary had directed the Admiralty to send Captain Sir William Sidney Smith – spy, mercenary and part-time diplomat – with a curious commission as naval officer and associate Minister to the Sublime Porte, or Turkish court. In finding a job for his cousin the Foreign Secretary simply ignored the command arrangements of St Vincent and Nelson, and Smith did not help matters by calmly assuming command of ships from Nelson's squadron.[23]

Nelson had spread his forces to the best effect: Rear Admiral Duckworth covered Toulon from Minorca; Smith was active, if unpredictable, on the Levant station where Troubridge would shortly arrive to attack the transports at Alexandria; Ball commanded the blockade of Malta. Nelson threatened privately to come home on 'health' grounds if Smith were not placed under his authority.[24] Nor was this an empty gesture: he asked Fanny to take a house in London, preferably the one his uncle Maurice had occupied near Hyde Park. He was further annoyed by the failure of the ministers to do anything for his family: the Prime Minister and the First Lord had not responded to his pleas to promote Maurice shortly after the Nile.[25] To make matters worse, one relative who was honoured, the newly promoted Captain Josiah Nisbet, continued to behave in a rough and doltish manner.[26]

The war continued to go badly on the mainland, with the French advance on Naples aided by treachery and cowardice. Only the lower orders, the *lazzaroni*, were prepared to fight for the King. They made the French pay dearly for the city, but were betrayed by their social superiors, who opened the gates of Fort St Elmo to the invader.[27] At Palermo Nelson, full of energy, ideas and optimism, was the mainspring of Bourbon resistance. He removed all the detested French émigrés from Sicily, tried to save the abandoned ships of the Bourbon navy from the French and stiffened the resolve of his hosts by promising not to leave Palermo. His widely spread forces were threatened by a rumoured French fleet from Brest arriving in theatre. If they came he would link up with Duckworth near Minorca, but he was confident the French would go to Toulon, not attack the British. He would defend Minorca only when it was attacked: he was prepared to run risks in order to recover the far bigger prize of Naples.[28] This analysis, the basis of his decision to ignore Keith's orders in July, was based on strategic judgement, not short-term or personal considerations.

To defend Sicily, meanwhile, Neapolitan troops were recovered from Leghorn, and local forces raised. Sicilians did not share the Neapolitan taste for alternative political systems, and their hatred of anything French was primeval: when a shipload of ophthalmia patients from Bonaparte's Egyptian army landed at Augusta, they were butchered by an angry crowd.[29] Amidst the chaos and bloodshed, Nelson received a letter from Admiral Lord Howe, and took the time to explain his tactics at the Nile to 'our great master in naval tactics and bravery': he stressed the importance of his 'band of brothers' of Howe's signal system, and that the state of the wind meant 'we always kept a superior force to the enemy'.[30] He might not have been one of Howe's school, but the praise of this Grand Old Man was worth more than any popular acclaim. Equally pleasing were the comments Elliot, now Lord Minto, had made in supporting the vote of thanks in the House of Lords; it was a timely boost to his flagging morale to discover how much his countrymen appreciated his services.

Neapolitan artist Guzzardi captured the exhaustion, illness and strain so evident in Nelson's letters.[31] He desperately needed rest, but the royal family depended on him, the Hamiltons and Acton, the English quartet who worked on[32] while prominent Neapolitans started to drift back to the mainland. Notable among them was Commodore Francesco Caracciolo, whom the king warned against serving the republicans.

Nelson was equally worried by the arrival of the Russians. He was not alone in finding a Russo-Turkish alliance odd, but he was unusual in the vehemence of his warning that the Russians were not to be trusted. He supported the Sultan, declaring 'I hate the Russians', while Admiral Oushakov was 'a blackguard'. He blocked Russian schemes to seize Malta by securing the reversion of the island from Ferdinand, who owned the freehold. If the French capitulated Ball was to take control for Britain and Naples.[33] Although the island was of little use to the British while they held Minorca or had access to the ports of Sicily or Naples, in French hands it would be a major problem.

When St Vincent backed his complaints about Smith, he declared himself content to stay, ill as he was, as long as he had the admiral's trust and the Queen's faith.[34] Without the support of the one man to whom he would defer, he would have gone home: he was at a low ebb, his spirit all but broken by the disasters of December. He even told Alexander Davison that 'my only wish is to sink with honour into my grave'.[35] This was impossible. He never lost his belief in a defining moment to die: he would find his own Quebec. On the same day and at the same desk he could pour out his flawed human thoughts and direct Mediterranean strategy with energy, penetration and that unique insight that elevated him above his contemporaries. He was something strange and rare.

As a French puppet republic was established to plunder the Kingdom of Naples, he sustained the various forces under his command. He had hoped to finish the siege of Valletta with an assault, but when it failed he immediately absolved Ball of any blame. When the Neapolitan government failed to send corn to Malta, he forcefully reminded Acton that the island belonged to the King of Naples. The same corn supplies, he told Ball, would be withheld if the Russians tried to act in the Islands. To preserve these supplies from pirates he worked to secure a truce between Sicily, Tunis and Tripoli, and to end a war between Portugal and Tunis. He recovered Moorish prisoners from the Portuguese flagship as a goodwill gesture, while flattering the Portuguese admiral, the Marquess de Niza, to secure his aid off Malta. Although Niza's ships were little more than window-dressing, they made it possible for Ball to carry on without Russian aid.[36] The North African pirate cities preoccupied Nelson, and would require a visit from his flagship during the crisis of 1799.

Nelson's clear strategic view took in the entire theatre. He understood that the 'Vesuvian' Republic would only survive until the Emperor joined the war in Northern Italy, drawing off the French troops. His priority was to preserve Sicily, seize Malta, bombard Alexandria and be ready for the Austrian attack.[37] Sicily would be safe if the people remained loyal, but he planned a second Bourbon evacuation just in case. Fearing Northern Italy would be overrun by the French before the Russians arrived, Nelson worked harder to bring the various allied forces, Turkish, Russian and Portuguese, into line, to secure Sicily and sustain the Maltese blockade. The key to the campaign was the port of Messina: if it could be held, Sicily was safe; if it fell, the game was up. To hold the fortress at Messina he turned to his old companion in arms, General Sir Charles Stuart at Minorca. Newly raised Sicilian forces were unready for a severe trial: the Neapolitans were untrustworthy and the citadel was too big to be held, as he had initially thought, by a garrison of marines and sailors under Troubridge. He needed a substantial force of British troops, at least a thousand, but preferably around three thousand. He requested Stuart's help. In the mean time he would place Troubridge's squadron off the harbour, once it returned from Egypt.[38] No one would land there without a fight. Once again the overland mail link gave him ample excuse to keep the First Lord informed.[39]

To secure British interests at Malta, meanwhile, Ball was given chief command ashore by Ferdinand. For the duration of the war the campaign would be waged under joint British and Neapolitan flags.[40] Nelson understood that the Maltese trusted the British to save them from the atheist French, the luxurious Knights and the indifferent Bourbons. He anticipated Ball becoming Governor after the island was taken, and stressed that the gift of a jewelled portrait of the Tsar would not stop him watching the Russian moves with the deepest suspicion.[41] He was convinced they wanted the Island for a future war with Turkey,[42] and politely warned Admiral Oushakov that the island was under British protection.[43]

The new Parthenopean Republic, proclaimed in Naples on 27 January 1799, was not a runaway success. While it satisfied the long-suppressed ambitions of the aristocracy, Freemasons, the intelligentsia and merchants, it had no popular support. The working classes preferred their vulgar, populist monarch, and the old order he represented, and it required the bayonets of a French army to keep the people committed to their own liberty. Outside the city the new regime had no support, prompting the King to send an agent to raise the royal standard in rural Calabria. Cardinal Fabrice Ruffo, a Prince of the Church, writer on military subjects and a local magnate, landed alone on 8 February 1799. Raising a core of support from his estates he formed a 'Christian' army of peasants, released prisoners and assorted ruffians. Initially Ruffo was not expected to achieve much, and was therefore given wide-ranging powers to act in the King's name. Instead his cause triumphed in terrible fashion. Unable to discipline his 'troops', Ruffo had to stand by as they rampaged through captured towns, butchering anyone suspected of Jacobin sympathies.

The campaign in Calabria became a triumphal procession, and by mid-March Ruffo was within forty miles of Naples. In Sicily, meanwhile, the arrival of a thousand British regulars had secured Messina. By the time Troubridge returned from Egypt on 17 March, without effecting much against the well-prepared French position, Stuart's arrival had released him to take command in the bay of Naples. He would impose a close blockade and support the counter-revolution. The steady improvement in allied fortunes encouraged Nelson to hang on to restore the Bourbons, despite his ill-health, before he went home. He could not, he informed his Commander in Chief, leave the court at Palermo.[44] The fact that St Vincent respected this decision, when he could have ordered Nelson to any position in the Mediterranean or sent him home, suggests that he shared Nelson's belief that it was the focal point of the campaign. While the Earl became fixated upon Minorca and the Spanish fleet at Cadiz, he left the active prosecution of the war to Nelson.[45]

As Ruffo's strength grew, Ferdinand reduced his powers, instructing him on no account to offer terms to the rebels.[46] The King would settle the fate of traitors, and took a severe line on any who had taken up arms against him. These instructions were sent to Nelson, to inform Troubridge's operations.[47] The counter-revolution had been promised Russian and even Turkish support, but the pace of Ruffo's advance was such that this only arrived at the very end of the campaign. Instead Troubridge cut off the city and supported Ruffo's advance, seizing two islands in the Bay of Naples on 3 April. This further undermined the already fragile authority of the Republic.

News that the French had attacked the Austrians in mid-March was welcome, but there was still much to be done. At Nelson's dictation King Ferdinand instructed Troubridge: 'always bearing in mind, that speedy rewards and quick punishments are the foundation of good government'.[48] Troubridge soon discovered that the people had no faith in the Parthenopean Republic, welcoming the royal revival. The Jacobin experiment would be over once the French retreated.

In Malta, meanwhile, the British government, in order to secure Russian support, had accepted the revival of the Knights of St John by the unstable Tsar Paul, and allowed the Russians to claim a role in the siege. Ball would require all his tact to adopt this new policy without disgusting the Maltese and compromising the siege.[49] It was in response to this ministerial volte-face that Nelson famously disparaged the utility of Malta to Britain once Naples was back in friendly hands. The same private letter lamented Spencer's failure to promote Maurice to the Navy Board.[50] Other personal correspondence of the same time shared thoughts about the lack of family rewards with brother William, while noting the death of the youngest brother, drunken Suckling. Fanny was warned not to come out to Sicily; Nelson would return with the Hamiltons once the Bourbons were restored.

Nelson's protestations that he only remained at Palermo in order to restore the royal regime in Naples, and thereby secure British interests, occur throughout his correspondence and must be taken seriously. The pleadings of the Queen, affecting as they must have been even at second-hand in Emma's translation, were as nothing to the strategic imperatives that directed his programme. He was the only man who could energise the Neapolitan cause and rescue the hooligan King from his treacherous subjects, securing the best naval facilities in the Mediterranean for his country.[51] Moreover, there were longer-term imperatives: by restoring Ferdinand, Nelson and Hamilton would cement the links with Vienna and drive the French out of the greater part of Italy. Improved conditions for trade would help fund the war, while damaging the prospects of the enemy.

For the next three months Nelson lived ashore at Palermo, in the Hamiltons' residence. This offered the political benefits of enabling him to work closely with the British minister and the exiled court. By living ashore, Nelson anticipated the practice of modern theatre commanders: a ship cannot be everywhere at once, and it is better to be at the hub than isolated at some unknown point on the rim of a wide-ranging theatre. But Palermo also offered more tangible and immediate comforts: good food, the society of leading figures and the unalloyed love of his hosts. It is often alleged that Nelson 'dallied'[52] at Palermo, gambling and amusing himself in the company of Lady Hamilton, 'cutting the most absurd figure possible for folly and vanity'.[53] Like most contemporary criticism, these comments came from a man with no personal knowledge of the situation; like any slander it had an element of truth. Nelson was inordinately vain; he loved the trappings of success, the decorations, awards, praises and tributes that showered over his poor battered head after the Nile. But it would be churlish and unrealistic to expect Nelson to have sustained the quasi-monastic discipline of his life afloat while his flagship lay at anchor in harbour. After three months of intense mental anguish, and a stunning blow to the head, he needed rest, but his country kept him at work. He was too famous to be granted leave. As for gambling, he is on record as never taking part, while his abstemious views suggest that he was never drunk. The criticisms, on closer inspection, dissolve into the mean-spirited carping of hostile witnesses. He had earned the right to enjoy a little pantomime at the end of the day, even one in which he was the chief character. He knew the difference between such off-duty trifles and the gasconades of Sir Sidney Smith, who all too often accompanied his public actions with 'a parade of nonsense'.[54]

Far from falling under the spell of his hosts, Nelson knew exactly what to expect. When the Queen belatedly sent money to help the Maltese, he advised Ball to have the bags opened and counted in the presence of witnesses, having no faith in the honesty of court officials.[55] Nor did he trust Cardinal Ruffo, the astonishing prelate-general and acting head of state. Closely connected by class and origins to many of the leading figures in the 'Vesuvian' regime, Ruffo took the view that the sooner the Jacobins were out of office the better, and was quite happy to excuse their error if he could avoid bloodshed, battle or the destruction of property. Such leniency did not accord with Nelson's view that treason would recur unless suppressed with exemplary force. The King and Queen realised that Ruffo's actions would undermine their regime, specifically withdrawing his authority to make any treaty or peace with the rebels. They rightly feared he would let the ringleaders escape. With Austria in the war, and the French evacuating Naples, there was no need to compromise with treachery.[56]

By early May, Ruffo had Naples surrounded, while Troubridge's squadron pushed up to the harbour walls. Outlying forts gave up without a fight, and the Jacobins took refuge in the two sea-front forts of Uovo and Nuovo. The remaining French troops wisely occupied Fort St Elmo, which commanded the city, and the other forts. Unable to comprehend the complex agendas of Ruffo and the court, Troubridge concluded that the Neapolitan officers sent to assist him were either fools or cowards. When he was asked to execute captured rebels his famously short temper was held with the utmost difficulty.[57] Clearly the Neapolitan authorities were anxious to shift the blame for anything unpleasant that occurred in this period away from themselves onto the slight shoulders of the British admiral. Overnight, however, the picture changed.

In a bold attempt to recover something from the double disaster of the Nile and the isolation of Bonaparte's army, the Directory ordered the Brest fleet into the Mediterranean. Admiral Bruix managed to get away without being seen by Bridport's Channel fleet. Bruix's orders to attack the allied forces in the theatre were so ringed about with clauses and qualifications as to suggest that he sought an excuse to avoid fighting.[58] The prospect of facing St Vincent and Nelson terrified him, and he was hardly comforted by the thought of being linked to a large Spanish squadron.[59] Both Bruix and Nelson knew that a combined fleet would be large, cumbersome and vastly inferior in ship handling and fighting qualities to a British force. With so many complex tasks to carry out, Bruix would not risk a battle, because it might cost him his mobility and the mission. So Nelson needed to place his forces between the enemy and their most likely target, confident St Vincent or Admiral Lord Keith would be hurrying along behind them, and confront the French with the choice of fighting his smaller force.

On 12 May Nelson received word from St Vincent that a French squadron had escaped from Brest and entered the Mediterranean. The attempt to link up with the Spanish at Cadiz failed, and it was now heading for Toulon pursued by a strong British force.[60] Recognising the threat to the almost defenceless island of Sicily, Nelson recalled his battleships from Leghorn, Salerno, Naples and Malta, forming a squadron off the western end of Sicily, to cover Palermo, and the blockade of Egypt.[61] Nelson returned to Palermo, to cover the blockade of Naples.[62] Hourly expecting the summons to join St Vincent off Minorca for a battle, he was being pressed to support the overthrow of the republic by the King and Queen, but this vital operation had to be put on hold until the enemy fleet had been accounted for.

Nelson was convinced the French would try to link up with the Spanish to attack Minorca and Sicily, the two islands that enabled the British fleet to operate in the Mediterranean. This may have given too much credit to the strategic insight of the enemy, but it was the worst-case scenario. Losing both islands would force another 1796 evacuation. He reckoned on nineteen French and up to twenty-five Spanish ships. Acting with customary speed and foresight he left Duckworth to decide whether to remain off Minorca with his eight or ten sail, or link up with St Vincent, advising him to keep at sea and not allow himself to be trapped in harbour. Duckworth would be joined by Troubridge and Ball, with the battleships from Naples and Malta. Even the Portuguese were drawn in, to make up the numbers. Nelson, acutely conscious of the strategic situation, and panting for another battle, stayed put at Palermo because 'this island appears to hang on my stay'. Once again, though, there were sound strategic considerations behind this apparently eccentric priority. St Vincent, Keith or Duckworth were all capable of beating the enemy fleet, but if Sicily fell in his absence then any battle would have been no more than a glorious distraction.

Nelson felt almost physically sick at having to defend the key island rather than lead the battle by seeking out the enemy, as he had a year ago. He elected to hold his position and fight once Duckworth and Ball had joined. Desperate to locate the enemy and his own ships, he detached the talented George Cockburn in his only frigate. Without his squadron he was outnumbered ten to one and could not fight with any hope of success. Yet even if, as appeared inevitable, he and his squadron were 'destroyed, I have little doubt but the Enemy will have their wings so completely clipped they may be easily overtaken'.[63] It was true that against Nelson, with Troubridge, Hood, Louis and

Hallowell in support, the inevitable Franco-Spanish victory would have been purchased at the cost of any strategic mission. Their sacrifice would have lived for ever, a fact that Nelson would have relished. But the cost of such a battle was forcibly impressed upon him by Hallowell, who chose that day to present him with a coffin made from the mainmast of *L'Orient*, 'that when you are tired of this life you may be buried in one of your own trophies'.[64]

Nelson's plan was predicated on his missing ships linking up: he expected to fight forty enemy ships with ten of his own. Though we do not know what the plan was, it would have exploited the advantage of a small, coherent and brilliantly handled force. There was even a fire-ship, which Nelson expected to use. He may have reflected on 'Cornwallis's Retreat', the finest tactical defensive action of the age.[65] Perhaps he considered the germ of the Trafalgar plan: destroying the enemy's cohesion, or their rigging – the 'wings' they needed to continue their cruise. The failure of his detached squadrons to join left him depressed. Even if the enemy came, he would be too weak to fight effectively – not that this would stop him.[66]

Having explained his inner thoughts to Emma, Nelson sent Fanny two sentences, neither of which rose above the matter of fact.[67] This disparity symbolised the end of his marriage, and the passion that would rule the rest of his private life. Emma was a high-profile public figure at the heart of the Anglo-Neapolitan alliance, a member of the inner circle of court. Nelson needed something more than quiet in his private affairs, and Emma was happy to provide a heady mix of adulation, attachment and action. Quite when he understood the depth of their relationship is unknown, but there was a growing intimacy, shared confidences, time alone, and a sense of deprivation when they were finally parted. It was, he lamented, 'to go from the pleasantest society to a solitary cell'.[68] He never wrote to Fanny like that.

Just as he had anticipated Bruix did not deign to trouble him. Unsettled by Keith's smaller force off Cadiz and battered by a storm, he headed for the safety of Toulon. Nelson was quick to resume his primary mission: the security of Sicily and the reconquest of Naples.[69] Just in case the enemy did arrive, he moored his eleven battleships across Palermo Bay in close order. He did not repeat Brueys' mistake. From Naples Bay Captain Foote reported an attack by the ships of the rebel commander, Caracciolo, and expected it would be repeated in greater force.[70] Nelson explained the strategic situation to Foote. The French were, as Nelson had expected all along, heading for Toulon, the Spanish were off Cape de Gatte, and St Vincent's fleet near Barcelona. It now seemed likely the enemy would escape, leaving nothing but 'the torment of blockading'. On this head, and many more, he was anxious to hear from St Vincent.[71]

When Duckworth reached Palermo on 6 June with four sail, including his long-awaited new flagship, the eighty-gun *Foudroyant*, Nelson was ready to go to Naples.[72] He was distressed to hear that the Earl was going home, worn to a shadow by four seasons of theatre command. Desperate for his support, more as a shield against anyone else than for anything positive he had been able to effect recently, Nelson begged him to stay, in a pair of emotionally charged letters that veered between blackmail and bribery. The war was nearly over, Emma would nurse him. But it was no good, St Vincent was too ill to 'hold a trust which I cannot exercise' – or at least that was his argument.[73] In truth he wanted the Channel Command.[74]

On 10 June Ferdinand and Maria Carolina begged Nelson to go to Naples, and take control of the situation with authority to act in the King's name and settle the business. But Nelson insisted that 'I will not risk a mast of any one of the squadron' – while there were enemy fleets at large this was wise. After embarking a small Neapolitan army Nelson left on the 12th. On 14 June, Nelson received a letter from the new Commander in Chief, Admiral Lord Keith, warning him that the enemy fleet, fresh from Toulon, had a fair wind to come down on his position, while the British fleet was unable to follow.[75] Keith detached two seventy-fours to reinforce Nelson, and spread his fleet to locate the enemy, but allowed St Vincent's orders to protect Minorca to override his judgement, and left Nelson to cover the central position with an inferior force.[76] With customary speed Nelson returned to Palermo, disembarked the troops and headed for the rendezvous off Maritimo, ready to fight thirty enemy ships, three of them three-deckers, with sixteen of his own, including three Portuguese units. He recalled Ball, but was determined to attack whenever the opportunity arose. It was the best defence for Sicily and Naples. He was disgusted by Keith's feeble conduct in being put off by the wind when within hours of the French, and to make matters worse Keith had not sent enough ships to join the fleet off Sicily.[77]

*

A few days earlier Ruffo's 'army' had driven the last remnants of the rag-tag republican army into the city, where they took refuge in the castles, leaving the city to the far-from-tender mercies of the peasants and the royalist townspeople. Anyone suspected of Jacobin sympathies was fair game for the most barbarous revenge, and Ruffo was unable to restrain these elemental forces, or to attack the castles. The commanding position of Castel St Elmo was held by five hundred French troops; the two smaller forts were occupied by Parthenopean troops and sympathisers. On 19 June Chevalier Micheroux, a Neapolitan envoy with the Russian detachment, granted the rebels an armistice. Ruffo had not been consulted, and was placed in a very awkward position. He rebuked Micheroux, but let the armistice stand, and on 22 June Micheroux drew up a capitulation. The terms were of little value, as they left St Elmo in French hands, and would do nothing to help if an enemy fleet arrived. The convention was fundamentally flawed because neither Micheroux nor Ruffo had the authority to negotiate with the rebels. Although Ruffo knew this he did not tell the Jacobins. Aware he was acting outside his authority, he did not write to his master in Palermo between 17 and 21 June, when he tried to prepare the way for an unauthorised and illegal treaty.

Rumours of Ruffo's actions had already reached Palermo, and Nelson was once more urged to go to Naples to end the business. He was unwilling to abandon his strategic position while the French and Spanish fleets were unaccounted for, but agreed to take the risk for no more than eight days.[78] On 21 June the State Council in Palermo agreed that Nelson would proceed to Naples with Hamilton to secure the unconditional surrender of the forts. There would be no negotiations.[79] Nelson left that day, rejoined his squadron on 22 June and set course for Naples. While on passage, however, he learnt that the rebels had been granted an armistice for twenty-one days, after which period they would evacuate the castles and be taken to France, if the French fleet did not come to their aid in the interval. The Jacobin leaders, more in hope than expectation, persuaded themselves that the French fleet really was coming, despite the contemptuous attitude of the French army, and the blatant way in which the country had been plundered to fund the war elsewhere. When they heard the French actually were at sea, the rebels broke the armistice which Ruffo had granted them, largely to prevent further destruction in a city already full of Calabrian peasants and local *lazzaroni* bent on plunder and anarchy.

The situation cried out for firm leadership. Nelson's state of mind was obvious: 'having ever found the conduct of these Italians weak and indecisive', he would go and finish the job. 'Let no one oppose me,' he told Hamilton, and he would settle the business in eight days: 'it will finish the War.'[80] Once he learnt that a detachment of the Channel fleet had reached the Straits to reinforce Keith, he was ready to run some risks.[81] To persuade the Jacobins that the French fleet was not coming he carefully positioned his ships to make the point to those ashore,[82] mooring his ships in a tight line across the harbour.[83]

Nelson rightly considered an armistice to be revocable by either side, on the arrival of fresh forces. His arrival, or that of the French fleet, would put an end to the situation existing when the terms were agreed. He believed that the French should give up within two hours and be sent home, and that the rebels must surrender to the mercy of their lawful sovereign. On his arrival he signalled Foote to annul the truce, and when informed that a formal capitulation had been agreed, maintained his determination to secure the immediate surrender of the castles. Unlike Ruffo, he had full power to act in the King's name, and was privy to his most recent thoughts. In addition, as the treaty had not been carried into effect, and the rebels were still in the castles, it could be annulled. On 25 June Ruffo refused to send Nelson's ultimatum to St Elmo, to warn the rebels that they had no option but to surrender to the King's mercy, or to assist the attack on St Elmo. However, he did admit that Nelson had the authority to overrule him. Nelson, knowing the views of the King, and the Queen, was well aware that Ruffo and Micheroux's treaty would be unacceptable in Palermo. He immediately sent a fast ship back to Palermo for further Royal orders.

Finding himself in an awkward position, largely through Micheroux's action and his own weakness, Ruffo now tried to slip out of his unauthorised treaty, warning the rebels that it would not be carried out and advising them to retreat inland. This, as he knew, was quite impossible. If caught outside the castles they would be massacred by the *lazzaroni*. By the end of the day Ruffo was coming round to Nelson's position, accepting his offer to land marines. The following morning Nelson agreed to carry out the terms of Ruffo's armistice, and the two rebel castles were evacuated. Knowing they could not escape by land, the rebels boarded small ships in the harbour in the hope of slipping away under cover of darkness. Some did escape. There is no contemporary evidence that Nelson ever told the rebels anything other than that they must surrender to the King, and on three separate occasions he explicitly stated that the rebels surrendered unconditionally.[84] They had no option: the castles would have fallen in a day or two, when the garrisons would have been slaughtered. The French troops in St Elmo were in an altogether different position. They were subject to the conventions of war, and were repatriated. The Queen reminded Nelson of the parallels with the Irish rebellion of 1798, when the small French contingent had been sent home but the Irish rebels left to the King's none too tender mercy.[85]

On 27 June a solemn Te Deum was celebrated, and Ruffo thanked Nelson and Hamilton for rescuing him from an awkward position. But Nelson's 'truce' with Ruffo ended early the following day when letters arrived from Palermo. The King, Queen and Prime Minister rejected all conditions and ordered Ruffo to abide by Nelson's instructions. Nelson immediately seized the rebel ships, and took several prominent Jacobins into safe custody. Once again Ruffo refused to act, and attempted to hamper the arrest of the suspects. Nelson even considered arresting him, a step for which he had full authority, but agreed with Sir William that it would be best to avoid trouble and await the return of the King.[86] Two days later Ruffo received royal orders to follow Nelson's measures; despite ample evidence of his supreme authority Nelson wisely chose not to humiliate Ruffo, who already knew he had displeased his King and exceeded his mandate. In a typically magnanimous gesture, Nelson spoke up for the Cardinal, and invited him on board the *Foudroyant*.

Such consideration was not extended to one prominent rebel. Commodore Francesco Caracciolo had commanded the Parthenopean gunboats in battle. The King and Queen were well aware of his treason by mid-May, naming him among a handful deserving death, a 'viper' who knew so much of the coast that he would constitute a standing danger to the King and the state if he escaped.[87] Nelson can have been in no doubt of royal opinion. Caracciolo tried to escape, but was captured on 25 June. Nelson knew of his arrest the following day, but Ruffo only handed him over to the admiral on the 29th. The timing coincided with Ruffo's loss of power, allowing blame once more to be shifted onto the foreigners.

As the designated Neapolitan Commander in Chief, Nelson properly convened a court martial for the Neapolitan Commodore. The court assembled on board the *Foudroyant* because there were no large

Neapolitan warships present. The court in the great cabin remained open to all interested parties, including several British officers who knew enough Italian to follow the proceedings. A majority of the Neapolitan officers found the Commodore guilty of desertion and of firing on the Sicilian frigate *Minerva*, an action in which royal sailors were killed. These were charges he could not rebut, and both carried a sentence of death by hanging. Acting in the King's name, and in accord with his legal obligations, Nelson ordered the sentence to be carried out that evening. Caracciolo asked for another trial, and when this was properly denied, that he be shot rather than hung. Such a mark of his rank was inappropriate to his crime, and he was hung at the yardarm of the *Minerva* at 5 o'clock that evening. As Commander in Chief of the Neapolitan Navy Nelson had carried out the King's stated policy and applied the law to the case before him. He had no personal role in the trial, and as the Court made no recommendation for clemency he had no grounds for altering the sentence.

With the rebels safely under his control Nelson moved to restore order, placing Hood in command of Castel Nuovo, and preparing the way for the resumption of royal authority. To secure the city he sent the ever-reliable Troubridge ashore in command of seamen and marines, with Ball as his second.[88] Acton wrote to thank him in the King's name and by his order for saving his honour by proper measures from a capitulation with the rebels. He was equally obliged to Nelson for seizing the rebels in the ships, and making Ruffo see where his duty lay. As for Caracciolo he 'had deservedly been a proper example for that capital' as the King returned to restore his authority.[89] The correspondence of the King's chief minister demonstrates categorically that Nelson was acting on the instructions of the Bourbon regime, as their appointed agent. He was not acting on his own authority.

If the scenes of horror that had greeted the downfall of the republic had been positively diabolical, it should be recalled that they pre-dated Nelson's arrival. Ruffo sought an armistice to protect the city from his own army, but order was only restored when the British took control ashore. As for the hapless, incompetent and misguided Jacobins, some 8,000 prominent and less prominent figures were arrested, largely those who acted for the republic in civil or military roles. Their fate was to be the central figures in a long-delayed public demonstration of royal power and restored authority. It was not a calm judicial process seeking the fine points of each case, more an opportunity to use the deaths of the obviously guilty to teach a lesson. Less than a thousand were punished; only 105 were condemned to death, and six of them were reprieved. Some 222 were imprisoned for life and 322 for shorter terms; 288 were deported and 67 were exiled. Few of the living would pay the full tariff of their offences.[90] While the execution of so many leading figures in literature and society was made into a parable of Bourbon vice, the final death toll was trifling when set alongside the human cost of setting up and supporting the Republic. The penalty for a failed rebellion, in time of war, as agents of the enemy was well understood. The posthumous lionisation of the rebels and their treacherous cause by writers with a variety of agendas has obscured the real issues of the Republic. It was the unwanted child of a French invasion, and perished once the bayonets that set it up were withdrawn. It perished of its own irrelevance, with a little help from Ruffo's Calabrese and the Neapolitan *lazzaroni*. Nelson made sure that the process ended with the proper submission of the rebels to the mercy of their lawful sovereign. Only in this way could the Kingdom of the Two Sicilies become a useful base for the British fleet, and a shared interest with the Court of Austria.

Ferdinand arrived on 10 July, tactfully taking passage on a Neapolitan warship. He arrived to find Caracciolo's corpse afloat, but the incident passed off when a wit advised the superstitious monarch that the traitor had come to beg forgiveness for his crimes. Ferdinand so far relented as to permit the rebel commodore a Christian burial in the fishermen's church. Unwilling to trust his person ashore Ferdinand held court on board the *Foudroyant*, while Troubridge forced the French in St Elmo to accept terms. The castle capitulated on 13 July, and Nelson immediately despatched Troubridge and Hallowell with a thousand marines and seamen to secure the key fortresses of Capua thirty miles inland, and at Gaeta a hundred miles to the north. This was an unusual employment for the high-quality personnel of the fleet, but there was no other source of disciplined and determined manpower with artillery skills.[91] Nelson saw no other way of clearing the kingdom of the French, to release his forces for the wider theatre. The arrival of orders from Keith, dated 27 June, to detach ships to protect Minorca was a problem, but Nelson had long believed that Naples was the bigger prize.[92] In explaining his actions to Keith he paraphrased the Articles of War: 'under God's providence His Sicilian Majesty . . . depends upon this fleet.'[93] The arrival of fresh orders from Keith, dated 9 July, to take all or most of his fleet to Minorca did not shake his conviction that he had been right. Although well aware that he was in breach of naval discipline, he promised Spencer that once the French had been expelled he would detach eight or ten ships to Minorca. The presence of up to 120 seamen and marines from each ship inland was the reason given, but strategic judgement was the occasion. He also prepared a formal defence of his actions for the Admiralty.[94]

As the French fleet was already heading out of the Mediterranean, with Keith in pursuit, the only threat to Minorca came from the Spanish, who were unlikely to take the risk. Whatever their object the French ships were leaving the theatre, and Nelson was confident Keith would pursue them all the way back to Brest.[95] His faith was misplaced: Keith bungled every stage of the pursuit, lacking the single-minded determination to close with the fleeing French.[96] Nelson was left to direct the theatre. To cover Minorca he despatched Duckworth with three ships and left the details to his 'well-known abilities and judgement'. Duckworth had begged that the Portuguese ships not be sent with him, lacking Nelson's sure touch with such ineffectual allies.[97] By the end of the month Capua and Gaeta had capitulated, and Naples had been secured largely by the efforts of the ships and men of the fleet. The flagship was back at Palermo in time for a grand festival to celebrate the anniversary of the Nile, and there she would have to stay as the coast of Italy was the main theatre, and no allied ships had put in an appearance.[98] A squadron was detached to the Gulf of Genoa to support the main allied army on 2 August, and three days later the newly appointed Commodore Troubridge was sent to operate against Rome and Leghorn. But Malta was Nelson's next object: to support Ball he despatched the flagship, complete with her marines, and authority to land them for ten days.[99]

Amid the tension of the restoration of the Bourbons, the new British Consul, Charles Lock, began a process that would confuse Nelson's biographers and blacken his reputation for two centuries. Lock, a cousin by marriage of Irish rebel Lord Edward Fitzgerald, Whig leader Charles James Fox, and Lady Holland, the society hostess, had been given the minor post as a sop to his wife's family, after failing to make anything of his previous opportunities. Hot-headed and self-important, he took offence at every slight, real or imagined, and rated his abilities far above those of his Minister, while blaming Emma for all his problems. He showed where his political sympathies lay by appearing at court functions dressed in a fashion associated by Ferdinand and most of his subjects with the Jacobins. When the Hamiltons embarked with Nelson for the recovery of Naples he was left behind; disappointed in his hopes of acquiring a house and some furniture, he began a sustained attack on the three people who had done most to save the Kingdom. These letters, circulated by his family, contain the first significant attack on Nelson's conduct in 1799. By 13 July Lock was complaining about the dishonour cast on the British by breaking the articles agreed with the Jacobins, revealing both ignorance and partiality. His imputation that Lady Hamilton was a hard-hearted monster directing affairs at the behest of the Queen dovetailed perfectly with the gossip of that faded *grande dame* Lady Holland, who already loathed Emma.

To compound his folly, Lock approached Nelson on the quarter-deck of the *Foudroyant* on 23 July, seeking a contract to supply the fleet with fresh beef and other provisions. It was common for the Consul to hold such contracts, but with his fleet so widely scattered, Nelson was content to leave matters as they were, with the ship's pursers conducting the business. Lock claimed to have seen evidence that one or more of the pursers was cheating. Not predisposed to favour Lock, who had already made a thorough nuisance of himself, Nelson demanded names and proof. When Lock tried to retract, Nelson summoned Hardy as a witness, and demanded that he repeat his complaint. Having been backed into a corner entirely of his own making, Lock became agitated. He seemed to be drunk, and it required the best efforts of the powerfully built flag captain to get him off the quarter-deck. The following morning Nelson set up an enquiry, and when the assembled captains and pursers found nothing amiss, the pursers demanded an apology from Lock, who had the bad grace to refuse, claiming that his conversation had been private.

Had Lock apologised Nelson may have let the matter drop, but instead he determined to pursue the question all the way to the Victualling Board in London. Realising what he had done, Lock called on his family to protect him from the consequences of his own arrogance. His defence, having no basis in fact, or law, relied on slanderous accusations aimed at Emma, Nelson and Sir William.[100] His exculpatory letters were the basis for the 'Black Legend' of Naples. Lock stayed behind after Hamilton was replaced by Lord Arthur Paget – another young man in a hurry who was overly fond of his own opinions. Paget listened while Lock poured vitriol into his ear. With such advice, Paget quickly alienated the court by his blunt and dictatorial manner, while blaming Sir William and Emma for his failings.[101]

Nelson may have overreacted to the stupidity of the Consul, but he was, as he had shown back in the 1780s, acutely conscious of his own dignity as an officer of the Crown, and of the need to ensure proper control of naval contracts. What would have sparked his ire even more than the arrogance of a young fool was the imputation that he, his captains, or the pursers, most of them veterans of the Battle of the Nile, were corrupt. A few days after Lock had impugned the honesty of his squadron, Nelson received a tribute of gratitude from Ferdinand, who well knew who had put him back on his throne. The King awarded him the Dukedom of Bronte, which included a Sicilian estate valued at £3,000 a year. The contrast between this token of royal esteem and the niggardly reward offered by his own country, especially the failure to do anything for Maurice, was not lost on him. For the rest of his life he would sign himself with some combination of the names Nelson and Bronte, and although the estate never produced much money, it was a real token of his achievements in the Sicilian cause. It was accompanied by a diamond-hilted sword, given by Louis XIV to his grandson Philip V of Spain, and passed on to Ferdinand with his Kingdom. Nelson received it as the Kingdom's saviour.[102]

The rest of August was dedicated to securing the stores required to refit the squadron and once more shifting his forces around theatre. He sent newly recovered Neapolitan galliots to support the squadron off Genoa, and demanded that Oushakov return the *Leander*, recovered at the fall of Corfu.[103] Nelson believed it high time the Russians and Turks used their fleets in the western basin. With the Russian hero Suvarov rampaging across Northern Italy, surely his countrymen were his best supporters? Troubridge could hand over at Naples and Leghorn when these unlikely allies arrived to concentrate off Mahon. Both Duckworth at Minorca and the force in the Straits were reinforced: the latter would blockade Cadiz and secure the oceanic trade beyond the Straits, a subject on which he was 'exceedingly anxious' to oblige the merchant community. Nelson had no fear for Minorca while the British fleet was in the Mediterranean.[104] Because Niza's Portuguese squadron would be adequate off Malta, Nelson persuaded Ferdinand to grant Ball the chief position ashore as Maltese leader. In this rank Ball could cooperate with Niza as an equal, rather than stay afloat as his ranking subordinate. This typical piece of forethought and finesse avoided inefficiency or offence.[105]

As if to confirm the talent of the temporary Commander in Chief, his new dispositions were adopted just as Admiralty sent almost identical orders.[106] After an apprenticeship of six years Nelson was ready to assume Hood's role as strategic director of the theatre, while drawing on St Vincent's approach to fleet support and discipline. The departure of the old Earl had broken the last link with his previous career, and no one else had the professional standing to direct his movements: it was not rank but ability that he followed.

However, the Admiralty had criticised Nelson's landing of marines and seamen for the operations at Naples and Capua, and issued a rebuke for his deliberate refusal of Keith's order to protect Minorca. His dilemma was simple: 'My conduct is measured by the Admiralty by the narrow rule of law, when I think it should be measured that of common sense.' Keith's orders would, if obeyed, have lost Naples.[107] Although Acton kept telling him he was the key to the salvation of Italy, he was disgusted by the failure of the Neapolitans to act up to their words: 'I will retire from this inactive service'.[108] He remained convinced the Austrian Chancellor Thugut was undermining the Neapolitans, and 'our English King of Naples'.[109] This may have been the Queen's opinion, but it was not wrong. The Austrian Chancellor saw the 1799 campaign as an opportunity to advance the Viennese empire in Italy, at the expense of the French, the Pope and the Bourbons, with the Russians doing most of the fighting. This policy had influenced his timing of the declaration of war and the direction of the allied advance. Ultimately it ruptured the coalition, leading to the withdrawal of the Russians. Such petty pilfering of principalities would be the downfall of the Emperor and his chancellor. The reward of their duplicity came with utter defeat at Hohenlinden in 1801.

Nelson knew such attitudes had ruined too many Mediterranean campaigns. The British cleared the seas only for their allies to fritter away the fruits of victory on internal disputes. He could see that naval warfare had to be made more effective – that Britain might wage war alone, secure the seas and sustain her trade. Only the largest measures, executed in complete harmony, stood a chance against the French. However, his clear-sighted approach was shared neither by Britain's shaky and procrastinating allies, nor by Nelson's petty-minded and conventional masters in London.

CHAPTER X

Subordination and Homecoming
1799–1800

With the authority of the Bourbon regime at Naples re-established, and the war swinging in favour of the coalition, Nelson would have been excused for leaving the stage. He chose to stay, however, despite repeated complaints of headaches, chest pains and near-blindness. He thrived on the responsibility of command, and when Keith departed with the main fleet in Bruix's wake, Nelson was the senior officer inside the Straits. The theatre was an unusual one, since the enemy did not possess a significant battle fleet. Instead the Royal Navy was conducting a range of important strategic tasks from Gibraltar to Alexandria, within a troubled coalition that necessitated watching 'friends' as well as foes. Under these circumstances, Nelson recognised the importance of the Commander in Chief occupying a central position to facilitate intelligence gathering and political contacts, while his flag would be the rallying point for the dispersed units of his squadron if an enemy fleet appeared.

In purely strategic terms, Syracuse would have been the best location for the operational fleet base; but political considerations made remaining in Palermo a more sensible choice, and Nelson was unwilling to sacrifice vital political leverage and strategic assets to save a day or two at sea. Nelson was becoming increasingly infuriated by the inability of the King and his ministers to see where their own best

A run ashore: 'The Jolly Tars of Old England'

interests lay, or to act to secure them. They constantly procrastinated about food and money for the siege of Malta, a Sicilian freehold, while Ferdinand would not go back to Naples, where his presence would have helped restore order and render his state a more effective partner in the war. Nelson was obliged to talk up the Neapolitan contribution to the ministers in London, while offering to mortgage his estate at Bronte and sell his trophies and decorations to fund the siege at Malta.

The main difficulty facing British naval commanders in the Mediterranean was the lack of a reliable military force under their control. The British army was too small, and too heavily committed to defensive tasks, to spare the men for a Mediterranean expeditionary force. The few British troops in the theatre were tied down at Gibraltar and Minorca. Nelson constantly badgered the generals to understand the big picture, to act on the spirit of their instructions rather than the letter, but only Charles Stuart had the necessary confidence in his own judgement, and political courage. Moreover, the command system did not permit the naval Commander in Chief to issue orders to the army. The result of this weakness was the interminable blockade of Valletta, where the French defenders were more numerous than the besieging marines and Maltese irregulars. A force of five thousand British regulars would have reduced the place in a month or two. Instead the operation tied down extensive naval forces for two years. Without troops, St Vincent, Keith and especially Nelson were left to rely on their allies, who were by turns unwilling, incompetent or absent. Rather than simply reporting his frustrations, Nelson landed seamen and marines, employing Troubridge as his general.

On 20 September Nelson received a package of official dispatches. One criticised his judgement in landing seamen and marines for service at Capua, and disobeying Keith's orders; while another, more welcome, conferred temporary theatre command on him, in the absence of Keith. (Nelson, who remained a Rear Admiral until 1 January 1801, did not have the rank to be placed in permanent command of the theatre.) A further dispatch set out the Admiralty's priorities among the strategic tasks of the fleet. The first task was to cooperate with the allies to drive the French out of Italy, specifically supporting the siege of Genoa. Next came the reduction of Malta, followed by the protection of Minorca. Fourthly he was to keep watch on the Spanish fleet at Cadiz, a task combined with securing the passage of Mediterranean convoys through the Straits of Gibraltar. The formation and escort of British and allied convoys was the fifth priority, while the redeployment of the squadron from the coast of Egypt, in the expectation that their task was at an end, rounded off the list. The same Board that had criticised his judgement then expressed their confidence that he would do all that he could with the forces under his command.[1]

Nelson's replies to the Admiralty dispatches show him vigorously defending his decisions over Capua and Minorca, stressing his concern for the honour of the King and Country, 'the dearest objects of my heart'. He also cited the opinions of Acton and Hamilton on the likely effect of a withdrawal while affairs at Naples were incomplete. He warned that the new instructions to restore the Knights at Malta, with the Tsar as Grand Master, would be unpopular, and he requested more ships, to replace those going home for refit and the unseaworthy Russians.[2] He expressed himself more strongly still, however, in letters to confidants. The third of the Admiralty's tasks for him had already been dismissed in a letter to Spencer: 'Minorca I have never yet considered in the *smallest* danger, but it has been a misfortune that others have thought differently from me on that point.'[3] And his real feelings on the Admiralty's censure were revealed to Davison:

> My conduct is measured by the Admiralty, by the narrow rule of law, when I think it should have been done by that of common sense. I restored a faithful Ally by breach of orders; Lord Keith lost a Fleet by obedience, against his own sense. Yet one is censured, the other must be approved.[4]

Nelson did not allow his feelings of being slighted to impair his command of the campaign, however. He was concentrating on Malta now: he sailed to Minorca to press for some British troops, and asked Oushakov to help. With Bruix gone, he anticipated the French would try to relieve the garrison from Toulon, where Nile escapee *Le Genereux* and other vessels were fitting out. Scouts were placed on the patrol lines of Toulon–Ajaccio and Lampedusa–Cape Bon.[5] At the beginning of October, he was celebrating the fact that Troubridge and Louis had taken Rome, accepting the surrender of the French garrison. He responded by sending his battleships to Minorca, offering a substantial naval defence to release troops for Malta.[6] To outflank the inevitable objections from the general at Minorca, he asked the Neapolitans to request that the British garrison at Messina be sent to Malta. To make sure they understood his purpose, he warned them that if Malta remained in French hands the Barbary corsairs would use the harbour to annihilate Sicilian trade. Brigadier Graham, in com-

mand at Messina, was also given the benefit of Nelson's views on theatre strategy and national policy, but both the King and Graham were
resolute. Ferdinand did not feel safe without British troops, and the
Brigadier would not move without orders. 'I am almost mad with the
mode of going on here,' Nelson lamented.[7]

Reports of thirteen French battleships off Cape Finisterre forced
another redeployment. Niza's Portuguese squadron had been recalled,
but on 3 October Nelson begged him to stay off Malta, while he
sought out the enemy. By 11 October Nelson was heading for
Gibraltar, but the following day he realised that the reported sightings
of the enemy had been false – just one of many unreliable fragments of
intelligence that exercised the mind of the admiral. Nelson returned to
Minorca instead to request the troops for Malta. General Erskine
admitted the island was in an excellent state of defence, but he was
about to hand over to General Henry Fox, and would not commit to
the new commander. No amount of naval protection would persuade
him to detach troops from Minorca, or redeploy those from Messina.
Nelson sent a sloop to report on Toulon, and hurried east, anxious the
French would try to reinforce Malta.[8]

Nelson was forced to return to Palermo, with nothing to show for
his cruise. Frustrated by Erskine's attitude, and the inability of the
Neapolitan government to pay the Maltese soldiers, Nelson kept up
the pressure on the general and spent his own money on the Maltese.
For a man of Nelson's temperament these were more than professional setbacks. He feared Malta might be lost; he believed the general was
wrong to ignore the changed circumstances, and that the war must be
prosecuted to the utmost.[9] He was frustrated that all his hard work
since returning to Palermo had not generated a single soldier, and that
his successes had not been given the credit they deserved, as he
revealed in a bitter letter to Fanny:

> I trust that one day or other I shall rest from all my labours. I still find it good
> to serve near home. There a man's fag and services are easily seen. Next to that
> is writing a famous account of your own actions. I could not do justice to those
> of my friends who rescued the Kingdom of Naples from the French and there-
> fore Parliament does not think of them.[10]

If Parliament underestimated the British contribution to the restoration in Naples, then the Neapolitans themselves could be accused of
no such thing; rather, they remained highly dependent, as Nelson
stressed to the Admiralty:

My own situation in this Country, certainly a very extraordinary one; for if I move they think the Country in danger, and that they are abandoned. If my flag is in a transport they seem contented.[11]

As Berry had resumed his post, Hardy, who carried the dispatch home, could inform the Board of the condition of the fleet, and the admiral. Nelson's mood was not improved by a letter from the Victualling Board, which appeared to sustain Consul Lock's claims. Wounded and angry, he exploded onto the page – 'I defy any insinuations against my honour' – and demanded a full enquiry. He also demanded Lock provide copies of any public letters concerning fleet supply.[12] A fortnight later Nelson demanded an Admiralty enquiry. Aware that Lock had used family influence to secure a private commendation of his actions, Nelson demanded he produce evidence, or withdraw. The following day, a humiliated Lock abandoned his claims, and the demand for an enquiry was withdrawn.[13] The determination with which Nelson pursued any criticism of his honour was typical.

Given his mental state it was perhaps fortunate that French attempts to supply the Malta garrison now took centre stage. This gave a suitable focus for Nelson's efforts, and provided a task that could be carried out by naval forces. Another letter begging Erskine to act reached Minorca after General Fox had taken over command. Fox responded quickly: his order that the Messina garrison go to Malta arrived on 25 October.[14] Nelson was also promised three thousand Russian troops, but the Messina garrison were the only men who turned up. Troubridge was instructed to sustain the claims of Britain and the Neapolitans, while avoiding friction. Niza, meanwhile, had been ordered home, but Nelson kept up a barrage of letters begging him to run the risk of disobeying, for a higher purpose.[15] His successful persuasion earned the Marquis a fulsome tribute of public and private thanks – perhaps more than the Portuguese ships deserved – when he finally departed in mid-December.[16]

Nelson was further angered by a new Admiralty complaint, alleging that he had not kept them fully informed of events. In response, he reminded the Board that he lacked the secretarial staff and extra pay of a regular Commander in Chief, and yet dealt with the greatest naval and political correspondence that fell to any senior officer. He never relaxed before 8 p.m. and rarely went ashore.[17] The dishonest conduct of Austria, Russian ambition and the hopeless sloth of Naples were making his task almost impossible: 'I am nearly blind, but things go so contrary to my mind *out* of our profession, that truly I care not how soon I am off the stage.'[18]

To make matters worse, just when he wanted to focus on Malta, Nelson had to respond to the complete failure of the Russian fleet to secure trade or cooperate with the allied army on the Tuscan coast. Despite the fact that the Admiralty had so reduced his force that there were no spare ships, Nelson had to ensure a British presence.[19] With ships and troops committed to the siege of Malta Nelson detached a squadron to the Tuscan coast. Henry Blackwood was sent in the frigate *Penelope* to watch for the Combined Fleet between Cape Spartel and Cape St Vincent. If the fleet was sighted he was to retreat, informing Gibraltar, Minorca and Malta.[20]

Minorca was the appointed rendezvous for the newly re-introduced Italian convoys.[21] Once Leghorn, the greatest market for naval stores in the Mediterranean, was recovered Nelson directed the Port Mahon naval yard to buy stores.[22] There were too few ships for the tasks in hand, while those that were available were almost all in need of refit. His best hope was that the new Consulate in France would mean peace.[23] This news followed the escape of Bonaparte from Egypt, which Nelson regretted. In a total war it was necessary that the French should all die in Egypt. Similar strategic concerns underpinned his views on belligerent rights at sea, an issue he would have occasion to fight over in less than eighteen months.

> I should be very sorry to see the doctrine established that free ships make free goods. Last war the circumstances of our situation forced us to acquiesce; but this war we take enemy property, wherever we find it.[24]

Such property provided the only good news of the month, rich prizes had been taken off Cape Finisterre by a frigate squadron at least in part under his orders. Davison was to press his claim.[25] It would take years, and two court cases, before St Vincent, who had hauled down his flag long before the action, would pay up.

In his anxiety to get on at Malta Troubridge put the *Culloden* ashore again, but Nelson was more concerned to exploit the latest intelligence haul, which showed how desperate the French Egyptian army had become for money and ammunition, and that their ships hugged the North African coast. It also indicated another sortie by the Combined Fleet.[26] Writing home he excused Troubridge's error, and hoped pressure from the land side would force the French squadron to leave

Valletta.[27] Although the newly appointed Commander in Chief Lord Keith shared much of his analysis, he was unduly pessimistic.[28]

Once again Nelson relied on Troubridge to infuse some energy into the critical point of the campaign, and he did not disappoint. Finding promised Neapolitan food supplies for the Maltese were not forthcoming, Sir Thomas could not stand back while men starved. Attributing Neapolitan inaction to treachery, he had grain ships seized from a Sicilian harbour on 5 January. Nelson had tried to help, but he could not cut through the obfuscation of Palermo with the same weapons that Troubridge deployed. While admitting 'nothing is well done in this country', he begged Troubridge to be more discreet: perhaps he could restrict his seizures to the open seas?[29] The Neapolitans were told that Troubridge had merely anticipated their King's orders.[30] Troubridge's agitated state of mind and hatred of the Neapolitans were reflected when he begged Emma not to spend so much time playing cards, as rumours were already reaching the fleet, to the detriment of Nelson's good name.[31]

Aware that Keith was coming to take command, Nelson briefed him on the key issues: lack of seaworthy ships, with only two battleships fit to face the winter, and the pressing need to get Ferdinand back to Naples. He stressed that the key to the theatre was the loyalty of King Ferdinand. He also stressed that he expected to remain on station, 'as I have been particularly placed here for the service of the King of Naples'.[32] On 16 January *Foudroyant* sailed for Leghorn, arriving on the 20th to meet Keith.

By stressing his particular relationship with the Bourbon court, Nelson had prepared his case for an early return to England if he was thwarted. While Keith was his superior in rank, he lacked the human and professional qualities that Nelson so admired in great admirals like Hood and St Vincent. Because Keith so obviously lacked the political courage and naval judgement to be his superior officer, Nelson found his demotion hard to bear. It also broke the link with Hamilton, who was no longer privy to his movements, because they were no longer Nelson's to determine.[33] He could not even go ashore on his own authority.[34] Nelson was attracted by the prospect of rejoining St Vincent's flag: the old Earl was now fully restored to health, with almost suspicious speed, and in command of the Channel fleet. St Vincent, too, hoped that Nelson would soon return to England, along with Troubridge, who was to be Captain of the Fleet.[35]

On his arrival at Palermo, Keith took a rather more robust line with the King, promising to come back only after Ferdinand had returned to Naples, as Palermo 'lay out of our way'.[36] It sounded clever, but did no good. Nelson, Keith and the squadron sailed from Palermo with reinforcements for Malta on 12 February. No sooner had they arrived than Nelson ignored Keith's orders, following his own opinion that the best position in which to intercept a French relief force was off the Barbary coast. He promptly fell in with the enemy flagship, the seventy-four *Le Genereux* which was being pursued by other ships. Nelson exploited the superior sailing of his flagship to catch her off Cape Passaro on the Sicilian coast on 18 February. The French, demoralised by the death of their admiral, surrendered after firing a single broad-side for the sake of honour.[37]

To Nelson's astonishment, Keith did not betray a flicker of emotion on hearing of this success, and promptly put the young Scots noble-man Lord Cochrane into the prize. Nelson sent Admiral Perree's flag to the Neapolitan Prince Leopold, destined for a naval career, and the French ensign to the City of Norwich, to join the sword sent after Cape St Vincent.[38]

Conscious that his disobedience might be another cause for censure, he sent his journal to Spencer – both to demonstrate that without his unilateral action the French ship would have escaped,[39] and in the hope that this new success would secure Maurice's promotion.[40]

Nelson's immediate reward was the command of the Malta block-ade, issued with the offensive instruction that Syracuse, or almost any-where other than Palermo, must be his base. With this proviso, he was left to his own devices.[41] Keith clearly had no man management skills: he had garnished a severe demotion with a personal insult. Nelson knew far better than Keith that Palermo was not the best base for the Malta operation. He had used it under very different circumstances, while serving as theatre commander. Evidently Keith had been influ-enced by the gossip about Nelson's infatuation with Emma, and the deleterious effect this was having on the service.

If Keith's actions were inept, then Nelson did not help his own case with his response. Ill and exhausted, he requested a few weeks of leave in Palermo with his friends, while the *Foudroyant* had a refit. He pointedly promised to leave Troubridge, his own choice for the post, in command off Malta.[42] By naming Palermo, Nelson gave the impres-sion that he was anxious to get back into Emma's boudoir. In reality, he was only using the opportunity of Keith's arrival to release himself from the exhaustion and tension that had been exacerbated by the impossibility of delegating his authority. And where else was he supposed to go to get the rest he had so handsomely earned than to the house of his only friends in the Mediterranean? This much was obvious from his letter to Hamilton the following day.[43]

It was clear to all concerned that Nelson's ailments had their origin in chagrin. Hamilton, who had lived with him for the past seventeen months, stressed that he had been deeply upset by Keith's orders, 'but he had wisdom enough to swallow the pill for the good of the service of his King and Country . . . I never met with his equal'. Ball knew Nelson had earned his rest: 'we shall not meet such another – such rare qualities seldom combine in one person.'[44] Nelson explained the problem to an old professional friend in more practical terms. Being superseded had taken 'from me all opportunity of my rewarding merit and obliging my friends'.[45] Consequently he was ill – but he assured Spencer he would answer the call to battle.[46]

On 18 March, while on passage to Palermo, Nelson experienced chest pains that convinced him he was close to death. Since there were no physical symptoms evident when his organs were examined, the ailment was almost certainly psychosomatic.[47] However, this did not prevent him from venting his feelings in bitterly ironic and somewhat melodramatic terms: he was ready to die at his post, if the Combined Fleet returned, 'but *we of the Nile* are not equal to Lord Keith in his estimation, and ought to think it an honour to serve under such a *clever* man'.[48] Despite his self-diagnosis, however, he did not plan to outstay his leave, and his flagship went back to Malta with orders to return to Palermo on 6 April.

No sooner had the *Foudroyant* rejoined the blockade of Malta than she completed the task begun eighteen months before in Aboukir bay. The eighty-gun *Guillaume Tell*, the last French battleship left from Brueys' fleet, was preparing to escape from Malta. She sailed at midnight on 29 March, keeping tight to the shore, but that consummate frigate captain Henry Blackwood took up the chase in HMS *Penelope*. When the chase began *Foudroyant* had been the most distant ship of the small squadron off the harbour, and Berry did not respond until given a direct order. Yet she made up the distance in the next six hours, demonstrating her speed, and Berry's skilful ship-handling.

By daybreak the *Guillaume Tell* had lost two topmasts and the mainyard to Blackwood's skilful harassing fire, allowing the sixty-four HMS *Lion* to engage. Captain Dixon fired into her bow, but he did not risk engaging the much larger and more powerful ship broadside to broadside, while the 'prodigious fire of musketry' from her 1,200-man crew made close combat impossible. As *Lion* dropped back to repair her rigging Berry brought *Foudroyant* into action with that unique combination of courage and folly that marked his career. It was not without reason that Nelson, who valued him as a friend and an ardent warrior, called him a 'blockhead'. Berry ran close alongside the French vessel and, without firing, summoned Rear Admiral Decrès to surrender. As *Foudroyant* ranged past, however, Decrès replied with two broadsides that reduced her rigging to the same state as his own. A chastened Berry then wore round and poured in two broadsides of double-headed shot before dropping back to repair his rigging and leaving *Lion* and *Penelope* to keep the French admiral busy. When *Foudroyant* returned, again at very close range, the battle continued for another ninety minutes, only ending when the French lost their foremast. Powerless to escape, Decrès surrendered. *Foudroyant* had lost eight killed, while the sixty wounded included Berry; the French, meanwhile, had lost two hundred men on the crowded ship.[49] Admiral Decrès lived to play a further part in Nelson's life, becoming Napoleon's Navy Minister in 1804.

In reporting the victory, Berry stressed how the ship's company had wished their admiral present: 'how we prayed for you, God knows'.[50] Ball was anxious Nelson might be upset at missing the end of the French fleet. He need not have worried: Nelson was characteristically generous.[51] He confessed that 'I am vain enough to feel the effects of my school', before complimenting 'his' ship: 'I love her as a fond father, and glory in her deeds.'[52] He was full of praise for Blackwood, too:

My dear Blackwood,
  is there a sympathy which ties men together in the bonds of friendship without having a personal knowledge of each other? If so, (and, I believe it was so to you,) I was your friend and acquaintance before I saw you. Your conduct on the late glorious occasion stamps your fame beyond the reach of envy: it was like yourself.[53]

On 4 April Nelson applied to the Admiralty for leave to return to England to regain his health.[54] He was sick, and felt disgusted at the ingratitude of his own country and betrayed by the Neapolitan ministers. Moreover, Hamilton too would be leaving: twenty-nine-year-old Arthur Paget had been sent out, at very short notice, to replace the ageing minister. Rather than troubling himself to learn about Naples or cultivate its ministers, Paget relied on Consul Lock, lending further credence to the 'Black Legend' that had gained currency from Charles James Fox's speech in the House of Commons in February. When Nelson learnt what Fox had said he was furious that his honour as a British officer had been impugned. Collecting the relevant papers to show that there had been no breach of faith, he sent them to Davison, with instructions to show them to George Rose, or some other minister, 'and if you think right, you will put them in the [news]papers'.55

On 24 April Nelson rejoined his ship, her battle damage repaired, and took passage for Malta via Syracuse. The Hamiltons were his guests and it was almost certainly on board, in late April, that his daughter Horatia was conceived – perhaps this is the meaning of his enigmatic communication to Fanny in June: 'My health at times is better but a quiet mind and to give content is necessary for me. A very difficult thing for me to enjoy. I could say much but it would only distress me and be useless.'56 The squadron off Malta was delighted to see their talisman; Ball obviously spoke more than he knew when he told Emma that Nelson's symptoms were 'brought on by anxiety of mind, I therefore rejoice at your being on board, as I am sure you will exert your powers to keep up his spirits, and the worthy Sir William will contribute much to it.' Despite his friendship with Emma, Ball had missed quite how intimate she and Nelson had become.57

Back in London, meanwhile, Spencer had finally realised that Nelson was ill: he had secured royal authority in early May for Nelson to come home, fearful his 'indifferent health' would not be helped by staying at Palermo.58 He stressed to Nelson that he was not being recalled; indeed, Spencer would prefer that he stayed until Malta fell, but if this were not possible, he should recover his health in London rather 'than in an inactive situation at a foreign court'.59 Nelson was quick to see the slight, intentional or otherwise, in Spencer's choice of phrase. 'I trust you and all my friends will believe, that mine cannot be an inactive life, although it may not carry all the outward parade of *much ado about nothing*.'60

Exhausted by seven years of war, Nelson had hoped to go home in his flagship, which was also in need of repair. However, Lord Keith, under strict instructions from the Admiralty not to send any ships of the line home, ordered Nelson to leave her behind. Nelson had planned one last visit to Malta, before he departed the stage with the Hamiltons, escorting the Queen of Naples to Leghorn for a royal visit to Vienna.[61] Keith, though, was concerned less with such diplomatic pleasantries than with the sudden shifts of fortune of the war in northern Italy: on 6 June Genoa fell to the allies after a long siege, but eight days later Bonaparte rendered the result irrelevant with his stunning, if fortunate victory at Marengo. The efforts of the Russians, Austrians and British over the past year were reduced to nothingness in a matter of hours. The Russians left the coalition, and the defeated Austrians signed an armistice and evacuated Piedmont, Liguria, the western half of Lombardy, Tuscany and Ancona. The brief period of Anglo-Austrian cooperation, and any hope of victory, was over. Even if Austria did not make peace, she would not resume the offensive. The rejection of Bonaparte's peace offer began to look like a mistake. Having belatedly developed a real Mediterranean strategy, the ministers learnt in late June that it was all over.[62]

While all this was unfolding, Nelson was on passage from Palermo to Leghorn, where he arrived on 15 June. Rather than oblige Nelson's wish to go home in his flagship, Keith ordered every available unit to help the evacuation of Genoa. After they had left the *Foudroyant*, Nelson and the Hamiltons waited until the Queen set off overland on 10 July, following her route via Ancona on the 12th. Far from relapsing into inactivity Nelson remained on duty to the day he landed.[63]

Nelson went home overland, which at least allowed him to accompany Emma, who was anxious to avoid a sea passage owing to her pregnancy. After a fraught and adventurous journey from Leghorn to Ancona, Nelson and the Hamiltons boarded a Russian frigate for a stormy passage to Trieste, which confirmed Nelson's opinion of Russian ships and seamen. Once in Austrian territory the journey became a triumphal procession, through Slovenia and on to Vienna, where Nelson became the centre of attention: everyone was desperate to see him and to touch his garments. He became a public spectacle.

The wealth, taste and sophistication that Nelson encountered in the Austrian capital cast the Court of Naples in a provincial light. Joseph Haydn had written a powerful 'Mass in Time of Fear' in D major in August 1798, which was first performed shortly after news of Nelson's victory reached Austria. Another performance on the Esterházy estate at Eisenstadt in early September 1800, given in the presence of the hero, seems to have cemented its identification as the 'Nelson Mass'. If it was not inspired by Nelson, the re-dedication was well earned, for Nelson had done so much to relieve the fear that prompted Haydn to produce one of his most powerful works. Haydn also set some English verses on the battle to music, and accompanied Emma when she sang them; this was probably more to Nelson's taste than a Catholic mass.[64]

Despite such entertainments, Nelson was subdued: the triumphal tour was, in reality, a rest cure for his shattered frame and exhausted mind. He wrote little and was happy to leave the performing to Sir William and the remarkable Emma, who fascinated everyone, including Haydn. For those whose ideas about public dignity were formed in the eighteenth century, there was something vulgar about the Nelson entourage, and about Emma's dominating, expanding presence – to which some critics made pointed reference, not that they suspected she was pregnant. The whole procession seemed showy, and inappropriate. But the world had moved on since 1793: nations that wanted to mobilise their people needed heroes, and Nelson was the only contemporary hero to win his fame defeating the French. He could be lauded in the Habsburg lands because, as an admiral, his triumph did not threaten the fragile self-esteem of the insecure Emperor or his nervous court. Consequently, popular adulation greeted him in every town and city.

The excitement he attracted was not the result of dazzling social accomplishments: far from the sea and ships, he seemed to have little to say, and he demonstrated no interest in art, music, literature, architecture or scenery. Though the weather was an abiding obsession, he passed mountains and medieval cities with indifference. Utterly dedicated to his profession, he had neither time nor education for culture. His reading was dominated by professional matters, coastal pilots,[65] naval biographies, texts on shipbuilding and charts, combined with the Bible, Shakespeare, recent English writers and the reviews. The classical world of Sir William, Lord Minto and other statesmen was a closed book; his linguistic attainments never stretched beyond a competence in French.

Despite the fame he attracted on the Continent, Nelson would have been anxious to discover how his countrymen would receive him, and concerned that the passage of time between his heroic achievements and his homecoming would dull the public's enthusiasm. He need not have worried. The collapse of the Second Coalition and the resurgence of the invasion threat made Nelson's return timely. The nation's need for a hero had grown, and no one else could challenge his centrality in the national consciousness.

When he landed at Great Yarmouth on 6 November, he was overwhelmed by the public response. He immediately wrote to the Admiralty reporting his arrival, and his fitness for service. He was less attentive to Fanny's needs: not only did he forget that had written for her to meet him in London, but he failed to open the letters she left at Yarmouth. Swept up in local celebrations, he left town and headed for Round Wood, where he may have hoped to greet and abandon Fanny, before pressing on for London with the Hamiltons to resume his career, and his chosen mode of life. Instead they finally met in London, and the break-up of the marriage took place in public, at the Admiralty and the opera. The tactical finesse, strategic forethought and careful planning that were the hallmark of Nelson at war were nowhere to be seen. In private matters he procrastinated, though he ultimately showed his decisive qualities when he refused to succumb to social pressure and go back to his wife. To have done so would have been feeble, and utterly incompatible with the confidence he showed in following his own judgment and rejecting superior authority in 1799. It was, if not 'heroic', certainly decisive and consistent.[66]

It may have been the crowd's adulation that brought him to a decision about the rest of his life. He was the hero, and he was entitled to live as he chose, not to submit to the dictates of convention. Like many another great man, he could set his wife aside, with a decent settlement, and take up with his new 'wife', soon to be the mother of his child. It is inconceivable that he could ever have settled into the parochial trifles of Round Wood, and the slight world that Fanny occupied. His life was a public one, and he needed the company of public figures, naval officers, statesmen, diplomats – and Emma, the confidante of a Queen. Though Fanny had done nothing wrong, she was not a fit consort for a hero, and she was unable to bear his children. The problem was that Fanny did not see this, and persisted with her attempts to win him back. This was profoundly embarrassing for Nelson, and made the whole affair much more public than it might otherwise have been.

It has been customary to see the events of 1798–9 as a watershed, a period during which Nelson slipped away from the upright conventional morality of his church and his age. This interpretation is a serious mistake. Nelson was a man of the eighteenth century, who took the same relaxed view as most of his contemporaries. A better context for Nelson's actions can be found in the irregular lifestyles of his family. Though his father was a clergyman, his elder brother Maurice lived with a woman who was not his wife, while his uncle William Suckling had a family of 'natural' children. Nelson's behaviour, in short, was scarcely unusual by the standards of his age; it was only his fame, and the problems that his behaviour caused hagiographers writing in the stricter moral climate of the Victorian era, that made the affair with Emma so notorious.

Nelson arrived home just as his country had need of him. Within weeks, crushing defeat at the battle of Hohenlinden would drive Austria out of the war, and with Russia already disengaged, Britain once again stood alone. He was anxious to serve immediately, aware that St Vincent had requested him for the Channel fleet.[67] Nor did Nelson waste any time calling on Spencer and his Admiralty Board. Lord Keith, recipient of so many letters about Nelson's ill-health, may have been surprised by Admiral Young's report of 10 November: 'He seems to have recovered perfectly from his fatigues and to be very well. He will immediately hoist his flag in the Channel Fleet.'[68] Spencer knew the political value of the hero. He had promised that Nelson would rejoin St Vincent and Troubridge in the 'Mediterraneanised' Channel fleet: 'it gave me very great satisfaction to find that he had no sooner set his feet in it than he applied in the most pressing manner for service; and expressed the strongest wish to serve under your Lordship's command.' St Vincent, meanwhile, though glad to have Nelson join his flag, sounded a warning note: 'he will tire of being attached to a great fleet, and want to be carrying on a predatory war (which is his metier) on a coast that he is entirely ignorant of, having never served in those seas.'[69]

In preparation for Nelson's return, Spencer sent Hardy to Plymouth to take the crew of HMS *Namur* into the *San Josef*. Spencer thought it was 'Nelson's peculiar right' to hoist his flag on this ship. 'I have at the same time told him that if his service should be required in a smaller ship he will of course not think himself ill-treated by being removed to one.'[70] The ship would of course be modified to meet Nelson's requirements.[71] That the stern of this majestic vessel featured on his coat of arms gave her a peculiar significance.

Meanwhile, Nelson had a busy social schedule in London: everywhere he went his coach was mobbed. On 10 November he spoke at a Mansion House dinner in his honour and thanked the Lord Mayor and the City for a two-hundred-guinea sword. The King was less enthusiastic, cutting him dead at a royal levee, an insult that may have been occasioned by his Neapolitan decorations, or the campaign he and Sir William had started to have Emma received at Court. Fortunately such wounds were salved by further demonstrations of public adulation: on 20 November he was introduced into the House of Lords, and on 3 December he was the guest of honour at a dinner given by a grateful East India Company, with Henry Dundas among the Cabinet ministers and City worthies in attendance.[72]

Such events reflected the fact that in the two years since his last visit to England Nelson had achieved a unique national status: his triumph at the Nile had raised him above all other admirals. It was in the character of an idealised romantic hero that he entered the popular consciousness. The country had long sought a deliverer, and now they had one he was followed everywhere.[73] His image was enshrined in the portrait by Lemuel Abbott, who created a heroic, almost divine figure, although he was not sure what sort of god Nelson had become.[74] Copies of his picture were produced for influential clients, while a print from Daniel Orme's picture had been a runaway success even before the Nile; all this, plus the cheap engravings that started to circulate, made Nelson one of the most recognisable faces in Britain.[75]

This Nelson mania was exploited in the work of the best political caricaturists of the day, notably James Gillray, whose memorable efforts linked the denigration of the Foxite Whigs (who were frustrated by Nelson's success, as they had wanted peace with France) with the boosting of Nelson as the executor of Government policy. Gillray produced three wonderful images: 'Nelson's Victory' simply showed the Opposition in suicidal despair; 'The Extirpation of the Plagues of Egypt' had the hero, one-armed, using a British oak cudgel to bludgeon the hostile crocodiles into submission. The two themes were integrated, meanwhile, in 'John Bull taking a Luncheon', which showed the corpulent embodiment of the country devouring ship-shape delicacies, while the great admirals, Nelson to the fore, competed to pile up more dishes. Outside the Whigs ran off, fearing they might be eaten.

Gillray's caricatures accurately reflect the polarisation of political opinion over Nelson and his Neapolitan exploits. Pitt and his ministers consistently upheld the actions of their hero: on 3 December 1798, indeed, Pitt had used his Budget speech explicitly to link 'the transcendent commander' with his own policies, and the determination of the political and mercantile classes. By contrast, Charles James Fox's Whigs and their press mouthpiece, the *Morning Chronicle*, accused him of bad faith, and pointed to the improper influence exerted by Emma.[76] Later, when the hero returned, the same paper pointed to Emma's condition, while caricaturist George Cruickshank was quick to find an earthy humour in their relationship. Criticism of Nelson mainly came from the Opposition in Parliament, however; for the country as a whole, the element of political opportunism in these attacks was clear, and there were in any case more important issues to deal with than Nelson's private life and the internal difficulties of Naples. Later, when the immediate political context of these contemporary attacks on Nelson's personal life and conduct at Naples was no longer obvious, they were misunderstood and treated as serious criticism, rather than political persiflage.

The years between the Nile and Trafalgar saw the construction of a new idea of 'Britishness': a political discourse that emphasised the social, ideological and imperial elements that distinguished Britain and her people from the tyranny, Jacobinism, militarism and chaos that had followed in the wake of the French revolution.[77] The stability of this new 'Britishness' was founded not on an army but on the Navy, which enabled Britain to defy external threats, secured her trade, and provided the nation with its first and greatest hero. Nelson was the pre-eminent symbol of this new cultural identity, the first to bring together England, Wales, Scotland, and in part Ireland. For some writers and artists, Nelson was presented as a saviour, an almost Christ-like figure: one artist even represented him on a tree, surrounded by his followers.[78] With Wolfe as John the Baptist, the older generation of admirals as prophets, and a 'Band of Brothers' as disciples, he had come to redeem his people through his own death. This powerful imagery explains why Nelson was a troubling figure for many in the Church of England despite his own orthodox religious beliefs.

By the time of his return from the Nile, Nelson was at the heart of the national effort, almost synonymous with this new notion of militant Britishness. This link was powerfully embodied on 31 December 1800, when Nelson and Hood conducted the King to his throne in the House of Lords, from where he delivered his speech on the opening of Parliament, with strong references to the conduct of Russia in seizing British merchant ships. In the New Year's Day promotion that followed, Nelson became a Vice Admiral of the Blue.[79] If Britain was going to survive the next year she would need someone to break the encircling grip of the entire continent. Britain, without a worthwhile ally, faced France and Spain in war, while Russia, Prussia, Sweden and Denmark were only waiting to extract crippling concessions that would destroy her strategy. Nelson's public role was obvious and vital; unfortunately, his private life still continued to dominate everyone's attention.[80]

It was an indication of how far his marriage had collapsed that Nelson spent Christmas with the Hamiltons at Fonthill, the fantasy Abbey of William Beckford, Sir William's fabulously wealthy, but unstable nephew. Beckford was also a social outcast, whose homosexuality was common knowledge; he hoped to use Sir William's poverty to secure social status, by making him a loan in return for being named as his heir. Amid such exotic company, Nelson met Benjamin West, President of the Royal Academy, history painter to the King, and creator of the epochal *Death of Wolfe*, which had redefined the art of death and the nobility of service for Nelson's generation. Here was a subject on which Nelson had strong views. The conversation began with Nelson confessing that he was no connoisseur of art:

> But he said, turning to West, 'there is one picture whose power I do feel. I never pass a print shop where your "Death of Wolfe" is in the window, without being stopped by it.' West of course made his acknowledgements, and Nelson went on to ask why he had painted no more like it. 'Because, my lord, there are no more subjects.' 'Damn it,' said the sailor, 'I didn't think of that,' and asked him to take a glass of champagne. 'But, my lord, I fear your intrepidity will yet furnish me such another scene; and if it should, I shall certainly avail myself of it.' 'Will you?' replied Nelson, pouring out bumpers, and touching his glass violently against West's – 'will you, Mr West. Then I shall hope that I shall die in the next battle.' He sailed a few days after and the result was on the canvas before us.[81]

This story was told many years later to a young American artist, by which time Nelson was dead, and West had attempted his death more than once. However, Nelson's fascination with Wolfe suggests the story contains a strong core of truth. He had served with men like Dalling and Jervis who were on the Quebec expedition with Wolfe, while that name and the example of heroic death had occupied a powerful place in his mental world picture from childhood. He was, at this time, profoundly depressed by his personal circumstances, and may well have seen death in battle – a death that would confirm his legendary status in perpetuity – as preferable to living with Fanny. Over the next two weeks he sat for at least eight artists, as if to ensure that his features were captured for posterity, and that his death would not go unnoticed.[82] They included a portrait for the City of Norwich by Sir William Beechey, one by John Hoppner for the Prince of Wales and a bust by Mrs Damer for the City of London. Beechey caught something of the quiet self-confidence that underpinned the naval leader, and perhaps reflected the decision he had made to end his marriage.

It is often said that Nelson's relationship with Emma, and the end of his marriage, revealed that while a genius afloat, he was a child ashore. The basic argument is Minto's, and it says more about Minto than it does about Nelson. Minto envied Emma's relationship with his hero, and Nelson his courage in setting aside his wife for someone altogether more interesting. The apparent schizophrenia set up by Minto absolves his biographers of the need to account for actions in public and private that appear contradictory. It would be more appropriate to see the private Nelson as a late developer. Owing to the emotional legacy of his childhood, his early entry into naval life, and long years afloat, he missed out on the social phases of his adolescence: he left home aged twelve, and came back at twenty-one – a captain, and half-dead. Nor, on the evidence of his fumbling attempts at courtship, did he pick up much more understanding before he married.

Away from the sea, he sought a simple life, an idealised version of the home he had known before his mother died. This is why he clung on to his brother William, a last link with his childhood. But Nelson did not sleep under his own roof until he was past forty, by which time it was too late for him to become a fully rounded social being like his contemporaries. Even when he had secured the quiet life ashore he craved, he never stopped being the admiral, and went back to sea whenever the duty bell rang. His need for public applause also demonstrated his arrested development; it was a child-like attribute that he never lost, though he had turned it to his own advantage by the end of his life.

In truth, examining Nelson's private life courts disappointment; it is a mistake to expect heroes to be heroic in every aspect of their existence. Emma argued that theirs was a great romance, and her version still attracts those who believe Nelson incapable of anything small. In truth his private life was small, short and trifling – worthy of note only because he did not trouble to abide by convention, and used his celebrity to escape the consequences of a foolish and immature decision fifteen years earlier. This decision did at least demonstrate some of his best qualities: by refusing to bow to social pressure and return to conventional marriage with his dull wife, he showed the same calm, decisive resolve that he displayed on more famous occasions. However, this does not mean that he was in the grip of a grand passion: the Nelson–Emma 'love story' is a posthumous creation, much embellished by two centuries fascinated by the human side of celebrity. In reality the pair spent very little time together, and Nelson no more thought of giving up his post for her than he had for Fanny.

It was a strong relationship, however, and its power lay in their respective talents and origins. Both had made their way to the top on merit, exploiting every opportunity nature or nurture could provide. Nelson had a family leg up on to the Navy List; Emma's looks opened doors, and not just to bedrooms. They were fascinating outsiders, and made no attempt to hide the fact, or to deny their relationship. They were wise not to make a parade of the affection until 1805, by which time no one was unaware, or at all bothered. By this time, Nelson had secured his domestic ease, only to lose it forever. But his road to a simple retired life opened in January 1801.

The Christmas holiday – nine days out of London with Emma and Sir William – gave Nelson time to think about his personal circumstances, free from constant demands for appearances, dinners and crowds. Using the same logic he applied to his professional life, he could weigh up his options, plan out his operations, and strike at the perfect moment. With his plan of campaign settled he was ready to face the world. But his return to London was saddened by news that old William Locker had died on Boxing Day, before he had visited Greenwich. On 3 January Nelson followed his mentor to the grave, and wondered if it would not have been better had it been his own. Over the next ten days he arranged to recover his papers from Fanny, dispose of the dreadful house at Round Wood, and arrange the financial details of the separation. He assigned Fanny £2,000 a year, his

Nile reward. This was a nice touch: the Nile had made him the national hero – surely it would buy him the personal happiness he craved? He would not be the first, or last, husband to abandon his wife after a change in his fortunes. He could only afford the gesture because the pension for his wounds was almost £1,000, double his half-pay as a vice admiral.

Nelson left London on 13 January, with brother William, and never saw his wife again. He was on the road for Plymouth, where his new flagship lay. By early 1801 rumours about Nelson's attachment to Emma were in wide circulation, with the clear understanding that Fanny had been set aside.[83] Fanny was the only person who did not understand what was going on, and her obtuse refusal to play the part Nelson had assigned her, to retire to the country and keep out of his way, made his situation difficult.[84] Fortunately for him, by the time Fanny realised what was happening, and started to make strenuous efforts to recover him, he was back at sea. He left the business of ending his marriage to Davison, and to a lesser extent his brother William, and went off to do what he did best. He would return to public notice on his own terms. The international situation was changing rapidly: the Austrians had finally made their peace with Bonaparte, and Naples would soon follow. But there were more pressing problems for Britain, and it was to them that Nelson was drawn.

PART THREE

The Years of Command

CHAPTER XI

Command in the Baltic Sea
1800–1

After eight weeks of domestic chaos and mental anguish ashore, Nelson wanted to get back to sea, and both Lord Spencer and St Vincent, now Commander on Chief of the Channel fleet, were anxious to oblige him. Over the next twelve months he would prove himself an inspirational symbol of British resistance, ensuring that he was the inevitable choice for the Mediterranean command when war broke out again.

With the failure of the Second Coalition British strategy changed. As Russia switched from ally to armed neutral it was clear that without a Continental ally, maritime power would be the key resource for Britain.[1] This suited Nelson and his approach to war. His contemporaries were reluctant to engage in coastal offensive operations, and showed little interest in grand strategy. Sir Hyde Parker's command of the Baltic fleet and Lord Keith's blundering and fractious direction of the Mediterranean naval offensive in 1800 and 1801 were significant examples of a wider problem. The Royal Navy needed to be reprogrammed for the new circumstances of total war for national survival. Statesmen, soldiers and sailors of the ordinary sort were bogged down by precedent and rules, but Nelson soared above them. Although his status as a national icon was clear, his role as the intellectual force behind national strategy was but dimly perceived in Whitehall. Most

Bombs in air: the attack on Copenhagen

still saw the Nile as a fortunate event, and the later campaigns around Naples as inglorious embarrassments. The Baltic campaign would be a salutary reminder that Nelson was irreplaceable.

The shift in strategy followed the failure of the Continentalist foreign policy that based British security on temporary coalitions with great powers. The inability of Austria and Russia to make any headway against the French on land left that policy in ruins. Now the British had to rely on sea power to counter French military prowess, limiting their successes to Europe, while hamstringing their economy. This new strategy had several requirements: to cripple or destroy the enemy's naval resources, to secure British assets, trade and interests, and to deny the enemy any opportunity to strike at Britain. The core of this strategy was an economic blockade, imposed by the fleet, based on the legal right asserted by Britain to stop and search any neutral vessel, to establish the ownership and destination of the cargo. This was the principal weapon in the national armoury, and so important that Britain would fight the whole world to uphold it.

The impact of the change in strategy would be particularly apparent to those standing on the sidelines, and exploiting the conflict for economic gain. The destruction of French sea-borne commerce, and the occupation of the Dutch Republic, left a large gap in the provision of shipping between the East and West Indies and the blockaded ports of French-controlled western Europe. This opportunity was being exploited by neutral shippers, notably Denmark, which had expanded its own small Asiatic trade to cover the carriage of Dutch goods from their far larger Eastern empire. This was an abuse of neutrality, but the British had largely ignored the subject until 1800 when the nature of the war began to change.[2] The new strategy required the imposition of truly effective blockades, and the application of the severe code of maritime belligerent rights developed in the mid-eighteenth century to deal with neutral carriers.

In 1798 Denmark had adopted an offensive neutral policy, using warships to convoy merchant ships her ministers knew were carrying Dutch goods past the British blockade. This revival of ideas from the 1780 Armed Neutrality was highly dangerous, and required far more adept direction than the Crown Prince could provide. After a few incidents the 'sovereignty of the seas' was asserted by the dispatch of British warships to Copenhagen in August 1800, and the two sides compromised, but wider events imposed a different outcome.

The unstable Tsar Paul of Russia, who had joined the Second Coalition full of enthusiasm, was now disenchanted with his allies. The Austrians had been more interested in securing territory in northern Italy than defeating France, while the failure of a Russo-British combined operation in Holland prompted severe recriminations on both sides. The final straw came in September 1800 when the British accepted the surrender of Malta, the most enduring fruit of Nelson's victory at the Nile. Initially the British had agreed to include their allies in the process, but Dundas's growing alarm about Paul's aims, and indeed his sanity, prompted a reconsideration, just as his new strategy of standing alone took shape. This transformed the role of Malta from a bargaining chip, which could be used to keep the Tsar sweet, into a front-line position of the utmost importance. A small island with a first-class harbour, already massively fortified, occupying the strategic choke-point between the two basins of the Mediterranean, astride key trade routes, Malta was an almost ideal possession for a maritime power in a global war. Unfortunately Orthodox Tsar Paul believed he was now the Grand Master of the Roman Catholic Knights of St John, and entitled to assume control of the island in their name. Both Nelson and Dundas had warned against this, while the final decision to exclude the Russians was greeted with relief by local commanders and the Maltese population. For Paul this was the last straw. He quickly manufactured an excuse to dismiss the British Ambassador, impound British merchant ships and sailors, and annex the smouldering Anglo-Danish trade dispute to revive the old Russian aim of excluding the British from the Baltic.

The Armed Neutrality convention, signed on 16 December 1800, made the minor powers cat's paws for Russian Great Power policies. Russia did not share the maritime commercial interests of her Scandinavian clients: she sought control of the theatre, and a rapprochement, or worse, with France. The British had long recognised this strain in Russian policy. Consequently Denmark, Prussia and Sweden were coerced into following a Russian programme, which had at its heart the assertion of dominance over their countries, and the establishment of the Baltic as a Russian *mare clausum* – a consistent aim of Russian policy since the days of Peter the Great.[3]

The combination of challenges now posed by the Tsar made a rapid and resolute British response inevitable. He threatened Britain's belligerent rights, the cornerstone of her strategy against France. Nelson had long understood this connection. If the blockade could be flouted by neutral shipping the French could rebuild their fleet with Baltic naval supplies, and resume their economic rivalry with Britain, securing funds for further fleet-construction programmes. If Britain accepted the argument, she would abandon her great-power status, and accept French hegemony over Europe. It would also give the Tsar control over the naval stores that Britain required: a diplomatic lever of such power simply could not be left in his hands. These issues were fundamental to Britain's very survival.

The powerful professional presence of St Vincent as First Lord of the Admiralty in Henry Addington's new government was highly significant. His knowledge and determination ensured the Baltic fleet left on time, and was adequately supported.

Pitt made a powerful speech in the House of Commons on 2 February 1801, responding to the temporary Whig leader Charles Grey, in which he warned that if Britain resorted to force, she would have to 'totally annihilate the foreign commerce and consequently the domestic industry of all those Countries who shall engage in such a Confederacy'. The British position would 'never be relinquished . . . till Her Naval Power be annihilated.'[4] He also used the occasion to pour scorn on the unpatriotic and misguided views of the rump opposition, who had expressed doubts about the justice of the British claims against neutral vessels, and the importance of the issue.[5] Stressing this was an point 'upon which not only our character, but our very existence as a maritime Power depends', Pitt demonstrated the legal basis of the claim, and pointed up the bad faith of the Danes in abrogating the agreement of August 1800. He condemned the call to wait for more details of the new Treaty, in case the powers should 'produce something like a substitute for the fallen navy of France', or the carriage of stores to the French so that they could rebuild their own fleet. This was not the time to let slip the means by which the naval power of France had been destroyed – and the House agreed.[6]

Having established the line of policy he thought appropriate, Pitt told the King that he would resign the following day. The time was ripe for change: with the failure of the Coalition the country was alone, and anxious for peace. An unprecedented rise in the price of bread sparked widespread disaffection, and there had been little glory to distract attention from the threat of French invasion, domestic unrest and high taxes. Fortunately for the country, the policy left in place by Pitt would bear fruit before the time came for peace with France.7

The formation of the Armed Neutrality threatened to have an early and serious impact on naval stores, especially hemp, which would 'make it necessary to economise our stores as much as possible'. Spencer issued a Circular order to economise, anxious to get the fleet in good order for the spring 'when it is not improbable that we may have a more extended naval war on our hands than we have ever yet had'.8 St Vincent, meanwhile, was quick to recommend an admiral for the situation:

> Should the Northern Powers continue their menacing posture, Sir Hyde Parker is the only man you have to face them. He is in possession of all the information obtained during the Russian armament [of 1791, when he was Hood's chief of staff], more particularly that which relates to the navigation of the Great Belt; and the *Victory* will be a famous ship for him being by far the handiest I ever set my foot in, sailing remarkably fast and being of easy draft of water.9

The recently expelled British Minister in St Petersburg, Lord Whitworth, reported that the Russian fleet totalled forty-five battleships, but only seven or eight were in tolerably good order: some had broken backs, and the rest were hardly seaworthy, needing serious repairs.10

By the New Year the issue had come to a head. Secretary for War Henry Dundas feared for the West Indies, and requested the Admiralty watch for Scandinavian ships leaving the Baltic.11 The situation was complicated by a shift in the Russian position. For the Tsar, Malta was the key: after the Russians had been excluded from the occupation, he embargoed British shipping, and by December Bonaparte was flattering Paul, who was treating for peace with France. The Russian shift alarmed Denmark and Sweden, whose diplomats proposed a compromise settlement of the neutral rights issue, but Foreign Secretary Grenville was prepared to use force to uphold the British interpretation. To concede anything would be a sign of weakness that could not be afforded by a nation standing alone against France and relying on seapower for her security and success: 'if we give way to them we may as well disarm our navy at once.' On 16 December, Grenville declared that it was better to fight, and 'though some temporary alarm will arise as to our commerce, we shall give more animation to the feelings of the Country, and go on, upon the whole, quite as easily as we should without it'.12 This message was conveyed to the ministers of the neutral courts at Berlin on 28 December 1800, and three days later the King's speech at the opening of Parliament made the issue public:

> If it shall become necessary to maintain against any combination, the honour and the independence of the British Empire, and those maritime rights and interests on which both our prosperity and our security must always essentially depend, I entertain no doubt either of the success of those means which, in such an event, I shall be enabled to exert, or of the determination of My Parliament and My People to afford Me a support proportioned to the importance of the interests which We have to maintain.[13]

By then it was too late. The neutrals had signed a convention in St Petersburg on 16–17 December, and this was ratified in early January. Their action was confirmed in London on 13 January 1801 by the Danish minister. Britain had to respond vigorously. Secretary for War Henry Dundas reviewed the Cabinet papers, and sent his thoughts on the situation to the Admiralty. His view of the Baltic was conditioned by the wider problems of the war.

> We must all agree that [we] have now the greatest stake to contend for that ever called forth the exertions of this country . . . the great trial of strength must be in the course of the ensuing summer, but that as to all Baltick operations the game is lost, which alone can make success certain, if we are not able to have a powerful fleet there the moment it is accessible, with the professed object of annihilating the confederacy of the North by the capture or destruction of the Danish Fleet.

He was well aware that the French armies were largely unemployed, and could be used to attack British interests anywhere in Europe; they might even be shipped to the Cape of Good Hope, the West Indies and Minorca. He called for a redistribution of naval forces to meet the danger. The French and Spanish battleships at Brest would be covered by St Vincent with sixteen three-deckers and eighteen seventy-fours, 'leaving two eightys and ten seventy-fours for the service of the Baltick and the North Sea'. This would be enough, by early March,

> to capture or destroy the whole of the Danish fleet. That accomplished the contest is over, and we will then have the power of transmitting . . . the knowledge of this splendid truth, that Great Britain contending for its maritime rights is a match for the whole naval force of the world combined against them . . . In our Baltick operations we stand in a different predicament from that we do in every other. In others we are upon the *defensive* and our force will be sufficient if we are able to cripple the efforts of our enemy so as to baffle their hostile attempts, but in the Baltick we must act with vigor on the *offensive*, for it is on such an exertion that the whole contest turns . . . the force for the Baltick should have

the first preference, and be of a nature so commanding as to leave no room for doubts of success.

To hasten preparations, the Admiralty was advised to use ships not thoroughly repaired, as they only had to last the summer.[14]

The fleet for the Baltic campaign had to be drawn from St Vincent's Channel fleet, which was reduced to meet the emergency, despite the presence of over forty French and Spanish ships at Brest. This also freed both Nelson and Admiral Sir Hyde Parker to join the campaign. St Vincent had recommended Parker as Commander in Chief largely to get him out of the Channel, though his rank and experience of fleet command, backed by Captain of the Fleet William Domett's mastery of fleet administration, promised a solid base for the campaign.[15] The old Earl was royally hoist on his own petard, however, when he became First Lord of the Admiralty before the fleet sailed: he ended up relying on a man he did not respect to execute the most demanding mission that had fallen to a British admiral. Nelson was ordered to hoist his flag at Plymouth on 9 January.[16]

Nelson had served under Hyde Parker before, in the brief period between Hotham going ashore and Jervis arriving, and he had not enjoyed the experience. In the intervening period, Sir Hyde had commanded in the West Indies and made his fortune. He had earned a reputation for energy and skill in his youth, but these qualities had not survived into middle age, while he was never overblessed with strategic insight or political courage. At sixty-one, Parker was a fussy, rather old-fashioned man; his mercurial subordinate was forty-two. The older man belonged to the limited wars of the eighteenth century, the younger to the total conflicts of the freshly opened nineteenth. Nelson was an obvious choice for the Baltic campaign, but in case the Baltic nations decided to avoid the blow – as they had as recently as August 1800, when Denmark backed down – he would be kept in reserve, behind the more conciliatory Parker.

The choice of officers and ships for the fleet was influenced by the requirement for local knowledge and smaller, older ships. Parker's flagship HMS *London* had been in service nearly fifty years, while the bulk of the seventy-fours dated back to the last war. These ships drew between one and two feet less water than the new, larger ships then serving in the Channel. This would be critical to effective operations against Baltic harbours like Revel and Copenhagen; and since a direct attack on such fortified places would be costly, it also helped that they were expendable. Regular units were supported by odd packets like the ex-East India merchant ships *Glatton* and *Ardent*. Human resources were very tight: the increased demands made by this extra squadron, and the consequent need for the existing North Sea fleet to keep the Dutch squadron covered, became evident when Rear Admiral Totty's short-handed flagship, the seventy-four *Invincible*, ran onto a shoal off Yarmouth and was lost with over half her crew.

During this period the Admiralty, prompted by Hyde Parker, selected a stream of captains and junior officers with local knowledge. George Murray had navigated the Great Belt, so he had to leave the large new seventy-four *Achilles* for the small, old *Edgar*,[17] while officers like Nicholas Tomlinson and Frederick Thesiger who had Russian experience volunteered for the campaign. Spencer consulted a number of officers about the demands of the theatre, receiving a very thorough reply from Hyde Parker. Leaving the Admiralty to determine how many battleships would be required, from the latest intelligence, Parker urged the need for a powerful flotilla, and six floating batteries to support smaller ships like gunboats and bomb vessels in shoal water, or attack 'low batteries or ships in a mole, or confined navigation'.[18] He also required six or eight good sailing armed cutters or luggers as dispatch boats, or as beacons on rocks and shoals. 'With these assistants I cannot but conceive the fleet will be able to make its way against every opposition the enemy can throw.'[19] Lieutenant Thesiger stressed the need for flotilla craft to deal with an enemy galley fleet, and to anchor over shoals. He was confident fireships could be used at Revel, where the harbour was made of wood, while Cronstadt was exposed to attack by bomb vessels.[20]

On 17 January Nelson and St Vincent, now First Lord of the Admiralty, discussed the prospect of the Baltic campaign at Plymouth. Anxious not to lose his new flagship, or the chance of the Mediterranean command, Nelson called for ten thousand troops to seize the Danish arsenal.[21] On the same day, Nelson was moved into the small three-decker HMS *St George* and placed under Parker's orders; the following day he was ordered to Spithead.[22] St Vincent, declaring that 'Lord Nelson will act the fighting part well',[23] was anxious to have him back in the Channel – 'the moment the business at Copenhagen is finished, the rest will be children's play.'[24]

While Nelson conducted his duties with his usual enthusiasm, his private thoughts were in turmoil. He had been happy to escape to sea, and was determined not to go back to Fanny. 'She is a great fool,' he told Emma; 'and, thank God, you are not the least bit like her.'[25] In truth Nelson was the fool: Emma was playing on his emotions by suggesting that the Prince of Wales was interested in adding her to his list of mistresses. The combination of joy at the birth of his daughter, and fear that he might lose his muse, prompted a daily ritual of letter writing that had been expressly forbidden by Fleet Physician Dr Trotter, who was trying to cure his ophthalmia.[26] He swore before heaven that he would make her his wife as soon as it was possible and begged, 'Let us be happy, that is in our power.'[27] His agony continued, though: 'Do not, I beseech you risk being at home. Does Sir William want you to be a whore to the rascal (The Prince of Wales)?' For his part, Nelson declared 'I might be trusted with fifty virgins naked in a dark room.' He was not going to change his mind whatever happened.[28]

His mood improved only when he found more immediate concerns to occupy his mind. On 27 January the appointments of Hyde Parker and Nelson were made public, and by the end of the month, bomb vessels, flat boats and other minor war vessels were being prepared. Ships set aside for the Baltic were ordered to stay close to home, and Parker was released from the Channel fleet.[29] The Foreign Office reported Danish opinion that Russia wanted to dominate the Baltic, while the Swedish fleet was old, but remained effective.[30] Nelson was quick to gather intelligence on Danish defences from General Simcoe, who had given a good deal of thought to the subject.[31] However, Parker did not share his intelligence, treating Nelson with a degree of high-handed disdain that offended his sense of how the service should be conducted, as well as his concept of politeness. The relationship only began to thaw when Parker found he needed Nelson's unique talents.

Someone else was looking to these talents to solve a problem. St Vincent was less confident about the campaign than he claimed in public: unless Hyde Parker had twenty thousand good troops under a proven general, he feared, 'he will do nothing. You know as well as I do that shells thrown from ships are impotent weapons, and will be laughed at when the first consternation is over.'[32] He was beginning to have second thoughts about Parker. The new Admiralty Board was sworn in on 20 February, and met immediately. St Vincent and Troubridge were the key players, while the Admiralty Secretary Sir Evan Nepean had been St Vincent's secretary back in the 1770s.

Nelson used his privileged relationship with the Earl and Troubridge to hasten the assembly of the fleet, and get it sent to sea.[33] The Board thanked Simcoe for his information, but there were nowhere near enough troops for him to be appointed. Instead the War Office detailed 781 officers and men of the 49th regiment and 114 from the Rifle company, under Lieutenant Colonel William Stewart, for this 'highly important expedition'.[34]

By late February the Foreign Secretary admitted that the Northern courts were refusing to recognise the ancient rights of the British Flag. The King was anxious to avoid the necessity of war, but with Denmark and Sweden actively preparing, Britain could wait no longer. The fleet would be sent to support the negotiation '& to bring it to a speedy and satisfactory conclusion'. If the Danes rejected British demands, 'then assert and vindicate without further delay the rights and dignity of His Crown, & if practicable to capture and to destroy the Navy and weaken as much as possible the maritime resources of Denmark in the Port of Copenhagen, or wherever they may be found and can be attacked.' It would require no fewer than twenty battle-ships, and smaller craft in proportion, 'to destroy the Arsenal of Copenhagen with the whole of the shipping in that Port.' Parker could accept the surrender of the fleet, shipping and arsenal in lieu of an attack.[35]

Nelson secured three days' leave in London, which he used to see his daughter, while Hyde Parker left London for Great Yarmouth on 26 February, and continued collecting charts, local experts, pilots and flotilla craft. Nelson went back to Spithead to hurry the fleet round to the rendezvous.[36] 'Time, my dear Lord, is our best Ally, and I hope we shall not give her up, as all our Allies have given us up.' He found Parker nervous about dark nights and fields of ice, but took comfort from St Vincent's approval. On 2 March Nelson left for Yarmouth with the bulk of the squadron and the troops. He had finally settled his private affairs, writing to Emma as 'My own dear wife, for such you are in my eyes and in the face of heaven'. Three days later he told Fanny that he wished to be left alone, and though he continued to fret about the prospect of princely interest in his 'wife' duty quickly became the main focus of his attention.[37] A despairing letter to St Vincent, speaking of this being his last campaign, prompted an upbeat reply from a master of man-management: 'every public act of your life has been the subject of my admiration'.[38]

Once at sea, however, Nelson focused his penetrating intellect on the campaign ahead. He had no doubt the Baltic navies lacked tactical skill, and reckoned he would beat them with no more than two thirds of their force. Arriving at Yarmouth on 7 March, Nelson was horrified to find Hyde Parker planning a ball: his letters to Troubridge and St Vincent generated a stinging rebuke for the Commander in Chief. St Vincent demanded that he leave immediately, both to refute rumours that he was delaying over trifles, which would create an 'irreparable injury' to his reputation, and because 'there are many, very many important questions that must be determined entirely by the prompt and vigorous execution of your orders'.[39] Hyde Parker sailed the next morning, missing his ball.[40] Anxious to master the issues, Nelson was appalled to find Parker would not share intelligence on the Copenhagen defences with him, and was reduced to begging Nepean to let him have Baltic charts.[41] He quickly identified the Captain of the Fleet, Domett, and Flag Captain Otway as cautious and unimpressive men who exacerbated Parker's indecision.[42] Nor was he amused to be given command of the van, with a pair of feeble sixty-fours to support his flagship.[43]

Two days later, fresh instructions from the Secretary of State for War shifted the focus eastward. Mild weather would allow the Baltic fleet to proceed sooner, and it was to head for the ports of Russia (particularly Revel) as soon as the current service would admit. Whether the Danish negotiations ended in peace or war, Parker was to proceed to Revel as soon as he had finished work at Copenhagen, locate the Russian division, and 'make an immediate and vigorous attack upon the same, provided this measure . . . would afford a reasonable prospect of success in destroying the arsenal or in capturing and/or destroying the ships without exposing to too great a risk the fleet under his command'. He was then to act successively against Cronstadt and the other ports of Russia, capture and destroy ships and annoy the enemy as far as possible, given usages of war. If the Swedes persisted he was to attack them also.[44] Sent on 15 March, the instructions reached Parker on the 24th, in the midst of a crisis about his route and purpose.[45]

Hyde Parker had favoured waiting for the Baltic fleets to come out into the Skaw for a battle, while Nelson was anxious to get at the Russians, whom he saw as head and heart of the conspiracy – he understood Russian aims and their seamanship from his time in the

Mediterranean. Nelson pressed Parker to move. Time was of the essence, and he was in no doubt that the fleet should pass the Sound, anchor before Copenhagen and support the efforts of the diplomats to find a peaceful solution. War or peace, it must be quick.[46] The diplomatic mission of Nicholas Vansittart and William Drummond was not going well, however. The Danish Foreign Minister Count Bernstorff, whom they met on 14 March, proved immovable, despite their promises and threats: 'The Count answered that the appearance of a British Fleet would make no difference in their resolutions.'[47] He also refused to accept their credentials unless the British embargo of Danish trade was removed. Their mission ended with Bernstorff's note of 16 March, so offensive in language and principles 'as to leave little doubt of the hostile determinations of the Danish Government'.[48]

On 19 March the fleet arrived in the Skaw to find Vansittart had been dismissed. It was time for war. On the 21st and 22nd gales forced the fleet to anchor. Late on the 22nd, Vansittart and Drummond joined the fleet from Copenhagen on HMS *Blanche*. Parker realised Bernstorff's letter was a declaration of war, and learnt of the preparations in hand at Kronborg and Copenhagen. He informed the Admiralty that the moment the wind allowed, the fleet would enter the Sound and 'put their orders into execution'.[49] Reports of two hundred cannon at Kronborg and floating harbour defences and batteries at Copenhagen shook Parker. He had expected to support the Danes against the Russians, and now decided to go direct to Revel through the Great Belt 'to attempt the destruction of the Russian ships at Revel which are expected'. If necessary he could attack Copenhagen from the south. However, the wind was against him, and he anchored. It appeared to him that the Danish defences were very strong: 'from the depth of water it will be very difficult to dislodge them without vessels of force, of a less draught of water than the ships of the line.'[50]

Nelson, appalled by Parker's procrastination, quickly compiled a sermonising letter, setting out the issues as he saw them and stressing the need to act immediately. The enemy was daily growing stronger; the British would never be better placed than they were at the present moment. The Government expected him to attack Copenhagen if the Danes would not negotiate. He had the honour and safety of England in his hands: 'never did our Country depend so much on the success of any fleet as on this'. Anxious to attack Russia, he was ready to lead a detachment to Revel, going through the Sound, or the Great Belt, as long as they acted now.[51] Perplexed and uncertain in the face of such tremendous responsibility, Parker called Vansittart and Nelson to the flagship on 24 March.[52] In view of the preparations at Kronborg and Copenhagen, they agreed to proceed through the Great Belt. Colonel Stewart, convinced the real object of Government policy was to strike the Russians, considered that attacking Copenhagen via the Belt was wrong, and a waste of time.[53] On 25 March, the fleet weighed at 3 a.m., but Nelson and George Murray of the *Edgar* went to Parker and persuaded him to go back to the previous anchorage near the Sound and resume the original plan. A squadron led by Nelson and Rear Admiral Graves would attack the defence line at Copenhagen.

The fleet sailed for the Belt, but Parker's staff persuaded him to return to the Sound route. The Belt was a longer, and more difficult passage: only Murray had navigated it in a battleship, and it would not be ideal for an attack on Copenhagen. On 26 March Nelson shifted his flag into the seventy-four, HMS *Elephant*, commanded by Foley. The name of this ship, while hardly euphonious to English seamen, was carefully chosen. The Danish royal badge was an elephant.

Lying at anchor, Nelson continued to bemoan the loss of time: now that there was no hope of reconciliation it would be best to go to Copenhagen. Hyde Parker's 'diffidence' and 'hesitation' over the past four days could not be justified.[54] Captain of the Fleet Domett, too, observed on 26 March that 'this delay is ruin to us, I hope the wind will soon be to the southward'.[55] He had to wait three more days. Nelson considered Domett the root of Parker's indecision but pitied them both for being placed in a situation that neither was equipped to handle, in which 'the spur of the moment must call forth the clearest decision and the most active conduct'. Now they were out of their depth Domett was indecisive, while Parker suddenly abandoned the high-handed and haughty tone he had presumed since Yarmouth.[56]

When the wind finally shifted on 29 March, Parker ordered George Murray of the *Edgar* to place the bomb vessels to fire on Kronborg and the town of Elsinore while the fleet passed. The impressive baroque fortress of Kronborg, associated with *Hamlet* and the scene of more than one memorable performance of the tragedy, was more symbol than substance. Although it served as a statement in stone of the Danish claim to collect Sound Dues – a tax on ships entering or leaving the Baltic, levied since the Middle Ages – it was in reality perfectly impotent. The sound was more than three thousand yards wide, and even if the Swedish batteries at Helsingor fired, ships could pass down the centre of the channel with impunity. It is revealing that Parker and Nelson did not know this: with this information Parker's indecision could have been avoided, and the attack mounted sooner.

On 30 March, Nelson's division led the fleet past the fortress, with the bomb vessels providing supporting fire. They were through the Sound by 9 a.m. without damage: as the Swedes did not fire the fleet shifted to the eastern side of the channel, far beyond the range of Danish guns. Some of the British bombs reached the target, and one remains stuck in the ceiling of St Olaf's Cathedral in Elsinore as a reminder of passing greatness. The fleet then anchored north-east of Copenhagen while Nelson led the reconnaissance on board the frigate HMS *Amazon*. Captain Edward Riou's ship-handling and insight made him an instant favourite. Nelson reported that the fire from the Kronborg had been a tremendous waste of powder and shot, and his opinion of the Danish defence line was no more complimentary: 'It looks formidable to those who are children at war, but to my judgement with ten sail of the line, I think I can annihilate them; at all events I hope to be allowed to try.'[57] Parker remained pessimistic, finding the defences 'far more formidable than we had reason to expect', but accepted Nelson's offer to command the attack, and gave him two more ships than he had requested. *Defence*, *Ramillies* and *Veteran* would move down from the main fleet to menace the northern part of Danish line and assist any disabled ships.[58]

The purpose of the attack was to clear away the Danish floating defences, exposing the dockyard, arsenal and the city to the fire of the fleet's seven bomb vessels. The Royal Artillery officers directing the mortar fire reported that:

> if the outer line of the enemy's defences afloat – that is, all the vessels to the southward of the two crowns island (Trekroner) – were removed, a bombardment would be attended with the best possible success; but that until that was done the attempt could be attended with none.

A Council assembled on the *Elephant* after dinner on 31 March, including Nelson, Parker, Domett, Foley, Fremantle, Riou, Graves and Murray. The next day, Nelson's division shifted to the starting position for the attack, the wind failing as the last ships reached position, just as Nelson had anticipated.[59]

That evening Nelson wrote his instructions for the attack on the Danish defence line. They were very detailed, and left little or nothing to the initiative of his captains. The navigational difficulties, the nature of the task and the importance of clearing the entire Danish line made 'mission-analysis' inappropriate. He arranged his forces to achieve a real firepower superiority, certain his ships could overwhelm the static Danish line. Yet as Clausewitz observed, no plan survives first contact with the enemy. When three ships went aground and the plan began to fall apart, he had the mental resources to reorganise and carry on.

Even with the wind in his favour, Nelson was still entirely dependent on navigating intricate shoals to get into the King's Deep. Only at 10 a.m. on 2 April did he find a willing pilot, who led the fleet from Murray's *Edgar*. Once Murray was under way, Nelson signalled the rest to follow. Firing began around 10.30. Soon afterwards his old favourite the *Agamemnon* failed to clear the Middle Ground shoal, spending the rest of the battle as a spectator. Other ships spent the entire day getting into position, and most of the flotilla were not ready until after the fighting. Nelson reacted quickly, signalling the *Polyphemus* to replace her classical sister. He also saw that the *Bellona* was too close to the shoal, but his signal was too late: she grounded, and was followed by the *Russell*, which lost her bearings in the gun-smoke. By word of mouth and flag signals, Nelson shortened and tightened his line of battle, to ensure he maintained a clear firepower advantage over the Danes, at the expense of leaving the Trekroner battery to be masked by Riou's frigates. To the consternation of his captains, Riou used his five frigates to extend the battleline north, and fill the space left by the missing battleships. This was Nelson's reward for an instant rapport with the brilliant frigate captain: Riou trusted Nelson, and acted like him. By the time all the battleships had anchored Nelson had redrawn his battle plan, concentrating on the south and centre of the Danish line, and maintained his superiority in numbers of guns. He was rather further away than he had hoped, as nervous officers feared the enemy were inside the shoal. In fact they were outside it, and the intervening waters were deep.

To the north, Parker's division was under way, but with the wind dead ahead the three supporting ships would be hard pressed to work up into action. Nelson's leading ship – appropriately named the *Edgar*, after the Saxon King who first established England's Sovereignty of the Seas – took up her position under sail, and under fire from the Danish ships. The other battleships followed. The range was short, around four hundred yards, and the Danish guns soon scored damaging hits. Captain Mosse was killed on his own quarter-deck as the *Monarch* dropped anchor. By 11 a.m. all the British ships were in action, *Elephant* flying Nelson's favourite signal, No. 16: 'Engage the Enemy more closely.'

For Nelson the tension was almost unbearable. He paced the quarter-deck, often talking with Colonel Stewart, who had seen nothing like the combat, or the admiral. 'I never passed so interesting a day in the course of my life or one that so much called for my admiration of *any* officer.' From a Peninsula War veteran that was high praise. Nelson was philosophical about the danger. When a round shot smashed into the mainmast, sending a shower of splinters across the upper deck, he turned to his companion and observed drily, 'It is warm work, and this day may be the last for any of us at any moment. But, mark you, I would not be anywhere else for thousands.' Who would not be inspired by such resolve? It is also, and perhaps more authentically, recorded that he declared: 'Well Stewart, these fellows hold us a better jig than I expected. However, we are keeping up a noble fire, and I'll be answerable that we shall bowl them out in four if we cannot do it in three hours.' Suitably prompted, Stewart noted that the British were firing faster, and as they also had more guns in action the result, as Nelson well knew, was inevitable. Brave as they were, the inexperienced Danes must be beaten – it was a question of time. A few weeks earlier Nelson had explained his views on gunnery to Berry:

> I hope, we shall be able as usual to get so close to our Enemies that every shot cannot miss their object, and that we shall again give our Northern Enemies that hail-storm of bullets which is so emphatically described in the *Naval Chronicle*, and which gives our dear country the Dominion of the Seas. We have it, and all the Devils in Hell cannot take it from us, if our Wooden walls have fair play.[60]

He had secured just such a position, and the Danes, be they men or Devils, would soon discover the truth of his remark.

Nelson's opposite number, Commodore Olfert Fischer on the old seventy-four *Dannebrog*, was well aware of the superior British fire. He faced the *Elephant* and William Bligh's *Glatton*, armed with sixty-eight- and forty-two-pounder carronades, firing shells. At four hundred yards every shot told: inside half an hour Fischer had to shift his pendant. Nelson had destroyed the enemy's flagship, and with it their cohesion. Soon the *Dannebrog* was on fire, while her gun crews were remorselessly scythed down. At 14.30 her flag came down, and the survivors went ashore. Her cable burnt through: she drifted north past the Trekroner fort, still ablaze, and at 16.30 she blew up, just like *L'Orient*. Long before that, several of the smaller Danish vessels had left the scene, unable to sustain the unequal combat with such powerful foes. By 14.30 the south and centre of the Danish line was beaten, but the ships were still in Danish hands. They could fire on the bomb vessels and had to be cleared away. To the north Commodore Fischer had to abandon his second ship of the day, the *Holsten*, at 14.15, taking his pendant ashore to the Trekroner before the ship surrendered.

While the smoke of battle hung thick and the situation appended uncertain, Parker watched from afar. At 13.15 he ordered signal No. 39, 'Discontinue the Action', to be hoisted, and enforced by firing guns. No one on the *London*'s quarter-deck that afternoon ever explained this action. Once again Parker's underlying irresolution burst through, propelled by uncertainty, anxiety and lack of confidence. Personally brave, he was unnerved by the responsibility of battle, not the shot and splinters. The signal applied to every ship, and was obligatory. Parker never said why he flew it. Nelson did not mention it in his official report, but he was once again faced with an order from a superior officer that he considered dangerous, and impossible to execute. Unlike Keith's foolishness over Minorca, this contained the seeds of immediate tactical catastrophe. Any attempt to get out of the King's Deep under fire from a position close to the Middle Ground would have left his squadron in chaos, with many aground, giving the Danes every prospect of a remarkable victory. When the signal was pointed out Nelson had it acknowledged, as was proper, but demanded that his own No.16 was kept aloft. He did not repeat Parker's signal. With Stewart and Foley at his elbow, he played out, legend has it, a little joke: saying, 'You know Foley, I have only one eye and I have a right to be blind sometimes,' he lifted his telescope to his right eye and announced, 'I really do not see the signal.' The more authentic report given by Minto the following month was: 'I have only one eye, and it is directed on the enemy.'[61] The exact words matter less than the sentiment: Nelson was going to disobey Parker, and face the consequences. He could see the Danish line crumbling, ships slipping out of the battle, guns falling silent and his own firepower superiority increasing with every minute. There was no reason to fear defeat: although the Danes were holding out a little longer than he had expected, they would be beaten within four hours. Only a heartbroken

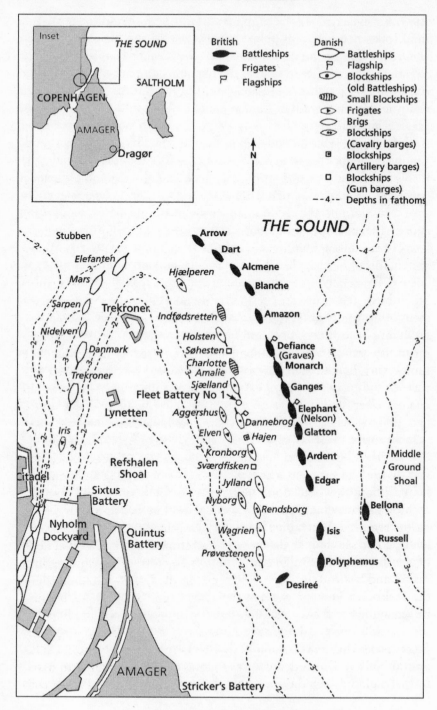

The battle of Copenhagen

Riou, far closer to the flagship, acted on No.39: 'What will Nelson think of us?' he lamented. As the *Amazon* showed her stern to the Trekroner, a round shot cut him in two. For Nelson this was 'an irreparable loss'.[62] Rear Admiral Sir Thomas Graves asked his signal officer to check Nelson's response, and elected to follow his commander, not Parker. The battleship captains shared his faith in their admiral, and stayed put.

Nelson followed up the signal incident with another stroke of genius. He had defeated the less powerfully armed Danish vessels, and if this had been a sea battle the Danes would have surrendered long before, their masts shattered. However, they were at anchor. So at 13.45 he went below and wrote a letter to the Danish Government, ordering Danish speaker Frederick Thesiger to take it by boat under a flag of truce along the disengaged side of the line. Thesiger landed at the Citadel at or before 15.00. The letter spoke of events that had not occurred when Nelson wrote, notably the capture of the Danish blockships, and warned of serious consequences if the Danes did not stop firing. Many have argued that this was a trick, a *ruse de guerre*, to escape a difficult situation. His own explanation was simple humanity, and he was not a competent liar. In reality his immaculate timing was the key. He knew how long it would take to get the letter ashore, and reckoned, very nicely in the event, that in an hour it would all be over, and his letter would be read by men facing utter defeat. He had not won when he sent the letter, but he had when it arrived.

It was also a neat political stroke, ending the battle and limiting the damage to Anglo-Danish relations. As he would stress to the Crown Prince, the real problem was Russia, so an emollient note, letting the Danes know they had done quite enough for honour, and warning them of the consequences if they did not see this, was just what the situation required. When the Danish Crown Prince received Nelson's letter, he could see that the defence line had stopped firing, and that none of the ships had an ensign aloft. Parker's squadron was working into range, and his leading ships were firing on the Danish forces north of the Trekroner. He took the hint that it was time to negotiate, because he knew the battle was lost. To avert the impending bombardment of the arsenal, dockyard and city he ordered a ceasefire, and sent his English speaking *aide de camp*, Lindholm, out to meet Nelson. On his arrival Nelson also ordered a ceasefire. The Danes wanted to avoid further fighting, but did not dare accept the terms that Parker conveyed to Lindholm that evening: to leave the Armed Neutrality and join Britain. With guns falling silent the British ships worked out of the King's Deep, although two went aground, including the *Elephant*. Nelson returned to the *St George* for the night, exhausted and anxious. He need not have worried: it was obvious to all who had won the battle, and what that said about the principal protagonists:

> What another Feather this is to Lord Nelson. I can't help thinking, what the difference of feelings there must be between him and the Commander in Chief, to let him get such a Victory, and the other to be looking on – for God's sake say nothing about this.[63]

The statistics of the battle told their own story: the British lost 254 dead and 689 wounded, the Danish losses were around double this. The British had taken twelve of the eighteen Danish vessels, but only the *Holsten* was worth refitting and sending home.[64] The rest were too old or unusual to warrant the cost of repairs. Most were stripped of any useful stores, bronze guns and equipment, before being burnt, usually at night.[65]

On the morning after the battle, all seven British bomb vessels lay in the King's Deep, ready for action. These ships were fitted with thirteen-inch mortars, firing two-hundred-pound shells filled with ten pounds of powder up to four thousand yards. This was far beyond the accurate range of any existing cannon, and as bomb vessels were small targets they could bombard a port or city with impunity. They were now in range of the dockyard, arsenal, the Royal Palace and key parts of the city. The Crown Prince considered fighting on, to prove his loyalty to his allies, but the result would have been useless sacrifice. Instead he pressed for a negotiated settlement that would appease the Tsar and the French: to accept the British terms risked the loss of Norway and the mainland provinces; to reject them would cost him Copenhagen and the fleet.

On 3 April Parker sent Nelson ashore to negotiate. Having completed his report and visited the ships that had fought so well the previous day, he landed at the Customs Quay with Hardy and calmly walked down the street to the Palace. The crowd showed no hostility: many wanted to get a glimpse of the hero. Nelson opened the business by flattering the Danes on their courage, and gave the Crown Prince two options: accept Parker's terms or disarm the fleet. The latter offered the Crown Prince and his Foreign Minister an opening. Anxious to attack Russia, Nelson was prepared to ignore explicit government orders, and open a political negotiation. He would settle for neutralising Denmark while the fleet set about Russia. He stressed that Denmark would not profit from a Russian-dominated Baltic, and that their neutral trade would not survive. He was anxious to get to Reval before the Russians could retreat to Cronstadt – indeed, he told St Vincent he would have been there two weeks earlier, except that Parker would not pass Denmark without a political settlement, fearing their batteries could stop his supplies. Such feeble conduct made him ill and anxious to go home.[66] His terms were lenient, because Britain held the Danish colonies and trade hostage, and could easily burn Copenhagen. It was best not to do so, because it would make reconciliation more difficult.[67] The purpose of the armistice was to move Hyde Parker.[68]

After six days of bluff and counter-bluff, the British settled for Danish neutrality for a period of fourteen weeks, the time Nelson believed he needed to deal with the Russians. The terms were made that much better for the Danes by news that the Tsar had died; they no longer needed to fear reprisals from their mighty ally. The British did not hear this news for another two days. While the negotiations were under way, Nelson placed a large order with the Royal Copenhagen Porcelain works,[69] an event still celebrated in the company's Copenhagen showroom!

While the negotiations dragged on Parker kept the bomb vessels ready, fitted out the *Holsten* as a hospital ship, and repaired the fleet so he could proceed as soon as he had finished with the Danes. His official dispatch contained effusive praise of Nelson's zeal. Fortunately for his peace of mind he had no idea that St Vincent had just written a reply to his letter of 23 March, expecting the complete destruction of the Danish fleet.[70] As soon as the armistice had been signed on the morning of 9 April, Parker exploited the terms, demanding water and fresh victuals. He also moved the bomb vessels.

Parker's report stressed that the armistice kept the fleet effective and the narrows open for the rest of the campaign, while any attack on Copenhagen would have rendered the critical bomb vessels useless for operations against Russia.[71] On 13 April the fleet passed over the Drogden Shallows into the Baltic, the two flagships having to take out their guns to reduce their draught. On the same day Captain 'Bounty' Bligh, now commanding the shattered *Monarch*, convoyed *Holsten* and *Isis* back to Britain.[72] These three ships were too badly damaged for local repairs. A frigate was sent to locate the Swedes, and offer them the same terms as the Danes. When she returned on 15 April, reporting that they were at sea off Carlscrona, Nelson had himself rowed from the *St George* to the *Elephant*, in case the fleet went into action while his flagship was disarmed.

The political situation in the Baltic, meanwhile, was changing rapidly. News of Paul's murder and the change of Russian policy reached London on 13 April, in time to influence the initial response to the battle. The Cabinet elected to exploit the new Russian policy, suspending the orders of 14 March to attack Reval and the other Russian ports. Now Parker should check if the embargo on British merchant ships had been lifted. He could suspend hostilities as long as the Russians were prepared to negotiate and the Revel Fleet did not attempt to leave harbour. Hostilities could be opened after twelve hours' notice.[73] Arriving off Carlscrona on 19 April, the Swedish fleet was sighted at a distance, and Parker signalled for a chase, but on further inspection it was clear that they were secure inside the rocky archipelago. As the fleet waited for reinforcements off Bornholm Parker was once more paralysed by indecision. Should he sail for Revel, or watch the Swedes?

Back in Britain there was no doubt who had won the glory. Lord Spencer stressed that Nelson 'need be in no anxiety about the feelings of the Country on your account. They give, as they ought, the whole merit in so very hazardous and difficult an attack to the man who carried [it] into execution, and the battle of Copenhagen will be as much coupled with the name of Nelson as that of the Nile.' Furthermore, 'the universal applause of a grateful nation and having already been looked up to as the best proof of our Glory in War, will most probably be blest as the principal instrument of procuring an honourable peace'.[74] The King and Parliament offered their thanks, while St Vincent sent the news to the Lord Mayor of London, praising Nelson for having 'greatly outstripped' himself and promising to attend to his wishes.[75] These wishes were, as ever, headed by the desire that his favourite brother Maurice be promoted. This was done: Maurice would have an extra £400 a year, but not a seat at the Navy Board. Davison reported him contented,[76] but Nelson himself was not. Sadly Maurice died suddenly on 24 April.[77] It was a terrible loss for a man who loved his family above all things.

On 20 April Colonel Stewart, who had been privy to much of the discussion, and all of the fighting, had arrived in London, taking with him the view of Parker's conduct that was held on the quarter-deck of the *St George* and the *Elephant*. The following day Parker was recalled because of his pusillanimous conduct, foolish handling of battle, and feeble negotiations. The Armistice was upheld, and Nelson was ordered to take command.[78] St Vincent now had a better appreciation of the battle, and stressed to Nelson that he had 'command of the Baltic Fleet, on the conduct of which the dearest interests of this Nation depend'. He must be ready for sudden changes in Russian policy, despite the death of Paul. He had commended Stewart to the King, but sent him back to the fleet as he would be 'of great use to you, both in treating and fighting, if there should be again occasion'.[79]

The Earl's explanation of his decision to the King was that:

> On a consideration of all the circumstances that have occurred since Sir Hyde Parker was first entrusted with the command of the Baltic Fleet, and the difficulties which he has raised on every occasion, wherein a prompt and vigorous execution of his duty has been required, he is under great apprehension that your Majesty's service will derive no advantage from Sir Hyde's continuance in that command.[80]

This was not entirely honest. Parker's real fault was that he did not comprehend war at the same level as his second in command, and lacked the political courage to act on his own judgement. Anyone going out with Nelson under their command was sure to lose their reputation. He would be given any credit, while they must explain a failure.

It had been Nelson's comments – relayed by Stewart, who shared his view – that persuaded the ministers to remove Parker for dilatory proceedings. They may also have been aware that the new situation required a new leader. Having broken the back of the conspiracy the British now wanted to ram home their advantage, securing a full retraction from the Tsar, and for this mission a fleet under the international celebrity Nelson would be far more powerful than one commanded by an officer who had so obviously failed.

On 21 April Rear Admiral Totty joined the fleet off Bornholm with reinforcements. The following day a Russian messenger from Copenhagen informed Parker that the Tsar had opened negotiations with London, and expected him to refrain from any hostile action against League members. Parker returned to Kioge Bay to wait for orders.[81] Inevitably Nelson found the delays that followed the armistice soul-destroying. Even by 20 April, he was writing to Emma that he was desperate to go home, and reminiscing about 'days of ease, and nights of pleasure' on a voyage from Palermo the previous year.[82] He also instructed Davison to tell Fanny that he wished to be left alone, threatening to live abroad for ever on his Sicilian estate.[83] The fact that he had the time to deal with private affairs suggests he was losing focus: there appeared to be no further prospect of action, or of being able to reward his followers.[84] Like Nelson after the Nile, Parker had burnt the captured ships, lacking the time and manpower to refit them while further service beckoned. St Vincent promised to pay handsomely for the one remaining ship and head money, but rejected the idea of a grant as ruinous.[85]

On 29 April, the Swedes sent a flag of truce. Sensing the campaign was over, Nelson requested permission to go home for his health. Parker, doubtless glad to see the back of his over-mighty subordinate, now there was no prospect of any further fighting, merely requested a surgeon's report 'for form's sake', and provided a passage in Graham Hamond's frigate HMS *Blanche*.[86]

St Vincent, meanwhile, was troubled by the strategic situation. He called a Cabinet to the Admiralty on 4 May and requested they sign new orders for the fleet, as the current disposition would enable the Swedes to join the Russians at Revel.[87] These were issued the following day. St Vincent approved Parker's conciliatory attitude towards the Russians and the suspension of hostilities that had been agreed following discussions with the Russian Minister at Copenhagen; now Nelson was to place the fleet to prevent the Swedish and Russian fleets joining at Revel or Cronstadt. He should inform the Swedes that he would not attack them if they stayed at Carlscrona. However Britain would be at war with Denmark at the end of the armistice period, if the grounds of dispute were not resolved.[88] The Admiralty was happy to press on, expecting the situation would ultimately return to the *status quo ante*: Britain already held the Swedish and Danish West Indian islands as a pledge for their future behaviour.[89]

On 4 May Parker learnt that his decision to suspend hostilities had been correct. But any satisfaction he took was short-lived; he was astonished by orders to resign the command to Nelson, who was to have sailed that day for the recovery of his health. Admiral Young reported that Parker received the decision 'with strongly marked indignity': he complained not only about the insufficiency of his forces, but also that Nelson had disobeyed his orders – ignoring the reality that had Nelson withdrawn, he would have exposed his force 'to certain destruction', as Young acknowledged. Now Parker waited on Nelson to deliver his public orders and instructions. The following day he resigned his command, and took Nelson's place on the *Blanche*. She ran aground passing through the Sound, and he was obliged to call on the Danes for assistance. It was a sorry end to a feeble command.

Although Nelson believed that the command had come too late, he was quick to assure the Admiralty that he would do the best that 'my abilities and a most wretched state of health will allow'. He remained convinced that his health was failing, constantly asking to be relieved, though without making an official request.[90] Stewart was convinced that Nelson's ill health was due to chagrin, not sickness, and Nelson himself realised, as he told Emma, that he could not leave until the business was finished.[91] He was anxious to do something decisive to show the Russians that Britain still had a fleet in the Baltic.[92] He took the best of the seventy-fours to Revel, while the sixty-fours, ex-Indiamen, the flotilla and other odd packets remained to watch Carlscrona. Had the war continued he planned to attack the twelve Russian battleships lying alongside a wooden mole at Reval. Now the mission had changed, he was to keep the Swedes and Russians divided, until the peace was secure, and dressed up his coercive visit as a compliment to the Tsar. If the Russians were still hostile he was ready to act.

Arriving off Revel on 11 May, Nelson was disappointed to find the Russians had moved their squadron three days earlier – the more so as he could see no reason why his force could not have destroyed them where they lay. As he reported to his confidant Vansittart, and through him to Prime Minister Addington, the British should have been off to Revel on 2 April, when the annihilation of the Russians fleet would have brought Denmark and Sweden, if not Russia, to their senses. The problem had been getting Parker past the Kronborg, or through the Belt; he seemed to want to wait in the Kattegat and fight the enemy there, 'a measure disgraceful to our country'.[93] His report to St Vincent was more measured, though equally menacing. 'We know the navigation, should circumstances call us here again.' He had gathered a wealth of hydrographic intelligence and other sailing information for this relatively unknown sea.[94] Next time it would be a lot easier.

The Russian response to the threat posed by Nelson and his squadron was extraordinary. They had sawn their way through thick ice, at enormous cost, to get the ships out of Revel before the British arrived, and were equally anxious to keep Nelson away from St Petersburg and the naval fortress/arsenal at Cronstadt. The Russians were well aware of their inability to match the impetuous, irresistible Royal Navy. Many British officers had served in the fleet of Tsaritsa Catherine, because they were far superior in all-round naval skills to their Muscovite contemporaries, and offered the Russian Navy a short cut to competence. This dependence only reinforced the sense of inferiority felt now that the British officers had been sent away, and British ships were coming. The forts at Revel and Cronstadt were weak: they would not have lasted long in the face of a determined British attack, directed by Nelson.

The Russians affected to be upset by Nelson's arrival, as a gesture open to 'misconstructions . . . at a moment of infinite importance to the interests of both countries'.[95] They asked him to leave the anchorage on 16 May. Well aware that the diplomatic discussions were in hand, he sent an emollient reply, hoisted anchor and stood down for Bornholm to rejoin Totty. As there was no chance of a battle and he had no desire 'to die a natural death',[96] he made an official application to be relieved on 17 May.[97]

Despite the disappointment of missing the enemy, and the chance of battle, Nelson continued to be the thorough professional. Anxious to keep his force efficient, he made careful use of captured stores and local food to improve the condition of the fleet. His fleet management was based on the existing routines established by St Vincent, and employed the standing Channel fleet report forms and orders. This was not merely to flatter the Earl: St Vincent had taken maintenance and health care to a new level, the better to keep his ships at sea, in front of the enemy, and away from the temptations of port.[98] As many of the Danish ships had been newly fitted out, he used their ropes to improve the rigging of several ships.[99] Nelson now had twenty-two battleships, forty-six other craft and not a man sick: 'a finer fleet never graced the ocean.'[100] He would do all he could to keep it that way, at the lowest cost.[101]

He also worked on the intelligence picture. Fremantle reported on

The first portrait of Nelson, by John Francis Rigaud, begun in 1777 when he was
appointed a Lieutenant, but heavily modified after his return to England as a heroic
Captain in 1780. The sword was a gift from his mentor, Maurice Suckling – patronage
enabled Nelson to reach a high rank early in his career, and this was a talisman he would
take with him in every battle, bar Trafalgar.

2 In 1785 Nelson's lifelong friend Cuthbert Collingwood painted him more as a boy than a man. Collingwood was a decade older than his friend, but as his junior on the Navy List he was condemned forever to follow in his footsteps from their first ship to their final command.

3 *Nelson Boarding the San Josef at Cape St Vincent*: George Jones added a touch of romance to the drama of the double boarding that made Nelson (with Suckling's sword in his hand) a household name. No one else had ever taken two enemy ships in such dramatic style, or taken such care to ensure the world heard of his achievement.

4 As his boat approached the beach at Tenerife, Nelson was hit in the right arm, which had to be amputated. Richard Westall's image of the wounded hero celebrated the quick thinking of Josiah Nisbet, whose tourniquet saved the Admiral's life. Despite his wound Nelson was careful to keep hold of his uncle's sword.

5 *The Battle of the Nile*: Thomas Whitcombe shows the moment the French ships opened fire, as *Goliath* and *Zealous* shaped to round the head of their line. The French have been caught at anchor, with the wind blowing down their line: they will be annihilated by the skilful application of overwhelming force.

6 George Arnaud's *The Destruction of L'Orient at the Battle of the Nile*: HMS *Alexander* remains close to the exploding French flagship, as debris is hurled into the night sky. Among the burning wreckage to land on her deck was one of Admiral Bruey's silver forks.

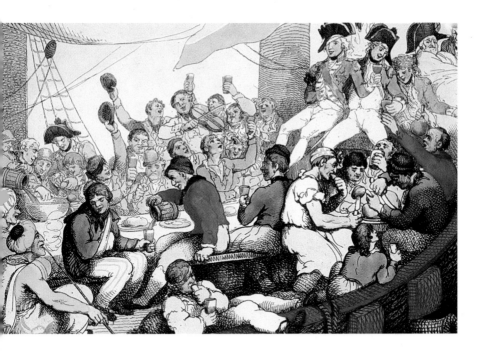

Nelson recreating with his brave tars after the glorious battle of the Nile: Rowlandson exaggerates Nelson's common touch, and misses the powerful religious element in his response to the triumph. However, such images helped to cement his popular appeal, and establish his central role in the national identity.

Nicolas Pocock's *The Battle of Copenhagen*, along with the other canvases commissioned for the official life, has become a standard way of viewing Nelson. After twenty years as a merchant ship captain, Pocock was a painstaking and exact painter of ships and coasts.

9 J. M. W. Turner's *The Battle of Trafalgar*: one of the most insightful artistic responses to Nelson. Commissioned by George IV, who recognised the magic of Nelson's life and was desperate to capture it for himself, the picture was ultimately given away by a King who did not understand the subject or the artist.

10 *The Death of Nelson*: Benjamin West's first attempt, engraved by James Heath, sold very well on publication in 1811. Despite its patent absurdity – having the crew as an audience on the upper deck, in the midst of a battle – it became the defining print.

11 Arthur Devis's *The Death of Nelson*: an altogether more impressive image than West's stylised inaccuracy. It catches the moment when the hero slipped away to join the gods, his earthly span at an end.

12 Nelson's uniform coat: complete with the hole caused by the fatal bullet on the left shoulder, this remains the most potent relic of his life.

13 Trafalgar Day 1905: the Navy League has dressed the column and a small crowd has braved the London smog to commemorate the centenary.

14 Benjamin West's *The Apotheosis of Nelson* of 1807, with Nelson posed as the dead Christ, carried in the arms of Victory to a mourning Minerva while Neptune watches. The signal 'England expects' gives the picture a motto. As a celebration of the cult of the hero, this combination of sacred and profane imagery was irreligious, if not blasphemous.

the Russian fleet and forts at Cronstadt, having been allowed to walk around the dockyard. The twelve ships from Revel were in poor condition, and none had been completely rigged. Most of the fleet was dismantled. It was obvious that hasty efforts had been made to put Cronstadt in a state of defence: a new fort similar to the Danish Trekroner was under construction and the flotilla was fitting out.[102] Stewart produced a plan of Revel Bay, which Nelson sent home to be lodged in the new Hydrographic Office, accompanied by his plan for an attack.[103] It was still there fifty years later, when his plan was revived for the Crimean War.[104]

Returning westward, Nelson encountered Lord St Helen's, the new Minister to St. Petersburg, at sea on 20 May. With becoming theatricality, he stressed his anxiety to be ready in case negotiations broke down, more to stiffen the arm of the envoy than from any belief that hostilities might resume. The Russian-speaking Lieutenant Thesiger and two luggers were sent with the envoy, to keep up communications.[105]

On 24 May Nelson rejoined Totty off Bornholm. The same day junior envoy Benjamin Garlike at St Petersburg reported the Russians would release the impounded merchant ships, and would also repair them. To preserve the Tsar's dignity, this would be described as an act of justice, rather than a response to English demands. The embargo had been lifted immediately after Nelson left Revel on the 17 May. England and Russia would negotiate an end to any differences without third parties; Russia would then dictate terms to Prussia, Sweden and Denmark. Garlike was confident Russia would not expect England to 'abandon any one of the principles of Maritime Law'.[106] This would be a complete success for British policy. St Helen's reached the Russian capital on 29 May. With the negotiations close to completion, Nelson suddenly found the Russian attitude friendly, but the invitation to St Petersburg came too late: he was already off Rostock, heading west.[107]

Back in London St Vincent had somewhat prematurely told the King that:

> Lord Nelson, who is in the habit of complaining of ill-health – has, it appears, received considerable benefit from the additional responsibility which has recently been thrown on him, and will, Lord St Vincent has no doubt, be able to continue in the command.[108]

Nelson's official request for relief galvanised the Admiralty, and a week later the King may have been surprised to learn that St Vincent was now 'very apprehensive, unless his lordship is immediately relieved, his life may be in danger'. It would be difficult to find a suitable flag officer, 'considering the present critical situation in the affairs with the Northern Powers'.[109] The following day he settled on Nelson's old friend Charles Pole. Already commissioned for an overseas command, Pole sailed on 7 June. Acknowledging a number of letters from Nelson, the Earl expressed his 'deepest concern' at his state of health:

> To find a fit successor, your Lordship well knows, is no easy task, for I never saw the man in our Profession, excepting yourself and Troubridge, who possessed the magic art of infusing the same spirit into others which inspired his actions . . . Your Lordship's whole conduct, from your first appointment to this hour, is the subject of our constant admiration; it does not become me to make comparisons. All agree there is but one Nelson; that he may long continue the pride of his country is [my] fervent wish.[110]

Admiralty Secretary Nepean agreed: 'I consider your indisposition to be a serious public misfortune in the present moment.'[111] Lord Hood understood the problem: 'It is undoubtedly to be lamented that the Russian fleet at Revel was not attacked when evidently at your mercy. This I imagine to be the primary cause of your complaints.' [112] Official permission for return on health grounds was sent the same day.[113]

Meanwhile, on 8 June a British government Official Proclamation lifted the embargo on Russian, Swedish and Danish shipping.[114] The government was anxious for the campaign to end; with a French invasion threatening, part of the Baltic fleet was moved to Cork even before Nelson came home. If any of the Baltic powers stepped out of line, they would be attacked without hesitation, but this looked increasingly unlikely.[115] The Danes were blatantly in breach of the armistice, equipping ships, reinforcing defences and parading French officers at the Crown Prince's elbow. Nelson, who had not yet received his permission to leave, sent Captain Sutton to isolate Denmark from Norway, and considered going back to bombard Copenhagen.[116] Not that he was worried by the prospect of fighting any combination of Baltic navies: though large in numbers, they were in every other respect insignificant.[117] Nelson knew the best use of his time was to make the fleet efficient and keep it fully stored, ready to go anywhere. His fleet-management skills had convinced St Vincent that he could command a major theatre in the future. The Earl rejoiced that Nelson's labours had 'finished so advantageously for your country and honourably to yourself'.[118]

Permission to return home finally arrived on 13 June. The campaign was over, and Nelson was anxious there should be no inquiry into Parker's conduct, which he characterised as 'idleness' rather than 'criminality'.[119] On 17 June the convention was signed at St Petersburg, after further Russian attempts to revive the old nonsense about free ships and free goods. When St Helen's countered by declaring that the King would not accept 'a principle so injurious to His most valuable interests', and was 'determined to combat its establishment at every risk, and by the most persevering & vigorous exertions', Count Panin gave way and signed.[120]

Two days later Nelson hauled down his flag in Kioge Bay, boarded the brig *Kite* and sailed for England, reaching Yarmouth on 1 July. He did not leave without thanking his fleet and subordinates. The junior flag officers spoke for many. Deeply affected by Nelson's approval, Totty promised to 'trace the Path to Glory which Your Lordship has so long pursued, to the eminent advantage of your country and your own immortal honour'.[121] Poor Totty did not get much further along the path, dying within a year, victim of the unhealthy West Indies command.

Nelson's last service in the Baltic was highly significant. He gathered the intelligence necessary to ensure the British could always come back. On 12 June he sent in 'remarks made on the passages of the Belt and drawings of the same, which I request you will be pleased to lodge in the records of the Admiralty, that they may be referred to in case they are wanted'. The Board minuted: 'Acquaint his Lordship that My Lords very much approve of his having employed the persons therein mentioned on this important service.'[122] Nelson's work on the charts continued. On 21 June *Alecto* and *Amazon* rejoined the fleet after passing through the Great Belt. *Alecto*'s captain reported the passage 'a very desirable one'.[123] Suitably impressed, Pole reported that no time would be lost, and no risk incurred, by coming home through the Belt, and he would be glad to make the attempt. He sent the sixty-four-gun *Polyphemus* and *Dart* 'to examine well the passage of the Belt'.[124] Four days later he reported to Nelson: 'We found the passage of the Belt all that could be wished for large ships.'[125]

It would be mid-July before Sweden and Denmark accepted the

Convention, dictated to them by London and St Petersburg, and until they did Pole remained with a squadron at Kioge, finally departing on 20 July. The fleet was given new instructions to pass the Belt, and after a slow but secure passage emerged into the Kattegat on 1 August. Pole's final report stressed that the Belt was much better for big ships. The Admiralty was very pleased and ordered that the report be sent 'to Mr Dalrymple [the new Hydrographer of the Navy] for his information'.[126]

Britain had defeated a massive threat to her security, and re-emphasised the value of sea control as a decisive weapon of war. Without Nelson, this would not have happened: not only did he guarantee the victory, he also created a highly efficient combat-ready fleet out of a collection of hurriedly manned old ships, and gathered strategically significant intelligence for the Hydrographic Office. The Baltic command showed Nelson at full power, despite his protestations of ill health. For France, by contrast, the Baltic campaign was a major defeat, and Bonaparte was among the few men to mourn the mad Tsar, who had been a vital asset in his war with Britain. Had Paul been able to continue his aggressive programme, Russia would inevitably have been humiliated and Bonaparte would have seized the chance to push his power further east, without Britain being able to influence affairs. But now Bonaparte was forced to concede the need for peace with Britain, and Nelson's next task would be to block his attempts to coerce her into unnecessary concessions. He landed at Yarmouth on 29 July, and lost no time setting out for London.[127]

CHAPTER XII

Defying Bonaparte

1801

With the end of the war in sight, the last remaining anomalies cleared away by the Baltic and Egyptian campaigns, Britain and France were in a position to negotiate. However, the peace process would see the role of the armed forces enhanced, rather than reduced.

Henry Addington's government lacked the heavyweight political figures of Pitt's team – but also the ideological prejudice that had prevented it from responding to a changing situation. While Foreign Secretary Grenville had been wholly opposed in principle to any peace with the French republican government, his replacement Lord Hawkesbury was more pragmatic, and with Cabinet concurrence opened negotiations with the French on 21 March. The British position was greatly improved by the battle of the Copenhagen Roads, and the subsequent collapse of the Armed Neutrality. The French position in Egypt was crumbling, and Malta could not hold out much longer.[1]

In early March Bonaparte sent Admiral Latouche Tréville to Boulogne to concentrate the ships for a planned invasion. This was a bluff: there were few ships available, and those at other ports found it very difficult to creep along the coast to join his command. The main purpose of the manoeuvre was to create the impression of a threat to combine with his overtures for peace – this was Bonaparte's favourite negotiating technique.[2] In May and June, Bonaparte, real-

Horatia, Nelson's daughter, aged two

ising his extra-European strength was slipping away, moved his troops to the Channel to increase his diplomatic leverage. The fact that the threat was not real was less significant than the determination it indicated. The French began to look to novel weapons, like Robert Fulton's submarine, prompting much ridicule in Britain. By late July the threat of invasion appeared to be growing, as new camps opened between Boulogne and Bruges. The public was alarmed: on 21 July the Army warned that invasion was imminent, the following day a mass rally of volunteers in Hyde Park demonstrated the national will to resist, and on the 24th the nation's hero was called on once again.

St Vincent created a new command for Nelson: he was to control all the ships and vessels on the coast between Orfordness and Beachy Head, without interfering with the existing North Sea, Nore and Downs commands. He was to position his forces along the coasts to block or destroy any invasion attempt, and attack enemy invasion craft in their assembly ports. St Vincent justified his decision to the local commanders by stressing that recent intelligence suggested invasion was highly probable. Therefore it was necessary to place the whole defence force under one officer, 'who will have no other duty to perform than that of attending to this important object'. These instructions were based on discussions with the Earl and Nelson, 'Memorandum on the Defence of the Thames Estuary etc.', combining stationary blockships and local craft with a concentrated sea-going force to intercept any attempt by the French to cross the channel. He considered forty thousand to be the smallest likely invasion force.[3]

It was an extensive command: six battleships, all of them small, shallow draught vessels, seven frigates, eleven sloops and brigs, thirty-two gun-vessels, seven bombs, four batteries and seven assorted merchant vessels.[4] Many of the larger vessels were old or ex-enemy units, and the smaller craft were of limited value – easily replaced and, like much of the Baltic fleet, expendable. Nelson arrived at Sheerness on 27 July, and within twenty-four hours he had imposed his ideas on the forces in the Thames and Medway – the mastery of navigation of these rivers that he had acquired in the 1770s had not been lost. Aware that he was building the defence system up from the foundations, he was in a hurry to get to Deal, consult Admiral Lutwidge and continue his inspection.[5] The easy communication with London, by mail, and the shutter telegraph between London and Deal,[6] enabled Nelson to consult the Admiralty on all important issues. This would be his first and only taste of command close to home.

St Vincent recognised the existing system was a shambles, and was happy for Nelson to restructure it more logically; but he also favoured bombarding Boulogne harbour, if it could be done without undue risk and without damaging Nelson's health.[7] Arriving in the Downs on 30 July, Nelson decided to proceed to the French coast.

He had consulted local community leaders on the Sea Fencibles, a volunteer corps of maritime professionals who were excused impressment in return for their services in an emergency. It was clear that these men needed to be promised they would not be removed from the coast, and even then they could not afford to give up their jobs until the emergency occurred. He took Captain Edward Owen, a talented coastal commander with excellent local knowledge, and Captain Fyers of the Royal Artillery, who had commanded the bombs at Copenhagen, to see if Boulogne was open to attack.[8] While St Vincent read the intelligence as indicating a real threat, Nelson quickly realised the British defences were improving so quickly that it was doubtful if the French would ever leave port.[9]

At Boulogne Nelson found only fifty to sixty boats, including many outside the harbour, and he decided to attack with bomb vessels. Nelson had seven bombs under his command, more than half the entire British force of this vital power-projection asset.[10] A similar force had been deployed to the Baltic. The conversion of such craft was the most obvious demonstration that the new offensive strategy was based on attacking from the sea, rather than relying on allied armies. While St Vincent warned him not to expect too much from a sea bombardment, he also revealed the thinking that would keep Nelson on this station until the peace was settled:

> Not only this Board, but the Country derives so much confidence from your Lordship's being at the head of our home defences that apprehension seems to be dispelled from the public mind.[11]

On 3 August Nelson tried the bombs, firing a dozen shells before the wind shifted. His object was to destroy the French invasion boats, which struck him as incapable of being rowed or sailed one mile towards England in the face of the existing naval forces.[12] The following day the wind shifted to the south-west and he resumed firing. Seven or eight French craft were sunk or badly damaged, and he reassured the Prime Minister that 'the French army will not embark at Boulogne for the invasion of England'.[13]

Satisfied he had shown the enemy they could not come out of harbour without being attacked, he issued a morale-boosting memorandum to the squadron, praising their skill and enthusiasm, before moving on to inspect the Dutch and Belgian ports.[14] Before he had gone very far, Nelson received Admiralty orders to persuade the Sea Fencibles to go to sea and put back to the Downs. Unwilling as he was to serve as a recruiting officer for the volunteers, he quickly issued a passionate call to arms: when the French meant to invade, every man owed a duty to his country, a duty already being fulfilled by the military volunteers. The seamen's task was to defend 'the sovereignty of the Narrow Seas, on which no Frenchman has yet dared to sail with impunity'.[15] The combination of patriotic appeal and the land example was well calculated, but ultimately unsuccessful. In truth he was less concerned by the French, now he had been to Boulogne, condemning the current alarm as a fabrication of 'some scoundrel [French] emigrant'. He thought the Flemish ports a more likely invasion base, but he had yet to visit them,[16] and St Vincent agreed:

> I have always been of the opinion that the real attempt of the enemy will be made from the Dutch and Flemish harbours, because of the great number of flat-bottomed vessels constantly employed in the inland navigation of those countries, besides that there is always a large body of troops in them.

Flushing, however, lay within Admiral Dickson's North Sea command. The bombardment of Boulogne had achieved more than the Earl had hoped, 'and much more in raising the spirit of the people here, to a degree not to be conceived'. It was a theme he returned to the following day, by now aware that Nelson was getting restive. 'The public mind is so very much tranquillised by your being at your post, it is extremely desirable that you should continue there.' To return to town now 'would have the worst possible effect at this critical juncture. I will explain farther when we meet.' The disposition of Sea Fencibles was left to him 'from the unbounded confidence we repose in you'.[17] Troubridge, by contrast, urged him to impress the Fencibles if they would not volunteer – a truly stupid idea, given the sensitivity of seafaring communities to the threat of the press, and the need to build loyalties and patriotism in the present emergency. Nelson decided the best policy was to leave the men alone until an emergency, trusting to their loyalty and self-interest to oppose an invasion. Besides, he was already very confident that the French 'cannot come'.[18]

Anxious to finish this command, which was costing him money he could ill afford,[19] he told Emma that he would come ashore by mid-September. Still in thrall to her, he promised not to dine out without her agreement. He longed for the company of the Hamiltons[20] – but however pleasant such thoughts were, as they had been when he was writing to Fanny half a decade before, they were but a brief daydream for a mind focused on the enemy, and plotting their destruction. The apologetic tone of his letters to Emma suggests that hers, which he destroyed, often made rather unpleasant reading. When she was not threatening to become the Prince of Wales's mistress, she was condemning him to stay out of company.[21] Fortunately he had more important things to do than discuss trifles with her; he never allowed his emotional torment to affect his professional judgement.

He was going to look into Flushing, the other potential invasion base, where the blockade was handled by one of his best officers, Edward Owen of the frigate *Nemesis*. Owen's mastery of coastal navigation, aggressive instincts and vision would find ample employment in the Channel on either side of the 1802 peace.[22] Owen lay off Flushing, reporting seven enemy vessels in roads, including a sixty-four-gun battleship. He believed they could be attacked by boats, but as this required a three-hour row from his current anchorage he was being rather optimistic in the face of strong currents. He was also well aware that the enemy could retreat under the cover of shore batteries or further down the Scheldt. If troops were available he advised taking Flushing or an offshore island; he volunteered for any operation and waited anxiously for Nelson.[23] Recognising another ardent spirit, Nelson wanted to attack, but only after a reconnaissance.[24]

St Vincent relayed another instalment of the French plan to bluff the British into a hasty and weak peace. Bonaparte had appointed himself Generalissimo of the Army of Invasion, declaring that 'we look to Flanders for the grand effort'. Consequently Flushing was one of the few places 'where any enterprise of the kind can be attempted with any reasonable prospect of success'. St Vincent also had the Hydrographer send every scrap of information on the port.[25] As might be expected, the old Earl favoured Troubridge's approach to the reluctant Sea Fencibles if they would not come out in adequate numbers, but he was pleased by Nelson's delicate handling of the three Port

Admirals with whom his command overlapped: 'It is, in truth a difficult card you have to play. Pray take care of your health, than which nothing is of so much importance to the Country at large.' The promise of the Mediterranean command remained the bait for Nelson; St Vincent told him that 'Our negotiation is drawing near its close and must terminate one way or other in the course of a few days, and I need not add how very important it is that the enemy should know you are constantly opposed to him.'[26]

As Nelson gathered intelligence from his commanders, he quickly perceived that the enemy had too few craft to mount an invasion. There were only two thousand troops at Boulogne, and boats enough for a mere 3,600 at Ostend. The conclusion was inevitable: 'Where, my dear Lord, is our Invasion to come from?' He was developing plans to attack Flushing, but being so close to London he would consult the Earl before risking a major operation. It did not help that he was being publicly ridiculed for this puny mode of warfare. His response would be to lead the fleet into Flushing, if the ministers agreed. He remained anxious for peace, and required nursing.[27] This last reference was doubtless his code for getting back to Emma. As he explained to Davison, there was simply nothing to be done 'on the great scale'.[28]

From his station with the Grand Fleet off Brest, Collingwood could see powerful French forces gathering to invade Ireland. But he knew that if they put to sea when the gales had blown the British ships away, they would be unequal to the elements. Nelson would do all he could to destroy the invasion shipping, despite the difficult navigation: 'however, he will make a fair experiment, and at least let them know what they are to expect when they venture beyond' their ports.[29]

Encouraged by news of the French capitulation in Egypt, added to Saumarez's victory in the Gulf of Gibraltar, St Vincent recognised peace was close. But he was not going to let his chief asset rest until the deal was done. His show of concern for Nelson's health was mere formality: he was convinced the ailments were all in the mind, and advised him to ignore the mischevous wits who were mocking his small-scale warfare. 'Be assured no service whatever can be of greater importance than that Your Lordship is employed in, and, as we have every reason to believe it cannot be of long duration, I trust in God that you will be enabled to go through with it.' Expecting the main French effort to be aimed at Ireland, with diversionary demonstrations at Dunkirk and Ostend, he would approve anything Nelson proposed with his existing force, but saw no need for consultation.[30]

Instead of setting course for Flushing, as everyone was expecting, Nelson had quietly developed a plan to capture or destroy the boats lying outside the harbour at Boulogne. He would have preferred the as yet unseen opportunities of Flushing, but for this he needed troops and other assets that were not available. His orders were highly detailed, using fifty-seven boats in four divisions to overwhelm the twenty-four enemy vessels. It was a large-scale version of the common British practice of cutting out enemy vessels with boats. His purpose was to expose the fraudulent French threat.

At Boulogne, Latouche Tréville was prepared: having no offensive object, he could deploy all his forces for a strictly defensive action. His preparations paid off: the line of boats outside the pier was prepared and fully manned, with a lot of heavy ground tackle and cables used to secure the craft in position, and to each other. He noted the preparations around the flagship, HMS *Medusa,* on the afternoon of 15 August, warning his men to expect a night attack. Nelson's plans were thorough, and would have been successful against most opponents, but this French admiral was a wily old fox. After dark, the four divisions of boats rowed in, but in the darkness they were separated by the wind and tide, arriving in fragments, one division missing the French flotilla altogether. The combination of limited attacking strength and well-prepared defences negated the usual British advantages in skill, daring and determination. One or two boats were carried, but the moorings could not be cut, and the French recaptured them with heavy supporting fire from the shore. Desperate to prove himself, and to earn post rank, Nelson's young favourite and *aide de camp* Captain Edward Parker pressed on, but suffered a horrific double fracture of the thigh, and had to be carried away. As the other officers were disabled the attack petered out. Unable to take part – for the want of an arm, rather than from any sense that vice admirals did not engage in boat work – Nelson was forced to wait and peer into the darkness as his men went to work, taking some comfort from writing out his anxieties to Emma.

By first light it was clear the attack had failed with heavy losses: forty-five killed and 128 wounded from nine hundred men. French losses were ten dead and thirty-four wounded. Nelson was distraught, the defeat compounded by terrible injuries to Parker and another young favourite. However, he rose to the occasion with characteristic flair. He reported the failure, and praised the astonishing bravery of his officers and men. He stressed that the object was worthy of their sacrifice, and passed on a report that the French had moored their vessels with chains. However, he did not flinch from taking full responsibility for the failure. Heavy losses among the best men from *Leyden* and *Medusa* would force him to postpone an attack on Flushing.[31]

Having read Nelson's letter and sent it to the King,[32] St Vincent knew the defeat would depress Nelson's spirits. He enlisted Addington to send an encouraging letter, while repeating his own commendation after the failure at Tenerife: 'It is not given to us to command success', and noting the 'zeal and courage' displayed. Nelson immediately communicated these sentiments to the squadron, and promised to take them to glory, if the French would only cast off their chains.[33] While his next letter to Emma still moaned because the Admiralty would not let him come to London on private business, he was already planning another operation.[34]

London gossip had it that Nelson attacked with no purpose, on some notion of his own. Even Hood repeated this canard,[35] wholly unaware that St Vincent was directing the campaign, leaving only the execution to Nelson. It was also unjust and ignorant. The attack, whatever the outcome, had shown the French that they could not leave ships on the coast without being attacked, and forced them to adopt extensive defensive measures, further reducing the slight possibility of an invasion.

St Vincent had no doubt it had been worthwhile; he stressed his unquestioning support for anything Nelson planned and the 'incalculable importance to your country' of his health. Addington argued that the Boulogne attack had confirmed British naval superiority, 'disinclining the enemy to contest it'. The losses were to be deplored 'but they have fallen in a good cause'.[36] Nelson agreed: 'Our loss is trifling, all circumstances considered.' He explained that St Vincent and Hood disagreed fundamentally on the best method of securing the coast: the former favoured a close watch, the latter pulling back everything onto the English coast apart from fast cutters.[37] He preferred offensive action, commending a smart piece of boat work that destroyed six French vessels, and a considerable quantity of naval stores.[38]

Flushing remained the preferred target, however. Troubridge sent every scrap of information, and Owen updated his report with new sketches and information. Nelson pressed Owen for more, sending detailed queries, hoping to replace his losses and arrive off Flushing ready for an immediate attack with thirty vessels. He would lead in with the *Leyden* and *Medusa*, and other craft would support, buoying the channel as he went.[39] When he arrived off Flushing, local pilots declared it impossible to attack or retreat without buoys, a fair wind and a suitable tide. Captain Owen had been too optimistic, ignoring sandbanks and tides: 'We cannot do impossibilities.'

The operation was 'out of the question'. Instead he would assemble a powerful force under Dungeness to counter any French moves. Closer inspection the following day only confirmed his decision, not least from the paucity of ships to be attacked, and the ease with which they could retreat.[40] He stressed the impossibility of the operation to Colonel Stewart, who knew as well as any man alive that Nelson would do whatever was possible. He also confessed a growing sense of frustration with his thankless task:

> I know that many of my friends think that my present command is derogatory to my rank. I cannot think that doing my best in the situation I was desired to hold can be so. My war, it is true, is against boats; but I have one consolation, that since my command not one merchant vessel has been taken by the enemy.[41]

The Earl accepted the decision to give up the attack on Flushing, and doubted the utility of a fireship attack on Boulogne. He let Nelson know that the peace negotiations were coming to a close, and promised to inform him as soon as the terms were settled. The problem would be keeping Nelson in command when he could not attack, and knew that peace was imminent.[42] He saw no reason to remain 'beyond the moment of alarm'.[43]

One strategy was the promise of the Mediterranean, which had some basis in reality: St Vincent wrote that the officers of the *St George*, apart from Hardy, were kept in place 'to be in the way of his Lordship on a future occasion, which I am not at liberty to communicate'[44] – though he meant the Mediterranean, of course. This promise was combined with a little moral blackmail. The Earl employed his trusted lieutenant Nepean to stress the point. Nepean claimed it was his personal opinion that it would be improper for Nelson to leave his post now; it would be 'an act which might injure you in the opinion of the public':

Your desiring permission to haul down your flag on the 14th, will do you an irreparable injury. Let me conjure you to abandon the idea. It is impossible things can remain long in their present state; but if at the period you have fixed upon for taking that step, the question of Peace and War should remain undecided, and it should really be an object to you to come to town for a few days, I do not think that the Board would offer the least objection to it, but rely upon it my dear Lord, that your relinquishing your command is the last thing you ought to think of.

He added that the service entrusted to him was honourable and flattering, it would not require him to be at sea very often, and he should now look only to the means of making himself comfortable at Deal 'till something may turn up that may be consonant with your wishes'.[45]

Although the Hamiltons and brother William and his wife were with Nelson at Deal, helping to lift the gloom of young Parker's continued struggle with his injuries, Nelson was anxious to leave. He had private affairs to settle: Emma had found him a house at Merton, and he was anxiously trying to raise £9,000 to pay for it. His solicitor William Haslewood negotiated the price down, while Davison loaned some of the money.[46] This would be the first house that Nelson lived in that he could call his own. Its attraction to Nelson was its location: only an admiral wrapped up in his duty would have selected a house just outside London, on the main road to Portsmouth. It was highly suggestive that for all the glory of his battles and the impact of his campaigns, he had trouble raising such a trifling amount to buy a low and undistinguished farmhouse.

St Vincent, whose own prize successes had made him very wealthy, should have been embarrassed to keep Nelson engaged on a station where there were so few rewards, had he chosen to reflect on the issue. Although a lack of concern with making money and complete indifference to keeping it explains some of Nelson's relative poverty, his country had not done enough to reward him, by contemporary standards, and he had reason to feel aggrieved. Such thoughts did not help him endure the last two months of his command. Soon after, he was obliged to sell the diamonds from various regal and imperial gifts, replacing them with paste.[47]

Matters were made worse by the continued newspaper squibs about Nelson's command, and there was even an attempt to blackmail him: £100 was demanded to prevent the publication of a hostile account of the Boulogne operation. And Nelson was hurt by the failure of his old friends, Troubridge and St Vincent, to recognise the human needs that underlay his call for release from duty. He had let both of them know of his inner turmoil, and could not understand how men he loved could treat him like this. Personal affections were at the core of his approach to war, and he was unable to disentangle them from the hard-nosed concerns that were driving policy in London. It is pointless to criticise Nelson for this failing, since it was inseparable from his whole approach to his duty. In reality, neither the Earl nor Troubridge was 'jealous' of him,[48] or anxious to do him down, as he began to suspect. There was no conspiracy against him, but it was necessary for the common good that he remain in command in the Channel until the French had settled.

Troubridge kept up the praise. All the world, he declared, was thoroughly satisfied with Nelson's arrangements, and felt at ease while he was afloat. He larded the compliments with news that Lord Keith and his captains in the Mediterranean had fallen out.[49] But for Nelson, the lure of the Mediterranean was beginning to pall: bored, unhappy and distressed by the lingering death of Parker, he claimed that he would soon be too worn out for that command. His views on the political situation, too, were gloomy:

> I pray God we may have Peace, when it can be had with honour; but I fear that the scoundrel Bonaparte wants to humble us, as he has done the rest of Europe – to degrade us in our own eyes, by making us give up all our conquests as proof of our sincerity for making peace, and then he will condescend to treat with us.[50]

If a peace on Napoleon's terms was not appealing, then nor were the alternatives any more attractive: 'I yet hope the negotiation is not entirely broken off, for we cannot alter the situation of France, or the Continent, and ours will become a war of defence.'[51] This style of war did not match either his preferences or his abilities. Still anxious to attack, Nelson decided that six French and Dutch battleships at Goree were the best target for a boat attack, if the weather was favourable.[52] St Vincent was less enthusiastic about the attack: he would not make a final decision until Nelson had spoken to a local expert, Captain Campbell, and ultimately decided that the operation fell into Admiral Dickson's command. His main preoccupation was peace.[53]

For all that St Vincent argued the Channel command was not unworthy of an Admiral of the Fleet, Nelson knew that any French move in the Channel would only be a diversion for the main effort to land in Ireland. As the Grand fleet was ready to block this move, he declared that 'if the war goes on, I shall hope to be employed against first rates', having only taken the Channel command 'at the desire of Mr Addington and Lord St Vincent'.[54]

By 20 September, Nelson was desperate to leave, especially as Sir William and Emma had gone back to London. However, he decided to scheme one last attempt on Boulogne, with a fireship commanded by Owen's younger brother, William. Plans were settled on 2 October: Owen would wait for a wind between west-north-west and north, set all sail, run the *Nancy* into the harbour just before high water and set her on fire, relying on wind and tide to take her up the harbour. The crew would get off once they were certain the vessel was on course. Just before the fireship set sail, the preliminaries of peace were signed, and Nelson used the telegraph to seek approval for the attack. The Admiralty demurred, and he lost the chance 'either to make Owen an Archangel or a post-Captain'.[55]

On 27 September Parker died, and Nelson confessed, 'I am almost grieved to death.' Despite his courage and his powerful sense that sacrifice was essential, he was never comfortable with death at the personal level: he did not like to be reminded of his own mortality, or that of those he loved. Parker had become an intimate, writing to Emma and handling much of the responsibility of the command. At the funeral, Nelson was seen leaning on a tree, sobbing uncontrollably. In a symbolic gesture, he had the dead man's hair cut off, and insisted that it be buried with him, a stipulation that was fulfilled. No one could replace Edward Parker in his heart – though Samuel Sutton, one of the heroes of Copenhagen, arrived in the *Amazon* to take over as *aide de camp* and deal with the routine of command.

Two days after Parker's death, Nelson turned to other business, reminding St Vincent that he had only taken the post to help the government, and that as no boat invasion was possible it was no longer a vice admiral's command.[56] The Earl decided to postpone offensive operations as soon as the preliminaries of peace were signed.[57] Nelson accepted the inevitable: he felt that the only alternative was to cut France off from all external trade, and go to war with all Europe and America to maintain the blockade.[58] In this he was absolutely correct. By the middle of 1812 Britain was indeed at war with almost all of Europe, and America, to uphold her economic war against the French Empire. It was a close-run thing, but Britain won through.

St Vincent was anxious to prevent any communication between

Britain and France, other than by official Dover–Calais message boat, and to keep Nelson at hand just in case the French tried any tricks.[59] The King agreed, having no faith in the present French government, and urging his ministers to keep up the defences.[60] Addington wrote to stress the importance of Nelson's remaining in post until the peace was settled. Nelson realised that this was 'to keep the merchants easy till hostilities cease in the Channel', and was happy to conduct this task: he took tremendous pride in the fact that not one English boat had been captured in the area under his command. Even if invasion was no longer likely, this was a good reason to keep the cruisers at sea. He promised Addington that once released he would get his health back, ready to 'take up the cudgels again', and ready for anything but a winter in the North Sea.[61]

On 14 October Nelson officially asked for permission to go ashore. The following day he learnt from the Admiralty that the preliminaries and a ceasefire had been signed.[62] The Earl could no longer refuse him permission to come to town, but until the definitive treaty was signed he must be continued in pay, 'although we may not have occasion to require your personal services at the head of squadron under your orders'. On 22 October Nelson began paying off his flotilla, and that evening he left for Merton. However, St Vincent was anxious to keep his absence from the public eye, stressing the need to restore his health.[63]

Addington, by contrast, hoped that Nelson would call at Downing Street. It would give him 'great pleasure to see, and to converse with [him], after the very interesting occurrences of the last three months'.[64] On 26 October he was introduced to the House of Lords in his new rank of Viscount, by Lord Hood, who had specifically requested the honour, and Lord Sydney. Four days later he made his maiden speech, seconding St Vincent's motion that the thanks of the House be given to Saumarez and his squadron with a short but powerful speech that stressed the importance to the fleet's success of naval education and sound doctrine.[65] Thereafter he made a number of speeches supporting ministerial policy, which were all the more significant because of the government's relative weakness in the Upper Chamber. On 3 November he upheld the terms of the peace as honourable and advantageous, while on the 13th he supported the Russian Treaty.

As he was still officially on leave, the new Viscount Nelson relied on Sutton at Deal to conduct the business of the squadron, collecting the details of those killed so that the Lloyds patriotic committee could make suitable payments to their families. Typically, his duty to his followers was uppermost in his mind, and perhaps the most outstanding example of this tendency was the Copenhagen medal question. Since 1794 it had become customary for the flag officers and captains at major fleet actions to be awarded a gold medal, specially struck to mark the occasion. Nelson already had a pair, for St Vincent and the Nile. He had moved heaven and earth to ensure Troubridge received the award for the Nile, despite his situation, and was anxious that those who had performed so nobly on 2 April should not be forgotten. He had raised the issue with St Vincent a month earlier: he would not wear his other medals until this injustice had been remedied.[66] The Earl was now caught in a very awkward position. With peace across Europe it was hardly the time to be noticing such services, especially as they were against a country with whom Britain was not officially at war, and in an action where the Commander in Chief had taken no active part. However, Nelson stated that he had been assured that medals would be awarded before he accepted the Channel command. St Vincent backtracked, denied any such promises had been made and reported he had recommended to the King and the Prime Minister that the measure would be inappropriate. Nelson in turn, declared himself 'thunder-struck' and 'truly made ill by your letter',[67] while the Earl feared the medal issue would open a Pandora's box of costly prize claims from the captors of the Danish and Swedish West Indian islands, which had all been returned.[68] Addington tried to fob Nelson off with a chat,[69] but the issue long outlived all three correspondents. Stewart raised it again with Addington and St Vincent in 1821, while Graham Hamond and other officers continued to question the justice of the decision until they died.[70] Not until the 1847 Naval General Service Medal was the event publicly noted with a bar for the battle, but by then there were few survivors, although Hamond used the occasion to resuscitate his claims.

The refusal of medals was indeed a monstrous injustice, inexcusable in a nation that sought to reward its heroes and encourage those who would follow. Nelson was equally offended by the City of London's failure to offer its customary vote of thanks on the Copenhagen victory: he never again dined with the Lord Mayor and City of London, or wore his other gold medals. As this refusal shows, his vanity never overrode his commitment to his followers: they had earned these marks of national and Royal approval in the hardest fought battle he had ever seen, and he would not be fobbed off with fine words.

It is an indication of the astonishing nature of Nelson's life that the first time he had ever slept in his own house was on his return ashore in October 1801. Nelson's house was ideally located for a senior naval officer expecting the call of duty in London, or back on the broad oceans. Strategically located at Merton, south-west of London and alongside the Portsmouth Road, it was no more than a modest farm-house without architectural pretensions, although a stream ran through the grounds. From the start, Nelson wanted it to be his house, and although Sir William and Emma would live with him, neither their furniture nor their servants were admitted. Nelson wisely left the decoration and improvements to Emma; his own taste went no further than battle pictures, portraits and trophies. Unfortunately, Emma's taste and style of living were far beyond the means of a vice admiral who had given half his pay to his cast-off wife, and a retired ambassador. By March 1803 she was broke. Fortunately Nelson never worried unduly about money: he was a good risk for a loan, as long as he lived to win more victories, and take more prizes. The Hamiltons also kept a house at 23 Piccadilly, doubling their costs for the dubious benefit of advancing Emma's social ambitions. Nelson had no need of an address in town, taking breakfast with Davison when attending the Admiralty or the House of Lords. Although ashore on leave, he remained on full pay and in command until the definitive peace treaty was signed in April 1803.

Emma assembled a cast of characters to people Nelson's semi-retired life ashore: the Nelson family, minus Fanny and Josiah; naval friends like Ball, Foley, Murray and Sutton; social outcasts including Clarence, who lived with Dorothy Jordan and their prodigious brood of bastards close by at Bushy; painters, musicians and local notables, like the bullion-dealing Goldsmid brothers and James Perry, editor of the *Morning Chronicle*. Minto came too, although he was rather censorious. This was enough for Nelson, who loved being surrounded by children and uncomplicated people, acting the genial host, free from the demands of war and strategy.

While Nelson preferred to keep his private life quiet and retired, his public role remained prominent. In local society Nelson was a charming and attentive host. He spoke to everyone at their own level, be they children, gardeners, city traders, statesmen or officers. Only when his astonishing mind was gripped by an issue of public policy did it slide effortlessly from the humdrum to the heroic. Like all great intellects, his focus and intensity were electric. After a life spent at sea and at war his mind was never disturbed by trifles. Even when describing his 'retired' life away from the 'noise, bustle, and falsity of what is called the great world', he inevitably slipped into reflections on high policy, statecraft and war.[71]

Nelson also had a less heroic side in private: he could be very dull company at times, as his friend Minto testified, and he was also a terrible hypochondriac. This was a family trait, one his father had elevated to an art form. Only a man of robust constitution, capable of living to an advanced age, would have survived the catalogue of disease and wounds that punctuated his career. But the bowel complaint that he brought ashore in late 1801 was different. It was alive: Lord Nelson had worms! This complaint did not reappear, however, unlike the mysterious psychosomatic heart spasms (in reality, acute nervous indigestion). Despite these minor ailments, the eighteen months ashore set him up to endure another campaign. Discussions with Dr Baird on the efficacy of lemon juice led him to ensure ensure his men were liberally dosed and able to stay the course as well, avoiding the dreaded scurvy, which affected the judgement as well as loosening the teeth.[72]

Among Nelson's domestic concerns, only his mistress and his child ranked above his family. He paid for William's son to go to Eton, and another £100 a year for his sister's children to be educated. This turned out to be a wise investment when Tom Bolton became the second Earl Nelson. He pressed the case of Colonel Suckling, secured the promotion of a Bolton cousin and worked endlessly on his political contacts to advance brother William to the bench of bishops.[73] In the event the Prime Minister had debts of his own to pay in that area, and too few prelates shuffled off their mortal coil for dull, greedy William to secure such an undeserved prize. While Nelson recognised his brother's faults, he never stopped trying because he believed the state owed him that much. Old Edmund, meanwhile, died on 26 April 1802, shortly after being reconciled to the life choices of his famous son. Nelson did not attend the funeral, possibly because it coincided with Emma's birthday, though Ball excused his actions on the grounds that it would have 'added considerable distress to his afflicted mind, without answering any one good purpose'.[74]

Fanny was with Edmund to the end, but his death removed her last link with the family while Nelson lived. Lord Glenbervie, who met her at Bath in 1810, considered that she had been grossly ill used, but was unimpressed with her personality: 'she is stupid, heavy, yet fond of talking if she can find a listener. One soon sees also that she is in her nature eager to attract attention, and hurt if she is not rated as a principal personage.'[75] She never did recover her role as a principal: there was no room for her in Nelson's life after the birth of Horatia, an advantage Emma exploited to secure Nelson's affection.

Emma, mistress of Merton, and of Nelson's heart, was in her element. While Sir William lived, the three of them would be together – this, along with Nelson's lack of concern to hide the situation, was the only unusual aspect to an otherwise mundane affair. Sir William was too wise to miss the events passing under his nose, and too cynical not to exploit them. His last years would pass in the company of the man he admired more than any other, and his devoted wife/nurse. In return for their support he played the chaperone. It was undignified, but not

Nelson in civilian dress with Lady Hamilton

unpleasant. Nelson never ceased to love his old friend, and it is likely they agreed that he would take on the expensive Emma while Hamilton left his money and estate to his nephew Greville.

With the child Horatia as her pledge, Emma had Nelson in chains – though he was besotted, anyway, readily accepting all her demands. Her campaign to discredit Fanny was a masterpiece of flattery, black-mail and power. She controlled access to Nelson, and used that control to force his family into line: even old Edmund had given in by the time he died. Emma, a whirlwind of energy and ambition, was always a step ahead of her men, scheming out the next option. When Sir William died she needed a 'reserve' patron, and lit on the Duke of Queensberry. She could not afford to be alone, and had skill enough to keep herself in the limelight. Whether she ever separated her need for Nelson as a protector from her love for him is unknown: she certainly possessed him and held his private life in thrall.[76]

Throughout his time ashore Nelson remained an admiral in waiting, a warrior at rest. He spent his energy urging the claims of his chosen followers, campaigning on the Copenhagen medal and prize-money issues, and negotiating with Lloyds Patriotic Fund for the families of those killed and wounded. One of the key elements in the creation and maintenance of an eighteenth-century naval 'family' was the patron's ability to distribute rewards, with prize money as the most obvious, if not always the most important example. Prize cases could run on for years: Nelson spent part of 1802 settling the distribution of money earned in Vado Bay back in 1796, and he also settled the more fraught question of the Copenhagen prize money.[77] In early 1803 Nelson pro-posed a round figure of £100,000; St Vincent finally settled on £60,000 and £35,000 head money – the timing suggests that the old Earl was anxious to remove as many causes of grievance as he could before Nelson went back to war.[78]

Although he had been a major public figure for several years, 1802 was Nelson's only opportunity to engage with British politics. Hitherto his political connections had been restricted to an intermit-tent, quasi-public correspondence with Lord Spencer at the Admiralty, and personal contacts like Minto. During the Baltic campaign he had corresponded with Prime Minister Addington, opening a curious rela-tionship with a worthy but ultimately dull politician. While Nelson was mercurial, brilliant and dynamic, Addington, the guardian of good order, sound money and stability, was the minister for the state rather than a party leader. After being picked by the King to continue the government, he gained the support of most independent men and proved remarkably popular. These were the very qualities that attracted Nelson. He had no time for faction; indeed, in wartime he thought opposition tantamount to treason. Addington and Nelson shared a simple patriotism built on unwavering loyalty: the admiral admired Addington's 'truly patriotic feelings' and trusted his judgement, while the Prime Minister listened carefully to Nelson's advice, and acted on it.[79]

Addington, moreover, needed Nelson. His very name was a guarantee of sound defence and success in war, while his vote in the House of Lords and his occasional speeches were a powerful reinforcement for Addington's Ministry. In turn Nelson raised key issues with the Prime Minister, having abandoned hope that St Vincent would concede on Copenhagen, prize or pensions. His appeals were carefully constructed. Nelson asked Addington to secure Royal sanction to wear a Turkish decoration awarded for Copenhagen, while noting that he would be far happier to wear the King's gold medal for the battle, 'the greatest and most honourable reward in the power of our sovereign to bestow, as it marks the personal services'.[80] Too astute to swallow the bait Addington secured the necessary permission, while holding out hope for brother William's episcopal ambitions.[81] This relationship worked because Nelson saw it as a 'friendship' as well as a political connection. It even stretched to cover the interests of those southern scapegraces the King and Queen of Naples, for whom Nelson acted as a local agent.[82]

If Nelson was never entirely satisfied with the official response to his requests for patronage and reward, he was wise enough to keep up the connection with Addington, as the best guarantee of future satisfaction. Later, he would consider the return of Pitt a change for the worse, and saw nothing to celebrate in the underhand and factious methods employed to bring down his friend.[83] The exact nature of the contact between Nelson and Addington from late 1802 is obscured by their presence in London, but the fact that it remained frequent and friendly is obvious from the sensitive national and personal issues on which Nelson wrote, and his contact with other members of the administration. It was also the period in which his rather awkward relationship with the Admiralty began to improve.

While they were all at sea, Nelson had been very close to St Vincent and Troubridge, but their translation to the Board of Admiralty changed the relationship. He expected them to treat him as close friends, as he would have treated them had the situation been reversed. That both men felt constrained to act as his 'superiors' grated. He found St Vincent distant and formal, and thought it ill became Captain Troubridge to lord it over Vice Admiral Nelson. In a barbed note to Troubridge he noted, 'when I forget an old and dear friend, may I cease to be your affectionate Nelson & Bronte.'[84] He was not the only officer to resent the stiff and formal manners of St Vincent's Board: it did not help that the old Earl was frequently unwell, and embarking on a highly contentious policy that would split the Cabinet and the service, making him many enemies.[85] Nelson had only secured a few patronage trifles from the Earl before the alarming events in Europe made his goodwill priceless.[86] St Vincent, narrow-minded, dogmatic and resolute, would not bend or admit his error. Both Copenhagen and the prize case made easy relations impossible, and it did not help that the Earl was not fully engaged with the rest of the government, which held a rather more astute appreciation of Nelson's worth.[87]

Nelson may have been at home at last, but he could not entirely relax: the Peace of Amiens was only a truce and the signs from Europe remained threatening, while his public fame and record made it obvious that he would be back in harness if war came again. There was no time to settle, and no excuse for turning his back on the task: once ashore, he focused his hard-won and finely honed talents on the higher direction of national policy and strategy. Nelson did not share the fears of Grenville and Windham that peace with France meant destruction, but he was not blind to the dangers:

> I am the friend of Peace without fearing War; for my politics are to let France know that we will give no insult to her Government, nor will we receive the smallest. If France takes unfair means to prevent our trading with other Powers under her influence, this I consider the greatest act of hostility she can show us; but if Bonaparte understands our sentiments, he will not wish to plunge France in a new war with us. Every man in France, as well as this Country, is wanted for commerce; and powerful as he may be, France would pull him down for destroying *her* commerce, and the war in this Country would be most popular against the man who would destroy *our* commerce. I think our Peace is strong if we act, as we ought, with firmness, and allow France to put no false constructions on the words, or on omissions in the Treaty.[88]

These were wise sentiments, although his analysis of France was optimistic. In the event the French were prepared to follow Bonaparte's chariot of glory for another twelve years, renouncing him only when the enemy reached Paris.

Nelson also discussed the future of the peace with Colonel Stewart. From his post at Shorncliffe, watching the French forces at Boulogne, Stewart doubted they meant to keep the peace. Nelson's views were based on a broader grasp of the issues. He thought Napoleon's demands on the Swiss would bring all Europe into concert against him, because it proved that his word was worthless. There was 'no sense but insolence in his present conduct'. He was confident the Ministers would not allow any French insult to pass, or accept any dictatorial language from them. 'This conduct and no other will secure my support.' Although Addington 'will not want a proper spirit to call forth, when it is necessary, the resources of the country, and make a popular war', he still hoped for peace.[89]

In late July Nelson and the Hamiltons set off to promote the claims of the new shipyard and facilities at Milford on Sir William's Welsh estate. Along the way the party, which included William Nelson, Catherine Matcham and their families, stopped at Oxford to receive honorary doctorates: Horatio and Sir William in Civil Law, brother William in Divinity. Although turned away from Blenheim Palace by the descendants of the great Marlborough, the English warrior hero of the previous century, the party was greeted with rapturous applause in every town it passed through, and as the news spread each destination tried to outdo the last. Who needed the chilly hospitality of the great, when the unalloyed love of the people was available at every coach stop? The party travelled from Burford to Gloucester and Ross-on-Wye, before taking a river journey to Monmouth where the reception surpassed anything that had gone before. The journey through Wales was punctuated by a stop at the impressive Merthyr ironworks, before pressing on to Pembrokeshire.

At Milford Greville had laid on a grand civic occasion: Sir William presented the New Inn with the Guzzardi portrait and Nelson gave a major speech, praising his Welsh friend Foley and the town that had gathered to hang on his every word. The return leg passed through more towns, including Swansea, where civic freedoms were granted and Emma sang 'Rule Britannia', with an extra 'Nelson' verse in case anyone missed the point. She did the same when they returned to

Monmouth, while Nelson gave a speech expressing his confidence that when a British army met the French, without relying on allies, it would be as successful as the Navy. Monmouth, after all, was the birthplace of the victor of Agincourt.

Nelson's 'triumphal progress' was already attracting attention in London, as the *Morning Post* noted: 'It is a singular fact that more éclat attends Lord Nelson in his provincial rambles than attends the King.' He gave the speech once again in Hereford, as ever mixing piety with praise for his followers. After another triumph at Ludlow, the party stopped for a few days with Richard Payne Knight, an old friend of Sir William, and author of a scandalous book on the cult of Priapus. Thereafter the party called at Worcester, placed a large order for china and took another freedom, at the cost of a speech. Further halts only added to the pandemonium that broke out whenever he appeared. Forewarned by the provincial press, midland towns were primed for a show, long starved of anything on this scale. At Birmingham he met manufacturing colossus Matthew Boulton, before stopping at Althorp, home of Lord Spencer. When the journey ended at Merton on 5 September, Nelson had harvested the full measure of his earthly glory in forty-six days, stamping his name on the nation.

In the process he had proved himself a truly inspired mass communicator: the style and manner that won the hearts of seamen and officers worked equally well with civic worthies and tradesmen. Unlike many professional politicans, Nelson had none of the patrician hauteur that alienated the middle class: he spoke to them in a language they understood, about things that for the first time made them feel proud to be British. With a woman of common stock as his muse, he proved that Britain had greatness among all its people: heroism, beauty and talent were not the province of the elite. Little wonder he carped to Davison on his return that popular applause was ample reward for his efforts, 'but the comparison is not flattering to King and Government'. He considered making a similar progress through the North the following year.[90]

For all his talk of being cut off from the centre of power, Nelson remained integral to the national cause. This became obvious when the political world returned to London in late 1802. Bonaparte had used the Peace of Amiens to clear up a few anomalies, and extend his control over subject and client states, in ways that the British ministers had simply not anticipated. By October his actions had thoroughly alarmed the ministers, and they prepared to mobilise the fleet. War could not be long delayed.

At the opening of Parliament on 16 November, the King's speech reflected a strong desire to preserve peace, but only with honour. Brought to town by the long running 1799 prize case, Nelson also discussed the European situation with St Vincent and Addington. It was a mark of their mutual esteem that Jervis's squalid conduct in the prize business did not ruin a vital command partnership. Nelson was more open with Minto on 26 September, arguing that the country needed to be much better prepared, and that he should have the Mediterranean command.[91] When war threatened St Vincent switched Nelson with Keith, the reliable 'Scotch pack horse', the right man for the job in both cases. Keith's Channel command was a monument of sustained labour and perseverance. He stood the task for six years: six months would have been too much for Nelson.

The issue that was likeliest to precipitate war was Malta. After discussing the subject with Nelson, Addington decided to go to war rather than give it up. Nelson advised him that unless it was in safe hands 'we had no choice but to keep Malta' – it must never belong to France.[92] By late February the only hope for peace, Minto argued, was to send Nelson to the Mediterranean to demonstrate that Britain meant business.[93] He was the British deterrent.

With his stock rising in Government circles it was time to ask for a favour. With Sir William dying and Emma's finances in ruins the hero had a problem: his income was quite unequal to his needs. From a gross income of £3,418, payments to Lady Nelson and other pensions and gratuities left him with a disposable figure of only £768, and he also had debts of £10,000. His only recourse was to ask Addington for an increase in his pension, noting that St Vincent and Duncan had each been awarded £1,000 a year by the Irish Parliament.[94] The following day, in the House of Lords, he let the Prime Minister know, 'I am your Admiral.'[95] Despite sending two reminders about the money he needed before he went to sea, nothing was done; instead he went on full pay, and opened the possibility of a prize windfall.[96]

By 22 March the future course was set: whether it was war or peace, Nelson had the Mediterranean command. George Murray, who had earned his admiration leading the attack at Copenhagen, would be Captain of the Fleet. Samuel Sutton would prepare the newly refitted

Victory for his flag, while Hardy took the frigate *Amphion*. The two men agreed to change ships, and share prize money. Nelson asked St Vincent, who had wanted to retire on health grounds but had been dissuaded by Addington, to find a ship for his nephew William Bolton, but did not trouble him for Berry, who would be left for the 'day of battle.'[97] Sir William, meanwhile, died in the arms of his wife and her lover on 4 April, but Nelson was too busy for mourning.

However important Nelson had become to the national self-image, it was his international reputation that would dominate the next conflict. His European tour had demonstrated a level of popular fame unknown to any other sea officer, and his name had become common currency on every continent. Even Bonaparte could not escape the phenomenon of Nelson worship. During the brief peace, British visitors flocked to see Paris, and the new First Consul, their curiosity piqued by long absence and the novelty of a European republican colossus. In the Consular quarters at the Tuileries Bonaparte had installed busts of two Englishmen. Charles James Fox earned his place as a friend of France; Nelson was there as a god of war.[98] Having fascinated the greatest soldier of the age, it is little wonder Nelson terrified the French admirals who served him.

The peace, short and unsatisfactory as it had been, was a vital intermission in the twenty-two-year Anglo-French conflict. It established the British willingness to sacrifice national interest to the wider cause of European stability, and exploded the Whig myth that opposition to France was selfish and partisan. Addington's determined effort to preserve peace exposed the dishonest, grasping policy of the French ministry and the underhand diplomatic methods and limitless ambition of Bonaparte himself. By May 1803, when the conflict resumed, there was little disagreement in Britain that it had to be fought, and fought to a finish.[99] That Britain and her people had the confidence to take on such a task reflected their new sense of national identity, shared purpose, and a common trust in the unique, iconic figure of Horatio Nelson. He, and he alone, had the presence and track record to stop the otherwise irresistible Bonaparte.

CHAPTER XIII

Master of the Mediterranean
1803–5

On 6 May 1803 Nelson achieved a long-held ambition: he was appointed Commander in Chief of the Mediterranean Fleet. With war inevitable, he waited for orders at Merton.[1] As soon as they arrived, he hurried down to Portsmouth, boarding his flagship HMS *Victory* on 18 May, the day war was declared.

Many of the causes of the war lay in the Mediterranean. After a succession of alarming, expansionist French moves – annexing Leghorn and Elba, dominating Spain, negotiating with the Barbary states, securing favourable access to the Black Sea and Russian trade, looking to resume unfinished business in Egypt, even extending the Republican empire to India – Malta proved to be the sticking point, as Nelson had anticipated. To give it up, as required by the Treaty of Amiens, would cripple British political influence, economic activity and strategic power in the Mediterranean. That would be to buy peace at too high a price.

The government had been preparing for war. In February the appropriately named sloop *Weazle* reconnoitred the Maddalena and other island groups on the coast of Sardinia, looking for sources of wood and water and to see 'how far those places may be capable of sheltering a Fleet'.[2] This was the ideal location for the watch on Toulon. In early March the government ordered the current Commander in

Bonaparte sees 'the writing on the wall': a caricature by Gillray

Chief, Rear Admiral Sir Richard Bickerton, to intercept and destroy the French fleet if it appeared to be heading for Egypt.[3] He was at sea before the outbreak of war.[4]

Addington's strategic choices were severely limited. It was 1801 all over again. France, including Belgium, Holland, parts of Germany and Italy, possessed a mighty army, led by a military dictator bent on further aggression, not least to stoke the fires of nationalism and spread the cost of his army. Britain could recover her command of the sea, impose a blockade and sweep up the newly recovered French colonies, aside from Louisiana, which Bonaparte cynically sold to the United States, well aware that he could hold it. The rest of Europe would remain on the sidelines. Austria was exhausted and nervous, Russia uncertain and Prussia hoped to make something of the inevitable conflict. The only threat to France would come if two of these powers went to war. While their mutual distrust equalled their fear of France this was unlikely.

Negotiations had been tried, accommodation attempted, but both failed. This time the Anglo-French struggle would be a war to the finish – total war, which only one regime would survive. For a man of modest political talent, Addington showed remarkable courage in taking on a massive, seemingly unwinnable war. He was forced to plan for a long war, one in which British economic power would wear down France. It could only be waged as a counter-attacking conflict. France's only hope of victory lay in an invasion of Britain, and Addington hoped they would make the attempt. It would be a mistake of the same nature as Egypt, opening the way for a decisive counter-stroke. Only after the annihilation of the French army at sea would the rest of Europe act.

With the income tax reformed and reimposed, Addington was confident that Britain could outlast France, while Nelson was the one British commander with the insight, energy and commitment to exploit a fleeting opportunity to crush the French. Bonaparte could not secure peace without crossing the Channel, and this left him stuck at Boulogne. Every month he waited made his presence more ridiculous. He could not hope to put to sea without being seen, engaged by the inshore squadron of Edward Owen, and wiped out by Lord Keith's fleet. It was this conundrum that made Nelson so confident the French fleet would be forced to come to sea. He knew they would not come out from Brest, where his old friend Cornwallis kept them tightly bound with a close blockade of astonishing commitment and professionalism. The Mediterranean, by contrast, was further from home, so although Nelson was taking a risk by leaving the way open off Toulon, it was done to secure the destruction of the enemy.

This cautious strategy governed the first year of Nelson's command. It unravelled in 1805 when Pitt forced the pace of diplomatic activity, creating the Third Coalition and giving Bonaparte a chance to escape, reconstruct his motives into an *ex post facto* strategy of genius, and secure a fresh lease on power with vastly greater resources through the inevitable failure of the Austrians and Russians at Ulm and Austerlitz.[5] A little more patience might have paid dividends.

To command the Mediterranean theatre required self-sufficiency, decisiveness and political courage, since it was a theatre where time and distance left much more for the admiral to decide than in the Downs, the Baltic or the Grand Fleet. With bases at Gibraltar and Malta, the British could divide the theatre into three areas: the eastern and western basins and the Adriatic. All were vital, but as long as the enemy fleet could be kept in the western basin, the other two areas only required cruiser squadrons. Consequently Nelson spent his time with the battle fleet in the triangle Naples–Gibraltar–Toulon, with a near-perfect central base on the Sardinian coast. The greatest danger was that the enemy fleet would escape to the Atlantic, to attack British trade and possessions or support an invasion of England or Ireland.

Britain's options in the theatre, though less dramatic, remained impressive. Naval power could cripple the movement of troops and economic activity by pressing close to the coast. Though the French could complete their conquest of Italy at will, they could not escape the Continent without a fleet. The presence of the fleet bolstered British diplomacy, encouraged friendly neutrals, and limited the impact of French threats. The blockade of France and her satellites led to widespread ruin, which greatly reduced the value of French territorial expansion as a mechanism for waging war with Britain.

Nelson worked closely with British ministers at Naples, the Ottoman Porte and Madrid; together with a constellation of minor diplomatic office-holders, they provided vital intelligence. As contact with London was intermittent, instructions tended to be general, and permissive. This left far more to the man on the spot than in the other major fleet commands, and explains why Nelson was the ideal commander. It was not his mastery of the Mediterranean or his importunity that gained him this command, but his instinct for acting on his own judgement and his political courage. He did not need to be supervised, or to refer back to London.

While the destruction of the Toulon squadron was at the core of Nelson's instructions, his role was far wider. He was to proceed to Malta, link up with the fleet, take over from Bickerton and discuss the situation with Ball, now Governor of the island. He would take station off Toulon 'to take, sink, burn or otherwise destroy any ships belonging to France, or the citizens of that Republic', and he should also seize any Batavian [Dutch] ships. He was to watch French proceedings at Genoa, Leghorn and other ports on the west coast of Italy for intelligence of plans to attack Egypt, Turkey or Naples, all places he was to secure. He should give such protection to British trade as was consistent with his other orders; he should also watch Spanish naval preparations – not offering any insult to Spain or her shipping if she remained neutral, but stopping Spanish warships from entering French ports or joining a French fleet. If he had any ships to spare he should place a squadron in the Straits to watch for French warships returning from an ill-fated expedition to St Domingo (modern Haiti). This general advice was the limit of the Admiralty's strategic and political guidance for the next six months, though it continued to require regular reports.[6]

On 20 May Nelson left Spithead with a north wind and driving rain, heading for the Grand Fleet rendezvous off Ushant. He was to ask Cornwallis if he needed the *Victory* before heading to his station. Also on board was Hugh Elliot, the new minister to Naples and brother of his old friend Lord Minto. The voyage established a key relationship for the forthcoming command, the two men being thrown much closer together then they had anticipated by the failure to find Cornwallis. After lamenting the loss of a favourable wind, they left the flagship behind, shifting into the frigate *Amphion*, commanded by Hardy. Cornwallis, as Nelson knew, would not keep his friend's flagship, so the whole incident took on the character of a farce.[7] It also underlined the Admiralty's obsession with the Channel fleet.

Once at sea Nelson wrote to Emma only every three or four weeks. He lamented that they were now on different elements, and asked her to take care of 'our dear child'. He also requested her to send Stephens' *History of the French Revolution*, perhaps to check if the author had profited from his advice.[8] Occasionally this correspondence was delegated to his secretary John Scott, who knew Emma. Some letters were partly dictated or written by Nelson, partly by Scott.[9] The emotional role of the letters was vital – they allowed him to dream of a real home, his 'wife' and child. But they did not distract him from his duty any more than his letters to Fanny in the 1790s.

After a brief stop at Gibraltar, to check on Spanish activity at Cadiz and arrange local convoys and patrols against the inevitable French privateers, Nelson hurried on to Malta. He sent Elliot to his post at Naples, armed with friendly messages for Sir John Acton, the King and Queen, recognising that it would not be in the Neapolitan interest for him to visit. With French troops already in part of the Kingdom, neutrality was the best policy for Naples, but Nelson was determined to keep the French out of Sicily.[10] This included censuring the captain of the *Cyclops* for seizing French ships in Naples harbour, a clear violation of neutrality. The ships were returned, and a public letter sent to Acton for the French minister to read.[11] Ferdinand, well aware of his exposed position, was very grateful for British support and Nelson's presence.[12] Nelson also wrote to the British Minister at Turin, offering his assistance to the King of Sardinia and to his Copenhagen colleague William Drummond, recently translated to Istanbul with letters for the Grand Vizier and Capitan Pasha, the senior Turkish naval officer. He wanted news from the eastern Mediterranean, fearing the French were moving into the Balkans.[13]

Nelson's return to the Mediterranean was the first indication to many that war had been declared, and while he hoped for prizes he promised Addington that 'You may rely on my activity in getting off Toulon.'[14] He had to assess the situation, analyse the intelligence and develop an effective counter to Bonaparte's strategy. His main problem was the relative lack of force at his disposal. The Malta garrison was less than five thousand troops, and he had been authorised to send half of these to Messina, but this would expose the island to a counterstroke. His fleet, meanwhile, was no larger than the French fleet at Toulon, and had nothing to counter the possibility of Spanish involvement, or to cover other tasks. He had to block Bonaparte in the Mediterranean, while other fleets cleared the seas and islands of the French, and protected the home base. There would be no reinforcements, few replacements and only limited quantities of dockyard stores.

Arriving at Malta on 15 June, Nelson found that Bickerton was already at sea off Toulon. He spent thirty-six hours ashore, discussing the situation with Ball and writing to the key players in the eastern basin. The senior army officer on the island, General Villettes, agreed to hold twelve hundred British troops, ready to occupy Messina. Nelson soon shaped a course through the Straits of Messina. Though the sight of Vesuvius must have stirred old memories, he could not go ashore without attracting French attention to the Kingdom, so he sent his dispatches and letters by boat. The political news was worrying, but a secret agreement between Elliot and Acton held out the best hope for Sicily. When danger threatened the British would occupy Messina. To forestall an attack Nelson's fleet would cruise between Elba and Genoa, blocking any French expedition south.

On 1 July Nelson ordered that Genoese and Ligurian vessels should be detained until the Admiralty responded to his request of that day for further advice. His rationale for an extended blockade encapsulated British strategy:

> It will make the inhabitants severely feel the baneful effects of French fraternity, and in the case of a co-operation with some of the continental powers, will make them ready to throw off the French yoke.

Sea power would squeeze France and her satellites, while steadily increasing economic pressure would break their resolve, weaken Bonaparte's grip on power and open the way for other states to combine with Britain.[15] The ministers were quick to agree.[16] Realising the French would try to evade the blockade by using neutral carriers, he sought a legal opinion.[17]

Nelson took care to send any contentious material through St Vincent, leaving it to his discretion whether it was passed on to the Admiralty Board or the Cabinet. He also explained his views to Lord Moira, the one figure in political circles he admired sufficiently to entrust with his proxy vote. To them he confided his fears. All Italy, save Naples, was already as French as France – Bonaparte clearly meant to recover Egypt and then, 'sooner or later, farewell India!' His greatest concern was that the Brest fleet would evade Cornwallis and descend on the Mediterranean, as Bruix and Ganteaume had in 1799 and 1800. If they did, French troops would move quickly, and the entire theatre would be lost beyond recall.[18] He relied on his ships in the Straits for adequate warning to bring any French force to action.[19]

Bonaparte's response to the outbreak of war, after a volcanic ill-tempered outburst, was to order the occupation of Taranto and the coast of Apulia, as a *quid pro quo* for the retention of Malta. This operation left General St Cyr's army ideally placed to march rapidly on Naples, paralysing the already feeble Ferdinand, and also opening a window onto the troubled Balkan and Greek territory of the Turkish Empire. The French might have attempted Sicily, using boats to cross the Straits of Messina, but not while the Royal Navy was at hand. Nelson also placed cruisers off Cape Spartivento, with orders to stop the French moving by sea, at any cost.[20]

If Bonaparte moved it would be to the east of Italy; Turkey or Egypt were long signalled, more for their diversionary value than any short term ambition. General Sebastiani's mission to Istanbul, and the insulting publication of his report on Egypt, had been one of the sparks that ignited the war. In both cases the Mediterranean Fleet was the ideal counter-attacking force, but it had to be concentrated, and directed with a degree of insight and vision usually found only in campaigns where a major intelligence advantage has been obtained. In this case the 'intelligence' was the product of Nelson's analytical mind, rather than code-breaking.

Covered by the fleet, British cruisers based at Malta looked after trade, the eastern basin and the Adriatic. Sicily, which fed and supplied Malta, was critical to the British strategic position. To keep the menacing French army in nearby Apulia on the mainland he deployed five cruisers. As he attempted to grasp the enemy's purpose, Nelson lamented the lack of ten thousand troops – who could have secured British concerns in the theatre and released his fleet for a more dynamic policy – but the men were needed at home, to counter the invasion threat. For an early warning of any French moves against Naples and Sicily, he relied on Elliot, Acton, and the presence of a British battleship in the Bay of Naples, which could repeat his evacuation of 1798. Nelson emphasised to Elliot and Acton that the safety of Sicily was vital: if it fell the Bourbons were finished, but while it held they had a chance. Above all, Sicily must not be risked to save Naples.[21] This was the lesson of 1798–9, seared onto Nelson's consciousness by that awful campaign.

General Villettes, meanwhile, was advised to have his two thousand men ready, but not to worry about baggage: any deployment would be short-term.[22] This was all the manpower Britain could spare, and there was little prospect of reinforcement from home – it would be two years before the Army could spare anything more than a handful of drafts from England and Ireland. This left the offensive and defensive burdens of the theatre entirely on Nelson's shoulders. Naples was feeble and had to bend to France; the Russians occupied the Septinsular Republic (the Ionian Islands) but would not help Naples. In 1804 French pressure removed Acton, leaving the conduct of government to Queen Maria Carolina, an energetic but inconsistent policy-maker who distrusted everyone.

As a fully fledged Commander in Chief, Nelson exercised considerable patronage: he could select junior officers, pick key subordinates, and influence the promotion of those he favoured. Clarence exercised his old friendship to secure a place, and Nelson agreed with him that the son of Admiral Lord Rodney 'should be a protégé of everyone'.[23] Troubridge's son was in the *Victory*, suggesting that any animosity generated by Sir Thomas's over-zealous conduct of Admiralty was temporary.[24] Admiral Lord Duncan sent his son Henry, and applied through his fellow Scot Lord Melville for his promotion. Melville sent this request in triplicate: Nelson responded quickly when he heard that old Duncan had died suddenly.[25] St Vincent, meanwhile, thought of little else than patronage, sending out a string of recommendations for noble youths, whose relatives had votes and influence. Nelson preferred those like old Sir Peter Parker's grandson and Lord Hugh Seymour's son, the progeny of naval friends.[26] He also made Minto's son a post captain.

The key to the next two years of Nelson's career would be the gathering, sorting and assessment of fragmentary scraps of intelligence from a wide variety of sources. He began well, when Captain Layman took a small French warship, with a remarkable haul of printed documents and books, signal codes for the fleet and the coastal telegraph, tactical and doctrine publications, charts and the state of the French forces off St Domingo.[27] Further captures constantly refreshed Nelson's understanding of the French order of battle.

The conduct of Spain was the single most important question facing Nelson. In peacetime, Spanish beef and onions and lemons from Catalonia were the key to the health of the fleet. But Madrid was in thrall to Bonaparte and likely to go to war sooner rather than later. The British Consuls at Madrid, Ferrol, Cartagena and Cadiz ran an excellent intelligence service, keeping Nelson abreast of the shifting policy of the Spanish ministry, and the state of their fleets. This reduced the need to detail scarce warships to watch Spanish ports.[28] Consul Duff at Cadiz promised that 'nothing shall be wanting on my part to procure and transmit every possible information; but the risk, or rather the *certainty* of their letters being opened here makes my Agents cautious in their details to me.' He sent sensitive material by ship.[29]

Another Consul, Spiridion Foresti in the Russian-occupied Septinsular Republic, was already known and valued by Nelson, who praised his dedication to the Foreign Secretary. While the tiny islands wisely remained neutral, they provided a wealth of material on French-occupied Italy and the Balkan littoral, amply repaying Nelson's faith.[30] Naval agent George Noble provided further insights from the commercial quarter of Naples.[31] Nelson's concerns went far beyond the confines of the middle sea. From India Arthur Wellesley, the future Duke of Wellington, took the time to send news and newspapers reporting his military successes.[32]

The trusty Davison, meanwhile, kept Nelson abreast of developments in Britain. In June 1803 he sent him a package of books; alongside works of modern history and poetry were several dealing with professional issues: the second edition of *Historical Sketches of the Invasions or Descents upon the British Isles* by Louis Giradin, a *Naval History of the Late War* by William Stewart Rose, and speeches by Lord Moira, the independent peer who held Nelson's proxy vote, and Richard Brinsley Sheridan, the eloquent Whig turncoat who now spoke for the Ministry.[33] The books were 'a treasure', Nelson replied, and so was Davison, whose links with the fringes of the British secret service, Lord Moira, the Prime Minister and Admiralty Secretary Sir Evan Nepean were invaluable to Nelson.[34]

Davison also kept an eye on Emma, although it was perhaps not wise of him to report a charming dinner with her and Charles Greville.[35] Now Nelson was back at work, his mistress-wife, child and home quickly assumed the character of a charming daydream: they provided warm memories of better days, but there was no prospect of going home until the job was done. His letters quickly started to resemble those he had written to Fanny in an earlier Mediterranean campaign. They contained more passion and earthly ambition, but that was the Emma effect. But they should not be taken too seriously: he used them to write out his frustrations with the weather, the enemy, the Admiralty and anyone else who had crossed him.

Nelson's main concern about Emma was to find an alternative means of support for her. Sir William left her with a small settlement – to be paid, with typical irony, by Greville. To supplement this, Nelson assiduously petitioned the Queen of Naples, who simply disowned her old bosom companion, the Duke of Hamilton and the British government. Emma had claims on all three, but none was anxious to help. Instead Nelson was left to hope that a successful commission would pay off his debts, and set them up for the future.[36]

When Nelson finally joined the fleet early on 8 July, his experienced eye quickly assessed the situation. The men were excellent, if a little short of complement, with high proportions of prime seamen on all ships. The eight battleships were being run ragged by a close blockade, showing signs of extensive hard service. Several, he soon discovered, needed dockyard attention. The two sixty-fours, *Monmouth* and *Agincourt*, were dreadfully slow under sail, 'and in these times are hardly to be reckoned with' in battle. Only seventy-fours would do, because they had thirty-two-pounder lower-deck batteries, while the sixty-fours made do with twenty-four-pounders. The French had seven battleships, all seventy-four or eighty-gun ships, with two more completing, five frigates and six corvettes. He could not afford to detach any battleships to patrol off Gibraltar, and was pushed to find one to support the Bourbons at Naples, to offer them a safe retreat.[37]

Nelson declared his pleasure that Bickerton, 'a very intelligent and correct officer', would be remaining. Within two days Nelson had assessed his talents, trusting him to reorganise the convoys and detachments when he went back to Malta. He was equally impressed by Captain Richard Keats, the pick of Clarence's nominees, and sent him to Naples. While the other captains were competent followers Bickerton and Keats could act alone.[38]

There was little point trying to run a close blockade of Toulon, since the weather in the Gulf of Lyons was boisterous, as he confessed to St Vincent: 'I am – don't laugh – dreadfully sea-sick this day.'[39] Furthermore the French had a major tactical advantage. The commanding hills around Toulon allowed them to watch the British far out to sea. To save his ships and disguise his movements, Nelson dropped back forty miles, relying on his cruisers for information. He was prepared to risk the French getting to sea because there were no strategic or economic targets closer than Sicily, Malta and the African coast. If they came out, he was confident he would catch them using his mastery of local weather patterns. Every day Nelson filled in his weather journal, the basic building block of his strategic judgement, and invariably used it to assess the possible destinations of any enemy ships that might get to sea.[40]

To exploit that knowledge he kept the fleet together while the frigates watched Toulon, rather than detach individual ships and leave his fleet weakened. He also decided that both Gibraltar and Malta were too far away to act as bases. By keeping his entire force together and varying the cruising regime, he hoped to lure the French out, and avoid the monotony that his friends off Brest experienced. The battle squadron would remain fully stored and watered, fit for a long cruise. For twenty-two months his ships waited, an unparalleled feat of management, medical provision, morale-building and will-power. At the Admiralty St Vincent, unable to do more than send an occasional replacement for his craziest hulks, and an inadequate supply of stores, could only marvel that the 'resources of your mind' could compensate for such widespread material deficiencies.[41] Nelson did not struggle to hold station with his ill-found ships – that way lay disaster. Instead he bent before the storms, left his rendezvous and waited for the weather to break.[42]

The strategic picture was clearing. Nelson doubted the French would leave Toulon without reinforcements from Brest, but he feared France and Russia were plotting to dismember Turkey.[43] His pleasantries and his name bore fruit in Istanbul, from where Drummond reported: 'The Turkish government has heard with particular pleasure that your Excellency has the chief command in the Mediterranean, your name stands no less here than it does everywhere else.' The Grand Vizier was highly impressed, while the Sultan had become noticeably more favourable to Britain.[44]

The final pieces of Nelson's system fell into place when the *Victory* reached the fleet on 1 August: Hardy exchanged with Sutton, and quickly hung Nelson's favourite picture of Emma in the great cabin, alongside one of Horatia.[45] The Reverend Alexander Scott served as an 'interpreter' in addition to his duties as Nelson's personal chaplain. Scott was an experienced intelligence officer, having worked in the Mediterranean Fleet since 1793, picking up Spanish and Italian with Hyde Parker and then St Vincent. He was an astonishing linguist: he read captured material in French, Spanish and Italian to Nelson, worked on cyphers, and handled foreign language correspondence. In 1803–5 his work with the Sardinian authorities and local people alone was priceless, while his intelligence-gathering missions to Spain and Naples were a major addition to Nelson's range of understanding.[46]

With Hardy to run the ship, George Murray to handle fleet administration and John Scott to deal with English correspondence, Nelson had a fine team. Moreover he had chosen these talented men because he liked them, which made his work far easier. Hardy, known as 'the ghost' from his silent perigrinations about the ship, his presence announced by the appearance of a bald head stooped far ahead of his feet, spent so much time walking with the admiral that he adopted Nelson's pace, rather than his own longer stride. Nelson's inner circle was completed by his steward Chevalier and servant Gaetano Spedillo, who ministered to his human necessities. If his days were taken up with routine and correspondence, he always found the time for exercise, walking back and forth on the quarter-deck for hours, and he entertained many of his officers over dinner, including the youngest. He would not step off his flagship for two years. It contained everything he needed to control the Mediterranean.

On 1 November the *Victory* anchored in Agincourt Sound, in the Maddalena Islands, exploiting a fine chart produced by Captain Frederick Ryves of HMS *Gibraltar*. Further local surveys improved access to the anchorage: now the fleet had a secure base, with 'water, brooms, sand, onions, some beef, plenty of sheep . . . but I suppose the French will take it now we have used it'.[47] The anchorage was only two hundred miles from Toulon. Here the ships could rest and take on water and fresh victuals. The supply situation needed careful oversight. Food would be drawn from Sardinia and the Barbary coast, while 'clandestine' methods secured vital supplies from Spain and even France – Gibraltar and Malta were simply too far away to supply fresh food.[48]

The arrival of Spanish lemons and onions soon cleared up an incipient outbreak of scurvy. Nelson's concern with nutrition had been influenced by his lemon-obsessed physician friend Dr Andrew Baird at the Sick and Hurt Board: 'I am clearly of your opinion that we must not be economical of good things for our sailors, but only take care that they are faithfully supplied.'[49] As Nelson explained to Dr Moseley of the Chelsea Hospital, who had treated his eye: 'The great thing in all military service is health; and you will agree with me, that it is easier for an Officer to keep men healthy, than for a Physician to cure them.' To Baird's lemons, Nelson added a personal preference for onions, fresh meat and plenty of fresh water. His own health was, he reported, indifferent, but 'I must not be sick until after the French fleet is taken.'[50]

There was nothing seriously wrong with him, frustration and mental over-exertion aside, so he was still telling the same story twelve months later. Although the fleet was remarkably healthy, he set up a naval hospital in Malta. This period is striking for Nelson's painstaking and professional management of his ships and fleets, and his mastery of the routine administration that kept the ships and men ready for a long cruise, a sudden battle or another year at sea. His record of fleet administration provides a rich source of detail on the everyday, the humdrum that was the reality of war at sea. No one else attended to the subject with such dedication.[51]

From the outset Nelson considered Sardinia the key to his strategy: it offered the only anchorages close enough to cover, if not blockade, Toulon, watch the Riviera, and intercept the French if they tried to make for the east or the Atlantic. 'If I lose Sardinia, I lose the French Fleet,' Nelson explained to Minto.[52] His concern that the French might seize it was real enough, after their occupation of Corsica and Elba. Without Sardinia his small force could not secure Sicily, Malta or Egypt. His constant demand that precautions be taken, either by purchase or occupation, finally produced results in March 1805. When troops were available, General Sir James Craig's instructions included the occupation of Sardinia among the contingencies to be considered, in consultation with Hugh Elliot and Nelson.[53]

With his strategy in place, Nelson spent the next year keeping everything in tune: ships, men, intelligence, logistics and options were all under constant review. It was a long wait, and offered few opportunities for his talent to flourish, but the nature of total war meant that everyone was prey to such pressures. He longed for the emotional release of battle, endlessly running the permutations of French strategy over in his mind. If his body and emotions were often in turmoil, these were merely the side-effects of concentrated mental commitment over the long months of waiting. The overriding aim was to get inside the enemy's plans, to out-think them and anticipate their next move. This, and only this, would set up the next battle of annihilation.

Cautious, sophisticated enemies like the French did not fight for pride, and rarely in anger. They knew that the British would accept any opportunity to impose their will in battle, to ruin their strategic combinations, and they rarely took the risk. In twenty-two years of war there were only six occasions when a major French fleet was engaged by a British force of similar strength. Only two proved decisive, and on both occasions Nelson was in command. That was not luck: his whole being had been dedicated to setting up those battles, always recalling the battles of Hotham, Bridport, Howe and, in a previous war, Lord Rodney. He would out-think the enemy, and then out-fight him. As he told Cornwallis, who faced the same problem off Brest, the French would wait in harbour until 'they have an object worth fighting for . . . I do not mean to say that they will merely think us an object worth coming out to fight, I never saw a Frenchman yet fight for fighting's sake, and I do not believe they will now begin.' He hoped with all his heart that Cornwallis would meet the French, an opportunity his old friend was denied.[54]

While Cornwallis and Keith kept the French locked up in port, Nelson left them an opportunity to get to sea. Ultimately this would draw Bonaparte into a major error: he would attempt to win the war with an inferior fleet, from widely dispersed bases, by grand strategic combinations. His only hope was to link up his forces, and avoid or overwhelm part of the British fleet before launching his invasion. Such complex strategic combinations were the core of his military thinking, and worked well in Western Europe, but they did not work in under-developed Eastern Europe and Iberia, nor at sea. Bonaparte never really grasped the tremendous gap in quality between his navy and the British, or the complex and unreliable nature of oceanic navigation in the age of sail. He seemed to think that wind and weather, tide and current should bend to his Imperial will. The threat the French could pose to British trade and overseas territories was real, but there was little chance they would divert such masters of strategy as Cornwallis and Nelson, St Vincent and Lord Barham, from Bonaparte's real objects.

In early 1804 the Admiralty, alarmed by the latest intelligence from Spain, sent two more ships: the first-rate *Royal Sovereign* and the seventy-four *Leviathan*. When they arrived Bickerton shifted his flag from the shattered seventy-four *Kent* into the three-decker.[55] Now the

French, under Latouche Tréville, chose to make an appearance just outside the harbour. This was all the encouragement Nelson needed. Well aware they would not seek battle, but might be forced into a harbour or roadstead, he issued his captains with the latest charts of the most obvious locations, which they were to study closely, and typically minute guidance for an attack on anchored ships. Each ship was to have four heavy anchors already attached to cables, and would send off the launch with the stream anchor and a hawser, ready to assist stranded vessels. The attacking ships should anchor to ensure 'mutual support for the destruction of the enemy'. Suitable sailing directions for Leghorn roads may have been written at the same time.[56]

As the anniversary of Nelson's return to the Mediterranean arrived, the French seemed as reluctant as ever to move. Instead Nelson had to deal with a trade war stretching across the theatre. As ever he exploited an unrivalled understanding of local wind, weather, currents and geography to frame his orders.[57] The fleet was spread across the region, with eight battleships, four frigates and two smaller craft off Toulon, two frigates outside the Straits of Gibraltar, two sloops inside, a frigate and four smaller craft cruising between the Greek archipelago and Ancona to protect trade, a frigate off Barcelona, and three battleships in movement, one at Naples and another to visit Algiers to discipline the Dey. Further ships were escorting convoys, undergoing repairs or carrying dispatches to link Malta, Naples, Gibraltar and other points.[58] While Nelson's mastery of the entire run of business in the Mediterranean was astonishing, he never overrode the judgement of those whom he had ordered to execute well-defined tasks. He always worked through the proper chain of command to avoid giving offence, or undermine the confidence of promising officers. If things went wrong he was the first to leap to the defence of a bold and decisive subordinate.[59]

With Admiralty rarely sending any mail much of his news came from the Paris newspapers that were sent from Spain, usually ten to fourteen days old. The translation of Bonaparte from Consul to Emperor in May 1804 prompted further reflections on the state of Europe: he hoped for peace, but with Pitt returning to power on 12 May the die was cast for a climactic campaign. While he would regret the departure of Addington from office, he declared that 'If Pitt is attentive to me he shall have my vote.'[60] For Nelson the main impact was the end of St Vincent's universally loathed Admiralty Board, although he regretted the departure of his friend Nepean. Nelson knew the faults of the Board, but blamed those surrounding the old Earl, especially Admiral Markham and Troubridge.[61] While he knew the new First Lord, Henry Dundas, only slightly, Nelson was confident he would improve the supply of ships and men.

Sardinia remained his main concern. To block the movement of troops to embarkation ports on the Italian coast and on Elba, he placed frigates close inshore, altering the nature of the blockade to meet particular circumstances. He hoped the pressure would bring on battle; instead it resulted in some smart boat actions and a few wounded men. While delighted that the French had come out of Toulon in mid-June, Nelson rightly feared they did so only to 'cut a gasconade' before scuttling back into safety. He waited with an inferior force for them to try their strength. He would not fight them too close to Toulon, where their damaged ships could retreat to safety, unless the wind was favourable. A month later he was wound up to highest pitch by another apparent sortie, but he continued to think very clearly, and work out the options. Whatever the pressure, Nelson never abandoned the analytical approach to his problems or resorted to blind panic.

The tension of his long wait finally broke when the French press published a boastful, dishonest dispatch by Tréville, claiming the British had run away. In an unguarded moment Nelson declared he would make the Frenchman eat it, if he had the fortune to capture him. Tréville died on 18 August, worn out, it was said, by constantly climbing to his observation post to look at the British fleet. After Tréville's death the French were noticeably less alert, despite sweeping the streets of Marseilles to man the fleet.[62]

As 1804 wore on the prospect of another winter running before the gales of the Gulf of Lyons began to pall, and the combination of exhaustion and boredom began to take a toll on Nelson's resolve. In mid-August he promised Emma he would be home for Christmas, if only for a rest. Anxious that another senior officer might take his command he wanted Bickerton to stand in, and suggested that King Ferdinand make an official application for his early return.[63] It was as if he doubted his own importance to the nation, as commander and talisman. Cut off from home, with little correspondence of any kind, he was losing faith in himself. He needed to recharge his emotional reserves with another infusion of public acclaim. Ferdinand took the bait, but also wrote through Elliot to urge Nelson to come ashore for the winter. This was not what Nelson wanted: 'Being on shore, either in Sicily or Naples, would not relieve my mind of the charge entrusted to me; for my thoughts would always be off Toulon, and I should not feel answerable for measures which I do not direct.'[64]

The Eastern Mediterranean and Adriatic required constant attention, with the Russians steadily building up their forces, and their influence. Nelson had long feared they meant to seize all of European Turkey.[65] Their presence at least made it unlikely the French would strike in that direction:

> Therefore; I rather expect they will, as the year advances, try to get out of the Straits; and should they accomplish it with 7,000 troops on board, I am sure we should lose half our West India Islands, for I think they would go there, and not to Ireland. Whatever may be their destination, I shall certainly follow, be it even to the East Indies. Such a pursuit would do more, perhaps, to restoring me to health than all the Doctors; but I fear this is reserved for some happier man.[66]

This was, he admitted a guess, but it was based on careful calculation.[67]

Other problems were looming, especially the possibility of war with Spain – not that he was behind in his preparations, having exploited a Spanish request to convey a cardinal from Majorca to Rome to obtain a full report on the defences and resources of the island. Pitt, satisfied that Spanish payments to France were a breach of neutrality, decided to force the issue. Orders to seize Spanish treasure ships were issued in mid-September, and on 5 October a brief action between four frigates from each nation in the approaches to Cadiz ended when one Spanish ship blew up and the others surrendered. Nelson did not think the situation had been adequately thought through, and would have preferred to be ready with an adequate force to seize Minorca.[68]

This new war arrived just as he heard that his official request for leave had been granted. He decided to stay, and kept his leave a secret. Painfully conscious of his impaired vision, he was thinking about taking a seat at the Admiralty as overall director of the naval forces of the state. Nor was this a delusion, as many have argued following St Vincent's acid asides. In truth, no one would have been better equipped to lead the officer corps by example and encouragement, rewarding merit and courage, rather than imposing harsh measures and blatant favouritism. Nor could any other officer have equalled his strategic insight and record of accurate analysis of complex situations.

The Spanish war had other consequences. With Nelson expected to return home on leave, the Admiralty despatched Sir John Orde to command a new station in the Atlantic approaches to Cadiz. He was Nelson's superior in rank, but had a smaller command, fewer ships and less responsibility. As Nelson chose not to go home, it appeared that Orde had merely been sent to reap his 'golden harvest'.[69] Having made a public complaint about Nelson being given the Mediterranean detachment in 1798 it would have been hard to pick an officer less likely to work well with him. He was not overly concerned about the money – 'God knows, in my own person, I spend as little money as any man; but you know I love to give away.'[70] But it was the apparent lack of faith in his ability to handle the station that rankled, especially as he had taken immediate steps to meet the need: his reinforcement of Captain Strachan off Cadiz had led to the capture of two frigates before Orde arrived.

Orde soon tired of a position that everyone knew was false, and which he could not fill with dignity or ability equal to his rank. Complaining that Nelson was interfering, he asked to be relieved in March 1805, and was taken at his word by return of mail. Orde was the same petty-minded blockhead who had tried to fight a duel with St Vincent five years before. It seems he had been sent only to annoy the old Earl, who was refusing to go back to sea until Pitt apologised for his remarks in the House of Commons on Admiralty administration during the Addington Ministry.[71]

Spain was no longer the sea power she had been in 1796. Her fleet had declined through capture and disaster and had not been adequately replaced. The national coffers had been emptied to buy off Bonaparte, while a terrible outbreak of yellow fever swept across southern Spain, hitting Cadiz and Cartagena particularly hard.[72] The situation was so bad that Orde was directed not to board any Spanish ships he might capture, but to take them into quarantine at Gibraltar.[73] Efforts to mobilise the Spanish fleet were crippled by the loss of craftsmen and seamen, the shortage of food and stores, and above all the lack of hard cash. Gibraltar too was affected by fever: over two thousand people died in a few weeks.

However, the French now demanded Nelson's full attention. Vice Admiral Pierre Villeneuve, Nile escapee and Napoleon's 'lucky' admiral, now commanded at Toulon. On 18 January he put to sea with eleven battleships, cruisers and six thousand troops. British frigates quickly reported back to Nelson, who moved to cover Naples and Sicily on the likely track of the enemy. Taking into account the strong winds then blowing, they could only be headed east, so he ran down to the Italian coast, through the Straits of Messina, and by 7 February was off Alexandria. There was no sign of the enemy. By 18 February he knew that the French, crippled by the wind on their first night at sea, had straggled back into Toulon – masts shattered, rigging strained and basic seamanship skills in doubt. Villeneuve was dismayed by the experience; Bonaparte was dismayed by his lack of resolution. Nelson, meanwhile, was concerned that the poor state of the *Royal Sovereign*'s copper made her too slow for such pursuits.[74]

The fleet had suffered no damage in the storms or the pursuit, however, and was ready for another cruise only days after reaching Sardinia on 8 March. Realising Orde had not been sent out to supersede him, Nelson decided to stay until the movements of the French fleet were clear. He was still expecting a battle.[75] A few days later Nile veteran Rear Admiral Sir Thomas Louis joined the fleet with flag Captain Francis Austen, then the best known of the Austen family.

The underlying purpose of Bonaparte's movements was unclear. Lying in Cawsand Bay, for a brief respite from the hard pounding off Brest, Collingwood recorded his view:

> The sort of dilatory war that he is now carrying on against us, is a new system, and of deep policy: – It is war against our trade & finances – a war the object of which is to subject us to great expenses, and diminish our means of supporting them – but experience will teach him the fallacy of his system very soon.[76]

This was a typically lucid and penetrating analysis by a master of war. Collingwood was Nelson's best friend in the service because he was one of the few men to view the world from the same level, and with the same clarity. Nelson agreed, regretting that Orde's command had broken up his system of Mediterranean trade protection, leading to the loss of one convoy, and risking many more.[77] By this time Bonaparte had switched from trade attack to deception plans to facilitate an invasion, and he continued to change his mind throughout the 1805 campaign. He might outwit Orde, but not Collingwood or Nelson.

Nelson stressed that the key to success in this titanic conflict lay in striking blows in Europe, not frittering away the national resources on 'buccaneering expeditions' to the Spanish empire.[78] According to the fleet surgeon's report, Nelson needed rest and the assistance of an oculist.[79] Nelson himself complained of 'heart' spasms, though they were later diagnosed as indigestion, brought on by tension, lack of exercise and poor diet – but he was worried that a return might be misinterpreted:

> The moment I make up my mind the French fleet will not come out this summer, I embark in the *Superb*. My health does not improve; but because I am not confined to my bed, people will not believe my state of health.[80]

By the time he wrote, however, the French were already at sea. The final campaign had opened.

CHAPTER XIV

To the West Indies and Back
1805

Between April and October 1805, Britain and France played out a complex strategic game on a vast scale. While it cost relatively few lives, the outcome would be crucial. Bonaparte was playing for the ultimate prize, the defeat of Britain by invasion; Britain tried to create a new Continental coalition to overwhelm the upstart Emperor. Both would be disappointed.

Bonaparte's invasion plans have exercised a grim fascination for the past two hundred years. For some they were the gravest threat to Britain between the Spanish Armada and 1940; for others a bluff. The latter seems more likely with the benefit of hindsight: when the French general staff investigated the issue very carefully at the end of the nineteenth century they concluded that the plans were never fully staffed, and showed little grasp of the realities of maritime warfare.[1] There were never enough troops at the Channel ports, or enough invasion craft to carry them, while the harbours were too shallow, the embarkation too slow and the prospect of getting across without a major battle too unlikely for the plans to have been real. This did not mean, however, that the threat was not perceived as serious at the time; its very existence had a fundamental effect on British policy.

Since his return to office in May 1804, Pitt had taken a more active approach to pursuing diplomatic links than the Addington Ministry –

Masters of war: Wellington and Nelson in September 1805

principally with Russia, but also Austria. He saw the solution to the problem of radicalised France in European terms. Only the combined efforts of the great powers could force France back into the state system, with a form of government that recognised the legitimacy of existing regimes, the sanctity of borders and of treaties. Without such a change the war would go on for ever. Addington had been content to wait for Europeans to see this for themselves. While he waited, he built up the defensive arm of British power, making the prospect of a successful French invasion less likely by the day. He increased the standing army, reformed the militia and used volunteer meetings to bring the total bearing arms to half a million. As the local forces improved, they would release the army for overseas operations.

After a year of sustained improvement, the defences of Britain were strong, and still Bonaparte had not moved. The key difference between Pitt and his predecessor lay in their offensive measures. Under the cover of the main fleets, Addington had begun to sweep up French islands and overseas bases, annihilated her trade and shipping, and denied her the chance to move outside Europe. It was economic war, and could be waged over the long term: sound money and economic stability would keep Britain going while the French economy collapsed. Pitt's focus, by contrast, was political: new alignments with St Petersburg and Vienna were his principal aim.

The key to the situation remained Bonaparte. His unlimited ambition and disregard for any form of international agreement not based on force made peace highly unlikely. Since the outbreak of war he had used the threat of invasion to keep the British pinned to their own shores, while reducing various clients and satellites on his borders to the status of French provinces. His long-term aims, which he took no pains to disguise, included southern Italy, Greece, European Turkey and Egypt. Ultimately, he wanted to throw the British out of India. While France held the Low Countries Britain would never make peace; while Bonaparte ruled without honour, disregarding the law of nations, any peace would be a delusion.

The Tsar was also concerned by French ambition, and favoured a European league of major powers, with British support, to block Bonaparte's schemes. By mid-1804 he had issued his demands, and recalled his ambassador from Paris. The obvious point of contact between Russia and Britain was the eastern Mediterranean, where mutual concern for Naples, the Greek islands and Turkey offered the potential for an alliance-building combined effort. British policy also favoured the restoration of the Kingdom of Sardinia, to block French hegemony in Northern Italy. To cement the new partnership Pitt agreed to send an army to join the Russians in Italy, but rejected the Tsar's demand that Britain return Malta to the Knights. Pitt was confident enough to threaten to fall back on a purely maritime war, leaving Russia to settle Europe on her own. Even so he continued preparations for a Mediterranean expeditionary corps to join the Russians in Italy.

When Pitt and the Tsar began to challenge French policy Bonaparte's bluff was called, and rather than attempt an invasion he abandoned the scheme, paid off his barges and looked elsewhere for a weapon. Spain, already paying heavy subsidies to avoid a worse fate, was drawn into the war, but Pitt struck first, intercepting treasure ships and crippling overseas trade in October 1804, before Spain was ready. The Spanish fleet would not be effective until the middle of 1805, so the only move that could challenge Britain was an attack on her trade and overseas possessions. In January 1805 Bonaparte ordered the Rochefort and Toulon squadrons to sea: they were to rendezvous in the West Indies, release the French ships at Ferrol and return united to a suitable French port. He also issued orders for the Brest fleet to land troops in Ireland, sail round Scotland and link up with the fleet in the Texel and the army in Holland. The latter disconnected scheme appears to have been a smokescreen, leaked for effect. The breathing space these moves would win could be used to drive Austria out of any Russo-British combination. The invasion plans and preparations were now explained away as a smokescreen for the creation of the Grand Army that would dominate Europe for the next decade. Yet when Austria backed gracefully out of a confrontation, and Britain rejected Napoleon's overtures for peace, he was left with no recourse but to revive the invasion plans.

Would Bonaparte take the initiative with his fleet, the only lever he could use to coerce Britain, before the new coalition could form and threaten his frontiers? He faced three powers: Britain was safe behind the Channel and Russia too far to the east to be attacked, but Austria was vulnerable, and hardly recovered from the Revolutionary wars. The threat from all three would be serious. He had to break up the combination before it could act. If he did nothing Britain could dispatch some of her tiny army overseas, link up with Russia and prompt Austria. For obvious political reasons, Bonaparte could not wait on the defensive like the legitimate monarchies he faced. His rule was based on military success and glory, not peace and stability.

After toying with an attack on India, Bonaparte developed a new plan to concentrate his fleets in the West Indies and swing back to Europe for an invasion. This grand plan has perhaps been taken more seriously than it deserved. Bonaparte never assembled more than ninety thousand troops on the Channel coast, and did not have sufficient harbour capacity or craft to embark them in fewer than four tides. His fleets from Brest, Ferrol, Cadiz and Toulon were to assemble at a distance, after escaping the British blockades, and cover an understaffed and unprepared 'surprise' invasion against an enemy who had been on full alert for twelve months. All this was to be achieved without a battle. The best that can be said for these schemes is that they occupied the attention of the British for several months, made use of a hugely expensive and otherwise unnecessary resource, and distracted everyone from his military designs. But the plan did not deal with the basic problem, one that his admirals understood only too well. If the French fleets managed to get to sea the British would concentrate on the Western Approaches off Brest, to cover the Channel, and the incoming trade. Furthermore, they would fight whenever the opportunity allowed, and any battle, whatever the result, would destroy the Imperial scheme.

The contemporaneous British plan to send General Craig with five to six thousand troops linked the British with Russia, met Nelson's long standing strategic concerns and opened a new front against the French. The troops would secure Sicily, cooperate with the Russians in Naples, and occupy Sardinia or hold Alexandria. However, Nelson had not heard anything from London since November; the last two despatch vessels had been lost – one wrecked, the other taken by Villeneuve in January. His own ideas were clear. Off Toulon on 10 March, he was certain the French were once more embarking troops. He worked through the options, decided that the French occupation of Sardinia, Sicily or Egypt would be an irreversible disaster, and developed a plan to catch Villeneuve, whichever direction he was heading – east or west. He would cover the former course; the latter would be blocked by a ruse, forcing Villeneuve into his chosen position. After running across to Barcelona, to be seen and reported, he would hold the fleet at Palmas on the Sardinian coast. The ruse would force the French to steer east, into the trap.

Villeneuve sailed on 30 March, well aware that Nelson was off Barcelona, heading south. The following day a neutral merchant ship betrayed Nelson's true position; Villeneuve immediately swung east of the Balearics, heading for Cartagena to pick up a Spanish squadron. Four days later Nelson, still unaware that the enemy was out, wrote to tell Emma that 'unless the French fleet should be at sea, or a certainty of its putting to sea, I shall move to the *Superb* on the day I have before told you'.[2] Later that day he learnt they were out, and had missed his trap. Deprived of his prize, Nelson had to satisfy himself that the enemy had not passed to the east before he could look to the west. He did not repeat his sortie to Egypt: instead the fleet was spread to cover the area between Sardinia and the Tunisian coast. He also had to ensure they had not doubled back and passed to the east of Sardinia, a threat that kept him pinned in place for days: 'I must not make more haste than good speed and leave Sardinia, Sicily, or Naples for them to take should I go either to the Eastward or the Westward, without knowing something more about them.'[3] He desperately needed unambiguous intelligence to guide his actions; without it he would not risk the key positions.

Villeneuve ran down to Cartagena, but would not wait for the Spanish ships to come out, heading for the Straits to release Admiral Gravina's force at Cadiz. On 8 April he was seen passing Gibraltar by Captain Richard Strachan in the seventy-four *Renown*; Strachan turned back and signalled Orde's squadron of five sail that the enemy was coming. Orde formed a line, but Villeneuve hurried past for Cadiz. Once Orde realised Nelson was not in hot pursuit, he sent a frigate to warn the Grand Fleet off Ushant of the possible concentration of enemy forces. He would follow the next day, if nothing changed overnight. This was sound doctrine, and good practice. If the Grand Fleet was overpowered Britain would lose the war: invasion or not, the loss of vital trade alone would be decisive. Orde took his battleships north, but left his cruisers to watch Villeneuve, sent warnings to Nelson, the West Indies and the homebound East India convoy. It was a solid performance, but too slow.

Villeneuve reached Cadiz on 9 April and signalled to Admiral Gravina to join him. Gravina hurried out with nine battleships, a solitary French ship and the eight Spanish ships then ready for sea. The course remained westward. They went away into the night, the Spaniards straggling after the French, and were lost to the British before Orde's cruisers could reach Cadiz.

These events coincided with the resignation of Henry Dundas, First Lord of the Admiralty, after charges relating to the improper use of public money were brought against him in Parliament. After some delay, he was replaced by his elderly cousin, Admiral Sir Charles Middleton, one-time Controller of the Navy with whom Nelson had corresponded back in the 1780s. Middleton was ennobled as Lord Barham to bring him into Parliament, but he was kept out of the Cabinet and the day-to-day running of the Navy. Instead he focused on the strategic issues, a subject on which Melville had been consulting him for some time. His central control, informed by the initiative and resource of numerous capable, confident frigate captains, and the consistent response of his fleet commanders to almost all the problems they faced enabled him to counter every move the French made, and often to anticipate them. It was a masterclass in pre-industrial strategy.[4] Once the enemy put to sea, every officer used his best endeavour to keep the main fleets informed, and to pass messages back to London where other intelligence sources – some accurate, others generated by Bonaparte's spies – were sifted and assessed. With Cornwallis or Gardner off Ushant, Calder off Ferrol, a squadron off Rochefort and Nelson in the Mediterranean, the cruisers knew where to look.

Suitably informed, Barham covered every eventuality. Although he was often too far behind events to pre-empt the enemy, his penetration varied from the acute to the sublime.[5] A detachment from the Grand Fleet, commanded by Collingwood, was put in hand, and the various options open to the French were considered. Craig's army heading for Italy was at risk, but smart cruiser work saw it put into Lisbon and, once Villeneuve had passed, rendezvous with Nelson at the Straits. Above all Barham ensured the Western Approaches to the Channel were secured by a force capable of defeating anything the French and Spanish could assemble. This simple strategic principle, based on long years of practical experience, and executed by competent and tested officers, would always defeat Bonaparte's elaborate combinations.

All this occurred without Nelson's knowledge. In position off Sicily on 10 April, he heard a rumour of the military expedition, and immediately set course for the Straits, to save it from Villeneuve. Instead he spent the next five days beating into a head wind to get round

Sardinia. Reliable news of the military expedition arrived just as he heard that the French were headed for the Straits. His first concern was the military force. On 18 April William Parker in the frigate *Amazon* confirmed the French had passed the Straits eight days earlier. Nelson had been outmanoeuvred, and hastened off to Gibraltar for more news. Not knowing where had they gone he left almost the entire cruiser force to cover Sicily, Sardinia and Egypt. Wherever the French were they would not profit from Nelson's decision to pursue them. Unless he could find more positive intelligence of the French destination he would retreat on the Grand Fleet, as Orde had done. News of the link-up with the Spanish persuaded him the enemy was heading for the Channel, and he responded accordingly, sending his route and rendezvous ahead so the Admiralty could redirect him if they possessed better intelligence.

Nelson heard the first official report of Craig's force, which had not sailed as soon as he had feared, shortly before he anchored at Tetuan on 4 May, to obtain water, beef and fuel for a long cruise. When Commissioner Otway at Gibraltar told him that it was generally believed the enemy had gone to the West Indies, he had to weigh uncertainty about their whereabouts against the possibility that they would seize Jamaica and break the vital West Indian economy. He would not act without evidence, and hoped that Parker in the *Amazon* would bring him answers from Lisbon. By 7 May, he was preparing himself for the cruise to the West Indies. Nervous tension left him tired, unwell, and emotionally drained: 'But my health, or even my life must not come into consideration at this important crisis; for, however I may be called unfortunate, it never shall be said that I have been neglectful of my duty, or spared myself.'[6] Throughout the crisis his main supports were the nearby comfort of Richard Keats, the best and brightest of his captains, and Alexander Davison, his oldest friend. His letters to Emma were largely professional, with a selection of endearments to garnish his continual absence.[7] There could be no more powerful demonstration of the division between his public and private lives: he was hers, but only when he was not at work.

Only on 10 May did the situation become clear. Nelson decided to head for the West Indies once he had seen Craig's army safely into the Mediterranean; he detached Bickerton to command the station in his absence, and left the sluggish *Royal Sovereign* to reinforce the troop convoy. Samuel Sutton in *Amphion* told him there was no sign of the

French to the north, while William Parker brought more positive news from Lisbon, including reports that the enemy had been sighted far out to sea, with full details of ships and officers. On 11 May Nelson left with ten battleships and three frigates. His choice of route was settled by Richard Hakluyt's two-hundred-year-old account of the English Atlantic voyages.[8] He was not afraid of a stern chase, or being significantly inferior in force. He expected to pick up ships in the West Indies: six of the line under Alexander Cochrane on the Leeward Islands station were the obvious reinforcement. More significantly, a battle would frustrate the French plans, whatever its outcome. Nor was he cutting himself off from the Mediterranean: if he was wrong, he told the Admiralty, he could be back by the end of June. Barham, typically, had reached the same conclusions five days earlier, but his response was overtaken by events.

Once he knew Villeneuve had got to sea, Bonaparte reviewed his plans, and revived the old idea of the Toulon squadron working round the north of Scotland to open the Dutch ports. Within a few days he had proposed an even more absurd combination that would release the Ferrol force, and then work up to release the Brest fleet by a combined attack on the British from inside and outside the harbour. Such elaborate plans might have worked on land, but at sea, without better means of communication than anyone possessed in 1805, they were absurd. Admiral Ganteaume would never escape from Brest while men like Admiral Lord Gardner or Cornwallis commanded the Grand Fleet. They knew that so long as the main French fleet was kept off the board the game was as good as won.

The Minister of the Marine, Admiral Denis Decrès, understood the realities of naval warfare. He had escaped the Nile, been captured on the *Guillaume Tell* and dined with Nelson. He warned Bonaparte, but his advice fell on deaf ears. It was the Emperor's habit to condemn any strategic choices that he had not anticipated as incompetent, inept or stupid. Equally problematic was his inability to take advice on issues that he did not understand. Decrès would have made better use of the French and Spanish fleets without Bonaparte's interference; he would not have tried to win the war with the sort of knock-out blow that the man of Marengo favoured. Bonaparte would prove, over and over again, that he could achieve the near-perfect synthesis of military triumph and political success, but only on his own element.

By mid-June the British had re-established the blockade of the main French and Spanish ports: Brest, Rochefort, Ferrol and Cadiz were guarded, while Cartagena was neutralised by the squadron off Cadiz and Bickerton's small force. The only pieces still moving on the global strategic chart were those commanded by Villeneuve and Nelson. It was also highly significant that when Collingwood arrived off Cadiz he instituted a strict blockade to deny the Spanish access to naval stores to fit out their fleet, rather than the more 'neutral-friendly' version the Admiralty and Foreign Office preferred.

Nelson sent a dispatch to the Admiralty as he passed Madeira on 14 May, the same day that Villeneuve anchored off Martinique. After that point Nelson was necessarily out of touch with London, but he had already sent a frigate ahead to warn Admiral Cochrane of his arrival. He hoped to find six battleships at Barbados, but Cochrane had left all but one of his ships at Jamaica. For Villeneuve, meanwhile, Bonaparte's orders to be instantly ready to combine with the Brest fleet precluded any major operations against the British islands, so he sent out some cruisers to gather intelligence and cut up the local shipping. New orders to widen the attack on British possessions only revealed Bonaparte's inability to maintain his focus on the big issues. His new return destination, if the Brest fleet did not arrive, was Ferrol. Villeneuve turned to attack Antigua and Barbuda.

Straining every nerve, and the fabric of his well-worn fleet, Nelson crossed the Atlantic ten days quicker than Villeneuve's motley armada, reaching Barbados on 4 June. He found Cochrane, and another battleship joined that evening. This gave him twelve of the line: he believed the enemy had eighteen, but the odds were not impossible. He had to act, and the security of the West Indian islands and trade justified the risk – he only had to locate the enemy.

Unfortunately local intelligence misled him. General Brereton on St Lucia reported the enemy had passed on 28 May, and seemed to be headed for Barbados or Trinidad. The latter was a likely option, and although Nelson had anticipated the enemy would be to the north, he felt that such precise intelligence could not be ignored. The clinching fact was that he had known Brereton on Corsica, and trusted him. Embarking two thousand troops from the Barbados garrison, he headed south on 6 June, issuing a new order of battle indicating that he intended attacking in two columns. Confident the enemy was at Trinidad, Nelson sailed into Port of Spain early on 7 June. He must

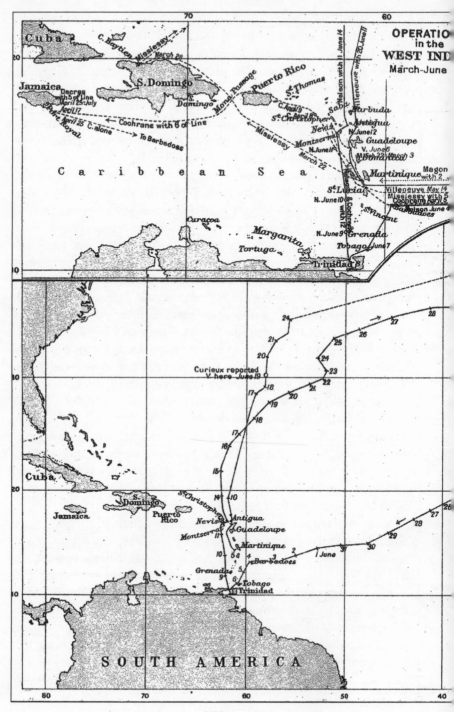

The trans-Atlantic chase (from J. Corbett, *The Campaign of Trafalgar*, 1910). Nelson's course is marked by the line originating west of Morocco on 12 May, reaching Trinidad on 7 June, and returning along a course that took him south of the Azores in early July. Villeneuve's return across the Atlantic is tracked from Martinique on 5 June to Finisterre on 22 July.

have expected to find the enemy trapped at anchor, their troops ashore, and a new battle of the Nile unfolding before him.

Instead he found the port empty. He had been right all along, and bitterly lamented Brereton's interference. Villeneuve had headed north, and along the way picked up a small convoy from Antigua, which the local merchants had insisted should sail before the island fell, only to run into the allied fleet. Now aware of Nelson's arrival, Villeneuve hurried back to Martinique, landed most of his troops, and on 10 June headed for the Azores. A combination of fear and the terrible condition of the Spanish crews made battle unthinkable: the only safety lay in flight. On 12 June Nelson was off Antigua, determined not to leave the theatre until he had hard evidence that the enemy had, as he suspected, headed home. Through the disappointment of being misled and missing his battle, he recognised the scale of his achievement: 'I have saved these colonies and more than 200 sail of sugar-loaded ships.'⁹ The brig *Curieux* carried home his analysis that the enemy was heading for Europe; he would pursue them. After landing the troops at Antigua and detaching Cochrane to guard the islands in case he was wrong, he headed off with eleven sail on 13 June, only to receive fresh information that the enemy fleet was larger than he had thought.

The West Indies voyage had been a major success: the enemy had been blocked and driven home after doing trifling damage. With the enemy in full retreat, Nelson planned to fight them in combination with other British forces as they approached Europe, rather than engage in mid-Atlantic with the odds two to one against. However, he would be alive to any opportunity to distress them, and to use his force to confound any other object they might have. He set a course for the Straits, but Villeneuve was bound for Ferrol and they did not meet. Instead the *Curieux*, heading for England, was soon in the wake of the Franco-Spanish formation, and watched them long enough to be certain of their course.

Barham's first thoughts, like Nelson's, were to expect Villeneuve in the Straits, but when the *Curieux*'s commander arrived on 8 July it was clear that Cape Finisterre was the intended landfall, and opening the blockade of Ferrol the object. Another brilliant example of cruiser work had given the high command priceless intelligence. Barham immediately wrote out new orders to reinforce Sir Robert Calder off Ferrol, both from Cornwallis's Grand Fleet and by giving up the blockade of Rochefort. Calder would cruise up to a hundred miles due west of Finisterre, Cornwallis could stand to the south-west a similar distance for ten days, while Nelson would deal with Cadiz. This was outstanding strategic insight, overall direction and good sense: it gave the local commanders adequate forces and good advice, and covered all three real options, Brest, Cadiz, and above all Ferrol, yet it left them at liberty to respond to local developments.

Bonaparte, then leaving Turin for Boulogne, had been defeated before he passed the Alps. Even when he knew Cornwallis had moved away, Ganteaume did not try to leave Brest, well aware that he would be spotted and pursued. He rejected the idea of rushing into the Channel out of hand – it was madness, the English would be after him immediately, and in overwhelming force. His twenty-two ships would face thirty or more, and be destroyed, while the invasion required two weeks, not twenty-four hours. For Ganteaume, who had witnessed the Nile from the quarter-deck of *L'Orient*, the English were an irresistible force. He saw Cornwallis's move to locate Villeneuve as a trap, not an opportunity. That the invasion force was not ready, either in men or ships, made the idea of leaving harbour absurd. By the time peremptory orders to enter the Channel reached Brest, Cornwallis was back in position.

On 22 July, Villeneuve and Gravina, with twenty battleships, met Calder's fleet of fifteen off Finisterre. In the fog and confusion, a partial action ensued, negating Calder's aggressive aim of cutting off the enemy centre and rear. It ended with the capture of two Spanish ships, and extensive damage to the rigging of several British vessels. Villeneuve put into Vigo, but Calder, having started well, so far misunderstood his role as to let him get away. He should have kept contact, ignoring the distant threat from the ships at Ferrol, and pushed his success to a conclusion. For this failure he would be court-martialled, losing his place as a fleet commander.

Hurrying back towards the Straits, Nelson hoped to overtake Villeneuve and engage him off Cape St Vincent, where he arrived on 17 July. He had overtaken them, but on finding the enemy had not passed the Straits or entered Cadiz,[10] he held on to meet Collingwood off Cadiz, before going ashore for the first time in two years at Gibraltar. Convinced the French intended concentrating their forces in the Western Approaches, to overwhelm the Grand Fleet and invade, Collingwood did not believe Bonaparte would have moved his ships for any lesser purpose. Nelson was not convinced. He was a Mediterranean man, and viewed the intelligence through a different prism from a Channel fleet veteran like Collingwood. While he waited for news, Nelson demonstrated his mastery of the theatre. Any reduction in ships in the central and eastern Mediterranean would gravely reduce British influence, so he tore up the Admiralty instructions and the existing deployments of Collingwood, Knight and Bickerton. His redistribution of the available forces was 'absolutely necessary' to counter the Cadiz and Cartagena squadrons and the privateer threat to trade, while protecting Sardinia, Malta, Sicily and Naples.

Only on 22 July, the day Calder fought his action, did the fleet drop over to the Moroccan port of Tetuan for water, wood and beef. Two days later Nelson had just raised anchor when news arrived from the north: learning of the *Curieux*'s intelligence windfall, he knew Villeneuve must be headed for the Bay of Biscay. Without wasting a boisterous wind, even to brief Collingwood, he set course for Ferrol. Adverse winds forced him to the west, and ultimately he had to head directly for Cornwallis's rendezvous. Unaware of Calder's action he did not know where Villeneuve was, or of the situation off Ferrol. He sent word ahead to the Grand Fleet, and to Ireland, which he thought the most likely point for the French attack. The relaxation of tension led to dark and grave reflections on the failure of his campaign:

> But for General Brereton's damned information, Nelson would have been, living or dead, the greatest man in his Profession that England ever saw. Now, alas! I am nothing – perhaps shall incur censure for misfortunes which may happen, and have happened. When I follow my own head, I am, in general, much more correct in my judgement, than following the opinion of others.[11]

Such insecurity may appear remarkable, but Nelson's ambition would be unfulfilled while there was still a war to win and fleets to annihilate. He approached the Grand Fleet rendezvous and home sunk in gloom, uncertain of the reception that would greet his return after a campaign without a battle. It was the very opposite of what one would expect from a man so long at sea, and absent from home, mistress and child. By now certain the enemy had put into a Biscay port, his health concerns began to reappear as he closed on the flag of another old friend, Sir William Cornwallis. He needed rest, and release from the incessant mental anxiety of planning a campaign, outthinking the enemy and sustaining the logistics, human resources and morale of his squadron.

Hearing of Calder's action and Villeneuve's arrival at Coruna, Barham agreed with Nelson, and on 3 August ordered a concentration off Ushant. This was not a simple defensive measure: Barham properly left Cornwallis at liberty to detach forces to exploit any opportunity the enemy offered for a counter-stroke. To prove the point the fleet that fought the decisive battle of the campaign would be a detachment from the Grand Fleet.

Villeneuve left Coruna on 10 August, planning to head for Brest or Cadiz as circumstances dictated. It took another three days for his fleet, now raised to twenty-nine battleships, to get to sea. Half of them had not been at sea for years, if at all; the rest, while improved in skill and battle-hardened, were hardly in first-class order. The Rochefort division of five was at sea, but could not be found. On 14 August Calder joined Cornwallis, and Nelson arrived late the following day. Cornwallis had instructions to send Nelson home: he, his flagship and the shaky *Superb* needed refitting. This left Cornwallis with thirty-six battleships, ten of them three-decked ships ideal for close-quarters battle. No combination of French and Spanish ships could defeat Cornwallis, the acknowledged master of the tactical defensive.

Bonaparte's many and complex plans were in ruins: his squadrons were no closer to Boulogne, barred by the solid mass of the Grand Fleet, while Keith's reinforced North Sea fleet was ready to annihilate the invasion shipping gathered around Boulogne, if it dared to put to sea. Now the game was shifting. In a campaign that reflected the nature of the war, the British had blocked every offensive move the French had attempted; now they were concentrated and ready for a telling counter-attack. By early August Foreign Minister Talleyrand knew the game was up, warning Bonaparte not to attempt the invasion.

On 13 and 14 August Bonaparte shifted his focus to the growing threat of an Austro-Russian attack, planning the campaign that culminated at Austerlitz. Yet rather than hold to the simple comfort of a massive concentration off Brest, Cornwallis immediately split his fleet. The day after Nelson arrived, he detached Calder south with eighteen battleships, including many from Nelson's fleet, to look for Villeneuve at Ferrol and stop him putting to sea. He knew the enemy might have over thirty ships, but this was all he could spare. He retained eighteen ships off Brest, including no fewer than ten three-deckers. It was a powerful force.

Bonaparte raged at Cornwallis's stroke of genius, something he had not anticipated, condemning it as a strategic blunder that risked everything. It was no such thing, as Barham acknowledged by ordering the same division, although he did not wish Calder to command. Cornwallis was in easy communication with the detached force, which was still under his orders, and Calder knew well enough what to do if he met the enemy, or heard of their whereabouts. The main threat that Villeneuve now posed was to the Anglo-Russian plans to attack in the Mediterranean, where Craig's army and a larger Russian force were assembling. The main British counter-attack depended on cooperation with Russia, and this would be impossible if the enemy commanded the Mediterranean. Villeneuve was also ideally placed to attack the immense homebound convoys from the East and West Indies. The loss of a major convoy would have ruined the economy, brought down the Ministry and possibly bankrupted the state. After an invasion this was the gravest danger that Britain faced, and was never far from the minds of all her great strategists, especially Barham, Nelson and Cornwallis.

The knowledge that Nelson was at sea, hard on his heels, had broken Villeneuve's spirit. Setting sail from Coruna on 13 August, he told Decrès: 'I do not hesitate to say . . . I should be sorry to meet twenty of them. Our naval tactics are antiquated. We know nothing but how to place ourselves in line, and that is just what the enemy wants.'[12] By 19 August Cornwallis knew the enemy was heading south, and sent fresh instructions to Calder, confident they lacked the stores for a long cruise, the troops for a landing, or any object beyond reaching the Mediterranean. Two days later Ganteaume came out of Brest Roads, and anchored under the batteries. Cornwallis had a major decision to make. Should he pull back, let the enemy out to sea and annihilate them, or drive them back into Brest? While he was desperate for a great battle, his response was determined by the strategic context. The next morning he led his fleet in. Although driven off by storm of fire from the shore batteries, his attack forced Ganteaume to scramble for safety, and made him unlikely to venture out again.

Villeneuve, meanwhile, had initially headed west for a rendezvous with the Rochefort squadron, but the presence of British cruisers, false news of a fleet nearby and numerous neutral ships reporting the British in strength to the north quickly changed his mind. He set course for Cadiz; the invasion plans of Bonaparte were over, his fleet was demoralised, her admiral already beaten and the allies bickering over who was to blame.

Arriving off Cadiz on 19 August, the Combined Fleet found Collingwood, forewarned from Lisbon, with three battleships and a frigate. Collingwood neatly stepped aside to allow them into Cadiz while covering the Straits. Once the enemy was in port he resumed his station, denying them access to food, naval stores and even sea-based intelligence. This was bold, but entirely in character. Bickerton sent his ships from off Cartagena: they arrived on 28 August, and Calder joined with eighteen more two days later. The enemy were now in a worse position than they had been in April. There were close on forty ships at Cadiz, but little food, and few stores. They were trapped by a force perfectly capable of knocking back any sortie, and demoralised from top to bottom.

Had Nelson, Barham, and the sound doctrine of the service defeated the most ambitious attempt ever made to invade England, or exposed the most outrageous bluff in the history of war? Bonaparte would assert both arguments on different occasions: the verdict on the real nature of the French schemes must remain open.

Never one to waste a scrap of information, Nelson continued to make notes on winds and currents as he headed north. When he reached the Grand Fleet, Cornwallis was expecting him, and sent word that he was not to stop, or to think of boarding the flagship so late in the day. 'I am truly sorry that you have not had your accustomed good luck in falling in with the enemy. I believe that was all that anyone wished for, being perfectly satisfied what the consequence would be.'[13] *Victory* and *Superb* were ordered to Spithead, while the rest of the squadron stayed with the Grand Fleet. Another old friend, Thomas Fremantle, commanding the ninety-eight-gun *Neptune*, understood what Nelson needed:

> You will, on your arrival in England find everyone disposed to do you entire credit, and at no period according to my judgement did you ever stand higher in the estimation of the public, and indeed we are much in want of all the ability the country can find.[14]

The combination of friendly words and the high praise appearing in the press must have speeded Nelson's recovery. His ailments were produced by stress and anxiety, not physical illness. He was relieved of anxiety about his reception at home, and knew that the enemy had not escaped. He trusted Cornwallis and Collingwood to finish the job, if he could not. It would be a far happier man who stepped off the *Victory* at Portsmouth.

On leaving for home Nelson thanked the officers and men of the squadron that had served him so well. He did not criticise Calder, but paraphrased the line St Vincent had sent him after Tenerife and Boulogne, that 'men cannot command success'.[15] Once he had been through the papers, they went across to Keats, with an invitation to dine. The two ships reached Spithead on 18 August, and went into quarantine the following day. The crews were in excellent health, requiring only vegetables and other refreshments to remove the scurvy. Nelson arrived at Merton early on 20 August, and was immediately summoned to London.[16] The day was occupied by meetings at the Admiralty, at Downing Street and at his prize agents, to see how his various outstanding cases were progressing.

News of Nelson's return spread quickly. Clarence called on 22 August, while old Lord Hood praised his handling of the campaign, and predicted he would soon be back at sea. Keats passed on his assessment of the public mood: 'all classes unite in one sentiment of admiration for your Lordship's judicious and persevering conduct'.[17] Nelson in turn praised Keats' judgement and courage, and reported that the ministers looked on him as some sort of conjuror. Despite the public acclaim, Nelson remained uncertain of his future: he was a Commander in Chief on leave, and the likelihood of his going back increased by the day.[18] Hood, still a confidant of Pitt, was convinced the enemy had gone to the Mediterranean, or to Cadiz. If so, Nelson would soon be back at sea.[19]

Although Pitt and Secretary for War Lord Castlereagh were anxious to see Nelson, Lord Barham was more reserved. He had not seen much of the hero since the 1780s, and was only won over when he read the journal of his campaign. The Admiralty required flag officers to keep a journal of proceedings, in which both their actions and their reasons were laid out. Barham recognised the breadth and penetration of Nelson's intellect, the wisdom of his decisions, the infinite pains he had taken to catch the enemy and his political insight. Discussions with Pitt and Castlereagh went so well that the Prime Minister, exhausted and burdened by the demands of the war as he was, considered riding over from Wimbledon to visit Merton. The West India merchant community was equally pleased, and requested an opportunity to present their vote of thanks in person. While Nelson emphasised that he had only been doing his duty, and praised the high state of the local military and militia forces, it was still a fine compliment, fit to stand alongside those from the East India Company, the Levant merchants and the City of London.[20] Nor was the Church unmoved. The Bishop of Exeter, a clerical friend of brother William, added: 'I ought also to congratulate my country upon the safe return of (under Heaven) its ablest protector, who is now ready at hand to defend us from the threatened attack of our vaunting enemy.'[21]

Yet despite the acclaim of great men, it was the effect he produced on the public that was simply astonishing. Minto was with him in a crowd:

> It is really quite affecting to see the wonder and admiration and love and respect of the whole world; and the genuine expression of all these sentiments at once, from the gentle and simple the moment he is seen. It is beyond anything represented in a play or a poem of fame.[22]

To be in his presence, to touch the hem of his garment, just to see him was enough. It was all too reminiscent of the final days of the Christian redeemer, and few missed the growing presentiment of triumph and tragedy.

In the brief period when Nelson was ashore, Bonaparte finally recognised that the Anglo-Russian coalition contained the seeds of a disaster. Austria would join, and even half-hearted Prussia seemed ready to make common cause. The failure of his grand naval strategy was obvious, Villeneuve had gone south, Ganteaume had been driven back into Brest, and the Rochefort squadron was simply lost. The key to the situation lay in the south, where the small British army that had cost Nelson so much anxiety was ready to land at Naples. It would link up with the Russians and the Austrians for a campaign to recover Italy.

By 23 August Bonaparte was satisfied that he could wait no longer: next spring there would be too many enemies, too widely dispersed. He must strike now. Decrès made it clear that any chance of invading Britain had passed, if it had ever existed. The army at Boulogne would move east, front-line units being replaced by depot battalions, although the Emperor himself remained to lend colour to the deception of Austria. On 1 September Bonaparte learnt that Villeneuve was at Cadiz.

Captain Henry Blackwood arrived at Spithead the same day with the same news, and posted up to the Admiralty. It was no mere courtesy that saw him stop off at Merton as he passed early the next morning. The fact that he found Nelson awake and fully dressed at 5 a.m. suggests the admiral had not thrown off the habits of shipboard life, and may have been expecting just such a call. Blackwood recognised that his news must bring Nelson back to the Mediterranean. Had Nelson lived anywhere else, the information would have taken days to reach him. Merton had proved its value as the home of a devoted public servant – on the right axis for naval intelligence, and an easy commute into town.

Later the same day, Nelson was at the Admiralty, Downing Street and the Colonial Office, discussing the strategic situation with the Prime Minister, the First Lord and Secretary for War. He persuaded the doubters that Cadiz, now blockaded by Calder and Collingwood, was the key to success. If the Combined Fleet had not already met Cornwallis or Calder it had to be destroyed, or at worst completely neutralised, both to secure the Mediterranean elements of the coalition war plan and to ensure the invasion threat, now waning, was not suddenly revived just as when Britain was sending her regular troops abroad. Nelson was clearly the man for the job: his return from leave would be hastened, his forces increased, and his theatre extended, as he expressly desired, to Cape St Vincent.[23]

Now Nelson could really influence the British response to Bonaparte's complex combinations. He had the opportunity to discuss the Mediterranean with ministers who were, albeit temporarily, anxious to listen. His emphasis on the need to secure Sardinia was quickly accepted, although his advice that General Mack was 'a rascal, a scoundrel, and a coward' came too late to prevent the catastrophe at Ulm. On 4 September Nelson was back at the Admiralty to settle his orders with Barham.[24] He showed them to Minto that night.[25] Fresh instructions went to Collingwood: *Victory* had been detailed to join Cornwallis on 30 September, but was reserved while Hardy reported himself fit for service.

Nelson would go to Portsmouth when his flagship was ready to sail, although his clothes, papers and furniture left Merton on 5 September.[26] Orders for Vice Admiral Sir Charles Cotton to take command off Cadiz were cancelled, and Calder was recalled to account for failing to renew his action. News that the camp at Boulogne was breaking up arrived the same day. The scene was shifting to the south:

the best that Britain could do to aid her partners was to act quickly in the Mediterranean, open the sea-lanes for Russian and Austrian troops, and secure the key islands. Nelson would command from Istanbul and Suez to Cape St Vincent, with wide latitude to act. His instructions were to prevent the enemy putting to sea and protect trade – everything else was left to his judgement.

By 6 September the new orders were nearly ready at the Admiralty, but there were still details to settle. Hydrographer Alexander Dalrymple and 'Bounty' Bligh provided new charts and other intelligence for his station; John McArthur sent his new book on courts martial; Nile hero Saumarez, now commanding off Guernsey, sent in Nelson's wine; while the Foreign Secretary promised to place a British consul on Sardinia, and found £40,000 to help Nelson secure the island.[27] With every minute a precious resource, Nelson cannot have been pleased by the bombardment of begging letters from friends, relatives, old shipmates and complete strangers, though he managed to answer many of the letters, and pressed Barham to appoint worthy men like Berry. His main concerns, however, were to secure enough ships to annihilate the enemy, and to keep Collingwood as his second.[28]

Nelson and Emma dined at James Craufurd's on 10 September, providing Whig circles with an opportunity to understand a hero they had affected to discount. Craufurd was a denizen of Devonshire House, the Whig social centre, and his guests included Lady Elizabeth Foster, mistress of the Duke and confidante of his wife, Georgiana, and her sister Harriet, Lady Bessborough. Lady Bessborough retailed the story to her lover:

> So far from appearing vain and full of himself, as one had always heard, he was perfectly unassuming and natural. Talking of Popular Applause and his having been Mobbed and Huzzaed in the city, Lady Hamilton wanted him to give an account of it, but he stopped her. 'Why', said she, 'you like to be applauded – you cannot deny it.' 'I own it', he answered; 'popular applause is very acceptable and grateful to me, but no Man ought to be too much elated by it; it is too precarious to be depended upon, and it may be my turn to feel the tide set as strong against me as ever it did for me.' Everybody joined in saying they did not believe that could happen to him, but he seemed persuaded it might, but added: 'Whilst I live I shall do what I think right and best; the Country has a right to that from me, but every Man is liable to err in judgement.[29]

The final thought expresses, as well as a civilian audience could understand, the terrible pressures of fleet command, and the awesome responsibility he took when making the great decisions of 1805. He knew that one wrong choice could ruin his reputation.

Lady Bessborough's well-drawn portrait of Nelson demonstrates that he was aware of his vanity, but kept it under control. Emma's part in the little exchange presages the part that she would play in the years to come, embellishing a particular version of the man she loved, but clearly did not understand. Nelson was no fool, even in smart society. He won over Lady Elizabeth by promising to deliver a letter to her son, serving with the fleet. It was a charge he executed with his customary consideration.[30] The significance of the dinner was not merely social, however. The inter-party struggle for power in the autumn of 1805, as both Pitt's ministry and his health began to falter, was intense. A projected Pitt–Fox coalition had been blocked by the King and every scrap of success was vital political capital. As a national asset of the highest importance, the opposition might need Nelson.

On 11 September Nelson went up to London again, calling at the White House in Richmond Park to see Addington, now Lord Sidmouth, where he explained and drew on a dusty table his concept of the ideal battle, cutting the enemy line in two places.[31] There was also another purpose to his visit, but Sidmouth refused the offer of his proxy vote.[32] Nelson was still interested in politics, and trusted this rather colourless figure above the great men of the age.

The following day he took his leave of Pitt, pressing him to ensure the fleet was adequate to the real need, to annihilate the enemy. Pitt undertook to do this, and when Nelson departed, he rose and accompanied him to his carriage: a gesture of admiration and respect that gratified Nelson's craving for recognition.[33] He called at the Admiralty on his way out of town, to ensure that the new edition of Sir Home Popham's signal code was sent to the fleet. This important addition to the signalling capabilities of ships and fleets had been devised by Popham a few years earlier, and tested in service. It enabled ships to signal specific information, rather than general predetermined statements, and was a major step forward in ship-to-ship communication. Nelson's concern to have the code for his fleet was typical: he had already used it, and could see that it would be of enormous value for the future. He took fifty copies with him when he sailed south.

During his last visit to the Colonial Office, on 12 September, he met his one-time Indian correspondent General Sir Arthur Wellesley in the

Minister's anteroom. According to Wellesley's account, this famous meeting of heroes began with Nelson rambling on about himself, in a vainglorious style more suited to public occasions. But everything changed once he discovered he was talking not just to a young major-general, but to a man he knew by reputation and correspondence – who had fought and won battles that did as much to keep India British as the Nile. Now Nelson changed tack: with astonishing swiftness, the conversation turned into a brilliant, incisive discussion of war, politics and strategy, between two professional, reflective warriors. Thirty years later Wellesley, by now the hero of Waterloo and Prime Minister, observed, 'I don't know that I ever had a conversation that interested me more.'[34]

The same morning – typifying the incessant demands on Nelson's time – he was summoned to Carlton House to meet his new 'friend', the Prince of Wales.[35] After the alarms of 1801 the Prince had not occupied much of Nelson's attention, but George, already descending into the opium-fuelled delusions that would dominate his later life, was anxious to touch the hand of glory, although his father had denied him any role in the war. The call, though it showed royal support to the national hero at the appropriate moment, the King being at Weymouth for sea-bathing, was quite unnecessary. Nelson had the admiration of the country, the love of the people, the respect of the political classes, and the acclaim of his profession. What need had he of Princes?

The Prince delayed Nelson and Emma's return to Merton, where they found their dinner guests Lord Minto, and neighbours James Perry and his wife, had already arrived. After a quiet evening with his friends and his mistress Nelson spent the following day, Friday 13th, at home. He took a chaise for Portsmouth around 10.30 p.m., arriving shortly before dawn. As he left, his thoughts and prayers were with his daughter, taking a last chance to entrust her soul to his God as she slept. He entrusted his own fate to divine providence, and if his life were cut short he relied on his God to 'protect those so dear to me'.

The next morning he walked through Portsmouth, took a boat out and hoisted his flag on the *Victory*. He was accompanied by two of Pitt's confidants, George Canning, Treasurer of the Navy, and George Rose, Vice-President of the Board of Trade. The crowd pressed in, touching his coat, kneeling, praying, crying and cheering: the short walk to the beach was later written up as the redeemer's entry into

Jerusalem. Whether Nelson picked up that impression, he was certainly moved, turning to Hardy and observing: 'I had their huzzas before, I have their hearts now!' Only now did he realise quite how popular he was.

CHAPTER XV

Trafalgar
21 October 1805

On 15 September the wind came round and the *Victory* left Spithead, accompanied by Blackwood's frigate *Euryalus*, then coasted for Plymouth to pick up two more battleships. Nelson was soon working on his official correspondence: there were presents and a royal letter for the Emperor of Morocco, offered in the hope of securing supplies for the fleet and the garrison at Gibraltar, along with intelligence of enemy movements. With Portugal under severe Franco-Spanish pressure, Morocco was the last source of water and fresh food near the Straits.[1] The Vice Consul at Tangier, James Matra, had just persuaded the Moroccans to relax their ban on food exports.[2]

Nor did Nelson forget those he left behind:

> I intreat, my dear Emma, that you will cheer up; and we will look forward to many happy years, and be surrounded by our children's children. My heart and soul is with you and Horatia.[3]

However, his head always overruled his heart: he had actively sought this return to sea, anxious that no one else should reap the rewards he saw as his right. Once he was out to sea, his letters to Emma returned to their usual subject-matter of fleets, winds and professional concerns.[4]

With the Combined Fleet in Cadiz, Nelson faced the age-old problem of persuading a reluctant enemy to come out to sea, where they

The 'Nelson Touch': Nelson explains his plan of attack

could be brought to battle. French and Spanish fleets had rarely chosen to face the risk in the preceding twelve years. Nelson's hopes of getting them to do so rested on a combination of possibilities and pressures. He would disguise his own arrival, and the strength of his fleet, hoping they might feel strong enough to face battle. He could also develop the strategy that Collingwood had applied, of an increasingly rigorous blockade: hunger and the lack of naval stores might leave the enemy with little option but to sail, or see the fleet reduced to a ruinous condition. Collingwood had extended the blockade to the small ports close by Cadiz.5 While Castlereagh agreed to a closer blockade, he stressed that it was only applicable if the ports were actually stopped up, and he reminded Nelson that the political cost of awkward relations with neutrals had to be borne in mind.6

Nelson would also review the offensive options. A direct attack on Cadiz harbour was out of the question: though Drake had managed it in 1587, and Lord Howard in 1596, the defences had been greatly enhanced since then. Nelson had lain off Cadiz long enough in 1797 to know that the best option was long-range bombardment using mortar vessels. There were also two brand new options: the developed Congreve rockets, and the floating carcasses, or mines, of the American inventor Robert Fulton, then using the cover name 'Mr Francis'. On the day Nelson resumed command, Castlereagh had sent him a note from Francis, who wanted to discuss his carcasses, which 'might do much execution in many cases of blockade'.7 Nelson was not overly enthusiastic about these new weapons, and despite some experiments at Boulogne, they would not be used in battle until after his death.

Off Lisbon on 25 September, Nelson urged Sutton to keep quiet about his movements, while Blackwood went ahead with a request that Collingwood should not salute him, or any other newly arrived ships. Two days later, Nelson rounded Cape St Vincent and entered his station. He fixed the fleet rendezvous off Cadiz, with a secondary location at Tangier. Late the following day he was off Cadiz, where he spent his forty-seventh birthday. He would not have been anywhere else for a king's ransom, even 'paradise Merton'. Having refused the offer of a seventy-four, Blackwood, the senior frigate captain, took command of the inshore watch.

Many officers came to pay their respects, and the more senior among them dined that night. Fremantle of the Neptune was greatly pleased to be given the place he had held at Copenhagen, as Nelson's second astern. Back on board the following day, to dine with the remaining captains, Fremantle 'never spent a pleasanter day'.[8] Duff, of the *Mars,* agreed: 'A very merry dinner. He certainly is the pleasantest Admiral I ever served under.'[9] Both men were contrasting the social opportunities Nelson provided with the complete absence of such occasions under Collingwood, who as Edward Codrington of the *Orion* observed, 'never communicates with anybody but upon service'. Codrington had longed for Nelson to resume command, 'that I may once in my life see a Commander in Chief endeavouring to make a hard and disagreeable service as palatable to those serving under him as circumstances will admit of, and by keeping up by his example that animation so necessary for such occasions'.[10] Even Calder was preferable to Collingwood: his last dinner brought together twenty captains who showed 'a strong desire to support each other cordially and manfully in the event of a battle'.[11]

Despite the presence of old friends, Nelson had taken command of a largely unknown fleet – most of the ships and captains had been detached from the Channel fleet, and consequently many had little experience of battle. He could rely on Collingwood, Louis, Fremantle, Hallowell and Berry, but there were many men whose conduct and capabilities were unknown. Nelson used these dinners with his captains to expound the tactical ideas he had already discussed with Keats and Sidmouth. The vital briefing was verbal:

> When I came to explain to them the 'Nelson touch', it was like an electric shock. Some shed tears, all approved – 'it was new – it was singular – it was simple!' and, from Admirals downwards, it was repeated – 'It must succeed. If ever they will allow us to get at them! You are, my Lord, surrounded by friends whom you inspire with confidence.'[12]

Before the prospect of an offensive action in Italy could be considered, Nelson had to address the danger from the Combined Fleet. The latest intelligence from Portugal reported that Bonaparte had issued sailing orders, but a Council of War had decided that this was not possible. Local sources reported growing Franco-Spanish friction, and that Admiral Decrès was coming to take command.[13] Much of the news was inaccurate, a garbled version of reality. Nelson was still short of ships. The enemy had thirty-five or thirty-six, while he had twenty-three, allowing for the six he needed to send for food and water.[14] Admiral William Young, now Commander in Chief at

Plymouth, reported rumours that the enemy would be forced to sea by hunger: his only fear was that the Brest fleet might head south, so Cornwallis had better be ready.[15]

After his discussions about weapons with Castlereagh, Nelson examined the prospects for an attack. It was possible the rockets might work: the Combined Fleet was crowded into the harbour area and might be hurried out by a bombardment, although he still put his faith in hunger. He adopted Collingwood's practice of detaining the Danish ships, then trying to get into the smaller local ports with French supplies from Bordeaux. The only purpose of the blockade was to force the enemy out.[16]

Rumours of an impending small ship attack were soon circulating, and ambitious young officers pressed forward to volunteer.[17] Royal Marine Artillerymen were coming for the two bomb vessels, fireships would follow and Blackwood was already working out how to use them: 'I am very glad to learn your Lordship intends to make the place too hot for them.' While sifting the best intelligence he could obtain on the winds and currents off Cadiz, both to anticipate the enemy putting to sea and to consider a fireship, carcass and rocket attack, Nelson warned Blackwood to be ready, but to keep the news to himself: 'there is no occasion for putting the enemy on their guard'. With two bomb vessels he would have a useful offensive force.[18]

As soon as he took command Nelson was immersed in a veritable blizzard of paperwork: 'with the business of such a fleet I am not very idle'.[19] On his birthday he spent seven hours writing, most of it routine fleet administration, and the load rarely lightened. Admiral Knight at Gibraltar summed up the effect when he confessed that Nelson's return had relieved him of a burden of responsibility that had made him ill.[20] Food and water were pressing problems, with so many ships so far from a major port or naval base. The only way to keep the force efficient was to send the ships away in rotation to revictual. Six battleships left the fleet on 3 October; three days later the next six ships had been nominated. Meanwhile, store ships and newly arrived units were distributing supplies round the fleet. 10 October was a particularly hard day in the office, with a mass of standing orders and paperwork passing Nelson's desk. Perhaps the most significant was a new form for reporting the casualties of battle in the manner required by Lloyd's Patriotic Fund; this would ensure early payment for sufferers, and the bereaved.[21]

The human dimension of fleet command was equally important to Nelson. His concern for his juniors, together with his anxiety to reward good service and promote the best men, made him the favourite admiral of every brave officer. He, like every admiral, had his favourites, but they were almost all men of the highest talent. When one of them, Sam Sutton, was invalided home from the *Amphion*, Nelson replaced him with Norfolk protégé William Hoste, who turned over his current command to Nelson's nephew Sir William Bolton.[22] When Berry turned up in the *Agamemnon* on 13 October Blackwood observed, 'Berry is such [a] bird of good fortune, that now he is arrived I feel that the enemy will make a bolt – which God send.'[23]

The impact of one supremely charismatic man on old friends and new devotees created a unique professional harmony in the fleet in a matter of days – no one else could have generated the same enthusiasm. To mirror this transformation of morale, the captains chose to paint their ships *à la* Nelson. His black and yellow colour scheme, with the gun-decks picked out by a thick black line, gave ships a chequerboard appearance when the gunports were lowered. In future years it would be the norm for all fleets. Codrington had been so impressed by the state of the ships of the old Mediterranean squadron that he had already done so, once he thought the *Orion* fit for the honour.[24]

Bonaparte's orders for the fleet to sail reached Cadiz on 26 September. Gravina reported fourteen Spanish ships ready, but reports that three more ships had joined Collingwood changed Villeneuve's mind. He did not yet know that the three-decked ship carried his nemesis, only that the enemy seemed to have thirty-one sail, far too many for his motley armada of thirty-three to deal with. On 2 October intelligence from Lisbon revealed that Nelson had arrived, with plans to attack, bombard or burn the Combined Fleet. There was little security for any supposedly secret measures. In response Villeneuve prepared a harbour defence flotilla. Although he could not see Nelson, or his fleet, he knew what lay just over the horizon. On 7 October the allied flag officers met in council: Gravina and the Spanish officers considered the enemy outside was not an 'inferior force'; and therefore they were not obliged to seek battle. Some French officers agreed, but others condemned such opinions, impugning Spanish honour and courage. The inevitable argument only ended when Gravina called a vote. They decided to stay put.

Admiral Lord Collingwood

At the same time Nelson, now aware that the Continental war was about to begin, had to prepare for a longer watch off Cadiz. This meant he had to detach a fifth of his fleet to resupply, or risk having to retreat and allow the enemy out. He would accept battle with an inferior force. Although Blackwood reported soldiers being embarked and every preparation for sea, he detached Rear Admiral Louis with six battleships to replenish their food and water, look at Cartagena and cover a convoy bound for Malta. His sympathetic and inspirational handling of Louis, who was desperate to stay, showed his charm and wit at their very best. Louis left on 3 October, taking with him Hallowell in the *Tigre*, halving the number of Nile veterans among the senior officers. Nor were the needs of his fleet his only concern. The entire Mediterranean theatre demanded Nelson's attention: if the situation off Cadiz was not resolved soon Malta, Naples and Sardinia would begin to draw off his forces. Little wonder he was anxious for battle.

The fleet now lay thirty to forty miles west of Cadiz, with a line of frigates connecting it to Blackwood, supported by an inshore squadron of fast seventy-fours commanded by George Duff in the *Mars*. Nelson had carefully selected his location: it would let the enemy out, but prevent the fleet being driven through the Straits by adverse weather, while remaining well placed to intercept the Brest fleet before it could contact Cadiz. Even so Nelson was desperate for more ships, to ensure he could turn any fleeting opportunity into a battle of annihilation. Once he learnt, as he did on 8 October, that Craig had orders to act in Italy or elsewhere in the event of a Continental war, he was certain the enemy was destined for the Mediterranean.[25] By 10 October he was confident he had penetrated the enemy's thinking, and could anticipate their moves, warning Collingwood where he thought they would be heading if they left harbour. He also issued his famous Tactical Memorandum to complete the process begun verbally in the Great Cabin of the *Victory*, explaining the 'Nelson Touch' to his captains.

The Trafalgar Memorandum of 9 October has been much debated: Corbett devoted a great deal of attention to the question of whether it was carried into effect, while the Admiralty subsequently undertook a minute investigation, published less than a year before the First World War broke out.[26] Both missed the key point. The memorandum should not be seen as a free-standing document, but in the context of the verbal discussions of 29 and 30 September, in which Nelson had set out the spirit of his idea. The concept was, as ever, to reduce the complex, demanding problem of arranging a fleet for battle, forcing the enemy to fight, and securing a complete victory into a set of basic ideas that could be easily understood. The written version contained the intellectual fruits of a career dedicated to the pursuit and destruction of the enemy. It distilled the history, techniques and possibilities of sailing-fleet tactics, through the prism of personal experience, and applied them to the situation he anticipated. It was not prescriptive, and anyone who had understood Nelson's career would not expect him to preclude the effects of chance, initiative, individual impulse, human error, weather or enemy action. What Nelson did give his captains was a priceless insight into his intellectual processes, a guide to the way he thought and the objects at which he aimed, together with the core concept of breaking the enemy formation in two places, to destroy two thirds of their fleet. Yet he did not elaborate on the other core concept: that the enemy's command and control should be destroyed in the process. This would be his task. Finally, he reminded them that 'something must be left to chance' and added 'in case Signals can neither be seen nor perfectly understood, no Captain can do very wrong if he places his Ship alongside that of an Enemy.'[27]

This last was the fallback position for the 'blockheads' without the wit to think for themselves. It was the least he expected, not a mantra for success in battle. Experience had taught him that not all captains were equal, and he did not know enough of his new team to rely on them all. This was why he was so careful to choose the ships that would be close to him in battle; all were commanded by men he knew and trusted – Fremantle, Keats (if he arrived in time), Louis, Hallowell and Berry. This was no mere form, or personal preference. It was vital that the flagship be supported by the best and brightest officers. Similarly, Nelson gave Blackwood permission to use his name to issue orders to any ships in the rear of his line on the day of the battle. He had an absolute trust in Blackwood's judgement.[28]

Unlike his predecessors, who commanded from the centre, Nelson would lead. He also massed his heavy ships, as far as their sailing qualities would allow, at the head of his two lines. He had long accustomed his fleets to follow his lead, placing the flagship at the head of the line when sailing. That he placed the flagship third in the line of battle was a concession to his subordinates, not a reflection of his ambition. He would lead, to control the pace and direction of the attack, select the point of impact and complete the vital task of destroying the enemy's command and control. Furthermore, he would lead by example. With the flagship ahead of them, no officer would have occasion to wonder, as had often happened in the past, what the admiral meant them to do; they could see with their own eyes, and had no harder task than to follow. He was careful to stress that the memorandum was not intended to fetter Collingwood's judgement, only to guide his thinking. The object was to annihilate the enemy, and get a 'glorious Peace for our Country'.[29] As he told Colonel Stewart, he expected Bonaparte would try an invasion, and only hoped to get at the enemy fleet soon.[30]

While Nelson kept his eye on the wind and weather, Collingwood found the inaction of the enemy hard to comprehend. With the war in Italy about to begin, surely this was the time to act? Early on the morning of 19 October, the enemy began to leave Cadiz. Nelson, almost fifty miles to the west, received the news a little over three hours later. Hearing that his relief, Admiral Rosily, was at Madrid, and unable to bear the thought of being superseded, Villeneuve decided to go to sea. News that Louis's squadron was at Gibraltar completed the picture: with an inferior enemy, he believed only twenty-two ships to his thirty-three, it was time to put to sea. The decision to sail was Villeneuve's, and Villeneuve's alone.

Blackwood's response demonstrated why Nelson placed such faith in him. He signalled along his chain of ships, and immediately sent off his two sloops, one to Nelson, the other to recall Louis. Nelson was so certain of his judgement that the fleet was already heading to cut Villeneuve off from the Straits before his Combined Fleet had cleared Cadiz harbour. Throughout the day Blackwood was 'talking to Lord Nelson' using the Popham telegraph system and the line of frigates.[31] By 1 a.m. on 20 October the fleet was in position at the entrance to the Straits. Nelson hoped to see Louis returning on the easterly wind, but that hope was misplaced: Louis was two hundred miles to the east, and did not finish his convoy work until the following day. Nor was the enemy where he had expected: they took so long to leave harbour that they arrived north of Nelson's position far later than he had anticipated. By mid-afternoon, however, they had been located, and with a strong wind blowing there was an opportunity for battle. Collingwood was summoned on board *Victory*. He urged immediate engagement, but Nelson was determined to wait. The enemy was too close to Cadiz, and it was too late in the day for a decisive action.

The enemy had spent much of their time trying to get into a specific formation, a regular line of twenty ships, equal to the force Villeneuve believed Nelson had – the remaining thirteen would be a reserve under Gravina. Gravina's force could counter any attempt by Nelson to concentrate on part of the main line. It was perhaps the only tactical solution to the threat Villeneuve faced, and may explain why he was prepared to offer battle. The problem for both fleets on 20 October was the shifting and squally wind conditions, which left the skilful British ships in a huddle for two hours, and the less experienced allies in chaos for many more. The telegraph kept up contact with Blackwood. By nightfall the enemy could be seen to the north of the British fleet, close to Cadiz. Nelson then hauled away to the southwest, leaving Blackwood to keep contact during the night, changing back onto a north-easterly course at 4 a.m. on the 21st. At daybreak, shortly before 6, the British fleet was in apparent disorder, just a crowd of ships. The enemy could be seen eight or nine miles to the north-east, heading for the Straits in a rough line. There would be time to fight and win a battle, but not much more, as the weather was going to break within twenty-four hours. Among those watching the events unfold it would appear that only Nelson had been studying the barometer.

Collingwood had shifted his flag into the newly recoppered *Royal Sovereign*, as ordered. Although Collingwood's original flagship, the ninety-eight-gun *Dreadnought*, was well-manned, and a formidable fighting unit, Nelson wanted his second-in-command in a ship with the speed to lead the line of battle. Nelson was a great believer in the superior fighting power of three-decked ships, but many of them sailed like haystacks. *Dreadnought*, Rear Admiral Lord Northesk's *Britannia* and the *Prince* were all sluggish performers.[32] Fortunately the new ninety-eights, *Temeraire* and *Neptune*, were in capable hands, and formed, with *Victory*, the spearhead of the British attack.

Nelson had begun a letter to Emma on 19 October, and left it open on the 20th: 'As my last writing before the Battle will be to you, so I hope in God that I shall live to finish my letter after the Battle.' He also wrote a note for Horatia.[33] These notes, along with the codicil to his will compiled on the morning of the 21st, were sensible precautions, not morbid presentiment, but there can be no doubt that as the enemy line loomed ever closer his thoughts darkened.

At daybreak on 21 October, Villeneuve, horrified to find that Nelson had five more ships than he had expected, abandoned his tactical concept of a powerful reserve under Gravina to reinforce the point of attack. He would have to make do with a line of battle, though he knew this formation would allow the full flowering of Nelson's genius. The light and shifting westerly wind and a heavy Atlantic swell made it difficult to form and hold a line. Nelson made no attempt to follow his memorandum, signalling the fleet to form in the order of sailing, and then to bear up and sail large for the enemy in the wake of the two flagships.

Over the next two hours, the British ships divided into two groups, gradually coming into line. Villeneuve responded by reversing course, heading north, back towards Cadiz, and ensuring his ships closed up for action. He must have feared an impetuous, unformed chase, the favoured tactic of old masters like Hawke. Nelson now signalled to steer for the centre of the enemy line, to break it in two places as he planned, and annihilate the rear and centre. Villeneuve had played right into his hands. Although Collingwood tried to rearrange his line, the speed of the attack, and Nelson's insistence on using every stitch of sail, left him leading a second ill-formed column of ships, heading directly for the enemy, about one third in from the rear. The Combined

Fleet set no more sail than necessary to keep station: they were not running away, they were waiting to fight.

Nelson remarked on this fact to Blackwood at about 10 a.m., and Blackwood voiced the opinion of everyone on *Victory*'s quarter-deck that Nelson should not continue to lead the line, but should command from the *Euryalus*. When that option was predictably rejected, they argued that he should let the two ships astern pass and revert to the established order of battle. Blackwood took the message to the *Temeraire*, while Nelson signalled Duff to take the *Mars* ahead of Collingwood, but without ordering him to shorten sail there was no way Nelson could stop his old friend leading into battle. To make his point Collingwood set *Royal Sovereign*'s studding sails: extra canvas to widen the sail area, increasing speed. Nelson was delighted – 'See how that noble fellow Collingwood carries his ship into action!' – and signalled for all possible sail to be set, hastening the moment of impact, and stretching out both lines, as the slower ships lost ever more ground to the swift.

In the light airs of that day the British ships closed at between two and three knots, no more than moderate walking pace. In the six hours between daybreak and the fighting, the officers and men of all three fleets had ample opportunity to think about what lay ahead. The ships were already cleared for action, the partitions, furniture and non-essential gear stowed away. The hammocks were up in nettings above the bulwarks, to reduce the danger from splinters. Many ships had musicians, and they played stirring and appropriate tunes as the ships closed: 'Hearts of Oak' was a particular favourite, along with 'Britons Strike Home', 'Rule Britannia' and 'The Downfall of Paris'. The sun was shining and the different colour schemes of the enemy ships were easily picked out. The one clear difference between the fleets was that the iron bands around the lower masts were painted black in Villeneuve's force; Nelson, with typical forethought, ordered his ships to paint the bands yellow, for identification in the smoke of battle.

21 October was a festival day for Nelson – the anniversary of his uncle's famous battle, and the autumn fair at Burnham Thorpe. Curiously, he forgot to wear his uncle's sword – the only time he went into battle unarmed. The enemy were little more than three miles away when he wrote out his last thoughts on the world beyond the looming fleet battle:

May the Great God, whom I worship, grant to my Country, and for the benefit of Europe in general, a great and glorious Victory . . . and may humanity after Victory be the predominant feature in the British fleet. For myself, I commit my life to Him who made me, and may his blessing light upon my endeavours for serving my Country faithfully. To Him I resign myself, and the just cause which is entrusted to me to defend.[34]

He then compiled a codicil to his will, leaving his mistress, her claims made clear, and his illegitimate daughter as a legacy for the country to support. Blackwood and Hardy witnessed the paper, but it had no legal force, as he must have known.

Shortly after completing his prayers and promises Nelson was back on deck. By now it was obvious to everyone that the enemy were going to fight: their bold display required an answer. His thoughts were quick, and to the point. He would use the new talking telegraph to send a personal message to the fleet, the sort of morale-boosting encouragement he had given the crew of *Victory* earlier in the day by walking about the ship and chatting with the men as they prepared for battle. He asked signal lieutenant John Pasco to send the message that 'England confides that every man will do his duty.' The key word was 'confides', meaning 'trusts': he was not trying to make his men do their duty, but telling them that he had complete faith in them. Nor was England the real basis of the message – in the face of the enemy men need something more immediate, and more personal. The focus of their loyalty that day was nearer at hand, it was the embodiment of England at sea, the deity of the oceans. The meaning was 'Nelson knows that every man will do his duty.'

Unfortunately 'confides' had not been reduced to a simple flag hoist in Popham's code, and Pasco suggested substituting 'expects', which had. Nelson accepted this change, and the signal entered the record. Collingwood, who lacked the human insight and warmth to see the need, or the opportunity, grumbled that 'We all know what we have to do.' He was almost alone in such thoughts, and once he knew the message he changed his mind. Like everyone else Collingwood was struck, exactly as had been intended, by the very personal message, one that touched the heart of every man in the fleet, and gave them a share of the divine magic that only Nelson could bring to the situation. As the message was relayed from the signal officers to the crew, ship after ship burst out in ringing cheers of approval. Nelson followed the message with two signals from the old book: 'Prepare to Anchor' and, as ever, No. 16, 'Engage the Enemy more Closely.' He would send no more.

Blackwood had been on board the *Victory* with Captain Prowse of the *Sirius* from early in the day, their ships running alongside the line. They would carry any last signals for the fleet, and as they were not involved in the fighting, could watch the battle develop. It was typical of Nelson that when fortune threw the hero of the *Guillaume Tell* action back into his fleet, he was on the most intimate terms with him again in a matter of hours, having absolute confidence in his seamanship, judgement and instinct. However, Blackwood could not get Nelson out of the flagship, nor the flagship out of the lead. Nelson knew the value of his leadership: he had given the men a morale-boosting message, now he would set them a morale-boosting example. In the days and months that followed, the conversations of Blackwood, Hardy, Alexander Scott and Doctor William Beatty were written out in a manner that suggested that Nelson could have avoided an obvious threat. They represented the admiral's actions as little more than bravado, and give no other purpose to his staying on his flagship, or wearing his own coat.

But there was no bravado about Nelson in battle. He had a deadly serious purpose in mind, and would not give anyone else the honour or the responsibility of winning the battle at a blow. He had to lead the line, and destroy the enemy flagship. Nor would he take off his coat, which he always wore. It is unlikely he even owned a plain uniform coat, and in any case, to hide from the enemy would be disgraceful. Collingwood was already setting a magnificent example, and it was unthinkable that Nelson should leave his ship, his post of honour or even shift his coat. After all men worshipped Nelson, the hero of a hundred fights, because he shared the dangers with them. How would the men of *Victory* have felt if he had left them at the last moment? What would the country have said if the battle turned out to be another 'Lord Howe victory' while Nelson watched at a safe distance?

Such speculation is unnecessary, for it is based on the wholly erroneous idea that Nelson entered battle with a death wish. This Victorian legend dealt with his 'shameful' private life by arguing that he knew that he was living an immoral life, and wished to expiate his crime through a glorious death. It is, like much more of the Victorian Nelson, utter nonsense. Nelson did not go into battle seeking a glorious death as the ultimate finale to his career. Though the idea had occurred to him at a particular time – the turmoil of his private life in late 1800, when he spoke to West at Fonthill, made such a death seem

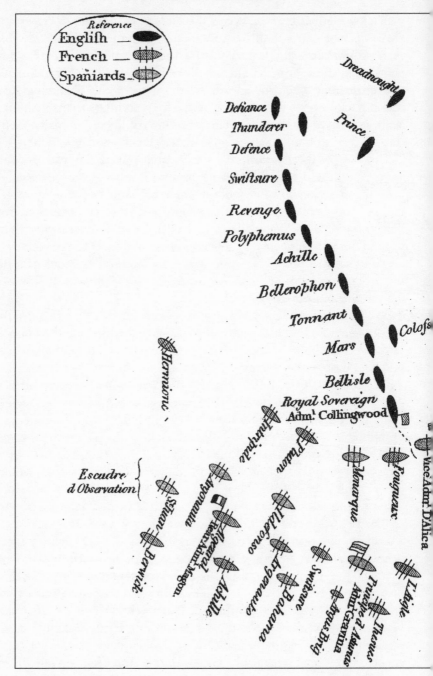

The battle of Trafalgar (from J. Corbett, *The Campaign of Trafalgar*, 1910)

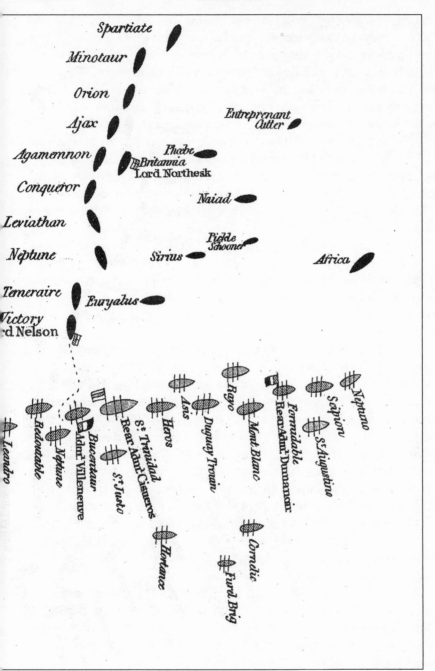

Spartiate

Minotaur

Orion

Ajax

Entreprenant
Cutter

Agamemnon

Phœbe
Britannia
Lord Northesk

Conqueror

Naiad

Leviathan

Pickle
Schooner

Neptune

Sirius

Africa

Temeraire

Euryalus

Victory
:d Nelson

Leandro

Redoutable

Neptune

Bucentaur
Adml Villeneuve

St Justo

St Trinidad
Rear Adml Cisneros

Heros

Asis

Duguay Trouin

Rayo

Mont Blanc

Formidable
Rear Adml Dumanoir

Sapion

St Augustino

Neptuno

Hortance

Cornelie

Furd Brig

Positions shown are at the start of the battle on the morning of 21 October.

attractive – this mood soon passed. His life had changed by 1805, and he was only too aware of the public fame and private comfort that would await him on his return from another glorious battle. He was already immortal, and had no need of his Wolfe moment. Wolfe was an unknown who achieved fame by the manner of his death; Nelson had become a national deity in life, a hero in the Homeric mould. He was too great to need death as the final distinguishing mark. He acted as he did on 21 October 1805 because it was his duty. He had to lead: the battle could not be controlled from anywhere else. It is highly significant that in the hour before contact he twice changed the attack plan for his line, which he could not have done from anywhere else. By 1805, death in battle was an occupational hazard for Nelson, not an object.

With the enemy waiting for his attack, Nelson held on in line ahead, to keep the ultimate point of attack uncertain; this would ensure the enemy could not counter his attack by reversing the van squadron. The two British lines appeared to be on slightly converging courses, while a shift in the wind left the Franco-Spanish force (the ships deliberately intermixed rather than in national formations) sagging in the centre, presenting a concave formation. Nelson aimed for the fourteenth ship in the enemy line, the target given in the memorandum, which was two ships behind Villeneuve's *Bucentaure*. However, the French admiral had not shown his flag, making the ship ahead of him, the massive *Santissima Trinidad*, an obvious target. Misleadingly informed that the enemy admiral was in a frigate, Nelson shifted his plan to cutting through the enemy van, and preventing it from getting into Cadiz, exploiting an opening that had suddenly appeared in the enemy line. Then, as the enemy rear opened fire on Collingwood, Villeneuve and his admirals displayed their flags. Nelson immediately headed for the bow of the enemy flagship; Villeneuve parried by closing on the stern of the *Santissima Trinidad*. Nelson simply shifted one place down the line, and went under the Frenchman's stern, despite a brave attempt by the *Redoutable* to close down the gap.

When the enemy opened fire on *Victory* shortly before midday, it was time for Blackwood to leave. As he climbed down the side of the ship, Blackwood tried to sound cheerful, trusting he would return that afternoon to find Nelson had taken the twenty ships he considered a good result. Without hesitation, Nelson cut him cold: 'God bless you, Blackwood: I shall never speak to you again.' It was a terrible send-off for a devoted follower, and quite out of character. These were not the final words of a man anxious to die, but of a man who knew that he would be surrounded by death within a few minutes.

Events bore out Nelson's analysis. As *Victory* closed on the enemy fleet, several ships were able to fire on her, mostly aiming into her rigging, trying to cripple her forward motion, while she was unable to present a gun for almost half an hour as she passed through the last eight hundred yards. This was the hardest part: to keep calm and endure a beating without the comfort of firing back. Within minutes, round shot were smashing through the flimsy bow of the ship, and the unprotected men on the upper deck. The first to fall was John Scott, Nelson's Public Secretary, who had been standing on the quarter-deck talking with Hardy when a ball cut him in two. As his mangled remains were heaved overboard, Nelson lamented the passing of a close friend. Soon after, the great ship's wheel was smashed to atoms, and the ship had to be steered from below decks, with commands relayed by voice. Then a double-headed shot, intended to cripple the rigging, scythed down a file of eight marines on the poop; Nelson quickly ordered Captain Adair to disperse his men, to avoid further heavy losses. Still Nelson and Hardy paced up and down on their chosen ground, the starboard side of the quarter-deck, not a foot from the smashed wheel, with splinters flying around them. One hit Hardy's shoe, tearing off the buckle. Once he was sure Hardy was not hurt, Nelson observed: 'This is too warm work to last for long.' He was right: fifty men had been killed or wounded, and they had yet to open fire. No wonder Nelson was impressed by the cool courage of *Victory*'s crew.

By 12.35 the concavity of the enemy line allowed *Victory*'s lower-deck guns to open fire on both sides as they closed, shrouding the ship in smoke, and providing some relief from the torment of waiting. Soon afterwards, she ran under the stern of the French flagship. The first gun to fire was the massive sixty-eight-pounder carronade on the port forecastle, blasting an eight-inch diameter solid iron shot and a case filled with five hundred musket balls through the flimsy stern galleries of the *Bucentaure*, followed by every one of the fifty broadside guns. The French ship shuddered under the impact of a hundred projectiles from the double-shotted broadside. Over two hundred of her officers and men were killed or wounded: Villeneuve was the only man left standing on the quarter-deck, and twenty of her eighty-four guns had been smashed out of their carriages. From inside the allied line, the French *Neptune* raked *Victory* and the *Redoutable* blocked her passage through the formation. Nelson's attempt to cut the enemy in two had ended with his ship trapped in the middle of the Combined Fleet, fighting on three sides. Unable to get through, Hardy asked which ship he should run into – Nelson left the choice to him. Hardy chose the *Redoutable*. Nelson would have preferred to keep his ship mobile, but there was nothing else he could do. Villeneuve's formation and the lack of wind had forced him to pile into a group of ships, not cut through a well-ordered line.

Once *Victory* had crashed into the *Redoutable*, Nelson was immobilised: he had sacrificed choice and tactics for all-out assault. While it was a significant modification of his memorandum, his overall concept survived. The impact of his line, headed by three three-decked ships, stunned Villeneuve, while the devastating raking fire they poured into his stern left him trapped on a crippled ship – immobile, unable to fight, signal, or escape. The allied centre was reduced to a collection of individual ships, and while they would fight with remarkable bravery they lacked the leadership and skill to meet the impact of the impetuous, irresistible British ships. Each British ship was, in itself, a superior force to an enemy of equal size and firepower. At close quarters the speed and regularity of British fire would overwhelm the allies, not immediately, but cumulatively. In the space of three hours the Franco-Spanish force collapsed, destroyed by gunnery the like of which had never been seen before. Nelson's attack had broken all the rules of tactics, treating a fleet in line waiting for a fight like one running away, substituting speed for mass, precision for weight, and accepting impossible odds.

Collingwood had picked out one of the Spanish flagships, the three-decker *Santa Anna*, raked her as he broke through the line, and ran alongside opening a furious battle that took over two hours to resolve. He fought alone for ten to twenty minutes, surrounded by enemy vessels, and even when the first group of his supporters arrived they too were soon fighting a far greater number of enemy ships. They survived and won the day because they hammered each of their attackers in turn, and by the time their performance was beginning to fall off the laggards came up and administered the *coup de grâce*. Big three-deckers like the *Prince*, *Britannia* and *Dreadnought* were the ideal answer to any Franco-Spanish rally. In fact the battle was won while the enemy had far more ships in the fight than the British: the real triumph was not one of twenty-seven against thirty-three, but twelve against twenty-two.

British casualties tell the story. Twelve ships fought the decisive phase of the battle, while those that followed them in profited from their work. Of those first twelve, the numbers of deaths were as follows: *Victory* 132; *Royal Sovereign* 141; *Temeraire* 123; *Neptune* 44; *Mars* 98; *Tonnant* 76; *Bellerophon* 150; *Revenge* 79; *Africa* 62; *Colossus* 200; *Achille* 72; *Defiance* 70.

Yet of all the men who died that day, one mattered more than the rest. It was not so much the death of Nelson as the manner of his passing that made the event memorable. Had he been cut in half by a round shot like poor Scott, or George Duff of the *Mars*, the final twist of immortality might have slipped from his grasp. He might have been trimmed back to fit a swift and sudden end, his life somehow reduced by the random nature of his death. If ever a man and his death were made for one another it was this man, on this day, under these circumstances.

Once the *Victory* was locked in combat with the *Redoutable*, the two ships grinding against each other, Nelson's work was done: he had broken the enemy formation, and his followers would complete the task and hold off the allied van, while Collingwood's ships dealt with the rear division. Nelson continued to walk with Hardy on the quarter-deck, more interested in the handling of the ships that followed than the battle at hand. The French ship alongside was desperately trying to clear *Victory*'s upper deck with musketry and hand grenades before boarding. This tactic made the upper deck of the *Victory* a very dangerous place: men were dropping on all sides. Nelson was discussing the handling of the *Leviathan* or the *Conqueror* with Hardy when, at about 1.15 p.m., a shot fired from the mizzen top of the *Redoutable* hit him on the left shoulder. The 0.69-inch-diameter lead ball smashed through his shoulder blade, punctured his left lung, cut an artery, severed his spine and lodged in the muscle under his right shoulder. Knocked to the deck, Nelson stumbled and fell into the pool of blood left by poor Scott. A Royal Marine sergeant and a sailor rushed to help, but Nelson knew what had happened, telling Hardy, 'They have done for me at last, my backbone is shot through.' For a man so given to hypochondria, this was a strikingly accurate description of the wound – and of its inevitable consequences, given contemporary medical practice. Hardy had three men carry him below to the cockpit, where Surgeon William Beatty was already hard at work on the mounting list of casualties.

In addition to the cacophonous roar and smoke of the guns, the shuddering motion of the ship as it ground against the enemy, this place possessed a unique horror. The low deck head, glimmering lanterns, moaning and screaming men, the stench of blood and the hurried work of amputating shattered limbs made this charnel house as close to hell as any living man could get. Alexander Scott, man of the cloth and veteran of many a battle, never forgot the cockpit of the *Victory* on that immortal day: it returned to torment his sleep for the rest of his life.

They placed Nelson against one of the great English oak timbers of the flagship. He repeated his diagnosis to Beatty, who had him stripped. An examination only confirmed the admiral's opinion, and when Beatty decided it was best to do nothing, Nelson insisted that he had more important things to do. Beatty left Nelson with the pursuer, his chaplain and intelligence officer Dr Scott, and his two servants. Above him, the battle with the *Redoutable* reached a crescendo: the French repeatedly tried to board, only to be driven back by heavy fire, and were finally all but wiped out by the *Temeraire*'s carronades. The French sailors in the mizzen top were shot down by two of *Victory*'s midshipmen, although it is unlikely they had understood what they had done. Nelson's fatal wound was a product of a clear tactical choice by Captain Lucas, and pure chance. The sharpshooters had missed the massive frame of Thomas Hardy, six foot four and heavily built, and picked out the slim, slight figure of the admiral. At 1.30 Lucas gave up: from his crew of 640, 490 had been killed and eighty-one wounded, and his ship had been reduced to a sinking wreck. By the time Nelson had reached the cockpit the threat to *Victory* had passed.

Conscious that he was in the presence of death, and could no longer avoid his fate, Nelson's thoughts constantly shifted from professional to personal, from points of detail to human destiny. There would be about his death something so astonishing, so implausible, and so moving that the attempt to replicate it has become a comic cliché. He asked Scott to remember him to Emma and Horatia, and to press their claims on the Government, through George Rose. Gradually Nelson lost all sensation below the chest: his spine broken by the musket ball, he was paralysed, but he could still feel intense pain, which broke up his thoughts into disjoined segments, and a gush of blood poured into his left lung every time his heart beat. He was hot, and thirsty, calling for lemonade and a fan.

Every time the crew cheered, his thoughts returned to the events of that day, and he was pleased to discover that another enemy ship had struck. For all the suffering he remained the same man, and on learning that the midshipman sent down by Hardy was the son of an old friend from the Nicaragua expedition of 1780, he begged to be remembered to his father. Not even the agony of death could destroy the human warmth that made Nelson unique.

At 2.15 Villeneuve, his ship destroyed, surrendered to Israel Pellew of the *Conqueror*. He had done all that a brave professional officer could – he had tried to fight the battle with hope – but the genius of his opponent, the power of the Royal Navy and the failure of Admiral Dumanoir to wear the van squadron round when signalled had doomed his brave effort. It was a far better performance than Villeneuve had given in 1798. He had not even managed to find death amid the slaughter that was the quarter-deck of the *Bucentaure*. That fate was reserved for Rear Admirals Magon and Cisneros, and several allied captains. And when Gravina died of his wounds, months later, he could hope for no higher honour than to join Nelson.

At around 2.30 Hardy was able to go below, in answer to Nelson's repeated requests: he reported that twelve or fourteen of the enemy were taken, and no British ship had surrendered. That last question betrayed Nelson's anxiety about the outcome of the battle. His other conversation was more personal: Emma was to have his hair and his personal possessions. Hardy could not linger, as the enemy van had finally turned – only to be hammered by the ships at the tail of the line, Codrington's brilliantly handled *Orion*, the *Minotaur* and the *Spartiate*. Hardy went back on deck and signalled the ships nearby to support the flagship. He also sent an officer to warn Collingwood.

When Beatty returned, having cut through his patient list, Nelson was composing his closing remarks, summing up his purpose and preparing for a scene he had been rehearsing all his life. His first effort, back at the Nile in 1798, had not gone well, but this time he knew his Wolfe moment had come: this was the greatest sea battle the world had ever witnessed, and he was going to win. Having double-checked with Beatty that he was doomed, he began to deliver his most affecting address. There were enough men around him to ensure that his words would not be lost: Beatty and Scott were literate men, and both would write up the last hours. His first thought was the entirely predictable, 'God be praised, I have done my Duty.' Then he considered the fate of Emma, and how she would deal with the disaster, suddenly unsure that his wishes would have any impact.

Hardy came back at around 3.30 to confirm a glorious victory, but as yet unable to satisfy Nelson's determination to have twenty prizes. 'Anchor, Hardy, anchor!' he demanded, his breath failing with the effort, as the rising sea reminded him of his weather forecast. Forgetting himself for a moment, Hardy said, 'I suppose, my Lord, Admiral Collingwood will now take upon himself the direction of affairs?' 'Not while I live, I hope, Hardy,' came back the sharp retort. 'Now, do you anchor, Hardy?' He then insisted that his body not be thrown overboard, a subject they had clearly discussed before that day. He also begged Hardy to look after Emma. The thought of Emma reminded him that something was lacking on the day of his death – human contact – and he begged Hardy to kiss him. After Hardy had knelt and kissed him on the cheek, Nelson declared, 'Now I am satisfied,' and gave his closing motto: 'Thank God I have done my Duty.'

Moved by the events he had witnessed and the composure of the dying hero, Hardy, unable to speak, kissed him again. By now Nelson was fading; he asked who it was, and when told added, 'God bless you, Hardy.' Unable to bear the scene any longer Hardy went back to the upper deck, burying his grief in the business of fighting and repairing a shattered first-rate.[35]

To ease his pain Nelson had his steward Chevalier turn him onto his right side. The relief was secured at the cost of shortening his life, since the move allowed the blood that filled his left lung to drain into the right: his breathing began to falter. 'I wish I had not left the deck, for soon I shall be gone,' he declared, before making something approaching a confession to Scott: 'I have not been a great sinner.' Scott and Chevalier took turns to rub his chest, which seemed to ease his suffering. As the pain of his final struggle for breath began to overwhelm him, he kept on repeating the line, 'Thank God I have done my Duty,' and Scott was convinced the last words he heard were, 'God and my Country'. That trinity of God, Duty and Country had inspired and shaped his life – he did not abandon them in death. Beatty, Scott and Chevalier were with him when he slipped away without a sound. It was shortly before 4.30 p.m., just as the fighting died away. Nineteen enemy ships had been taken, and one blown up, set ablaze by firing from the tops.

The cost of victory was high: seventeen hundred British killed and wounded, six thousand enemy casualties and nearly two thousand prisoners. Many lives were lost, along with almost all the prizes, in the storm that followed. The shattered ships, unable to work or keep their holds clear of water, were abandoned or burnt – among them Villeneuve's flagship, and the mighty *Santissima Trinidad*. Collingwood chose not to anchor, which was the right decision in the circumstances.

Throughout the fleet, the end of the battle brought some relief, although the need to secure the prizes and repair the rigging in the face of the looming storm meant few had any rest. News that Nelson was dead had been trickling through the fleet for some time, and the absence of his flag from the *Victory* confirmed the news. The boat crew who went to warn Collingwood could not keep their feelings from those they met: grown men, hardened by the sight and sound of battle, wept like children. They were not ashamed of their grief. In private, hard men like Blackwood were unable to control their emotions, seeking an outlet in writing home. His wife Harriet was the only person he could confess to:

> I do not, even at the risk of distressing you, hesitate to say that in my life I never was so shocked, or so completely upset as upon my flying to the *Victory*, even before the action was over, to find Lord Nelson was then at the gasp of death . . . Such an Admiral has the Country lost, and every officer and man, so good, so obliging a friend as never was. Thank God he lived to know that such a Victory, and under circumstances so disadvantageous to the attempt, never was before gained. Almost all seemed as if inspired by the one common sentiment of conquer or die . . . Lord Nelson . . . has left cause for every man who had a heart never to forget him . . . I hope it is not injustice to the Second In Command, who is now on board the *Euryalus*, and who fought like a hero, to say that the Fleet under any other, never would have performed what they did under Lord N. But under Lord N. it seemed like inspiration to most of them.[36]

No one knew Nelson better than Collingwood, who opened his wonderful General Order of thanks for the officers and men of the fleet the following day with the lines:

> The ever to be lamented death of Vice Admiral Lord Viscount Nelson, Duke of Bronte, the Commander in Chief, who fell in the action of the 21st, in the arms

of Victory, covered with glory, whose memory will be ever dear to the British Navy and the British Nation; whose zeal for the honour of his King, and for the interests of his Country, will ever be held up as a shining example for a British seaman.

The report to the Admiralty of the same day was in the same vein: it was a powerful document, written by a master of the English language. Yet these calculated elegies did nothing to lessen the emotional impact of the news – in the fleet, the Admiralty, or across the nation. The King was rendered speechless and Pitt could not sleep: the triumph was cancelled out by the loss.

Beatty placed the body in a cask of brandy, and after the *Victory* had been repaired at Gibraltar replaced the preservative with spirits of wine. The hero went home in his own cabin, in a barrel lashed to the mizzen mast. When the tension of the storm had passed, Collingwood had time to reflect, and wrote to their old friend from Antigua, Mary Moutray:

> It was about the middle of the action, when an officer came from the *Victory* to tell me he was wounded. He sent his love to me and desired me to conduct the fleet. I asked the officer if the wound was dangerous and he, by his look told what he could not speak, nor I reflect upon now without suffering again the anguish of that moment.

To William Cornwallis he conveyed another part of Nelson's meaning: 'He will live in the memory of all who knew him as long as they have being.'[37] Numerous letters flowed from the pen of the heroic Collingwood, letters that penetrated to the very core of his friend's genius:

> He possessed the zeal of an enthusiast, directed by talents which Nature had very bountifully bestowed upon him, and everything seemed, as if by enchantment, to prosper under his direction. But it was the effect of system, and nice combination, not of chance. We must endeavour to follow his example, but it is the lot of very few to attain to his perfection.[38]

PART FOUR

Nelson after Trafalgar

CHAPTER XVI

Death and Transfiguration
1805–85

In the months that followed his death Nelson was transformed from living hero into a national god. The greatest warrior that Britain has ever produced, and the finest naval commander of all time, passed from the mortal realm as he would have wished, in the moment of victory, surrounded by a crowd of worshippers, including the essential scribe to transmit his dying wishes and capture the moment for eternity. The scene was doubly affecting, for the hero had died slowly, drowning in his own blood as a ruptured artery filled his lungs, and remained conscious throughout. His final thoughts interleaved professional concerns, warning Captain Hardy to prepare for the imminent storm, while desperately seeking absolution, and some last sign of human warmth. To Hardy he conveyed his concerns for his funerary arrangements, and then entrusted to him the impossible task of securing a national reward for his mistress and child. The manner and location of Nelson's passing completed his legend; it was the ideal romantic death.

The death scene has been attempted in oil, pencil and ink, celluloid and video tape, but it remains impossibly moving. Only great artists have risen to the challenge. While most biographers and artists have seen death as final it was, for Nelson, only the passage to immortality. Here his wishes, and those of the state he served, coincided perfectly.

Misplaced zeal: *The Death of Nelson*, by Benjamin West (detail)

Already the greatest celebrity of the age and a romantic icon, his trans-formation would be, by turns, contrived, pre-ordained, and irre-sistible. Each succeeding generation would modify the image to meet its own needs for edification, education and example.

The public reaction to Nelson's death was universal, as numerous writers have testified. Samuel Taylor Coleridge was in Naples the day the news arrived:

> ... and never can I forget the sorrow and consternation that lay on every coun-tenance ... Numbers stopped and shook hands with me, because they had seen the tears on my cheek, and conjectured, that I was an Englishman; and several, as they held my hand, burst, themselves into tears.[1]

In Britain the news was received in silence, any cheers for the victory quickly stifled by the opening line of Collingwood's dispatch. *The Times* rose to the occasion, stressing his unique abilities, national importance, and unequalled glory, as well as his piety. Up in Cumbria, meanwhile, Coleridge's friend Wordsworth was unable to stifle a tear: his 'Character of a Happy Warrior' weaves his public lament for Nelson with the expression of his personal grief at the loss of his brother in a shipwreck. It featured an idealised Nelson, for Wordsworth took a Foxite view of Naples.[2]

The consequences of Nelson's death for public life were immediate. A day of National Thanksgiving for the Victory was set for 5 Decem-ber, and observed with becoming solemnity across the country. All religious buildings were crowded, while the clergy strove to express the national mood; collections totalling over a million pounds were devoted to the relief of the wounded and bereaved. For Pitt, however, the news of Nelson's death ended his career, so great were the hopes he had placed in the hero, both strategic and political. Pitt lingered on another two months, but did not live to see Parliament reopen, and passed away shortly after Nelson's state funeral. His own interment was on a smaller scale, with none of the glory so evident at Nelson's.

For those who had been closest to Nelson, his death had sharply diverging results. William Nelson was advanced by Pitt to the rank of Earl: he was provided with a pension of £6,000, and £100,000 to buy a suitable house.[3] For Emma, however, the story would have a slow, tragic denouement. Denied the chance to attend Nelson's funeral, she retreated dramatically to her bed to read over his letters. Nelson's request that the nation should provide her a legacy was never accept-ed, since Pitt died before he could act on his determination to honour the hero's wishes. His successor, Lord Grenville, was hostile to Emma, and the new Earl Nelson also turned against her, grubbing after 'his' money. While Nelson's friends advanced Emma's claims, if only for his sake, they soon discovered that she had no legal rights. She also proved impervious to the sound advice of supporters such as Addington, Rose and Hardy. Unable to capture another admirer, her beauty and her allure fading, Emma ran through the money Nelson left her and sold the house at Merton. By 1814 she was in prison for debt, and only got out with help from old friends of Nelson. She even sold his letters, which quickly appeared in print, doing nothing to help her cause or his memory. The one asset she never cashed in was Horatia: she never even admitted that the child was hers, although she did concede that Nelson was her father – this much was obvious from Horatia's slight physique and striking, angular face. Emma eventually died in poverty at Calais in January 1815, in the brief period between Bonaparte's two abdications. Horatia, however, was rescued by her Matcham relatives, and lived a long and largely happy life, the wife of a country parson.4

Pitt left the arrangements for Nelson's funeral to the Home Secretary, Lord Hawkesbury. The funerary obsequies would be the most elaborate of the age: Nelson would be buried with all the pomp and circumstance the state could muster, without a thought for the cost. Yet this was no gesture of farewell: the purpose of the ceremony was to capture the essence, the spirit and the name of Nelson for the nation. In a break with tradition, Nelson was not interred in Westminster Abbey, but would be placed under the crossing of St Paul's – the cathedral of the City of London, the commercial heart of the Empire he had secured – as the central figure in a new national pantheon. This met the hero's wishes, although the decision was taken by the King following an initiative by Hawkesbury:

> As Westminster Abbey is at this time so very crowded with monuments, and as it was thought proper to lodge the Standards taken from your Majesty's enemies in the different naval victories in the last war in St. Paul's, your Majesty will perhaps consider that Cathedral as the fittest place for this melancholy ceremony, as well for the erection in future of such monuments as it may be determined to raise to the memory of those who have rendered considerable naval or military service to their country.5

Because this would be a state funeral the chief mourner would be

Admiral of the Fleet Sir Peter Parker, not Earl Nelson. However, the Prince of Wales was quickly emerging as a principal figure in the process: he wished to take centre stage as the chief mourner, but the King forbade such a fundamental breach of royal protocol, although he did not stop the royal princes attending in their private capacity. Prince William, as a lifelong friend, had reason enough to mourn the man; George knew only a national symbol he had met but once. Though he claimed Nelson as a 'dear friend' and sought to control the production of the authorised biography, he did nothing to meet Nelson's wishes: there was no glory or credit in helping Emma, and the subject was rather too close to home. Although occasionally generous, George was already descending into an opium-fuelled world of self-delusion, in which he, rather than any real heroes, would win the war.[6] While George never claimed to have led the line at Trafalgar, as he did the cavalry at Waterloo, he recognised the magic of Nelson's life, and tried to appropriate it for himself.

Nelson's heroic national status was not contested. The state interred him as a modern deity, and the people accepted him as their deliverer, without instruction. Every aspect of the funeral was calculated to impress. The coffin was reckoned the most elaborate yet seen, heavily decorated with trophies, emblems and reminders of his earthly fame. It enclosed Hallowell's simpler work made from the mainmast of *L'Orient*. They would be placed under a great sarcophagus made for, but not used by, Cardinal Wolsey, nearly three hundred years earlier. Nelson was the first commoner to be worthy of such a monument.

On 23 December, Nelson's body was transferred from the *Victory*, anchored at the Nore where his naval career had begun, into the official yacht *Chatham*, for the journey down-river that he had known so well in life. Scott accompanied the dead hero on this last saltwater journey, in clerical attire. After receiving marks of honour and mourning – muffled bells, and minute guns – all down the river, the body was landed at the Greenwich Hospital, and taken into the care of Lord Hood until arrangements for the funeral were complete. The date was finally set only on 27 December, and work hastened at St Paul's.[7] As the day approached Hood found the crowds of thirty thousand and more gathering outside the Hospital intimidating, and pleaded with Hawkesbury to send a strong force of cavalry to keep order. The local magistrates reported that 'they never saw anything like it before'.[8]

On 4 January the public was admitted to pay its respects to Nelson's mortal remains, elaborately displayed in the magnificent Painted Hall, itself a temple to naval glory and national might. A party of men from the *Victory* arrived to help to convey their admiral to Whitehall on 8 January; dangerously large crowds again pressed to view the ceremonial embarkation of the coffin, and many people were injured. Once safely afloat, a carefully managed procession of boats followed the four barges that conveyed the official party and the coffin. The nineteen admirals included newly promoted Eliab Harvey, who had supported his admiral so nobly in the *Temeraire,* while Peter Parker and Lord Hood rightly took the chief places, having given him his post-captaincy, and his chance for glory. At the last minute, somewhat incongruously, Orde was substituted for an indisposed colleague. Among the captains were many Trafalgar heroes: Hardy, Bayntun, Laforey, Rotherham, Moorsom and Blackwood. Lieutenant Pasco, newly made a captain, carried a banner. The Lord Mayor followed; the full panoply of the City of London and the great commercial companies was on display. The river was empty of other traffic, and all along the banks crowds paid their respects and ships lowered their colours. A strong wind opposed the procession, but the coffin was landed as intended at 3.30, and despite a sudden rain squall it was conveyed to the Admiralty. Large crowds gathered outside, desperate for a sight of glory.

The following morning the land procession from the Admiralty to St Paul's received a powerful reinforcement of soldiers and eminent persons. Carriages and troops had been formed up well in advance, and when the grand ceremonial funeral car began to rumble out of the Admiralty at noon there were more than two miles of official procession to follow. The procession was so long that the leading elements had arrived at St Paul's before the last of the followers passed out of the Admiralty forecourt. The route was lined with soldiers, to control the mass of humanity that crowded the streets. The funeral car was a black monster, shaped at the bow and stern to resemble the *Victory*, and drawn by six of the King's black horses. An advance guard cleared a path through the warren of streets around Charing Cross, then ahead of the funeral car came the chief mourner and his supporters, peers and Privy Councillors, all in rank, and finally the Princes of the Blood Royal – in reverse order, ensuring the Prince of Wales was the last man ahead of the mourning party and car.

Lady Bessborough watched the two days of solemn processions and funeral service, and recorded her impressions for her lover, a young diplomat in St Petersburg:

> I do not in general think that grand ceremonies and processions are the Genius of the English Nation, and therefore they usually fail; but in this instance I must say I never saw anything so magnificent or so affecting . . . Amongst many touching things the silence of that immense Mob was not the least striking . . . The moment the car appeared which bore the body, you might have heard a pin fall, and without any order to do so, they all took off their hats. I cannot tell you the effect this simple action produced; it seemed one general impulse of respect beyond anything that could have been said or contrived. Mean while the dead march was played in soft tones, and the pauses filled with cannon and the roll of muffled drums.[9]

At Temple Bar the Lord Mayor and other dignitaries of the City of London greeted and joined the procession, the Mayor on horseback, bareheaded and carrying the City sword. Troops took up position around the west door of the cathedral as the procession arrived, and the body was carried inside, where many mourners had been seated for hours. Shortly after 2.00 p.m. the service began; but it was not until 5.33 p.m., after the words 'and his name liveth evermore', that the coffin was lowered into the crypt by concealed machinery. After the Garter King of Arms had completed his duties, the seamen charged with folding the *Victory*'s flag and placing it in the grave ripped it into fragments, each taking a piece as a memento – he was, after all, their admiral. The ceremony was over shortly before six, but some mourners lingered for hours, awestruck by the finest public ceremonial laid on in England since Elizabethan times, and the most magnificent funeral ever staged. It was well worth the £14,000 it had cost.

The mortal remains had been placed in the centre of the City of London's cathedral, where the power of commerce, the state and the Church of England intertwined. Bound up with power, policy and piety, Nelson had become the totem and talisman of a state fighting for survival. He might be dead and buried, but the very public performance that surrounded his interment ensured that his name and example would live on. Public burials have always been political occasions, but no British funeral has ever matched the intensity of Nelson's interment. His rites combined the human tragedy and adulation accorded to Diana, Princess of Wales, and the regard for public services accorded to Churchill with a unique atmosphere of danger. Napoleon was master of the Continent: only the Navy and Trafalgar stood between his armies and the coast of Britain. Grief, fear and reverence combined with the numbing cold to chill the souls of all present. After a century in which public funerals had been in decline, the Romantic era, the tensions of total war, and a growing sense of national identity ensured that when the nation's god-hero was killed at the moment of victory his rites would be on the grand scale. The staged pageant, the Lying in State, a grand water procession, land procession, and an interminable, if majestic service were calculated to impress. The Church, in every outpost across the land, was quick to seize upon the event for a morally uplifting and very Anglican interpretation. The crowds were immense, and the cathedral full to capacity.

The scale and substance of the majestic funeral, with a unique assembly of naval heroes, royalty and the great, with no expense spared, did much to reconcile the nation to their loss, and in the longer term to recreate the name of Nelson as the national talisman, now translated in glory to watch over an endangered island. The state had created a very specific Nelson, but this 'official' version would be contested.

Trafalgar and the death of Nelson forced some profound questions on a stunned nation. What did Nelson stand for? What was the inner meaning of Trafalgar? How could Nelson's legacy be used for the future, and how could such a unique life be interpreted for the common good? For the King, Nelson's 'transcendent and heroic services . . . will prove a lasting source of strength, security and glory to my Kingdom.' The Prince of Wales, who disagreed with his father on every other issue, said much the same, in his own way: 'His very name was a host of itself: Nelson and Victory were one and the same to us, and it carried dismay and terror to the hearts of our enemies.'[10] Sidmouth spoke for the political class when he concluded 'that he inspired all around him with the same gallant enthusiasm and ardent zeal in the service of his country which he felt himself'.[11] Lady Londonderry provided a more elegiac and more intimate summation. 'Had I been his wife or his mother, I would rather have wept him dead, than seen him languish on a less splendid day. In such a death there is no sting, and in such a grave everlasting victory.'[12]

The first artistic responses came in the popular prints. The caricaturist James Gillray, sharp critic of greed, stupidity, corruption and folly, saw the core of the business. Despite his savage assaults on every other figure in contemporary British life Gillray never doubted Nelson's genius, and treated his undoubted vanity with the lightest of touches. His death scene of December 1805 had the hero dying in the arms of the King, who took Hardy's place, with Clarence as a common sailor, and Emma a large, mourning Britannia. Above, the angel of victory summoned Immortality with a trumpet blast.

As soon as the *Victory* reached Spithead, on 4 December, she became a shrine, whose principal pilgrims were artists seeking a way to tell the story and secure a prize. Benjamin West missed the mark this time: his picture placed the scene on the upper deck, and lacked any of the warmth and drama that made his earlier painting such a success. Absurdly, he placed the entire crew on deck as an audience, in the middle of the battle! West had followed his own *Death of Wolfe* too closely. His audience would no longer tolerate stylised inaccuracy. He produced a second study, now located in the cockpit: the composition was better, but the central figure remained stiff and unengaging. West could not find the medium in which to convey Nelson's magic. That said, the original picture, produced as a partnership with a leading engraver, became the popular 'death': it attracted thirty thousand paying viewers in the summer of 1806, and was shown to the King, while fifteen hundred good prints sold at premium prices in 1811.[13]

One-time East India Company draughtsman and undischarged bankrupt Arthur Devis,[14] one of the lesser lights of English painting, took longer to absorb the atmosphere. Taking passage on *Victory* as she passed up the English Channel to her final destination at Chatham, he absorbed the key roles of the ship as the shrine, and of the crew as disciples. He also assisted Dr Beatty at the autopsy, sketched the fatal musket ball, and accepted the doctor's commission to paint a portrait. Devis was among the last to see the face of the dead man and his *The Death of Nelson* was more moving, more accurate, and more nearly right than any other image. Devis's Nelson lies bathed in an unearthly radiant light, one that had no place, or source, in the cockpit of a battleship, surrounded by a crowd of adoring disciples. While he portrayed Nelson a trifle too dead, Devis instinctively saw what West had missed. Nelson's death was the transfiguration of a mortal man into a divine being. While West condemned the composition as 'A mere matter of fact (that) will never . . . excite awe and veneration', the moment of immortality will always belong to Devis, and he rightly took the five-hundred-guinea prize offered by the publisher Joshua Boydell for the best death scene of Nelson. However, the West engraving of 1811 outsold the Devis, which appeared in 1812.

Meanwhile, a far greater artist than either Devis or West, J. M. W. Turner, was at Sheerness on 22 December to sketch the *Victory* as she entered the river, and he went on board at Chatham. He quickly filled a notebook with brilliant sketches, striking poetry, notes and rather inferior attempts at figures and portraits. As ever, the perspective he adopted was unconventional, striking and highly effective. Turner shows us the moment the fatal shot was fired, viewed from high in the *Victory*'s rigging. Dwarfed by towering masts Nelson falls while the battle rages round him; Turner had pinpointed the defining moment for his *The Battle of Trafalgar, as seen from the Mizzen Starboard Shrouds of the Victory*. The picture was first exhibited in June 1806, and after some reworking, reappeared in 1808.[15]

Turner recognised, as few contemporary artists did, his national role, and the need for a British identity: a way of seeing the world that would draw the nation together. While his landscapes defined a new cultural sensibility, his epic treatment of Nelson and the scarcely veiled classical allusions of his Carthaginian pictures would harness the state's determination to resist Bonapartist tyranny.[16] The Battle of the Nile had inspired Turner's first battle scene, but Trafalgar took the subject and the artist to new levels. The sea was the dominant focus of his artistic endeavour: his Channel was a vast expanse, to which he gave the elemental strength to defeat invasion, and his ships stood much taller than reality allowed, the better to convey majesty and power. Following his first *Trafalgar*, which was widely criticised for the blotchy figures, Turner returned to his métier, the seascape, with *The Victory returning from Trafalgar*. Here the ship, bearing the body of Nelson, runs past the Isle of Wight. Following the convention of the genre, the great ship is shown in three positions, with fishing boats in the foreground to represent the people of Britain. Their placing is essential, for this Channel is a wide watery space, bounded by the high white cliffs of the Needles, a combination standing between Napoleon and the conquest of the world. Turner's paintings are the most power-ful images to be inspired by Nelson, and the ultimate expression of his impact on the age.

The series of 'death' paintings was completed by West's third pic-ture, *The Apotheosis of Nelson* of 1807. This time the aged artist caught the mood of the time. This Nelson, posed as the dead Christ, is carried in arms of victory to a mourning Minerva, while Neptune watches. The famous signal, 'England expects', gives the picture a motto. The piece has been much misunderstood. West took the figures and composition from a recent canvas by a minor artist, although the original inspiration came from the religious masterpieces of the renaissance and the sculpture of Ancient Greece. The meanings are clear, if a trifle laboured: Nelson has succumbed to man's tragic destiny, but died a glorious and well-rewarded death. This time West met his own ambition, providing a worthy scene. He wanted the image to 'excite awe and veneration', and did not see how this could be achieved if Nelson were represented dying in the hold, like a man in prison. His death had to meet the highest ideals of the Romantic age if it was to inspire a nation. West may not have been aware of the irony, but he could only do justice to Nelson by returning to an art form he had subverted thirty years earlier.

One artist who stood against the tide of Nelson idolatry was William Blake, critic of Kings, empires and war. Blake, who was sympathetic to the American and French Revolutions and dreamed of an older English 'liberty', had a marked dislike of British naval power, which he saw as a 'sea-monster' that would 'harrow and strangle nations'.[17] Blake's response to Nelson was deeply ambivalent: he did not share the euphoria that followed the victory at the Nile, because it had revived enthusiasm for war at a time when peace was in prospect, and he had seen nothing out of the ordinary in Nelson before 1805.[18] Nelson's death, however, changed everything: now Blake understood the inner meaning of the man and his status as a secular god and national icon. Yet Blake's response would be radically different to that of his contemporaries. Shorn of his physical being, but still affected by human weaknesses, Nelson became one of Blake's 'detestable Gods' of war.[19] The artist transformed the hero into a truly majestic character, one of the darkest forces in his mystical demonology. These reflections culminated in his 1809 picture: 'The Spiritual form of Nelson guiding Leviathan, in whose wreathings are infolded the Nations of the Earth'. Leviathan, the serpent-like symbol of naval power and imperial tyranny, is wielded by Nelson to crush other nations. Though the 'crushing' imagery was inspired by an event two years after Nelson's death, when Britain despoiled neutral Denmark, in Blake's mind Nelson remained the presiding genius of the war. This picture – and its companion piece, 'Pitt guiding Behemoth' – have been variously interpreted as a belated, if unconventional concession to the patriotic impulse of the age,[20] and as altogether more radical statements.

Blake himself was clear: Pitt and Nelson were 'contemptible idiots who have been called Great Men of late years',[21] and he was interested only in their meaning. Unable to avoid the mood of the age Blake concedes Nelson's heroic status, showing him in an ideal, naked form, arm and eye restored, as any self-respecting classical artist would. Yet the effect is quickly discounted, for Blake was no admirer of military heroes. Calling Nelson 'the heroic villain', and showing him naked with female figures in the coils of his serpent, Blake makes his meaning clear. Nelson has moral failings at the human level, and like many of Blake's imaginary heroes has been led astray by a malign female spirit. The figure is surrounded by a halo of lightning bolts, but they point inwards, reinforcing the anti-heroic quality of the image. The meaning was more obvious in his first sketch, where two bolts of lightning strike Nelson on the right shoulder and the groin. One of these bolts has been loosed by Christ, a figure almost hidden in the jaws of Leviathan. For all Blake's objections, the heroic is still evident; even Blake's exhibition catalogue of 1809 quotes Nelson's final signal, 'England expects', suitably amended to include the arts.

Blake's images were among the most powerful of the great mass of works in oil, stone and ink that would appear in the decade between Trafalgar and Waterloo, reflecting the nation's need to capture and flaunt Nelson's totemic image. Only when the course of the war finally turned in 1813, and the downfall of Napoleon loomed, did the need for Nelson decline. He was replaced by lesser figures: the new heroes of a war that would be won, not the talisman of survival against all odds.

The literary response to Nelson's death was just as strong as that of painters, and no less varied in the quality and outlook of the work it generated. Newspapers and journals poured out accounts of the hero's life and death, and the events surrounding his interment. Book-length treatments were published within weeks, usually hastily assembled from news clippings and gazettes, most lacking both literary merit and insight into Nelson's genius. The exception to this run of mediocrity was an essay by Samuel Taylor Coleridge, who had spent much of 1804 and 1805 as Public Secretary to Sir Alexander Ball at Malta, in which capacity he had corresponded with Nelson and written papers on aspects of Mediterranean policy. In his obituary essay on Ball, Coleridge considered the qualities that allowed some officers to rise above the ordinary. The key assets included an open mind, and the ability to assemble, sift and exploit the ideas of others. Nelson, according to Coleridge:

> with easy hand collected, as it passed by him, whatever could add to his own stores, appropriated what he could assimilate, and levied subsidies of knowledge from all the accidents of social life and familiar intercourse. Even at the jovial board, and in the height of unrestrained merriment, a casual suggestion, that flashed a new light on his mind, changed the boon companion into the hero and the man of genius; and with the most graceful transition he would make his company as serious as himself. When the taper of his genius seemed extinguished, it was still surrounded by an inflammable atmosphere of its own, and rekindled at the first approach of light.[22]

Though Coleridge was not an expert on the naval profession, he understood men, methods and genius better than any other English author, and recognised the magic that made Nelson special:

> Lord Nelson was an admiral every inch of him. He looked at everything, not merely in its possible relations to the naval service in general, but in its immediate bearings on his own squadron; to his officers, his men, to the particular ships themselves, his affections were as strong and ardent as those of a lover. Hence, though his temper was constitutionally irritable and uneven, yet never was a commander so enthusiastically loved by men of all ranks, from the captain of the fleet to the youngest ship-boy. Hence too the unexampled harmony which reigned in his fleet, year after year, under circumstances that might well have undermined the patience of the best-balanced dispositions.[23]

Coleridge's absence from the host of Nelson biographers remains a matter of profound regret: his breadth of learning, intellectual sympathy and acute penetration, allied to his experience of public office and friendship with Ball, would have provided the ideal perspective from which to understand Nelson's life and work.

Even before Nelson's body had returned to England, it was clear that an official life would be required. The Bishop of Exeter warned the new Earl that many ill-informed books would appear, making it wise to have an authoritative account. William Nelson agreed, and soon after the funeral he advertised in the newspapers for an author to undertake the task, thereby antagonising John McArthur, who had already spoken to the Earl on this subject and whose work had already been announced. McArthur's object was to pre-empt the 'numerous, uninteresting and clashing accounts' by providing 'one full, genuine, authentic detail of the most interesting parts of his life, illustrated by correspondence, properly selected', and he was not impressed by the qualifications of the potential author, a Reverend Mr Nott, that the Earl had suggested. At this point the Prince of Wales intervened, calling in the Earl on 16 February 1806 and insisting that the Reverend James Stanier Clarke, his librarian and chaplain, be involved.[24] Clarke, who had served as a naval chaplain, was a prolix author on maritime subjects, and the first editor of the *Naval Chronicle*. With the Prince and Clarence leaning on him, the Earl gave way, although he stubbornly refused 'to suffer the least scrap to go out of his own possession'.[25] Clarke and McArthur, old colleagues on the *Naval Chronicle*, agreed to work together, with McArthur as the lead author, as he had already assembled materials for the project, and commissioned 1,500 guineas' worth of paintings and illustrations. He had also secured two hundred advance orders.

McArthur had begun the work with Nelson's sanction, but despite his qualifications the Earl decided that Clarke should stand first on the title page.[26] The Prince's librarian quickly assumed the directorship of the project, and wrote to the Earl to ask for 'such recollections as illustrated your brother's character when a boy and a young man'.[27] He had also asked Dr Beatty for an account of Nelson's last hours, and was horrified when he heard that the good doctor intended to publish this under his own name, with the Prince's blessing. His efforts to prevent this were in vain: the *Authentic Narrative of the Death of Lord Nelson* was published by Cadell and Davies in 1807, long before the official *Life* would be ready. Undeterred, however, Clarke worked his way through the small sections of the archive of correspondence that Earl Nelson was gracious enough to loan, and secured fresh material from many who had known the hero.[28] McArthur, too, borrowed letters from many sources, notably the Hood family, whom he had served for many years – though unlike Clarke, he did not return them once he had made use of them.

The book was ready to publish in the middle of 1809, but was held back because London was deserted. It would cost nine guineas, and the two volumes weighed in at over twenty-one pounds.[29] Much of the cost of the book had gone on art works commissioned to embellish the product: West's third 'death', the *Apotheosis of Nelson,* was a frontispiece,[30] while Nicholas Pocock's pictures of the great battles and ships and Richard Westall's bland action scenes illustrated the text. With the Prince at their elbow, the authors had gone for size and presentation, hoping to impress their audience by production values. However, the book's price and format restricted its readership, while shorter and cheaper rival works arrived sooner and swept the market clean. Moreover, despite its monumental length, it was unworthy of its subject: as a contemporary review pointed out, it was neither a biography, nor a collection of correspondence, but a blundering attempt to combine the two. A key part of the problem was the lack of a strong editorial grip on the project. Clarke was a weak man, and allowed others to impose their own agendas on the project – not just the Prince, the Earl and even the resurgent Fanny, but also hostile witnesses like Captain Edward Foote. It was also discovered later that Clarke had 'improved' the syntax of Nelson's letters, making his wonderfully direct English read like the work of a pretentious literary parson.

The initial print run cannot have been large, and many copies were pre-sold, but sales were so moderate that the publishers saw 'little hope of it ever repaying your and our advances, or anything like'. By late 1812 there were still 320 sets of the two-volume edition in stock: the publishers were still some £1,500 out of pocket, but were now anxious to close the account.[31] In 1814 some copies were offloaded to the book trade, although McArthur was still trying to drum up business in the West Indies.[32] By 1818 it was time to 'remainder'. In truth the book had been a sorry production, uninspired, unremarkable, weakly compiled and produced in an absurd fashion that deprived it of its natural readership. Few men have been so unfortunate in their 'official' biographies – and it is even more unfortunate that the text, despite having long been discredited, continues to influence writing on Nelson.

By late 1809 there was a substantial body of literature on Nelson, and Robert Southey – poet, historian and critic, as well as Coleridge's long-suffering friend, brother in law, and supporter – was busy surveying it for John Murray's *Quarterly Review*, the leading intellectual journal of the Tory establishment. The importance of the commission was reflected by the fee: £20 per page, rather than the usual £10. Southey bore his own grudge towards Clarke, who had been given the post of Historiographer Royal which Southey had sought. For Southey, the fact that 'a most extraordinary blockhead' should have been allowed to work on this subject was an insult to the memory of the hero, and the literary world.[33] Southey poured all his art and venom into a notice that emphasised the faults of the official life and Clarke's proven incapacity to undertake it.[34]

At Murray's bidding, Southey began to prepare a book of his own, and he was soon dining at the Admiralty with John Wilson Croker, Admiralty Secretary and another regular *Quarterly* reviewer. Croker persuaded the First Lord of the Admiralty to subsidise the project by drawing the maps in-house.[35] The book appeared in 1813 and was dedicated to Croker. Although his creative spark was radical, Southey was well on his way to becoming a Tory establishment figure when he addressed this national subject. His object was to complete the process begun at St Paul's: to reclaim Nelson for the establishment, who needed to be reminded of his transcendent achievements, and their singular failure to follow up the funeral with any other appropriate monuments. For Southey, their lukewarm response contrasted markedly and unfavourably with the celebration of Nelson's achievements among ordinary people. Southey was anxious to show the country that its leaders were men of character; however, he also used Nelson to show that the aristocracy had no monopoly on leadership, or virtue.[36] His book would inspire young officers, teaching them command, leadership, humanity and the care of their men. He also highlighted the political courage that illuminated Nelson's entire career: that implicit reliance on his own judgement that made him the greatest of all commanders.

Southey's book, despite its flaws, set a standard that none has matched. Its power and eloquence derive from the literary skill of the author, and the simple, powerful style of Nelson's own writing. Moreover, Southey wrote at a time of pressing national need, in the darkest hours of the struggle with Napoleon, which added urgency and purpose to his narrative. The tone is uplifting, but carefully balanced: this is Nelson warts and all, and the book includes a stinging indictment of Nelson's handling of the Neapolitan counter-revolution, and his relationship with Emma.[37] The initial print run of three thousand copies sold out immediately, and a second edition was in hand by September.[38] Despite (or perhaps because of) the objections of Emma,[39] who had but a few months to live, the book remained in print, running to a fourth edition in 1830. At a very reasonable five shillings it found a ready market among the increasingly literate populace, establishing itself as the standard life.

Coleridge and Southey were not the only poets to subscribe to the cult of Nelson. The hero found a still more passionate devotee in Lord Byron, who used Nelson to define the heroic in his masterpiece, *Don Juan*:

> Nelson was Britannia's god of war,
> And still should be so, but the tide is turn'd;
> There's no more to be said of Trafalgar,
> 'Tis with our hero quietly inurn'd;
> Because the army's grown more popular,
> At which the naval people are concern'd[.]

Early drafts of the first line use 'the popular', or 'the people's' in place of 'Britannia's'.[40] All three are effective, while the second gives a particular twist to the line concerning 'the naval people'. In contrast to Southey, Byron was setting Nelson against the post-war Tory establishment, dominated by two men he hated: Castlereagh and Wellington.

No writer was more influenced by Nelson than Byron; the beautiful but flawed poet had even self-consciously imitated Nelson in his first portrait, commissioned from a naval painter in 1807. As the grandson of an admiral, Byron had a familial disposition towards the naval model of heroism, and this was only strengthened by his personal love of ships and the sea. References to Nelson litter Byron's work, from *Childe Harold* to *Don Juan*, and also his more private thoughts. Even his death – in the midst of war, seeking an engagement with the enemy, before he could grow old and lose his looks – knowingly followed Nelson's model. What Byron found in Nelson was the model for his pose, another man prepared to defy convention in following his own genius. From this image Byron created the romantic hero, and worked hard to match the ideal, in art, artifice and action. The idea of 'erotic obsession', which became, through Byron, a central trope of European Romanticism,[41] quickly came to cast a backward reflection on Nelson. Nelson's relationship with Emma was refashioned as Byronic, and his eighteenth-century morality converted into romantic rebellion. In truth Nelson was the original Romantic hero and Byron the imitator: after all, what glory is there in the poet's art?

In *Manfred* Byron was preoccupied by the concept of a superman, a 'Titanic figure half way between the mortals and the gods'. The connection with Nelson, the immortal memory, is obvious. The connection grew with time. Byron returned from the Mediterranean in 1811 on board HMS *Volage*, in company with HMS *Amphion*. The two ships were returning in triumph from the battle of Lissa. As the enemy closed in Nelson's brilliant protégée William Hoste had flown the signal, 'Remember Nelson' from *Amphion*'s masthead to inspire his men.[42] Byron took the opportunity to discuss the battle, along with their adored admiral, with Hoste and his officers,.[43] Once ashore the connections continued to pile up. Among the wealth of Byron portraits the defining 'romantic icon' was painted by Richard Westall in 1813.[44] Westall had created the 'romantic hero' pictures of Nelson for Clarke and McArthur's book only four years before. He went on to fulfil other Byron commissions;[45] his illustrations for the largely autobiographical *Don Juan* only reinforced the connection. So highly did Byron regard the subject that he forgave Southey his politics and his poetry to praise the famous 1811 review.[46] For Byron death was a frequent companion: friends and school-fellows were struck down by war and disease, making mortality a constant feature of his life. He would die trying to be a 'Nelsonic' hero, not a poet. Nelson is the real-life hero at the heart of his oeuvre.

By the time Byron's tribute was produced, more durable memorials to Nelson in the form of statues and monuments were beginning to appear. These were the ultimate expression of public interest: accessible to all, including the poor and the illiterate. Dublin was the first city to respond to the public demand for a monument to Nelson, and subscribers to the project included the future Duke of Wellington, then in Irish Government, who gave £100. A horseback procession of the Anglo-Irish elite attended the laying of the foundation stone by the Lord Lieutenant, but the pillar, designed by Norfolk architect William Wilkins, had a mixed reception, and a chequered history. James Joyce referred to it in *Ulysses* as 'the statue of the one-handed adulterer', while nationalists always associated it with British rule. In 1966 it was blown up by the IRA in a remarkably neat operation.[47]

In 1813 a memorial was erected in Liverpool, symbolically located between the Town Hall and commercial Exchange in Mansion House Quadrangle. Over £9,000 was raised in public subscriptions for the memorial, reflecting the importance of Nelson's career to a seaport trading with the West Indies. The large, complex plinth was overloaded with meaning and allegory. The design, by Westmacott and Wyatt, placed the dying hero across the lap of Britannia, with four prisoners, an enraged sailor, Death and Victory in attendance. The combination of contemporary dress and classical nudity makes this an uneasy and confused rendering.[48] Hermann Melville, in town thirty years later as an unknown American sailor while his ship changed cargoes, was fascinated by the meaning and majesty of the image, and would give it a place in *Redburn*.[49]

Edinburgh, Glasgow, Birmingham and Bridgetown, Barbados, all put up memorials, although the latter is now in danger of following the Dublin pillar into oblivion as an inappropriate reminder of a colonial past. Attempts to commemorate the hero in his native Norfolk were delayed by the inability of the great and good to decide where to put the pillar. After nine years, and the return of peace, they selected Great Yarmouth, the last place in the county that Nelson had visited. By 1819, Wilkins' 144-foot high structure, crowned with an artificial stone Britannia looking toward Burnham Thorpe, was complete.[50]

London, the obvious location, had been slow to act, and even slower to complete the task. The House of Commons discussed the issue in 1816, but nothing was done. However, the clearing away of the slums, stables and warren of lanes between Charing Cross, St Martin in the Fields, Whitehall and St James's provided a suitable space, while the addition of the National Gallery in the early 1830s provided a focal point, and in 1835 this central space was named Trafalgar Square. The King – Nelson's old friend William – wanted to appropriate the place and stand in splendour on a level with his brother Frederick, Duke of York, already atop a nearby pillar, but he was wise enough to accept the inevitable. After William's death a committee was formed to collect money for a Nelson memorial, and its members included Wellington, Hardy, Cockburn and Croker. The Navy was canvassed, and if HMS *Snake* was typical, the officers and men donated anything from one to four days' pay.[51]

The design finally selected, by William Railton, was based around a column copied from Augustus's Temple of Mars Ultor in the Roman Imperial Forum. The choice was no accident: the Roman temple had celebrated the transformation of a dead hero – Julius Caesar – into a god, linking him with the god of war and the establishment of an Empire that would last for ever.[52] The parallel was clear. Nelson, 'the greatest naval hero that the history of the world can record',[53] had transcended human limits to become the national god of war, and personify the vengeance of the nation. It was also the last word. Trafalgar had set the seal on Britain's naval mastery for all time, and the combination of Nelson and the Augustan column formed the ultimate expression of global maritime power. The conscious identification of Imperial Britain with Imperial Rome, a tendency emphasised by Gibbon seventy years earlier, was becoming ever more frequent. Rome provided an example, an artistic language and a warning to the classically educated British elite.

Since the eighteenth century Rome had been a source of inspiration for British architects, providing the ideal artistic language in which to express themes of empire and power. The Napoleonic conflict, the ultimate imperial struggle, had pitted the French version of Rome, personified by Bonaparte and his eagle-topped armies, against Nelson and the sea power of the British Empire. Both regimes used Roman motifs, models and icons to stake their claim to be the true inheritor of the all-embracing sway of Rome. With France's political ambitions curtailed after 1815, Britain could lay claim to the imperial mantle. British architects were busy in Rome, measuring the remains, ready to translate them to modern use. From the mid-1820s onwards, British architecture would be Roman, with the opening shots being the triumphal commissions of the Marble Arch and the Constitution Hill Arch. These projects were ordered by George IV, as part of his attempt to appropriate the glory of defeating Napoleon for himself. His brother Frederick, Duke of York, was given a Trajanic/Napoleonic column, but the column that followed would be more remarkable, and more powerful. Built at the height of enthusiasm for Roman architecture, Nelson's column was the ultimate expression of British power, written in a language that the entire civilised world could read.[54] While the legislature was Gothic, reflecting the origins of British democracy and constitutional practice, and the Greek classical style was appropriate for culture, the British Museum and the National Gallery, Roman architecture stood for power, international connections, and also commerce – hence the Roman style of both the new London Exchange and the Foreign Office.

The column and statue were in place by November 1843, but it would be another twenty-four years before Landseer's bronze lions completed the design.[55] Despite the delay in execution, the success of the composition was and remains obvious. Hitler's view of it as the 'symbol of British naval might and world domination' is testimony to this – he had planned to take it back to Berlin if his invasion project of 1940 were successful. The symbolic power of the location was no less

The Nelson Column on Trafalgar Day, 1897

apparent to the Frenchman, Hippolyte Taine: when he visited Trafalgar Square in 1852, he could not bring himself to give the space its name, reserving his vitriol for the heroic figure far above him – 'That hideous Nelson, planted upon his column like a rat impaled on the end of a stick!'[56]

While Nelson's statue was being hoisted to the top of the column, another literary monument was in progress. Sir Nicholas Harris

330

Nicolas had served in the Royal Navy from 1808 to 1816, before beginning a legal and literary career. In 1843 he began work on his magnum opus, *The Dispatches and Letters of Lord Nelson*. This required him to locate, check and publish all the Nelson correspondence he could find, an enterprise that has never been repeated. Nicolas believed that Nelson had not received his due from his country:

> She owes to him a Name synonymous with Victory, which, with almost talismanic power inspires her Sons in the day of battle with a confidence that ensures success; and She is indebted to him for an Example to ages yet unborn, of the most ardent loyalty, the most genuine patriotism, the most conscientious sense of duty to his Sovereign and his Country, and of the highest professional skill, combined with the most generous disposition, the kindest heart, and the noblest aspirations, that ever graced a Public Man.[57]

Convinced that Nelson's own words would do full justice to his career Nicolas claimed to have omitted only a few items connected with Lady Hamilton, and the names of a few living individuals who had been criticised.[58]

On applying to the second Lord Hood for access to correspondence cited in the official life, Nicolas discovered that this was not in family hands, but apparently remained with the papers of John McArthur, who had recently died. Though his family had returned a few letters, both Hood and Nicolas were convinced they had many more. On inspecting this correspondence Nicolas realised the need to see the rest: 'there is not one that escaped his [Clarke's] mutilations and suppressions.' It was clear that the McArthurs were holding on to important papers, and Nicolas suggested that 'possibly a letter from your Lordships Solicitor would do good'.[59] With Nelson still a relatively controversial figure Nicolas found it necessary to allow his donors to edit the material: 'I would use them under any restriction you might think fit to impose.'[60]

On Trafalgar Day 1844, only eleven months after the completion of the column, Nicolas sent Lord Hood the first volume of his work. Nicolas was disgusted by the behaviour of the McArthur family, and hardly less so by a Mr Lamb, who refused to let him have copies of the letters in his collection 'lest it should injure the mercantile value of the originals'.[61] That Nicolas compiled seven stout volumes in little more than two years is monument to his industry. The column and the *Letters* rounded off a period of forty years in which the less edifying aspects of Nelson's life, real or imagined, had faded. What remained was his heroic image, and his totemic qualities.

The death in 1837 of Nelson's old friend, King William IV, symbolised the end of an era in the national understanding of Nelson. Now there were few men left who had known the hero in life. Two years later, Hardy ended his days, as Hood had, as Governor of Greenwich Hospital. Cockburn hung on until 1852, and Graham Hamond until 1862, but the longest-lived of Nelson's captains was the precocious young commander of the *Amazon*: Admiral of the Fleet Sir William Parker, Bt., died in 1866, fifty-one years after Trafalgar. The passing of these old men cleared the way for a new Nelson who would meet the needs of a new age.

William's niece and heir was well aware of her naval heritage. She was introduced to the key aspects of the naval story as a child, in a conscious programme to prepare the little German princess for a British future. Victoria read Southey's biography in 1830, aged ten, later telling the author that she had enjoyed it.[62] In July 1833, the fourteen-year-old princess cemented her links with naval glory by boarding HMS *Victory*, accompanied by her mother, the Duchess of Kent: she paid close attention to the Nelson relics and sat down to dine with the men.[63] A month later, the Princess and her mother sailed from Portsmouth around the Eddystone lighthouse on board the frigate HMS *Forte*. The cruise provided the impressionable girl with a powerful appreciation of Britannia's right arm in action. The price of glory was also obvious: Captian Pell had lost his leg in battle.

On Trafalgar Day 1844, Victoria, by now Queen, visited HMS *Victory* again, this time accompanied by her husband, Prince Albert. Those present, who included Trafalgar veteran Captain Moubray, noted that Her Majesty had been 'visibly affected' by the occasion.[64] Albert, too, understood the shrine's significance. Though his central German origins made the sea and the Navy novelties, he soon saw how essential they were to his adopted country. He increasingly identified with Britain's naval past, a link symbolised by his acceptance of the dedication of Nicolas's edition of Nelson's correspondence.

When Albert began commissioning fresco work for Buckingham Palace, Osborne House and the new Palace of Westminster, he gave one of his favourite artists, the Irish Romantic Daniel Maclise, the immense task of capturing Waterloo and Trafalgar for the Royal

Gallery at Westminster.[65] These would be vast pictures, forty-five feet long and twelve feet deep, accompanied by sixteen smaller pictures of British valour, and the death of Nelson would once more be joined with that of Wolfe. These military scenes would serve the same function as the splendid Armada tapestries, destroyed with the old House of Lords, but this time Nelson would be the central figure, reinvented as an example to future generations.

However, it would be many years before Maclise started work on his Nelson. In the interval, his friend Clarkson Stanfield produced two major Nelson canvases, establishing him as the marine artist of the era. Following royal commissions, including his 1832 *Portsmouth Harbour*, with *Victory* taking centre stage, the United Services Club commissioned him to paint a Trafalgar for their imposing new building (now the Institute of Directors). Stanfield represented the state of the battle at 2.30, sacrificing art for historical accuracy. The picture is full of ships, but short of meaning. Despite being a very wooden image, it was immediately more popular than Turner's romantic interpretation.[66] A decade later Stanfield produced a more compelling composition, *The* Victory *Being Towed into Gibraltar*, for Sir Morton Peto, the engineering contractor who had put up Nelson's Column. It shows the battered flagship and her sad cargo being towed to safety by Thomas Fremantle's *Neptune*.[67] While a far better reproduction of the sea than Turner's 1806 *Victory*, it lacked his emotional engagement. Stanfield reproduced what he had seen; Turner's pictures were the creation of a towering imagination.[68]

Between 1844 and 1865 Stanfield served as curator of the gallery that had been established at the Royal Naval Hospital at Greenwich, overseeing an important programme of cleaning and restoration that kept the art and the space in good order for another century.[69] The original impulse for this gallery had come from William Locker, Nelson's old captain, a Deputy Governor of the Hospital and a minor but discerning collector of Nelsoniana. His 1795 proposal that the Painted Hall be used as a National Gallery of Marine Paintings to generate revenue for the charity that ran the Hospital was finally taken up in 1823 by his son Edward Hawke Locker, Secretary to the Hospital and Civil Commissioner. The younger Locker augmented the existing collection by securing twenty-nine pictures from George IV, who had tired of naval glory, and commissioning major paintings to fill in gaps in the coverage of naval history.[70] In 1829 the King handed over two majestic sea-battle pictures, de Loutherbourg's *Glorious First of June* and Turner's overwhelming *Trafalgar*.[71] The collection of paintings was supplemented by relics, most notably the famous bloodstained coat, found by Sir Harris Nicolas in 1845; Albert bought it for £150 and placed it in a sealed case among Stanfield's newly refurbished pictures.[72] The remarkable price paid reflected the quasi-religious significance of the artefact.

Most of the visitors to the Greenwich collection read its history lesson in a conventional linear manner, as a record of Britain's rise to imperial power on the oceans. These viewers knew exactly what Nelson meant: he had given them the empire of the world, and its trade flowed past the building. In this way the Victorians began to strip away the wonder and the magic of Nelson and his greatest battle. The literal images that were increasingly favoured in the gallery were not devoid of meaning and power, but their concern with fact and form invited an unthinking response. Stanfield's images played a major role in the development of the Victorian understanding of the Nelson cult, while his restoration of the Painted Hall and cleaning of many older pictures preserved the best work from previous generations.[73] He oversaw the introduction of a new, popular aesthetic to the Nelson story.

The new ideas on heroism were no less evident in the literary responses to Nelson generated during the Victorian era. Thomas Carlyle was among the most influential makers of Victorian culture, and no writer saw history in grander terms than he did: for him, it was 'poetry, prophecy, biography and social criticism – all in one'.[74] He wanted to create modern prose epics, to provide the Victorians with a past that helped them plot the course ahead. His 1839 essay, *Heroes and Hero Worship*, helped to shape a new sensibility, elevating the great men of the age to a quasi-religious status – and he did not ignore Nelson. Indeed, a brief biography of Nelson was among Carlyle's earliest writings, composed for an encyclopaedia in the early 1820s. If his source was Southey, the approach was altogether more elevated. Carlyle saw no reason to discuss the 'only stain' – the story of Carracioli – 'and his fervid though pure attachment to Lady Hamilton'.[75] Carlyle's Trafalgar was the capstone on the naval greatness of England, while Nelson's life was distinguished by 'unremitting exertion of a mind gifted with the most acute penetration, the loftiest ardour, the most inflexible determination; and the last scene of it was fitly, though mournfully, adapted to its general tenor'. For Carlyle, 'Nelson's name will always occupy a section in the history of the world, and be pronounced wherever it is understood, as that of a HERO.'[76]

Carlyle's approach to history, as the work of great men recorded for example, enjoyed a long popularity, though few aspired to match his elevated conception of purpose, or achieved his insight. Investing every ounce of his being in his work made Carlyle a unique talent, and if his theme endured, his intensity could not. Over time his thoughts became common currency, but their deeper meaning was lost. The Victorians put their heroes on pedestals and looked to them for uplifting examples, but this process inevitably reduced them to a homogenised stereotype: Christian hero, moral, pure, chivalric and evangelical. While some of their contemporaries might come close to this model, it was only through a strenuous editing process that it could be reconciled with the biographies of earlier heroes such as Nelson.

The first Victorian *Life of Nelson* was produced by Thomas Pettigrew (1791–1865), a surgeon and antiquary whose father had served as a naval surgeon on the *Victory*, though long before Nelson's day. While best known for establishing Horatia's paternity beyond doubt, Pettigrew also dealt with the folly of the 'Black Legend' of Naples.[77] The book coincided with a renewed interest in Nelson that was closely connected to the French naval revival, a link symbolised by Petti-grew's dedication to Lord Auckland, First Lord of the Admiralty at the time the book went to press – though he died suddenly before it appeared. Pettigrew had access to private correspondence Croker had withheld from Nicolas, and also received liberal support from the Admiralty, notably from two of Croker's relatives. Unfortunately for the causes he espoused, Pettigrew's literary style was rather heavy-going: while his treatment of the material and his analysis of the evidence were an improvement on Clarke, his prose was a steady procession, quite incapable of competing with Southey even if the text had been shorter, and published in a cheap format. The book stirred up a newspaper controversy, principally over Emma and Horatia, and quickly went into a second edition. Yet it soon faded from the limelight, and remains largely unknown. The Victorians already knew about Nelson, and while Pettigrew had evidence and ambition, he lacked the talent to change their minds. His book did succeed, however, in drawing attention to the nation's failure to honour Nelson's wishes for Emma and Horatia. He provided enough evidence to revive the claim, and after a prolonged discussion during 1852–4 between radical MP Joseph Hume and successive Prime Ministers, a Civil List pension of £300 was raised, to be split between Horatia's three daughters.[78]

Like Nicolas before him, Pettigrew's methods and values were those of an age increasingly interested in the past, and the practical lessons, moral examples and future prognoses it could offer. However, the impact of both works would be limited by their cost: the later volumes of the Nicolas edition, the most 'interesting' by any calculation, did not sell well, and the series was not reprinted until 1997. Instead the growing popular appetite for Nelson biography would be satiated by Southey – taken entire, or in essence.

The Society for the Promotion of Christian Knowledge (SPCK) had produced a *Life* in 1837, an abridgement of Southey's text. However, it retained Southey's damning verdict on Nelson's public and private affairs at Naples in 1799 – a poor return for Nelson's active support of the SPCK.[79] Despite this condemnation the book still managed to end on a morally uplifting note: it hinted at immortality, although carefully ascribing the idea of sanctity to simple sailors, and concluded with an uplifting eulogy of Nelson as 'a martyr patriot'.[80] The function of the edition was to provide for the intellectual needs of the newly literate classes, with a 'suitable' text, moral if not religious. In an age influenced by Carlyle's vision of the heroic Nelson remained the quintessential figure, the ultimate hero, romantic icon and the national talisman.

Daniel Maclise's inclusive fresco of Waterloo for the Royal Gallery at the Palace of Westminster was finally completed in December 1861 – the same month that Albert died, victim of an unromantic complaint occasioned by the medieval, but hardly chivalric, drains of Windsor. With one big wall covered the artist moved to design 'Trafalgar: the Death of Nelson'. For this his research was meticulous, as befits the taste of the time, and incorporated the famous coat that his patron had secured, along with visits to the *Victory* and samples of rope, fittings and other gear. The composition includes over seventy life-sized figures on the upper deck of *Victory,* with the fallen Nelson in the arms of Hardy at the focal point. There is no glory or triumphalism here: the price of success is shown life-sized and with disturbing power.[81]

Maclise's picture reflects a new mood: while the hero falls, mortally wounded, death and mutilation surround him, at the heart of the image. Moreover, Nelson's blood can be seen on the deck, along with that of his men, something the previous generation of artists had scrupulously avoided – gods do not bleed. Here, however, all are united in duty, and death, and the sacrifice is far more democratic than had been allowed hitherto. This Nelson is not a god – just one of many men to die that day.[82] Perhaps without realising it, Albert had succeeded in 'dethroning' Nelson: by demoting him from the divine status he had been accorded by an earlier era, a metaphorical space was opened up for a restored and newly respected monarchy.

The picture took nearly two years to execute, using a complex new fresco technique that Albert had sent Maclise to learn in Germany. By the time it was finished, the great project to embellish the Houses of Parliament was collapsing: Albert 'had been the directing mind and without his determined support the enterprise would probably have ended sooner'.[83] Anxious to save money, and unimpressed by the relative unpopularity of the two battle pieces, the Commission cancelled Maclise's remaining work, and the smaller paintings were never executed. Yet the Nelson was universally praised as a masterpiece of narrative art in the high romantic style.[84] The *Art Journal* concluded: 'We are a maritime power, but it is the only picture which we yet possess entirely worthy of our naval history.'[85]

Such judgements reflect the triumph of literalism over the ethic of an earlier age. For the mid-Victorians, Nelson simply could not be the chivalric hero, the ideal knight: his flaws were too great, and his sense of duty too sophisticated. The moral climate, too, had noticeably chilled, and conduct that had attracted adverse comment in 1800 was now considered absolutely immoral. The problem was how to make use of the greatest hero of all without condoning his life. Daniel Maclise met this task head-on, and succeeded brilliantly. His scene presented the House of Lords with a demonstration of duty, heroism and democratic carnage.

By 1865 the country had humanised Nelson, and his status was steadily being reduced. In an age of minor wars and dangerous exploration, he was vulnerable to being displaced by the temporary heroes of the day – priggish lightweights like Admiral Sir Edmund Lyons, who explicitly courted comparisons with Nelson during the Crimean War. Such men, however, knew nothing of the danger of invasion, or high-intensity combat. Mid-Victorian Britain never had to meet the challenge of total war: the rivalry of the Second Bonapartist Empire, unlike that of the First, was dismissed with a pair of arms races. Consequently, the need to develop fresh versions of Nelson was limited. However, this comfortable world would not last indefinitely, and a new Nelson would be needed when the external environment darkened. The only question was what form the new image would take.

CHAPTER XVII

Nelson Revived
1885–2005

During the peaceful years of the late Victorian era, once the French threat had been annihilated by the German armies, interest in Nelson fell away. He seemed an inappropriate and even unnecessary figure in an era whose character was symbolised by its Prime Minister, William Ewart Gladstone, a man who combined moral fervour, liberal reform and tree-felling in one remarkably industrious nineteenth-century package. As the scourge of the Neapolitan Bourbons, Gladstone's view of Nelson was obvious. He also disliked the Navy, and hoped to cut it back in order to abolish income tax. But he overlooked the fact that the masses he wished to enfranchise depended for their daily bread on free access to the sea.

The populist journalist William Stead, editor of the influential *Pall Mall Gazette*, using confidential figures supplied by Captain John Fisher RN, started a campaign to highlight 'The Truth about the Navy'. In search of allies, Stead sent his first editorial to the Poet Laureate, Alfred, Lord Tennyson, long a public critic of defence economies. Suitably roused, Tennyson produced a simple but emotive popular appeal, which appeared in *The Times*, and the *Pall Mall Gazette*, on 23 April 1885.[1] 'The Fleet' left no one in any doubt about where Tennyson stood: Gladstonian economics had gone too far, and it was time to reinforce the defences of the country. With a poet's sen-

Vivien Leigh and Laurence Olivier (with erroneous eye-patch) in
Alexandar Korda's *Lady Hamilton* (1941)

sibility, Tennyson invoked Nelson and the Fleet as the exemplars of English greatness: 'The Fleet of England is her all in all . . . and in her Fleet her fate.' The poem reflected the national mood, and Gladstone listened. Within weeks a supplementary naval estimate, the 'Northbrook Programme', had been placed before Parliament, and passed into law. The following year the first new life of Nelson for three decades appeared, and was soon followed by others: no sooner had the country realised it needed to improve the Navy than Nelson resumed his central role in the national identity.

Harsh economic competition from Europe and the United States, rising levels of naval spending across the globe, and the looming prospect of another major war created a growing sense of crisis. Patriotism was popular, and patriotic figures equally so, as something to which frightened people could cling. The use of Nelson's image multiplied, and the 1890s were the prime decade for Nelson biographies, with seven significant publications. Children, too, were taught by the Cambridge Junior school history textbook that 'Nelson thought a great deal about duty; and that he was very brave and daring, and that he was also kind and tender-hearted' – Emma, Naples and the more contentious issues were ignored, as Nelson was used to teach the men and women of tomorrow citizenship, patriotism and moral values.[2] Little wonder they grew up to prefer his moral 'failings' with Emma: by making Nelson a symbol of conformist excellence, educators in the new age of compulsory schooling turned him into a priggish bore. Nelson's Victorian eminence – though nothing to do with the man himself – was later subjected to much criticism, and the notorious private life was brought out to expose the hypocrisy of Victorian society.

The naval revival reached a peak in 1891 with the Royal Naval Exhibition at the Chelsea Hospital. In a grand spectacle designed to demonstrate 'the relation between Britannia's naval expenditure and naval responsibilities', Nelson was the central figure, and a full sized mock-up of the *Victory* the dominant image, complete with a 'Death of Nelson' by Madame Tussaud's, based on the Devis picture. Between 2 May and 24 October almost two and a half million visitors attended, inspecting everything from Nelson artefacts to modern ships, guns, engines and boilers. A smaller travelling version of the show then toured the major cities, gradually selling off artefacts.

The exhibition was followed in 1894 by the formation of the Navy

League, whose purpose was to campaign for naval expansion and to inform the people about the importance of naval supremacy, on which the British Empire depended for trade, food supply and national existence. The chief fund-raisers for the League were City firms, involved in trade, banking and investment, through the London Chamber of Commerce. They were joined by a powerful list of retired admirals, and unemployed captains, who lent a veneer of naval authority to the proceedings. The League's organisers were careful to link Nelson with their message. 'Nelson's life and death, it was foreseen, might be utilised to personify British Sea Power to the children, if not to the veterans of British democracy throughout the world.'[3] They also made full use of Trafalgar Square, celebrating Trafalgar Day in 1896 with a massive gathering that offended liberal opinion-formers and prompted George Bernard Shaw to suggest that it would be better to pull down Nelson's column.[4]

The Navy did not participate in such events, preferring to exploit the signs of popular enthusiasm for additional battleships in more discreet discussions with the Treasury. Unlike the League, the Admiralty had consistently failed to exploit the symbolic power of Nelson's image. In 1892 the only other Nelson ship left, HMS *Foudroyant*, was sold, and quickly passed on to a firm of German ship-breakers. This prompted a public outcry, but the Admiralty refused to reconsider. Privately they told one critic that they did not wish to see the ship preserved because she had 'discreditable' associations – a reference was to the liaison with Emma, the suppression of the Neapolitan revolution and the execution of Caracciolo. A private citizen saved the ship, and restored her to provide seamanship training for underprivileged boys. Sadly she was wrecked on Blackpool beach in June 1897.[5] The 'discredit' has persisted to this day: the Royal Navy has not reused the name. The remaining Nelson ship would have to wait for her salvation.

The Navy League's propagandising use of Nelson was accompanied by an altogether more cerebral appropriation of his legacy. While the Chelsea exhibition had been opening the eyes of the nation at large, the theoretical argument for naval power was being set out in clear and exemplary form by an American naval officer. In his two 'Sea Power' books of 1890 and 1892, Captain Alfred Thayer Mahan argued that the basis for success in the modern world was the possession and use of an ocean-going battlefleet navy, capable of securing access to colonies and markets. Mahan's purpose was to persuade his countrymen to build such a navy, and join the British in a partnership to lead the world in the twentieth century. Mahan was praised and lionised in Britain, and his books changed the intellectual climate. Even Gladstone recognised them as the books of the era; and in 1894, aware that the tide of opinion was running against his policy of low tax and small defence budgets, he resigned rather than accept increased naval spending.

The previous year, the Navy Records Society had been founded by naval historian Professor John Knox Laughton and the Director of Naval Intelligence Captain Cyprian Bridge. Their purpose was to assemble, digest and publish the most important material on the naval past, as a source of ideas, doctrine and education for the modern Navy. The Society brought Laughton into close contact with Mahan, who came to rely on 'the naval historian' as a living resource from which he drew information, archival advice, support and companionship. Over time their relationship deepened as the two men recognised their shared interests. Nelson dominated their work between 1895 and 1900. With the centenary of his greatest achievements looming, many aspects of the great admiral's life and career were thrown under the spotlight. A debate about who was 'responsible' for the nature of the attack at the Nile was only a foretaste of what was to come.

Laughton produced three major Nelson books: a single-volume edition of his correspondence in 1886, a brief life in 1889, and the more broadly based *The Nelson Memorial: Nelson and his Companions in Arms* in 1896. Though Laughton remained a man of the mid-nineteenth century, and took a rather defensive attitude to the more scandalous aspects of the story, he opened a new era in Nelson scholarship, from which important results would flow. Mahan, meanwhile, more political scientist than historian, was concerned to use the hero as 'the embodiment of the Sea Power of Great Britain', to teach naval strategy by example. His 1897 *Life of Nelson* followed the argument of his earlier texts, but shifted the focus to the individual, to show how Nelson used 'sea power' to decisive effect. He was the first senior naval officer to examine Nelson's life, and his book, written in a ponderous, stately style, found a ready audience: the reviews were universally good, and within a year it had sold over five thousand copies in Britain at a imposing £1.80, making it the best-selling naval biography of the age.

Mahan used a limited range of sources, and his approach was literary and impressionistic rather than academic, which led him to perpetuate a number of the less credible Nelson embellishments, notably those provided by Emma. He also decided – bizarrely, and on the basis of little more than a single sentence – that Nelson was no seaman. It was unfortunate, too, that in his creditable effort to save Nelson's reputation, Mahan criticised Captain Foote's self-justificatory 'Vindication' of his conduct in Naples.[6] Mahan's comments provoked Foote's grandson, Francis Pritchett Badham, to mount an assault on Nelson's veracity, and as an aside, on the integrity and scholarship of his two advocates.[7] Badham sent his attack on Mahan and Nelson to the leading British historian Samuel Rawson Gardiner, for publication in the prestigious *English Historical Review*. Despite his friendship with Laughton, Gardiner concluded that he and Mahan were wrong, and published Badham's paper.

The Neapolitan Revolution has been interpreted by Italian liberals, notably the Neapolitan historian Benedetto Croce, as the beginning of national regeneration and the movement for independence, 'when modern Italy, the new Italy, our Italy was born'.[8] Because Nelson helped to restore the corrupt Bourbon regime and suppress the movement for Neapolitan autonomy, his actions have always been portrayed in the darkest terms by Italian historians – and by those liberal British historians who had sympathies with Italian nationalism.[9] This politically motivated interpretation has cast a long shadow over Nelson's otherwise glorious career.

Undeterred by such attitudes, Laughton and Mahan addressed the evidence and began to uncover the facts. After three years' hard work they overwhelmed Badham, and then demolished the host of ill-informed, hostile critics who refused to see the truth. While Laughton worked at the sources, Mahan prepared a series of reports and papers that culminated in the comprehensive revision of his chapters on Naples in the second (1899) edition of his *Life of Nelson*. The chapters were significantly longer, and adopted a scholarly approach to the use of evidence. This was the only time Mahan ever rewrote one of his books. Eventually the two men amassed enough evidence to secure a victory. Having published Badham, Gardiner was mortified to find that his old friend Laughton, and the famous American, had been right all along, and advised using the Records Society, of which he was a Vice-President, to settle the matter. Laughton set H. C. Gutteridge, a young Cambridge graduate, to work on the Italian archives. Gutteridge's Records Society volume of 1903, *Nelson and the*

Neapolitan Jacobins, was the culmination of their efforts.[10] The evidence in Gutteridge's collection was conclusive, exposing the frauds and malpractice that lay behind so much of the hostile evidence. Taking its cue from Bonaparte and Alexandre Dumas, a version of the Neapolitan past had been created that bore scant relationship with the events of 1799.

By 1900 Laughton had made the Royal Navy historically aware, and taken the past into the core of naval thinking, creating a discipline and a professional body in the process. Yet though the work of Laughton, Mahan and Gutteridge was undoubtedly successful in changing policy, it had less impact on popular opinion about Nelson: they were understandably infuriated by the careless repetition of the old myths in the prestigious *Cambridge Modern History*. Still more debate on Nelson's tactics was prompted by the centenary of Trafalgar. This time Laughton stood aside, passing the task to his friend Julian Corbett, a key member of Admiral Sir John Fisher's unofficial staff, who provided a masterful analysis of the Trafalgar campaign, British naval tactics, and the application of maritime power in national strategy. Corbett's *Campaign of Trafalgar* was a historical monograph that doubled as a modern teaching text, linking the events of 1805 to the needs of officers in 1910: it was the culmination of the work begun in the early 1890s, and gave the Navy a Nelson they could understand.[11]

Just how much Corbett's work was needed became obvious during 1907, when politicians, admirals and generals discussed the threat of invasion. Their historical understanding was so weak that both the army and the navy accepted that Nelson had been 'decoyed' to the West Indies by Villeneuve. Here Bonaparte's lies proved more credible than Nelson's truth.[12] Little wonder the Navy was happy to accept the simplest of pasts, in which Nelson always attacked: this avoided the need to do as he had done, to think, reflect and analyse the demands of war at sea in the broadest context.[13]

The Entente that Britain had signed with France in 1904 settled the squabbles of the preceding thirty years, and allowed the two powers to cooperate in the face of the growing German threat. It had the added effect of muting the celebrations of the centenary of Trafalgar, since the Foreign Office was concerned to avoid upsetting French sensitivities. The Admiralty ordered the fleet not to make any special display;

the Navy Records Society, which had naturally planned to commemorate the event, also took the Admiralty's advice and restricted its activities. Earl Spencer, the Society's President, agreed to a public lecture on some aspect of Nelson's career, but stressed that it was 'important that . . . the address should not include anything which might wound the susceptibilities of France or of any other foreign nation'.[14] Admiral Lord Charles Beresford, then commanding in the Mediterranean, was similarly instructed to avoid triumphalist display, but ignored the order and reviewed three thousand men on the parade square at Malta. The event was handled with becoming dignity, and reflected more on the loss of the hero than the victory.[15] The idea that we should forget our past merely to avoid upsetting the sensitivities of our current friends is absurd, and does not show the country in a particularly favourable light – Trafalgar is a matter of historical fact.

The apologetic tone adopted by the Government left the centenary of Trafalgar to be marked by relatively unimpressive events. There was a Navy League wreath-laying ceremony in Trafalgar Square, and an exhibition of relics at the Royal United Services Institution on Whitehall. New books appeared, although few of any significance. One exception was the tribute of the Polish novelist, Joseph Conrad, who reminded Britons that Nelson was a supremely professional seaman. For Conrad, the attack at Trafalgar was a wonderful example: from his own experience as a seaman, he realised how great were its chances of failure, and how faint the wind on which it relied. In general, however, the nation was still content to attribute Nelson's achievements to 'character' and get by on myths and make-believe. It was his courage and self-sacrifice that the Victorians and Edwardians found so ennobling about Nelson: his devotion to 'duty' chimed in with the service ethic of the age, while his Christian values were modernised to suit current tastes. Nelson was portrayed for the general public in remarkably simplistic terms: the educational efforts of Mahan and Laughton had not reached a popular audience.

Nelson's greatest importance continued to reside in the way in which he influenced those responsible for ensuring the Navy's continued readiness to meet a maritime threat. The two leading figures of the Edwardian Navy, John Fisher and Lord Charles Beresford, were particular devotees of Nelson, in ways that reflected their very different personalities. Both earned their public fame at the bombardment of Alexandria in 1882. Beresford, son of an Irish peer, had every advantage money and social rank could bestow. He was a fine leader and a fair sailor, brave and loyal. He enjoyed politics, and often took an independent line. Not over-blessed with intellect, he made the best of what he had, and while he spoke well, he tended to prolixity. Fisher, five years older, had a head start, and the brains and determination to keep his lead. Son of a failed tea-planter in Ceylon, he entered the Navy with few friends, and made his way almost entirely on merit. A human dynamo of ideas, activity and administration, he mastered the new technologies of electricity, torpedoes and artillery to become the leading voice in debates on new weapons and tactics. Both men favoured reform, but fell out when they reached the highest ranks.

Beresford co-wrote a charming illustrated Nelson book to promote the Navy League.[16] Its aim was to widen access to the story of Nelson, who 'taught the lesson which all our people should take to heart, that while the British Empire maintains its naval strength, the freedom of its people and the security of its borders may be successfully preserved against any hostile combination of military powers.' Rather than investigate Nelson's supposed faults, Beresford asked his audience not to concern themselves with 'that which is small and pitiable, and regrettable'.[17] Fisher also understood the essence of Nelson: he frequently quoted his correspondence and ensured that the Edwardian navy was well aware of the Nelson heritage. He built the fleet that fought the Battle of Jutland, and the battleships that served on that day used, quite deliberately, many of the same names as those at Trafalgar, for he was planning a second Trafalgar. The names associated with Nelson had huge symbolic power for the Navy, but were not always appropriately used, as the chequered history of the name 'HMS *Nelson*' demonstrated.[18] Only Fisher had the confidence to associate himself with Nelson. The first two battleships ordered by his Admiralty Board were the *Lord Nelson* and the *Agamemnon*. He went on to add *Dreadnought*, *Temeraire*, *Neptune*, *Superb*, *Vanguard*, *Bellerophon*, *Colossus*, *Orion*, *Conqueror*, *Thunderer*, *Ajax*, *Collingwood*, *St Vincent* and *Audacious*.

As far back as 1871, Commander Fisher had demonstrated a sound grasp of the Trafalgar memorandum and how it would be applied to steam ships. Fisher knew Mahan's works, chose 21 October 1904 as the ideal day to take up the office of First Sea Lord, and cited Nelson as the example for new measures wherever possible. The fact that his first Commander in Chief had been Sir William Parker also gave him a living link with Nelson.[19] At the heart of Fisher's naval reforms lay the new cadet college at Dartmouth, a striking building replacing the old wooden hulks that had been the entry point for officer cadets for half a century. The college was consciously laid out as a shrine to two gods, Nelson and the King. The opening of Dartmouth prompted a sudden rush to donate suitable Nelsonian artefacts and pictures to the college,[20] reinforcing the buildings' quasi-religious atmosphere.

In one vital respect, however, Fisher completely misunderstood Nelson. Seeking an admiral to emulate the hero in the next war he chose a mild-mannered, self-effacing technocrat: 'Sir John Jellicoe. Phenomenally young and junior. He will be Nelson at Cape St Vincent until he becomes "Boss" at Trafalgar when Armageddon comes along in 1915 or thereabouts – not sooner!'[21] It must surely have been obvious to Fisher that Jellicoe was quite unlike Nelson: he was closer to Lord Howe in his approach to the service, and afflicted by a level of uncertainty, doubt and caution quite alien to his supposed model. Nonetheless, Fisher made the Nelson–Jellicoe connection again in 1911 when reporting to the new First Lord of the Admiralty, Winston Spencer Churchill, and reminded him of the point in July 1914.[22] Only great men like Fisher can make such big mistakes.

On his retirement in 1910, Fisher was created a baron: like Nelson he had risen on his own merit. Despite their differences of character and areas of expertise, Nelson and Fisher were the two admirals of genius to serve the Royal Navy between the eighteenth century and the twentieth. In 1913 Fisher was annoyed to hear that the statue of a general was about to be moved into Trafalgar Square, to make a space for his old friend King Edward VII outside the Athenaeum:

> When Nelson looks round London, he only sees one naval officer, Sir John Franklin, and he died from ice, not war! Where are Hawke of Quiberon, Rodney, Cornwallis, Howe, Benbow, and all of Nelson's Captains? Was this country made by sailors or soldiers? If monuments [are] any guide, then the sea had no victories for us![23]

The nineteenth century had produced no naval heroes worthy of a statue in Trafalgar Square. It remained to be seen whether the twentieth would do so.

In 1914 the Royal Navy went to war with more ships, men and guns than the enemy. Buoyed up by an almost sublime self-confidence the British accepted risks, made mistakes, and in almost all cases escaped punishment. The public expected a second Trafalgar, entirely unaware of the very different situation pertaining in 1914. In Nelson's day the British had to pin the French fleets in harbour, to secure their ocean communications. In 1914 they had only to wait and watch: if the Germans wanted to go anywhere other than the Baltic, they would have to come right past the main British base at Scapa Flow. Britain, as the historians had demonstrated, could cripple Germany by staying at home. Furthermore, Nelson could take risks because he never commanded the main British fleet, but the second or, in 1801, the third fleet: if he lost it would not be fatal. In 1914–18, by contrast, the defeat of the Grand Fleet would have meant the end of the war for Britain, and her allies: Jellicoe, as Churchill pointed out, was the one man who could have lost the war in an afternoon. This was an awesome responsibility to place on any man, let alone a constitutional worrier who was overly concerned by technical flaws. Furthermore, Jellicoe did not have a 'Band of Brothers' to work with: he had a collection of solid fellows who would do as they were told, but who lacked the wit and the confidence to function in the fast-moving and complex situations the war would throw up. Unlike Nelson, these men had grown up in a peacetime navy of neatness, drill and good order. Without experience of war to fall back on, they needed clear instructions, and solid routines.

As a result, the one great naval battle of the war – Jutland, 31 May 1916 – saw Jellicoe hammer the High Seas Fleet. Rather than risk his own fleet late on a gloomy afternoon, however, he was satisfied that he had driven the enemy away from their ports, and planned to complete the task the next morning. This was sound, judicious and avoided unnecessary risk; but it also gave the Germans an opportunity to scuttle home, and the next morning Jellicoe found the enemy had gone. Jellicoe's counterpart, David Beatty, had by contrast been more aggressive in commanding his Battlecruiser fleet, pushing home his attacks, but Beatty lacked the calm professional detachment that Jellicoe used to keep control. He sacrificed advantages in numbers and firepower in a thoughtless quest for action, which cost him two of his ships and the lives of over two thousand sailors. Beatty was striving, misguidedly, to emulate Nelson: his failed attempt reflected a comprehensive misunderstanding. Though Beatty looked the part, and took big decisions with confidence, he lacked the reflective mind and professional dedication that informed Nelson's judgements.

The Great War at sea was won by sound, reliable officers, men who might have found Sir William Cornwallis and Earl St Vincent more suitable models than Nelson. For more than four years they blockaded Germany, and at the end Germany collapsed.

However, the lack of a great sea battle left many dissatisfied with the Navy's performance. There was little sacrifice to set against the massive cost of victory on land. Without a smashing battle victory, a second Trafalgar, the whole myth of Nelson and the Navy seemed to be diminished. Rather than celebrating their victory over everything that the Germans had thrown at them during the war, the Royal Navy's officers fell into a nasty, futile feud over who was responsible for not winning at Jutland. Jellicoe, who made no mistakes and took no risks, was contrasted with Beatty, who had done both. Beatty started the argument, but Jellicoe's quiet dignity and professionalism won more support than Beatty's blatant rewriting of the battle.

Fisher's *Lord Nelson* served throughout the war with her sister, the *Agamemnon*. Both ships took part in the ill-fated Dardanelles offensive, where *Lord Nelson* was slightly damaged. Later Lord Kitchener used her as his headquarters. For much of her career she was a flagship; she finally went for scrap in 1920, long rendered obsolete by the Dreadnoughts. By then the *Victory* was in a parlous condition, her time afloat over. Fortunately the Admiralty was prepared to sacrifice a dry-dock to give her a permanent home. In January 1922 the old ship made her last voyage. An eminent committee of admirals and experts raised money and oversaw the restoration. They wanted to reconstruct the actual ship, and devoted their efforts to tearing away the things that had been inspired by Trafalgar: the stronger bow and stern that would have reduced casualties had she, or her type, ever repeated the bow-on attack. In this way the physical aspect of the story was preserved, to be seen by millions, and would inspire fresh generations to worship at the shrine of the hero. This was an age of literal, accurate reconstructions, putting the pursuit of detail above understanding. The men of 1922 should not be condemned, for without them there would be no ship. But they left it a bare shell: hull, rig, guns and a few trifles to support the plaque on the quarter-deck marking the spot where he fell.

In 1928, the reconstruction complete, she received royal approval from another sailor King, George V. The temple of Nelson worship was now easily accessible to the public, which had not been the case while she lay out in the harbour. Millions could go on board and gain direct access to Nelson's story. Nelson had been reinvigorated as a national, naval deity, but only time would tell if the 'war to end all wars' was the end of strife. If it was then the antiquarian reconstruction of *Victory* would serve as a suitable epitaph for an age; if not, the Navy and the nation would need rather more of Nelson than a memory.

In the same year that the *Victory* began her restoration, the Royal Navy faced up to a very different threat. The cost of the First World War left Britain indebted to the United States, and soon the relationship between the old imperial power and the new naval colossus was deteriorating. For the past two decades Britain's alliance with Imperial Japan had been the basis of her Far Eastern security, and Japan had adopted the Royal Navy as the model for its own fleet. Proving adept pupils, the Japanese annihilated the Russian navy in 1904–5, to considerable American alarm. Tension between the US and Japan was exacerbated by arguments with over China during the First World War, and the result was a naval arms race in the Pacific. Unwilling to be left behind as the size of battleships continued to escalate, Britain prepared to build her own monster ships. The Americans then used their economic power to call an arms-limitation conference at Washington, which ended the Anglo-Japanese alliance, cut the size of all major fleets, limited the number and size of future warships, and called a ten-year holiday in battleship construction. The Americans had got what they wanted.

Naval arms limitation penalised Britain, which depended on the Navy for security, prosperity and communications, to a far greater extent than continental powers like the USA, Germany or France. Even Japan, as an East Asian power, was less affected. As no limitations were placed on armies and air forces, the treaty greatly reduced the relative effectiveness of naval power. The Washington Treaty had been necessary, but it created as many problems as it solved, and left Britain unable to rebuild the Royal Navy to the strength necessary in the 1930s.

The treaty did at least have one positive short-term consequence. The sudden end of battleship construction left the Americans and Japanese with new ships fitted with sixteen-inch guns: Britain, with no new ships nearing completion, secured the right to build two of this type. This was a priceless opportunity to make a statement about Britain, and reassure the Dominions and the Empire that sea communications were still secure. Consequently the lead ship was named HMS *Nelson*, her sister the *Rodney*. When she entered service on Trafalgar Day 1927 she was the most powerful ship afloat. *Nelson* served as the fleet flagship until 1941. It was appropriate that Nelson's name should adorn the mightiest vessel afloat, representing what was still the pre-eminent naval power. *Nelson* was the ultimate expression of Britain's desire for peace, using the power of her name and her artillery to deter aggression. Throughout her peacetime service the ship carried one of the hero's less famous coats, a tangible connection with glory.

A less benign celebration of Nelson occurred at the Royal Naval College at Greenwich in June 1933: a grand pageant staged by its Admiral President, Sir Barry Domvile, a committed fascist, and scripted by the deeply unpleasant historian Arthur Bryant.[24] The attempt to appropriate Nelson as a fascist hero would be amusing if it were not so appalling – fortunately a sense of the ridiculous prevented the British taking such posturing seriously. Domvile, once the navy's most promising young captain, spent the Second World War locked up as a threat to national security; Bryant, who had run with the appeasers and fascist apologists, was more nimble, and took thirty pieces of silver to write Churchillian history.[25]

An altogether less dangerous approach to the cult of the hero was taking shape across the road in the buildings of the old Royal Hospital School. The school was about to move, and the buildings would be transformed into the National Maritime Museum, under the direction of Geoffrey Callender, lately Professor of Naval History at the Royal Naval College, and editor of the critical edition of Southey. The new museum would be based around the Painted Hall collection begun by Edward Hawke Locker, and the Navy's own museum, both of which had been in the Naval College buildings. This gave Callender the lion's share of the great Nelson relics: the coat, swords, the best pictures and numerous other items. With the support of shipping magnate Sir James Caird he was able to extend the collection into new areas, but he never forgot the central place of Nelson to any institution devoted to the history of Britain and the sea. The purchase of important manuscript collections and the creation of a research culture soon made Greenwich the prime destination for Nelson scholars. The restored *Victory*, meanwhile, had its own museum in Portsmouth dockyard, and over time this developed into The Royal Naval Museum, another important collection of Nelson artefacts, archives and ephemera.

*

At the outbreak of the Second World War the Navy found itself once more under the political direction of Winston Churchill. His record of interfering, overruling and making mistakes in 1914–15 must have made the signal 'Winston's Back' seem more warning than encouragement to many senior officers. However, this time his finest qualities would be in evidence. In the darkest period of the war, from the fall of France in May 1940 to the German invasion of the Soviet Union in June 1941, Churchill's belief in ultimate victory, his confidence in the Navy, and his constant references to Nelson imbued his leadership and his speeches with a conviction that no one else in British public life could match. Churchill called Nelson to aid the war effort with far more skill than had been the case a generation earlier. It was perhaps fortunate that his popular book *The History of the English Speaking Peoples* had reached Trafalgar in early September 1939,[26] leaving the subject fresh in his mind. The connection was recalled when he spent a day with the Home Fleet a week later, on board the flagship, HMS *Nelson*; and in February 1940 he observed, 'The warrior heroes of the past may look down, as Nelson's monument looks down upon us now, without any feeling that the island race has lost its daring or that the examples which they set in bygone centuries have faded.'[27] Churchill's admiration of Nelson was evident everywhere, from the bust of the hero that featured in his study at Chartwell to the naming of the Admiralty cat. The feline Nelson, a fine black creature who was often stretched out across Churchill's bed as he dictated and discussed the war, had to be evacuated to Chequers when he became frightened by the anti-aircraft guns.

It was not just Churchill who made better use of Nelson in the Second World War. The over-centralised, stiff tactical instructions the Royal Navy had used during the First World War were neither in the tradition set by Nelson, nor particularly successful. The approach taken during the Second World War was closer to that of Nelson: officers were enjoined to seek close-range engagement, where the outcome would be decisive, at lower fighting ranges than rival fleets. The 1939 Fighting Instructions opened with a truly Nelsonic injunction:

> Captains, whenever they find themselves without specific directions during an action or are faced with unforeseen circumstances which render previous orders inapplicable, must act as their judgement dictates to further their admiral's wishes. Care should be taken when framing instructions that these are not of too rigid a nature.[28]

It was under this system that the navy recovered the initiative, élan and aggression that had made Nelson's fleets so effective.

On taking over as Prime Minister in May 1940, Churchill faced the gravest crisis since 1805: France was about to surrender, Italy had joined the war and Japan was increasingly hostile. Throughout August, as invasion threatened, Nelson's heroic example was never far from Churchill's thoughts. He used Nelson's line about the want of frigates as the basis for his plea to Roosevelt to supply old destroyers, and told the House of Commons that the government was acting on good precepts in attacking enemy invasion harbours. 'As in Nelson's day, the maxim holds, "our First line of Defence is the enemy's ports."' Churchill compared the crisis to 'when Nelson stood between us and Napoleon's Grand Army at Boulogne'.[29] When the crisis passed his dining club bought him one of Nelson's gold snuff boxes, with subscriptions from over sixty people, including Lloyd George, J. M. Keynes, Air Marshal Lord Trenchard, Admiral Lord Chatfield, Edwin Lutyens and H. G. Wells. This distinguished list of donors clearly considered that Churchill had earned the right to be linked with the original owner.[30] Later in the war, of course, Churchill would go further and establish himself as a modern equivalent to Nelson, the subject of an equally powerful legend. Only a man so immersed in the naval and military history of Britain would have found inspiration in the past at such times, and only one who shared Nelson's strong streak of personal vanity would possess the self-belief to stand out against the prevailing gloom.

Churchill's idolisation of Nelson found sustenance in his repeated viewings at Chequers of Alexander Korda's *Lady Hamilton*, produced in 1941. Although Churchill could not resist observing to the director that he had erred in having Big Ben chime fifty years before it was completed, *Lady Hamilton* became his favourite film, and he never tired of hearing Laurence Olivier deliver the portentous line: 'You can't make peace with dictators' – not surprisingly, since he had written it himself! Though Vivien Leigh's Emma was too thin, and Olivier's Nelson had an accent quite unlike his thin nasal Norfolk drawl, this Nelson undoubtedly stood for Britain – the Britain of the Blitz, defying the tyrant. Like the original he had a dry humour, but unlike the hero of 1805 he was fashionably understated and reserved, his upper lip inappropriately stiff.[31] Churchill's staff came to find the film a little wearing, and the senior officers who received Churchill's

Nelsonian missives after he had viewed it cannot have found advice such as 'No Captain can do very wrong . . .' particularly welcome.[32]

The year after Korda's film was released, an edited version of Mahan's *Life* was published by Penguin, pioneers of the cheap paperback. The unnamed editor cut 'a considerable amount of material, dealing with Nelson's early career and domestic life'. In his foreword, A. V. Alexander, First Lord of the Admiralty, stressed that the book would enable thousands 'to learn from Mahan something about the creation by Nelson of the tradition of Britain's mission at sea, which has done so much to make today's victories possible.' Alexander also implied that Mahan's book had been chosen to express the nation's gratitude to the Americans, now that all had combined under 'the flags of freedom'.[33]

The physical locations associated with Nelson, too, played an important role as a focus for national identity throughout the war. Down in Portsmouth, the *Victory* was visited by countless heads of state, military leaders and other worthies, paying tribute to the man who died saving Europe from tyranny. She was hit by German bombs, but fortunately no serious damage was done. Her survival, like that of St Paul's, only increased the talismanic quality of the man. HMS *Nelson*, meanwhile, served throughout the war, being mined twice, and hit by a torpedo. After forming the backbone of the initial British war effort, securing command of the sea and escorting several crucial Malta convoys, she spent the second half of the war supporting a succession of amphibious landings, on Sicily, and Salerno in July to September 1943. The success of these landings led Italy to seek an armistice, the official ceremony taking place on board the *Nelson* in the Grand Harbour at Malta on 29 September 1943. In June 1944 *Nelson* supported the D-Day landings, and completed her service operating on the Malayan coast against the Japanese. At the end of the war, the natural focal point for the VE Day and VJ Day celebrations was Trafalgar Square: civilians mixed freely and jubilantly amid a sea of uniforms from many nations. However, the man the square commemorated passed out of the minds of the nation, as it turned from war to peace, from danger to opportunity. Nelson, like Churchill, was a hero for times of war: now new heroes were needed.

In the aftermath of a second total war, Britain was exhausted and bankrupt – and yet she recovered, as the Beveridge Report and the arrival of the Welfare State gave people a new belief in their leaders and new enthusiasm for the future. Perhaps it was time to shed the old ideas of Britain, and the old heroes who sustained it? The Empire, rigid class barriers, deference and deprivation were consigned to the history books, and with them went much of the justification for Nelson. Having been transformed by the late Victorians into the creator, or saviour of their Empire, he was now guilty by association of all the crimes and misdemeanours that it soon became fashionable to load onto Britain. He was a symbol from the bad old past, and would soon be subverted and mocked. Once again the historical Nelson was irrelevant to this process: it was the Victorian image, not the Georgian hero, who earned the ridicule of the anti-imperialists. Even the strategic pattern suggested the time had come to abandon Nelson: in an age of jet bombers, ballistic missiles and atomic bombs, surely the future lay with air power?

After the war HMS *Nelson* resumed her role as Flagship of the Home Fleet, but only briefly, and after a period in the training squadron she was sold in February 1948, suffering the ultimate indignity of being used to test RAF bombs before being scrapped. She was replaced not by a new aircraft carrier, or a powerful cruiser, but by a concrete accommodation block in Portsmouth – an absurd waste of the most powerful name in naval history. It is inexplicable and shameful that this situation should continue into the twenty-first century: no other navy in the world would waste the names of their greatest naval heroes – Nelson, Collingwood, Drake – on barrack blocks and training establishments. Surely Britain can find a ship to honour the greatest name in naval history?

Nelson's family fared little better after the war than the ship that bore their name. Their pension had expired in 1913, and the family had not prospered: Trafalgar House had to be sold, which allowed several treasures to be acquired for the nation. The spark of genius had touched only Horatio: his brothers had been dull fellows, and the descendants of his sister were no better. Brother William's dynastic hopes had rested on his son, also named Horatio, but he died in 1809, and the title passed to his nephew Tom Bolton, who had changed his name to Nelson. His son, the third Earl, was politically active, if undistinguished. Unfortunately the family had no money beyond the Parliamentary pension and the grant that purchased their estate near Salisbury – without a major injection of funds or another man of genius the Nelsons were doomed to return whence they came. Meanwhile Horatia's family, the Nelson-Wards, were numerous, and her descendants still bear a resemblance to their famous ancestor.

Nelson must have seemed a complete irrelevance in the post-war world, and there was no interest in large scale projects that would revitalise his memory. When the last French seventy-four from Trafalgar, HMS *Implacable*, needed preservation, the Navy was not prepared to help: in 1949 they towed the old warrior out into the Channel, and blew her up. Not a few officers were heard to say that the Navy would be better off with less of Nelson, or none at all – this was not a reflection on the man, of course, but on the simplistic, boring story that had been taught at Dartmouth for decades, using pious texts as dated as the architecture of the building. The heady days of Fisher's Edwardian Admiralty reforms were but a distant memory, and the Navy wanted to be modern.

In 1946 the twentieth century's major Nelson biography appeared, half a decade too late to meet the pressing national need, but welcome nonetheless. Carola Oman's seven-hundred-page masterpiece reflected two significant trends: first, the growing interest in Nelson's private life, which she handled with commendable balance, and second, the steady increase in access to Nelson material. It was a book for a nation at war, about heroes and their proper setting; it has challenged all those who follow to do the job as well for their own day. Among the post-war studies, Tom Pocock's 1987 book is particularly noteworthy, distilling a lifetime of travel, research and reflection and adding many new insights. Yet, for all the Nelson books, there can be no 'definitive' life: Southey used his Nelson to set a standard for popular biography; Mahan, Oman and Pocock offer rich insight based on serious research, personal aptitude and the spirit of their age. Future works – and no doubt the bicentenary of Trafalgar in 2005 will bring several – will reinterpret Nelson and the meaning of his heroism in the light of the preoccupations of their own period.

The events of the post-war years seemed to make Nelson, if anything, still less relevant to contemporary Britain. The Suez crisis of 1956 was interpreted by many historians as the end of the British Empire, and of any independent role for Britain in world affairs; though the Navy did well in its assigned task, the discredited cause did it no favours. This, with the further cuts in naval spending announced in 1957, made Nelson's model of naval dominance seem still more remote. In 1966 the Irish Republican Army decided it was time to end Nelson's occupation of O'Connell Street, blowing the top off the Dublin pillar. The skill they displayed should have warned the Government that they intended to remove the six counties from Great Britain by similar means. Britain's entry into the Common Market in 1973 seemed to settled the issue: Britain was now no more than a middle-ranking European state; Commonwealth trading connections were cut, and the Empire was history. The mood of the time was summed up in the first major text of the modern naval-history revival: Paul Kennedy's *The Rise and Fall of British Naval Mastery* (1976). Kennedy consciously reworked Mahan's 'sea power' approach to argue that Navy and Empire were intimately linked by economic factors, the decline of industry presaging the decline of British power.

Trafalgar Square, meanwhile, became better known as a site for political protest – against Margaret Thatcher's infamous 'poll tax' in 1989, for example – than for its association with imperial greatness, glory and national self-confidence.[34] More recently, it has taken on a third function as the epicentre for national celebrations of sporting triumph. When the teams being celebrated have been English rather than British, as with the rugby World Cup triumph of 2003, the flag waved has been the St George banner so well known to Nelson and the Royal Navy. The first Mayor of London, Ken Livingstone, has transformed the atmosphere of the square by pedestrianising the platform linking it with the National Gallery, and by banning the sale of feed to end the infestation of filthy, disease-ridden pigeons. Fortunately for Nelson his image has been far above the political battles and triumphant partying, and he has been spared such indignities as are now commonly heaped on memorials of the famous dead.

The national role of the Royal Navy was thrust into unexpected prominence in 1982, when Britain went to war on her own account for the first time in a generation. In a last desperate ploy for political popularity, the Argentine military junta had invaded and seized the British South Atlantic dependency of the Falkland Islands, known to the Spanish-speaking world as 'las Malvinas'. Ironically, Prime Minister Thatcher had just signed off the 1981 Defence Review that would have annihilated the Navy's ability to act outside the North Atlantic Treaty area. Fortunately the Argentines did not wait for the cuts to take effect. First Sea Lord Admiral Sir Henry Leach argued that the Navy could and should do the job: what, he asked, was the point of having a navy if it were not used to oppose blatant aggression? If Britain did nothing her word would be ignored, and her international standing severely depreciated.[35] It was the decisive moment in the history of post-war Britain. Were the purveyors of gloom and despair, of decline and fall right? Was Britain fit only to limp along in the wake of other nations?

Leach's resolve paid off. Thatcher's confidence was bolstered by this determined professional man, making his case with not a little of that political courage Nelson had prized so highly.[36] A task force under Admiral 'Sandy' Woodward sailed eight thousand miles from home and took on the entire Argentine air force with twenty-four untried Sea Harriers. The critical moment came when the Argentine Navy threatened to attack the task force: the danger was nipped in the bud by the nuclear powered submarine HMS *Conqueror*, named for the seventy-four that Nelson had been admiring at Trafalgar just before he was hit. She sank the cruiser *General Belgrano* in a textbook attack. Even so, the task force took heavy losses, but the same spirit that had been so evident since Nelson's day ensured the army was put ashore and given unconditional support.

One short war a long way from home reminded the British why they had a Navy, and everyone else that the Royal Navy was still the best, even if it had ceased to be the biggest. Navies are about people, not ships, and the Royal Navy has had the best people since the sixteenth century – as Nelson put it, 'I knew what stuff I had under me.' For Prime Minister Thatcher, whose political fortunes were made by the conflict, the war rekindled the spirit of the past, allowing Britain to find herself once more.[37] The national identity created in Nelson's day had survived the vicissitudes of war and peace, changing social and economic conditions, and the introverted maunderings of declinists.[38] If the expression of those ideas occasionally verged on the disgraceful, notably when the *Sun* printed the headline 'Gotcha!' over a picture of the *General Belgrano* sinking, this should not confuse the point. The British national identity, shaped in war and consciously designed to meet the demands of total conflict, mass social mobilisation and the threat of invasion, had no room for refined attitudes and liberal platitudes. They were a luxury for peacetime.

The 1981 Defence Review disappeared along with its unpopular author, and domestic policy took centre-stage for the next few years as

Thatcher embarked on a radical reconstruction of British economic and social policy whose effects are still felt today. In 1989 the Cold War – for thirty years an excuse not to think about defence policy – ended with striking speed. It found Britain already partly prepared: the Royal Navy had re-established a global role after 1982, and this was merely confirmed by the fall of the Berlin Wall. The British, having defined their cultural identity in war, remain more bellicose than their European neighbours,[39] and Britain is the only western European nation with armed forces capable of acting at short notice at the highest level.

Nelson continued to occupy an important place in popular culture in the post-war years: the trend of concentrating on his private life, already evident by 1918, persisted, with Emma the key element of his story. Terence Rattigan's 1969 play *Bequest to a Nation*, developed from a 1966 television play and filmed in 1973, speculated on the nature of their relationship, focusing on the brief period they spent together at Merton in 1805. By contrast *Lady Hamilton*, a mildly pornographic German film of 1968, treated the subject with less delicacy, and the evidence suggests this might be the right genre. In 1982, with immaculate, if entirely fortuitous timing, a television series entitled *I Remember Nelson: Recollections of a Hero's Life* was broadcast. The final episode was postponed until the Falklands war was over, as the focus on death at Trafalgar was judged incompatible with the maintenance of good morale in the forces. By the late twentieth century, the tendency to idolise the dying hero was seen as suspect: Barry Unsworth's *Losing Nelson* (1999) offered a distinctive, alarming view of obsession, presenting the worship of Nelson as a sociopathic complaint.

Nelson retained his fame among the general public, however, as the BBC's *100 Great Britons* programme of 2002 showed. Nelson was the only warrior voted into the top ten, far outstripping his contemporaries: he could still excite the nation, though doubtless this had as much to do with Emma as Trafalgar.

Among the more interesting manifestations of Nelson worship since his death has been the mythical status often accorded to artefacts from his career. Even in his lifetime, his letters were used as gifts and favours: Lord Hood used those he received as a form of currency.[40] After 1805 they were traded, bought, and hoarded with religious devotion, as were physical remains, from the famous uniform coat to swords, furniture and china. Such artefacts have always attracted high prices, but the £117,000 paid for a single letter in November 2003 (admittedly one with a particularly salacious theme) suggests something more than enduring celebrity. The last remaining source for 'genuine' relic material is the *Victory*, now approaching the end of a massive restoration programme to coincide with the bicentenary. The replacement of decayed oak with teak generated a large pile of timber, with old copper bolts and sheet. These remains have been transformed into something resembling fragments of the True Cross, each with a certificate of authenticity. Moreover, the early years of the twenty-first century have witnessed a remarkable upsurge of interest in Nelson in his native Norfolk: a new museum has been opened in Great Yarmouth, a town he passed through on three occasions, and in October 2003 the Heritage Lottery Fund announced an £850,000 grant to restore Wilkins' Nelson monument.

If continued interest in relics from his lifetime and memorials to his achievement is one aspect of Nelson's legacy, a more important one is found in the activities of the Royal Navy. The brief, salutary Falklands conflict of 1982 and the years that followed demonstrated that the 'declinist' doom and gloom that had dominated post-war analysis of Britain's position in the world was based on erroneous assumptions: contrary to popular belief, the British Empire, that wonderful construct of capital, commerce and trade that Nelson had fought to secure, was alive and well. The flag might have come down across the globe, but the continuing economic power of the informal empire is demonstrated by Britain's position as the world's fourth largest economy, an astonishing fact for so small a country. Britain remains the world's largest maritime trading economy, with a unique range of international interests. This fact is reflected in the sophistication and professionalism, if not the size, of her navy: the heirs of Nelson continue to sail the world's oceans in support of British interests.

Nelson's example, moreover, is still considered relevant by the men and women of today's Navy. In 1996, the official handbook *British Maritime Doctrine* opened with a clearly formulated explanation of how Nelson used doctrine to facilitate the most effective use of forces, citing the Trafalgar memorandum as the obvious example. His concern to enable his officers to use their initiative, while taking care to provide basic guidance in case all else failed, remains an outstanding example.[41] The Royal Navy is perhaps more comfortable with Nelson now than it has ever been: his legacy is now properly studied, rather than simply parroted in hackneyed old phrases.

In 2005 Britain, and the world, will commemorate the two hundredth anniversary of Nelson's death, and of his finest achievement. This time the naval pageant will be adequate: Spain and France will join every other fleet with a soul at Spithead, and HMS *Victory* will emerge from her restoration to serve as the focal point for worship. The museums at Portsmouth and Greenwich will present new and old versions of Nelson, while the bookshelves and souvenir stalls will groan under a weight of memorabilia. And then it will all be over.

Before we return the British national hero to storage for another century, we should take care that we have brought our Nelson into the twenty-first century, and understood how he fits into our national identity. Like Nelson we need to ask questions, make up our own minds. Over the past two centuries we have created many Nelsons, far removed from the man of flesh and blood: there is a Nelson to suit every need. Having been deified, worshipped, damned and occasionally ignored, he remains the national icon of the British state in adversity. His greatness lay in rising to every challenge, in working above and beyond the professional expertise of a naval officer to become a strategist, statesman and diplomat in pursuit of his nation's interests. He had the courage to act when others waited for orders, and the genius to be right on almost all occasions. In a secular age he remains an inspiration, tangible proof that mankind can achieve immortality. Nelson remains the ultimate expression of those qualities that made Britain wealthy, secure and free. If we value such things we must honour his memory: a public holiday on Trafalgar Day should surely be instated.

We may know little more about Nelson than that he lost an eye and an arm, loved Lady Hamilton and stands in majesty in Trafalgar Square, but that should be enough to encourage fresh questions. Who was this man that he should have been rendered in stone, and placed above his countrymen? In the process we might learn more about who we are, and what it takes to create and sustain a modern state. We need to understand Nelson because he, and the culture of his age, still define the way the British see themselves in the world, and the way the world sees them. Any Nelson we create today will be ours, but it must be securely based in the historical events of his life: we must balance our needs with his truth. If we know him well we might agree with Cuthbert Collingwood – the man who understood him better than anyone – that he was 'the glory of England':

> His loss was the greatest grief to me. There is nothing like him left for gallantry and conduct in battle. It was not a foolish passion for fighting for he was the most gentle of all human creatures and often lamented the cruel necessity of it, but it was a principle of duty which all men owed their country in defence of her laws and liberty. He valued life only as it enabled him to do good, and would not preserve it by any act he thought unworthy . . . He is gone, and I shall lament him as long as I remain.[42]

Appendix, Sources, Notes
and Index

Appendix: 'The Black Legend'

Every great man has his critics – the greater his fame, the more serious the criticism. In the process the truth is often ignored.

Nelson's role in the suppression of the Neapolitan republic and the execution of Caracciolo gave rise to a wholly unwarranted attack on his public character and moral integrity. The attack was given credibility by the repetition of highly critical verdicts by his greatest biographer, Robert Southey, back in 1813. Since Southey, the public and private events of Nelson's period in and around the Neapolitan court have customarily been considered as a parade of weakness and error. His private relationship with Lady Hamilton, which eventually became intimate, is enmeshed with his public actions – the immorality of the former is seen to taint the latter. The 'Black Legend' – namely, that Nelson betrayed an armistice freely given by a British officer and a Neapolitan cardinal to the defeated Jacobin rebels in Naples, and caused the judicial murder of the Neapolitan officer Francesco Caracciolo – is still frequently believed, despite the fact that these accusations have been demonstrated to be false in all but one of the major studies of Nelson. The fact that they are still being repeated demonstrates the enduring power of malicious gossip and human credulity, as well as a woeful lack of research.

In point of fact, Nelson had full authority to act in the King's name at Naples; the armistice was unauthorised by the King, as Cardinal Ruffo knew, and Captain Foote was deceived into signing it. The Jacobins, as a group, and Caracciolo as an individual, were victims of their own folly. They had taken the opportunity of a French invasion to repudiate their duty to their sovereign, and used French bayonets to set up a republic over the broken bodies of the common people who had fought to uphold their King and their country against a foreign invader. At a time when the fate of Britain hung in the balance, Nelson acted on his professional and political judgement, backed by his admiral, the King of Naples, and the British Minister. To have connived in the escape of the rebels would, as the Queen stressed, have threatened the very existence of a useful ally, at a time when Britain had very few. The French troops were allowed to surrender and leave, but the rebels were not. Caracciolo was guilty of throwing off his allegiance, and ordering the rebel ships under his command to fire on those of his erstwhile King, killing loyal seamen. He had no cause for complaint about his trial, or the sentence, and it was customary for the sentence to be carried out without delay.

The issue of Naples was brought into the public domain by Charles James Fox, *soi disant* leader of the rump Whig opposition, and no friend of the Bourbons. After a long absence from active politics, Fox rose in the House of Commons on 3 February 1800 to suggest, on the basis of Consul Loeti's self-serving letters, that the 'atrocities' attrib-uted to France were paralleled by those that followed the reconquest of Naples, and that a party of rebels in Castello dell'Uovo had made terms with a British officer for safe passage. The fact that the restored Bourbon regime had taken revenge on a parcel of noble-born traitors was undisputed, but this was not Nelson's responsibility. He had no occasion to intercede between the traitors and their sovereign: lest it be forgotten, the counter-revolutionary excesses were entirely the work of an enraged population, fuelled with religious and political loyalties that Nelson did not share. His detractors forgot that the atrocities in Naples only ended when Nelson placed the Jacobins on the ships in harbour, under his protection and out of reach of the enraged *lazzaroni*. Order on shore was only re-established when naval personnel took control of the key points. Nelson ended the bloody chaos and anarchy that followed Ruffo's occupation, and handed over a tranquil and settled city to the King.

Although it was dismissed by the House of Commons, Fox's public imputation of bad faith stuck, and when Nelson heard about it he was moved to respond immediately. His rebuttal of Fox's attack satisfied the government, but unfortunately the matter did not rest there. In 1801 Helen Maria Williams, a pro-republican authoress and long-time French resident, produced *Sketches of the State of Manners and Opinions in the French Republic*, a dire book that included a highly inaccurate account of the Neapolitan affair. After eulogising the rebels, she accused Nelson of tricking them out of the castles.[1] Nelson read the book, and a copy with his marginalia is among his papers. He dismissed her remarks, noting that Foote's agreement 'was fulfilled most religiously'. Three years later he advised a prospective historian that the Neapolitan sections of her book were 'either destitute of foundation, or falsely represented'.[2]

John Charnock's 1802 biography was distinguished by his access to Locker's collection, and the disclaimer of anything more than a desire to 'correct the defects and mistakes of such miserable sketches as have already appeared'.[3] While the book is not particularly enlightening, his account of the central incident at Naples bears re-reading:

> Cardinal Ruffo had moreover ignominiously signed a disgraceful armistice and convention, not only with the French general, but also with the Neapolitan rebels. The terms of the Treaty, however, which had been agreed to with the Prince Carracioli and others who were the principal leaders of the revolution, Lord Nelson refused to accede to.

These leaders paid for their crimes, 'under a sentence regularly passed on them by the court constituted to take cognisance of their offences'.[4] This was clear enough, although Caracciolo had not signed any documents. Significantly Charnock produced a book entirely free of Emma.

After Nelson's death there was an unseemly rush to print any thing that might pass for a book about him, and many peddled the Fox-Williams line. Even when they managed to take a more correct perspective, they invariably confused the issue.[5] The one early publication to have some claim to authenticity was James Harrison's book. Emma's object, as its editorial director, was to deal with 'the many dishonourable insinuations which have been promulgated by bold speculators on public credulity'.[6] She argued that Nelson lamented Caracciolo's fate, and would have recommended him for clemency 'if it was not so at odds with the temper of the people, and would have operated against the King's interest; without preserving the culprit from the worst effects of their fury.' Yet there is nothing in Nelson's own writings to support this construction: it is more likely to have been Emma's view.[7] However Harrison included one of the many letters in which Nelson called Ruffo's armistice 'infamous',[8] and this proved too much for Captain Foote. Foote was still disturbed by the events of 1799, and appeared to believe that Nelson's letter attached some of the stigma to him. In 1807 he publicly asked Harrison to remove the offending passage, but as his letter stirred up enough interest to warrant a second edition, Harrison did nothing. Confused and angry, Foote published a *Vindication* of his conduct. This unfortunate epistle worked from the assumption that the only way to clear his own name was to blame Nelson. Foote took from Williams' book the explanation that Nelson's conduct could be attributed to the influence of Lady Hamilton, and adopted it in order to avoid attacking the national hero directly – though he argued that 1799 'was the only occasion upon which the character of Admiral Lord Nelson has been found materially defective'. He then proceeded to quote Fox's partisan and feeble speech, despite saying he was not of Fox's party. While observing that it would be best to 'bury the transaction in oblivion', he did exactly the opposite.[9]

Foote's paper war with Harrison attracted the attention of the official biographer, Clarke, who proceeded to enter into an ill-advised and inconclusive dialogue with the disturbed captain.[10] In truth, neither Nelson nor Harrison had meant to insinuate anything about Foote: the 'infamous' armistice was the work of Micheroux and Ruffo, and Foote merely had the misfortune to be misled by two men far less scrupulous than himself. But Foote simply would not accept that Ruffo had tricked him. Clarke was 'laid on his beam ends' by Foote's attitude, and despite all the evidence in his hands that established Nelson's case, he continued to correspond with a man who clearly could not be advised. Somewhat obsequiously, he assured Foote that supporting Nelson's conduct 'surely cannot in any way prove that I wished to attach blame to you'. Foote, by contrast, considered that it was impossible to vindicate both himself and Nelson. He was not appeased by the proof sheets of the relevant chapter, and decided to republish his *Vindication*, with Clarke's correspondence attached. This just added another confused and bitter text to a catalogue of hostile, judgmental, ill-informed or downright dishonest works, from which the 'Black Legend' would be created.

Clarke, meanwhile, was being fed hostile commentary on Emma by the Earl and Fanny. Initially he was disposed simply to follow the Williams line when preparing his authorised 'Life' – then he read the papers and shifted his position much closer to Nelson's.[11] Clarke's purpose was to recover Nelson from his association with Emma, while using her as a convenient excuse for any conduct that appeared questionable. His biography pivots around the events of 1798–9, but the fact that the whole issue is based on a false premise – the same that so troubled the hero of Barry Unsworth's *Losing Nelson* – escaped Clarke. Nelson's faults are attributed to the fact that he 'enjoyed a delightful, but dangerous relaxation in the extraordinary talents and captivating flattery of Emma, Lady Hamilton'. This, with his ill-health, 'led him to indulge a confidence which was fatally adapted to mislead his affectionate disposition, and to warp his judgment'.[12]

Because Clarke lacked the confidence to produce his own account, and did not know how to deal with Foote's pamphlet, he then began quoting large sections of Foote's work almost verbatim, as if he could buy off a deluded monomaniac. He also stated that Emma was present at the trial and execution of Caracciolo and other Jacobins – this is absolutely false, and demonstrates better than anything the origins of his confusion, and the purpose of his judgement. With Earl William controlling access to the papers, he was obliged to tell a particular story. But his weak, inconclusive and shuffling account of what he knew to be the central story of the book was never going to convince anyone that Nelson was innocent of the imputation of dishonourable conduct. It is typical of Clarke's incompetence that he did not see through Foote's very partial recollection of the events: Foote's barge had been prominent among the craft that seized the Jacobin ships on the King's orders, and Ferdinand had rewarded him for his services.[13] And in his anxiety to exculpate Nelson by blaming Emma, Clarke overlooked that fact that although Nelson would fall passionately in love with Emma, he had not done so in July 1799. It would be January 1800 before they accepted the inevitable, and even then Nelson was far too professional to allow his private passions to override his public duty.

Clarke's failure was the more remarkable because it appeared in the official life, a work intended to serve as a timeless lesson to the country, and the basis for the political, clerical and financial claims that the Earl was going to make. Clarke had a duty to demolish the petty, politically motivated and spiteful attacks that had been made on Nelson's conduct in 1799. Rather than trying to see both sides and meet Foote halfway, he should have taken a clear line, following Nelson's own robust and consistent defence. Emma – whatever the faults of Harrison's book, and they are many – produced a far better account of what happened in 1799. By imposing Clarke on the Earl, the Prince of Wales served his supposed friend vey badly, leaving his reputation in tatters and open to ill-intentioned and ignorant attacks.

Clarke's incompetence gave the 'Black Legend' the stamp of official credibility. He and he alone was responsible for elevating it above the petty, partisan sniping of 1800–1. By leaving the final text in such an unsatisfactory fashion, Clarke gave every subsequent writer a licence to take the story further. Robert Southey missed a golden opportunity to deal a mortal blow to his *bête noire*, Clarke, when he compiled his eulogy of Nelson. Instead of following the correspondence which Clarke published, or that provided by Harrison, or consulting his friends Croker and Barrow for better materials, Southey repeated the Williams/Foote version, adding fresh nonsense of his own invention. When he served up this concoction in his elegant prose it became the definitive statement of the 'Black Legend'. The explanation this time lies not in Southey's one-time radical politics – his loyalties were now increasingly Tory – but rather reflected his own personal life. Through his writing, Southey was supporting his sister-in-law and her children, who had been abandoned by his old friend Samuel Taylor Coleridge.[14] It is hardly surprising that under these circumstances Southey chose to make the abandoning of his marriage Nelson's greatest sin – but it is inexcusable that he did so in violation of the evidence, and vilified Emma for faults which he had invented. Clarke had not imputed any improper motive or conduct to the trial of Caracciolo, but such an event – with a hero, a villain, and a Lady Macbeth to push the drama along – appealed hugely to Southey's poetic sensibility. Southey described the public and private events at Naples as, 'a stain upon the memory of Nelson, and the honour of England'.[15] That such unmitigated nonsense should have persisted in the popular consciousness for close on two hundred years is evidence of the influence that can be exerted by great literature, for Southey's accusations of dishonourable public conduct, which have been widely followed ever since, are entirely without foundation.

Croker, to whom the book was dedicated, had a far better appreciation of the subject, and made his views clear in April 1814, when Harrison published the Nelson–Emma correspondence:

> The fame of Lord Nelson is, as his life and services were, public property; and we absolutely deny the right to which any unworthy possessor of a few of his private notes may pretend, to invade (by the publication of what never was intended to pass the eye and ear of the most intimate and confidential friendship) to invade, we say, that public property, and lower the reputation of the hero and his country.[16]

He concluded by wishing the letters were forgeries.[17] In 1817 Harri-son's publisher, Thomas Lovewell, was bankrupted and Nelson's letters to Emma were put up for auction, together with other papers still in his possession. Croker moved quickly to purchase them privately, and kept the fact hidden, seeing no reason to parade Nelson's weakness in public. He was wise to suppress the material on Horatia's parentage.

William James, the pioneer of modern naval history,[18] was out of his depth dealing with complex political issues, and found himself overwhelmed by the mass of evidence. He accepted the 'Black Legend' largely from Foote's version, and cited Clarke, Harrison and Williams. James missed the point that Nelson had royal authority for his actions, and had been specifically directed to that end, while those who had made the agreement he annulled did so without authority.[19] In a book devoted to the quantifiable analysis of naval actions, and which is otherwise bereft of political detail, or the personal lives of officers, the passage makes strange reading.

James was followed by his bitter rival as the naval historian of the Napoleonic Wars, Edward Pelham Brenton. Captain Brenton was a protégé of Earl St Vincent and a Whig partisan. He added a new horror to Southey's criticism of Emma, inventing the idea that she forced Nelson to take her in his barge to view Caracciolo's corpse swinging in the breeze, an event that later gave her nightmares.[20] This was pure fabrication and, like much of his output, biased and unreliable. Admiral Sir Francis Collier, who had been on board the *Foudroyant*, condemned the passage as 'an arrant falsehood'.[21]

Meanwhile, the treatment of this subject in works of a more general nature tended to be brief, impressionistic, and repetitively incorrect. Lord Holland, Fox's nephew and political heir, blamed Emma's 'baneful ascendancy of Nelson's mind' for his 'indefensible conduct' at Naples. Holland's memoirs were edited for publication after his death by his son and wife, and the latter had always hated Emma, who outshone her in society. The damage that such spiteful nonsense could occasion was soon evident. Holland's Whig version was adopted wholesale by the editor of George Rose's papers. The Reverend Leveson Vernon Harcourt combined party ties with family piety in his editorial interjections, which damned Nelson, and added Brenton's attack on Emma and Caracciolo's execution for good measure. The irony was that Rose was a committed Tory, and the papers Harcourt blundered into had been sent to him by Nelson so that he could rebut Fox's attack.[22] What Rose would have made of this travesty of his intentions is not hard to guess. Lord Brougham, another old radical, and blundering Scots Tory historian Archibald Alison invented new horrors to add to those created by earlier critics.[23] Their efforts reflected the enduring power of a lie. By the time Commander Jeaffreson Miles penned his *Vindication* in 1843 the facts of the matter had been quite forgotten. The case had been settled against Nelson, and the only question was how much more artistic colour and moral outrage could be added to the original picture. As Miles saw all too clearly, the fame of the national hero was being traduced by ignorant, petty and stupid men, without a scrap of evidence, or understanding.

The power of the 'Black Legend' was reinforced by disappointed, disgusted Neapolitan exiles. The British, as Ruffo had observed, became unpopular for burning the fleet at the evacuation of Naples, so the returning government sloughed off as much responsibility for unpleasant or unpopular actions onto their saviours as possible. This fitted into a growing nationalist history, which often lionised the rebels for their ideals, while conveniently forgetting that they existed only as the creatures of a French army, and that they were profoundly unpopular with their fellow Neapolitans. At the same time the chief actors in the royalist cause, Ruffo and Micheroux, made sure they told their own versions of events: to exculpate themselves without offending Ferdinand, they shifted the blame onto the British. The feeble and foolish work of Clarke and Southey gave them an ideal opening: if even the 'official' British biographers were unable to reject the 'Black Legend' it must be true.

The subsequent unpopularity of the Neapolitan Bourbon regime led to guilt by association, and when French writers added their efforts to the picture the story became further confused. The first major account from the Neapolitan perspective – that of Colletta in 1838 – was highly critical, as might be expected from a man who had served the Bonapartist French regimes of Joseph and Murat, and been exiled for his part in the rebellion of 1820. His book is 'a prolonged and solemn denunciation of Bourbon rule'. The careful, classical style and calm wording of the text[24] should not disguise the venom, and the context, of the book.

The final stage of a process already long divorced from reality came when it took literary shape. Alexandre Dumas the elder (1802–70), the son of a Revolutionary general who died after a spell in a Neapolitan gaol, and an uncritically romantic Bonaparte worshipper, was among the more significant contributors to the Black Legend. For ever linked with *The Three Musketeers* and *The Count of Monte Cristo*, which made his name and his fortune, Dumas's ability to construct pacy and compelling action narratives, loosely based on historical events, made him the most dangerous of all Nelson's critics. He understood the power of the romantic hero, but his bias and his nationality denied him any appreciation of Nelson. It was as a fundraiser and pamphleteer rather than a historian that Dumas worked for Garibaldi during the overthrow of the Bourbons in Naples. His reward was the unsalaried post of Director of Works, which he held between 1860 and 1864. This gave him access to the state archives, which he plundered for a series of articles that appeared in *L'Independente*, the local newspaper he edited. The articles were collected into the ten-volume polemic, *I Borboni di Napoli*, in which bowdlerised and mangled translations of documents were used to 'prove' the guilt of Nelson.

Imbued with the Jacobin principles of his heroes, and having some experience of overthrowing two Bourbon regimes, Dumas was the hired pen of a new regime seeking to establish legitimacy on the basis of the crimes of their predecessors. His agenda was hardly complex. He had been involved in an anti-Bourbon plot as far back as 1834, and had used the events of 1799 in his novel *Le Corricolo*.[25] Dumas's four-year sojourn in Naples also resulted in a major novel, *La San-Felice*, in which Nelson and Emma featured, although not to their advantage. The book was a great success in France, despite its inordinate length. These texts gave the old romantic Bonapartist the opportunity to exact some posthumous revenge. In the process he muddied the waters, and hampered future scholars, by abstracting much of the evidence he had so obviously abused.[26] Only when these frauds and fabrications had been exposed could the debate move on. The fact that this took another forty years is not untypical of the power of myth over fact in Nelson studies. It is perhaps more surprising that the myths have become part of the Italian national consciousness, and are still retailed on the streets of Naples.

While the downfall of the Bourbon monarchy in 1861 provided an opportunity to open the archives, and vilify the old regime, the Bourbons did not give up without a fight. The deposed King of Naples retreated to Rome, and tried to repeat Ruffo's campaign of 1799, with insurrections funded with royal gold and Papal benedictions. It took the new Kingdom of Italy years to suppress these movements, stretching the fragile political union of north and south to the limits.[27] This was hardly the political environment in which Italians, of any persuasion, would take a detached perspective on the original restoration of the detested Bourbons.

The debate over Naples was reopened in Britain at the end of the nineteenth century by Mahan and Laughton, who wanted to remove the stain from the hero's name. They had adopted Nelson as the central figure in a campaign to educate the nation about the Navy – if his personal feelings had led him to act in an illegal or immoral way towards the Neapolitan rebels, then he could not be employed to serve this agenda. But this new defence provoked another furious outburst of ill-informed nonsense from a member of the Foote clan. The debate was intense, but the vehemence of Nelson's detractors concealed a complex web of misinformation, personal malice, partisan politics and changing agendas. The case for Nelson was set out with ample footnotes in the second, revised edition of Mahan's biography.[28]

The facts of the matter were set out once again in 1903 in a significant new work of scholarship, H. C. Gutteridge's *Nelson and the Neapolitan Jacobins*, which drew on as much evidence as could be uncovered in London, Naples and Rome.[29] Gutteridge discovered that the evidence had been largely distorted, with nothing of consequence to dispute Nelson's account of the events, and he established Nelson's integrity beyond reasonable doubt. But this was not an attractive version for those pursuing a rounded story. Every hero needs his fall, every great man his nemesis. Consequently few Nelson biographers have accepted the evidence assembled by Gutteridge, or the fallibility of the Neapolitan version,[30] and as a result the 'Black Legend' retains much of its power to this day.

The questions raised about Nelson's conduct at Naples go to the heart of the historical process. If serious academic enquiry cannot change the way the past is viewed by academics, let alone by the wider community, we are entitled to ask whether academic history has any purpose. Most biographers have accepted the 'crimes' of 1799, and then sought apologetic and unconvincing explanations. They shift the 'blame' for his actions onto Emma, or Queen Maria Carolina, or suggest that a concussion incurred at the Nile was still warping his judgement a year later. These arguments are quite untenable. Nelson handled the events of that summer with his customary skill. He had full authority to act in the King's name, unlike Ruffo; his firm and decisive intervention prevented further bloodshed, restored order ashore, and preserved the lives of the rebels from the fury of the populace. The traitors he saved had been abandoned by their erstwhile friends, the French, and were being slaughtered by their own countrymen. Nelson and his men stopped these murderous excesses, and handed the rebels over to the lawfully constituted authority. Of those seized by Nelson only 99, a small percentage, suffered the penalty decreed by the law of the land. In Britain such treason was punished far more severely. There is no evidence that Nelson allowed his public duty to be influenced by his private feelings, on this or any other occasion throughout his career, and in any case, he and Emma became lovers only in January 1800.

It should be stressed that the enemy in Naples was doubly threatening. The Parthenopean Republic had followed the French in overthrowing royal authority: this was an ideological war between legitimate royal authority, absolute or constitutional, and republican revolution. Yet from the start a major British political party identified these Neapolitan ideologues with the heroes of the British constitutional revolution of the seventeenth century,[31] the founding fathers of 'The Whig Interpretation of History'.[32] The link with contemporary Foxite Whiggery, and more especially the post-1832 resurgence of liberalism as an export, which took root in Italy after 1860, gave the initial identification a posthumous veracity that was wholly unwarranted.

The 'Black Legend' was created by Whig sympathy for a Neapolitan Republic of which they knew only that it was led by the intelligentsia, and suppressed with the help of the British government. The subsequent horrors of the later Bourbon regime, which stood against the liberal trend of post-1830 Europe, the triumph of the Italian constitutional monarchy and 'British' political values, reinforced a negative image of Nelson. To find the national hero upholding a autocratic, debauched and cruel regime that had been consigned to the dustbin of history could be explained by referring back to Southey. Southey set up the Jacobins as model patriots, their 'revolution' dignified by association.[33] His version made for great literature – but it happened to be untrue. Though this was demonstrated by Gutteridge, and reinforced by Callender, the 'Black Legend' keeps on coming back. Sometimes it seems that the truth is simply not enough.

List of Sources

ARCHIVES

The National Archives (formerly the Public Record Office):
  Admiralty Papers (ADM)
  Foreign Office Papers (FO)
  War Office papers (WO)
  Pitt/Chatham Correspondence PRO/30/8/-
National Maritime Museum, Greenwich:
  Croker, Phillips, Monserrat, Girdlestone, Nelson, Keats, Hood, Yorke
British Library:
  Nelson, Bridport, Liverpool, Davison, Vansittart, Nicolas, Pettigrew,
  Althorp, St Vincent, Lord Aberdeen.
  Additional (Add.) and Egerton (Eg.) manuscripts
Nelson Museum, Monmouth:
  Nelson Papers
Duke University Library, North Carolina:
  Admiral Sir Graham Hamond
  John Wilson Croker
University of Michigan, Ann Arbor:
  John Wilson Croker

PRINTED DOCUMENTARY COLLECTIONS

(Place of publication is London unless otherwise stated.)

Anon. *The Letters of Lord Nelson to Lady Hamilton; with a supplement of
  Interesting letters by Distinguished Characters.* 1814
Aspinall, A. ed. *Later Correspondence of George III.* Cambridge, 1962
– *The Correspondence of George, Prince of Wales.* Cambridge, 1963–71
Baring, Mrs. ed. *The Diary of the Rt. Hon. William Windham MP 1794–1811,*
  1866.
Battaglini, M. & Placanica, A. *Leggi, Atti, Proclami ed altri Documenti Della
  Repubblica Napoletana, 1798–1799.* 4 vols. Naples, 2000–2
Bickley, F. ed. *The Diareis of Sylvester Douglas, Lord Glenbervie.* 1928
Buckingham, Duke of. *Courts and Cabinets of George III.* 2 vols. 1855
Churchill, R. S. ed. *Churchill. Companion Volume II,* Parts II and III. 1965
Corbett, J. S. and Richmond, H. *The Private Papers of George, Second Earl
  Spencer.* 4 vols. Navy Records Society 1913–14, 1923–4
Manuscripts of Cornwallis Wykeham Martin. Historical Manuscripts
  Commission, 1909
Coupland, R. ed. *The War Speeches of William Pitt the Younger.* Oxford, 1915
The Cumloden Papers. nd.

Curry, K. ed. *New Letters of Robert Southey.* 1965

Desbrière, Colonel E. *Projets et tentatives de débarquement aux Iles Britanniques 1792–1805* 5 vols. Paris 1900–2

Duffy, M. ed. *The Naval Miscellany VI.* Navy Records Society, 2003

Fortescue Manuscripts (at Dropmore; Lord Grenville's Correspondence) 10 vols. Historical Manuscripts Commission, 1892–1927

Fox, C. J. *Speeches During the French Revolution.* 1924

Gilbert, M. ed. *The Churchill War Papers I: The Admiralty.* 1993

Granville, Countess. *Lord Granville Leveson Gower, Private Correspondence 1781–1821.* 2 vols. 1916.

Greig, J. ed. *The Farington Diary.* 1922–3

Gutteridge, H. C. *Nelson and the Neapolitan Jacobins: Documents relating to the Suppression of the Jacobin Revolution at Naples, June 1799.* Navy Records Society, 1903

Hamilton, Sir R. V. ed. *Journals and Letters of Sir Thomas Byam Martin. Vol. III* Navy Records Society, 1901

Hannay, D. ed. *Letters Written by Sir Samuel Hood (Viscount Hood) in 1781–2–3.* Navy Records Society, 1895

Harcourt, Rev. L. V. ed. *Diaries and Correspondence of the Rt. Hon. George Rose.* 2 vols. 1860

Hughes, E. ed. *The Private Correspondence of Admiral Lord Collingwood.* Navy Records Society, 1952

Lambert, A. ed. *Letters and Papers of Professor Sir John Knox Laughton: 1830–1915.* Navy Records Society, Aldershot, 2002

Lang, C. Y. and Shannon, E. F. *The Letters of Alfred, Lord Tennyson Volume III.* Oxford, 1990

Laughton, J. K. ed *The Naval Miscellany Vols. I and II.* Navy Records Society, London, 1901

– *Letters of Lord Barham. II–III.* Navy Records Society, 1909–10

Leyland, J. ed. *The Blockade of Brest 1803–1805.* 2 vols. Navy Records Society, 1900 and 1901

Lloyd, C. ed. *The Naval Miscellany Vol. IV.* Navy Records Society, 1952

– *The Keith Papers, selected from the Papers of Admiral Viscount Keith. Vol. II.* Navy Records Society, 1950

Londonderry, Lord. *Correspondence, Dispatches etc, of Lord Castlereagh.* 12 vols. 1851–3

Marder, A. J. ed. *Fear God and Dreadnought: The Correspondence of Admiral of the Fleet Lord Fisher of Kilverstone. Vol. II 1904–1914.* 1956

Morrison, A. ed. *The Hamilton and Nelson Papers.* 2 vols. 1893–4

Morriss, R., ed. *The Channel Fleet and the Blockade of Brest 1793–1801.* Navy Records Society, Aldershot, 2001

Naish, G. P. B. *Nelson's Letters to his Wife and other Documents.* Navy Records Society, 1958

Nicol, J. *The Life and Adventures of John Nicol.* Edinburgh, 1822

Nicolas, Sir H. N. *The Dispatches and Letters of Vice-Admiral Lord Viscount Nelson.* 7 vols. 1844–6

Pool, B. ed. *The Croker Papers.* 1967
Rawson G. ed. *Nelson's Letters from the Leeward Islands.* 1953
Smith, D. B. *Letters of Admiral of the Fleet the Earl St Vincent; 1801–1804.*
  Navy Records Society, 1922 and 1927
Steffan, T. G. and Pratt, W. W. *Byron's Don Juan,* 2 Vols. Austin, Texas, 1957
The Windham Papers. 2 vols. 1913

BOOKS

Acton, H. *The Bourbons of Naples.* 1956
Albion, R. G. *Forests and Seapower: The Timber Problem of the Royal Navy.*
  Cambridge, Mass., 1926
Arthur, C. B. *The Remaking of the English Navy by Admiral St Vincent, Key to
  Victory over Napoleon.* Lanham MD, 1986
Auerbach, J. A. *The Great Exhibition of 1851: A Nation on Display.* Yale, 1999
Barker, J. *Wordsworth: A Life.* 2000
Battesti, M. *La Battaille d'Aboukir: Nelson contrarie la Stratégie de Napoleon.*
  Paris, 1998
Beatty, W. *The Authentic Narrative of the Death of Lord Nelson.* 1807
Behrman, C. F. *Victorian Myths of the Sea.* Athens, Ohio, 1977
Bennett, G. *Nelson the Commander.* 1972
Berckman, E. *Nelson's Dear Lord: A Portrait of St Vincent.* 1962
Beresford, Lord C. and Wilson, H. W. *Nelson and his Times.* 1897
Beresford, Lord C. *Memoirs.* 1916
Berry, Sir E. *An Authentic Narrative, drawn up by an Officer of Rank.* 1798
Billing, V. *The Panorama of the Battle of Trafalgar: Painted by WL Wyllie RA.*
  Portsmouth, 2002
Boase, T. S. R. *English Art, 1800–1870.* Oxford, 1959
Bold, J. *Greenwich Hospital.* Yale, 2000
Bolger, W. and Share, B. *And Nelson on his Pillar, 1808–1966.* Dublin, 1976
Bourchier, Lady. *Memoir of Sir Edward Codrington.* 2 vols. 1873
Brenton, E. P. *The Naval History of Great Britain.* 2 vols. 1837
Brewer, J. *The Sinews of Power: War, Money and the English State 1688–1783.*
  1988
British Maritime Doctrine BR 1806. 1999
Burrows, E. H. *Captain Owen of the African Survey, 1774–1857.* Rotterdam, 1979
Butlin, M. and Joll, E. *The Paintings of J. M. W. Turner.* 2 vols. Yale, 1977
Butterfield, H. *The Whig Interpretation of History.* 1931
Carlyle, T. *Heroes and Hero Worship.* Everyman edition, 1908
– 'Nelson', in *Montaigne and other Essays.* 1898
Cavanagh, T. *Public Sculpture of Liverpool.* Liverpool, 1997
Chancellor, V. E. *History for Their Masters; Opinion in English History
  Textbook, 1800–1914.* Bath, 1970
Chandler, D. *The Campaigns of Napoleon.* 1967
Charnock, J. *Life of Nelson.* 1802
Clarke, J. S. and McArthur, J. *The Life of Admiral Lord Nelson, KB, from His*

Lordship's manuscripts. 1809; 2nd edn, 1840
Clarke, W. K. L. *A History of the SPCK.* 1959
Clausewitz, C. von. *On War,* transl. Paret, P. and Howard, M. Princeton, 1976
Coleridge, S. T. *The Friend I,* ed. Rooke, B. 1969
Colley, L. *Britons: Forging the Nation 1707–1837.* 1992
Conrad, J. *The Mirror of the Sea.* Collected edn, 1923
Cook, R. *The Palace of Westminster.* 1987
Cookson, J. E. *The British Armed Nation, 1793–1815.* Oxford, 1997
Corbett, J. S. *The Campaign of Trafalgar.* 1910
– *Some Principles of Maritime Strategy.* 1911
Cordingly, D. *Nicholas Pocock, 1740–1821.* 1986
Corlett, E. *The Iron Ship.* Bradford-upon-Avon, 1975
Cornwallis-West, G. *The Life and Letters of Admiral Cornwallis.* 1927
Crook, M. *Toulon in War and Revolution.* Manchester, 1991
Crook, J. M. and Port, M. H. *The History of the King's Works VI 1782–1851.*
    1973
Darby, E. and Smith, N. *The Cult of the Prince Consort.* Yale, 1983
Deane, A. *Nelson's Favourite: HMS Agamemnon at War, 1781–1809.* 1996
De la Gravière, Capt. E. Jurien, *Sketches of the Late Naval War.* transl. Capt.
    Plunkett RN. 2 vols. London, 1848
Desbrière, Col. E. *The Campaign of Trafalgar.* transl C. Eastwick. 2 vols.
    Oxford, 1933.
Dupin, C. *Voyages dans la Grand-Bretagne. Vol. IV.* Paris, 1821
Eardley-Wilmot, S. *Life of Vice Admiral Lord Lyons.* 1898
Edgerton, J. *Making and Meaning: Turner, The Fighting Temeraire.* 1995
Ehrman, J. *The Younger Pitt.* 3 vols. 1969, 1983, 1996
Erdman, D. V. *Blake: Prophet Against Empire.* 3rd edn. Princeton, 1977
Eyre-Matcham, M. *The Nelsons of Burnham Thorpe.* 1911
Feldbaek, O. *The Battle of Copenhagen, 1801: Nelson and the Danes.*
    Copenhagen, 1985; English edn transl.Wedgewood, T. 2002
– *Denmark and the Armed Neutrality:1800–1801. Small Power Policy in a
    World War.* Copenhagen, 1990
Fenwick, K. *HMS Victory.* 1959
Foote, E. J. *Vindication of his Conduct when Captain of HMS Seahorse etc.*
    1799. 1807; 2nd edn, 1810
Foreman, A. *Georgiana, Duchess of Devonshire.* 1998
Fortescue, J. W. *A History of the British Army, Vol. IV.* 1906
Fraser, J. L. *John Constable.* 1976
Frost, A. *The Precarious Life of James Mario Matra.* Melbourne, 1995
Fry, M. *The Dundas Despotism.* Edinburgh, 1992
Gardiner, R. ed. *Fleet Battle and Blockade.* 1996
– *Nelson against Napoleon: From the Nile to Copenhagen.* 1997
– *The Campaign of Trafalgar 1803–1805.* 1997
Gash, N. *Lord Liverpool.* 1984
Gatty A. and Gatty, M. *Recollections of the Life of the Rev. A. J. Scott DD.*
    1842, reprinted as *Nelson's Spy?* Bridgenorth, 2003

George, D. *English Political Caricature: 1793–1832*. Oxford, 1959

Geyl, P. *Napoleon: For and Against*. English edn. 1949

Gilbert, M. *Churchill Vol. III*. 1971

Gill, E. *Nelson and the Hamiltons on Tour*. Monmouth, 1987

Girouard, M. *The Return to Camelot: Chivalry and the English Gentleman*. 1981

Gooch, G. P. *History and Historians in the Nineteenth Century*. 1913

Goodwin, P. *Nelson's Ships: A History of the Vessels in Which he Served, 1771–1805*. 2002

Gordon, G. A. H. *The Rules of the Game: Jutland and British Naval Command*. 1996

Gore, J. *Nelson's Hardy and his Wife*. 1935

Guerin, W. *Horatia Nelson*. Oxford, 1981

Harbron, J. *Trafalgar and the Spanish Navy*. 1988

Hardman, W. *A History of Malta during the Period of French and British Occupation, 1798–1815*. 1909

Harrison, J. *The Life of Horatio, Lord Viscount Nelson of the Nile*. 2 vols. 1806

Hemmings, F. J. W. *The King of Romance: A Portrait of Alexandre Dumas*. 1979

Heuser, B. *Reading Clausewitz*. 2002

Hill, D. *Mr Gillray: The Caricaturist*. 1965

Hill, Adm. J. R. *The Prizes of War: The Naval Prize System in the Napoleonic Wars, 1793–1815*. Stroud, 1998

Hobhouse, H. *Prince Albert; His Life and Work*. 1983

Hoffman, F. *A Sailor of King George: Journals of Captain Frederick Hoffman RN 1793–1814*. 1901

Holland, Lord, ed. *Memoirs of the Whig Party*. 2 vols. 1854

Holmes, R. *Coleridge, Darker Visions*. 1998

Hood, D. *The Admirals Hood*. 1940

Hornsby, C. ed. *The Impact of Italy: The Grand Tour and Beyond*. 2000

Howard, M. *The Causes of Wars*. 1983.

Imbruglia, G. ed. *Naples in the Eighteenth Century: The Birth and Death of a Nation State*. Cambridge, 2000

James, W. *The Naval History of Great Britain*. 6 vols. 1836

James, Admiral Sir W. *The Portsmouth Letters*. 1946

– *The Durable Monument: Horatio Nelson*. 1948

– *Old Oak: The Life of John Jervis, Earl St Vincent*. 1950

Jupp, P. *Lord Grenville, 1759–1834*. Oxford, 1985

Kennedy, L. *Nelson's Band of Brothers*. 1951

Kennedy, P. M. *The Rise and Fall of British Naval Mastery*. 1976

Lambert, A. D. *The Crimean War: British Grand Strategy against Russia 1853–1856*. Manchester, 1990

– *The Foundations of Naval History: John Knox Laughton, the Royal Navy and the Historical Profession*. 1998

Laughton, J. K. *Nelson*. 1895

Lavery, B. *Nelson's Navy: The Ships, Men and Organisation, 1793–1815*. 1989

– *Nelson and the Nile: The Naval War against Bonaparte, 1798*. 1998.

Le Donne, J. *The Russian Empire and the World 1700–1917: The Geopolitics of Expansion and Containment.* Oxford, 1997

LeFevre, P. and Harding R. eds. *Precursors of Nelson: British Admirals in the Eighteenth Century.* 2000

LeFevre, P. and Harding, R. eds. *Contemporaries of Nelson.* 2004

Levy, J. *The Royal Navy's Home Fleet in World War II.* 2003

Littlewood, K. and Butler, B. *Of Ships and Stars: Maritime Heritage and the Founding of the National Maritime Museum, Greenwich.* 1998

Lucas, J. ed. *William Blake.* 1998

Lukacs, J. *The Hitler of History: Hitler's Biographers on Trial.* London, 1997

MacCarthy, F. *Byron: Life and Legend.* 2002

Mace, R. *Trafalgar Square: Emblem of Empire.* 1976

Mackay, R. *Fisher of Kilverstone.* Oxford, 1973

Mackenzie, J. M. *Propaganda and Empire: The Manipulation of British Public Opinion, 1880–1960.* Manchester, 1986

Mackesy, P. *The War in the Mediterranean, 1803–1810.* 1957

– *Statesmen at War: The Strategy of Overthrow.* 1974

– *War without Victory: The Downfall of Pitt, 1799–1802.* Oxford, 1984

McNairn, A. *Behold the Hero: General Wolfe and the Arts in the Eighteenth Century.* Liverpool, 1997

Mahan, A. T. *The Life of Nelson: The Embodiment of the Sea Power of Great Britain.* 1st edn, 1897; 2nd edn, 1899; reduced edn, 1942

Marder, A. J. *The Anatomy of British Sea Power: Naval Policy 1880–1905.* 1940

– *From the Dreadnought to Scapa Flow. Vol. I 1904–1914.* Oxford, 1961

Martin, T. *Life of the Prince Consort.* 5 vols. 1875–80

Miles, J. *Vindication of Admiral Lord Nelson's Proceedings in the Bay of Naples.* 1843

Minto, Countess of. *Life and Letters of Sir Gilbert Elliot, First Earl of Minto from 1751–1806.* 3 vols. 1874

Mitchell, L. G. *Charles James Fox.* Oxford, 1992

Morgan, K. O. *Callaghan, A Life.* Oxford, 1997

Morriss, R. *Cockburn and the British Navy in Transition: Sir George Cockburn 1772–1853.* Exeter, 1997

Newsome, D. *The Victorian World Picture.* 1997

The Norfolk Pillar. Norwich, 1977

Oman, C. *Nelson.* 1947

Pakenham, T. *The Year of Liberty.* 1969

Paret, P. and Moran, D. eds. *Carl von Clausewitz: Historical and Political Writings.* Princeton, 1992

Parissien, S. *George IV: The Grand Entertainment.* 2001

Parker, H. *Herman Melville: A Biography Volume One 1819–1851.* Baltimore, 1996

Pettigrew, T. J. *Memoirs of the Life of Vice Admiral Lord Viscount Nelson.* 2 vols. 1849

Phillimore, A. *Life of Sir William Parker, Vol. I.* 1876

Pitt, V. *Tennyson Laureate.* 1962

Pocock, T. *Remember Nelson: The Life of Captain Sir William Hoste.* 1977
– *Young Nelson in the Americas.* 1980
– *Horatio Nelson.* 1987
Prentice, R. *A Celebration of the Sea.* 1994
Pugh, P. D. *Nelson and his Surgeons.* 1968
Raine, K. *Blake and Tradition.* 2 vols. Princeton, 1968
Ralfe, J. *Naval Biography.* London, 1828
Ramage, N. H. and Ramage, A. *Roman Art: Romulus to Constantine.* 2nd edn.
   Cornell, 1995
Ramsden, J. *Man of the Century: Winston Churchill and his Legend since 1945.*
   2002
Richards, J. *Films and British Identity: From Dickens to Dad's Army.*
   Manchester, 1997
Ritcheson, C. R. *Aftermath of Revolution: British Policy Towards the United
   States, 1783–1795.* Dallas, Texas, 1969
Robbins-Landon, H. C. *Haydn: The Years of 'The Creation', 1796–1800.* 1977
Roberts, A. *Eminent Churchillians.* 1994
Rodger, A. B. *The War of the Second Coalition, 1798–1801: A Strategic
   Commentary.* Oxford, 1964
Rodger, N. A. M. *The Wooden World: An Anatomy of the Georgian Navy.* 1986
– *The Insatiable Earl: A life of John Montagu, 4th Earl of Sandwich.* 1993
Rose, J. H. ed. *Pitt and Napoleon: Essays and Letters.* 1912
– *Lord Hood and the Defence of Toulon.* Cambridge, 1922
Rosenberg, J. D. *Carlyle and the Burden of History.* Harvard, 1985
Ruskin. J. *The Harbours of England.* 1895
– *Nelson and the Hamiltons.* 1969
Russett, A. *George Chambers, 1803–1840.* 2000
Sacchinelli, P. *Memoire storiche sulla vita del Cardinale F. Ruffio.* Naples, 1836
Schama, S. *Landscape and Memory.* 1995
Schroeder, P. W. *The Transformation of European Politics, 1763–1848.* Oxford,
   1994
Schurman, D. *Julian S. Corbett 1854–1922.* 1981
Sermonetta, Duchess. *The Locks of Norbury.* 1940
Shannon. R. *Gladstone; Vol. I, 1809–1865.* 1982
Sherwig, J. M. *Guineas and Gunpowder: British Foreign Aid in the Wars with
   France, 1793–1815.* Harvard, 1929
Shine, H. and Shine, H. C. *The Quarterly Review under Gifford.* Chapel Hill,
   NC, 1949
Smith, E. A. *Lord Grey, 1764–1845.* Oxford, 1990
Southam, B. *Jane Austen and the Navy.* 2000
Southey, R. *Life of Nelson.* Callender edn, 1922
Sparrow E. *Secret Service: British Agents in France 1793–1815.* Woodbridge, 1999
*The Spectacular Career of Clarkson Stanfield 1793–1867: Seaman, Scene Painter,
   Royal Academician.* Newcastle, 1979
Stanhope, Lord. *Life of Pitt.* 4 vols. 1867
Stanley, A. P. *Life of Thomas Arnold.* 1844

Storey, M. *Robert Southey: A Life*. Oxford, 1997

Syrett, D. and DiNardo, R. eds. *The Commissioned Sea Officers of the Royal Navy: 1660–1815*. Navy Records Society, 1994

Sumida, J. T. *Inventing Grand Strategy and Teaching Command: the Classic Works of Alfred Thayer Mahan Reconsidered*. Washington, 1997

Taine, H. *Notes on England*. 1995

Talbott, J. E. *Pen and Ink Sailor: Charles Middleton and the King's Navy 1778–1813*. 1998

Taylor, G. *The Sea Chaplains. A History of the Chaplains of the Royal Navy*. Oxford, 1978

Testa, C. *The French in Malta 1798–1800*. Valletta, 1997

Thatcher, M. *The Downing Street Years*. 1993

Thomas, W. *The Quarrel of Macaulay and Croker; Politics and History in the Age of Reform*. Oxford, 2000

Thorne, R. G. *History of Parliament 1790–1820. Members G–P*. 1986

Tracy, N. ed. *The Naval Chronicle: The Contemporary Record of the Royal Navy at War*. Consolidated edn. 5 vols. 1999

Report of a Committee appointed by the Admiralty to consider the tactics employed at Trafalgar. 1913

Tucker, J. S. *Memoirs of Earl St Vincent*. 2 vols. 1844

Unsworth, B. *Losing Nelson*. 1999

Vincent, E. *Nelson, Love and Fame*. Yale, 2003

Walker, R. *The Nelson Portraits*. Portsmouth, 1998

Ware, C. *The Bomb Vessel: Shore Bombardment in the Age of Sail*. 1994

Wareham, T. *The Star Captains: Frigate Command in the Napoleonic Wars*, 2001

Warner, O. *A Portrait of Lord Nelson*. 1958

Waters, D. W. *The Art of Navigation in England in Elizabethan and Early Stuart Times*. 1958

Weston, N. *Daniel Maclise: Irish Artist in Victorian London*. Dublin, 2001

White, A. J. *The Political Life of Cavour 1848–1861*. Oxford, 1930

White, C. ed. *The Nelson Companion*. Gloucester, 1995

– *1797: Nelson's Year of Destiny*. Gloucester, 1998

White, J. *Professional Life of Lord Nelson*. 1806

Williams, H. M. *Sketches of the State of Manners and Opinions in the French Republic*. 2 vols. 1801

Wilson. G. *The Old Telegraphs*. 1976

Wilton, A. *Painting and Poetry: Turner's Verse Book and his work of 1804–1812*. 1990

Wolffe, J. *Great Deaths: Grieving, Religion, and Nationhood in Victorian and Edwardian Britain*. Oxford, 2000

Woolgar, C. ed. *Wellington Studies III*. Southampton, 1999

Yarrington, A. *The Commemoration of the Hero: 1800–1864. Monuments to the British victors of the Napoleonic Wars*. New York, 1988

Ziegler, P. *Addington*. 1965

– *King William IV*. 1971

ARTICLES

Baker, M. 'Lord Nelson and John Bowsher', *Mariner's Mirror* 86 (2000), pp. 310–12

Breihan, J. R. 'The Addington Party and Navy in British Politics, 1801– 1806', in Symonds, C. L. ed. *New Aspects of Naval History*. Annapolis, 1981; pp. 163–89

Cannadine, D. 'The Context, Performance and Meaning of Ritual: the British Monarchy and the "Invention of Tradition" *c.*1820–1977', in Hobsbawm, E. and Ranger, T. eds. *The Invention of Tradition*. 1982

Colomb, P. 'Nelson', in Laughton J. K. ed. *From Howard to Nelson*. 1899

Crimmin, P. K. 'Letters and Documents relating to the Service of Lord Nelson's Ships, 1780–1805: a Critical Report', *Historical Research* 70/171 (1997), pp. 52–69

Croker, J. W. 'Nelson's letters to Lady Hamilton', *Quarterly Review* (1814)

Czisnik, M. 'Nelson and the Nile: The Creation of Admiral Nelson's Public Image', *Mariner's Mirror* 88 (2002), pp. 41–60

Davis, J. A. 'The Neapolitan Revolution: 1799–1999: Between History and Myth', *Journal of Modern Italian Studies* (1999), pp. 350–8

Eastwood, D. 'Patriotism Personified: Robert Southey's *Life of Nelson* Reconsidered', *Mariner's Mirror* 77 (1991), pp. 143–9

Fulford, T. 'Romanticising the Empire: The Naval Heroes of Southey, Coleridge, Austen and Marryat', *Modern Language Quarterly* (1999), pp. 161–96

Gooch, J. 'The Politics of Strategy', *War in History* 4 (2003), pp. 424–47

Jordan, G. and Rogers, N. 'Admirals as Heroes: Patriotism and Liberty in Hanoverian England', *Journal of British Studies* 28 (1989), pp. 201–24

Kenney, J. J. 'Lord Whitworth and the Conspiracy against Tsar Paul', *Slavic Review* 36/2 (1977), pp. 216–19

Lambert, A. 'Maintaining the Image', in Gardiner, R. ed. *Warship 1991*. 1991
– 'Sir William Cornwallis', in LeFevre, P. and Harding, R. eds. *Precursors of Nelson: British Admirals of the Eighteenth Century*. London, 2000, pp. 353–75
– 'HMS *Foudroyant* and *Trincomalee*', *Maritime Life and Traditions* 17 (2002), pp. 46–59

Monaque, R. 'Latouche Tréville: the Admiral who defied Nelson', *Mariner's Mirror* 86 (2000), pp. 272–84

Noszlopy, G. T. 'A Note on West's 'Apotheosis of Nelson', *Burlington Magazine* 112 (1970), pp. 813–17

Pratt, L. 'The Naval Thanksgiving of 1797', *Journal of Maritime Research* (2000)

Roberston, J. 'Enlightenment and Revolution: Naples 1799', *Transactions of the Royal Historical Society* VIth Series, 10 (2000)

Rodger, N. A. M. 'Image and Reality in Eighteenth Century Naval Tactics', *Mariner's Mirror* 83 (2003), pp. 280–96

Salmon, F. 'The Impact of the Archaeology of Rome on British Architects and their Work 1750-1840" in Hornsby, C. ed. *The Impact of Italy: The Grand*

Tour and Beyond. 2000, pp. 219–44
Southey, R. 'Lives of Nelson', *Quarterly Review* (1810), pp. 218–62
Tomlinson, B. 'The Battle Sanctified', in Duffy, M. and Morriss, R. *The Glorious First of June*. Exeter, 2001
White, C. 'Nelson's 1805 Battle Plan', *Journal of Maritime Research* (2002)
– 'The Wife's Tale: Frances, Lady Nelson and the Break-up of her Marriage', *Journal of Maritime Research* (2003)
– ed. 'The Public Order Book of Vice Admiral Lord Nelson July–October 1801' in Duffy, M. ed. *Naval Miscellany VI* pp. 221_55

Exhibition: *Mad, Bad and Dangerous: The Cult of Lord Byron*. Exhibition at the National Portrait Gallery, Jan–Feb 2003
Unpublished Ph.D. thesis: Colville, Q. 'An analysis of the significance of material culture in constructing notions of class among male Royal Naval personnel, 1930–1960.' University of London, 2004

Notes

INTRODUCTION

1 The Articles of War, 1749, second article
2 Lukacs, *The Hitler of History: Hitler's Biographers on Trial*, p. 73. Genius is, of course, a value-free concept. Hitler was undoubtedly one, as was Napoleon.
3 Howard, M., *The Causes of Wars*, 1983, p. 215–16.
4 Clausewitz, C. von, *On War*, ed. P. Paret and M. Howard, Princeton, 1976, p. 87.
5 Cookson, *The British Armed Nation, 1793–1815*, pp. 38–95
6 de la Gravière, J, *Sketches of the Late Naval War*, 2 vols., trans. Captain Plunkett, 1848, provides a clear-eyed assessment of the issues.
7 Rodger, 'Image and Reality in Eighteenth Century Naval Tactics'
8 This system opened a Pandora's box of problems for admirals who wanted to micromanage their fleets. See Gordon, *The Rules of the Game: Jutland and British Naval Command* for a powerful study of the problems this would cause between Trafalgar and Jutland in 1916.
9 Collingwood to Alexander Carlyle 24.8.1801; Hughes, ed. *The Private Correspondence of Admiral Lord Collingwood*, p. 130
10 Collingwood to Admiral Pasley 16.12.1805; Nicolas VII p. 241
11 Heuser, *Reading Clausewitz*, pp. 72–3

CHAPTER I

1 For details of this, and every other ship on which Nelson served, with a wealth of period detail and operational history, see Goodwin, *Nelson's Ships: A History of the Vessels in which he Served, 1771–1805*
2 Goodwin, p. 35
3 Nelson to Cornwallis 1790; *Manuscripts of Cornwallis Wykeham Martin*, pp. 341–2
4 Clarke and McArthur (1840) [hereafter C&M] I p. 24
5 C&M I p. 14.
6 Nicolas I pp. 21–2
7 Vincent, *Nelson, Love and Fame*, p. 33
8 McNairn, A., *Behold the Hero: General Wolfe and the Arts in the 18th Century*. Liverpool, 1997
9 Pocock, *Young Nelson in the Americas*, offers a comprehensive and rewarding study of this episode.
10 Lambert, 'Sir William Cornwallis', in LeFevre and Harding, *Precursors of Nelson*
11 Mahan p. 27, Oman, p. 40 and Warner p. 38, attribute it to his merit. Southey, Laughton and Vincent pp. 42–3 simply accept the appointment.

12 Nelson to Suckling 14.1.1784; Nicolas II p. 479
13 Jenkinson to Sandwich 12.2.1781; Add. MS 38,308 f. 81
14 Rodger, *The Insatiable Earl: A life of John Montagu, 4th Earl of Sandwich*, pp. 176–9. See also Sandwich to Jenkinson 19.1.1781; BL Add. MS 38,217 f. 253
15 Nelson to William Nelson 7.5.1781; Nicolas I pp. 42–3
16 Jenkinson to Sandwich 10.4.1781; Add. MS 38,308 f. 113
17 Walker, *The Nelson Portraits*, pp. 13–18
18 Hood to Pigot 22.11.1782; Hannay ed. *Letters of Lord Hood; 1781–83*, p. 15
19 C&M 1. p. 52. The anecdote was supplied by the Duke after 1805 and is therefore suspect.
19 Nelson to Locker 25.2.1782; Nicolas I p. 723

CHAPTER II

1 Goodwin, pp. 106–13
2 Goodwin, pp. 113–17 lists the offences, and the number of lashes awarded.
3 According to his first lieutenant James Wallis, who retailed the story to C&M [1840] p. 143. There is a complete transcript of this memo taken from Add. 34,990 in Rawson ed. *Nelson's Letters from the Leeward Islands*, pp. 47–54. Pocock, *Young Nelson*, p. 194
4 Ritcheson, *Aftermath of Revolution: British Policy Towards the United States, 1783–1795*, pp. 3–17, 218–21
5 His letters to William frequently refer to this fraud. See 29.12.1786; Nicolas I p. 204
6 Nelson to William Nelson 29.3. and 2.4.1784: Nicolas I p. 101–2
7 Brewer, *The Sinews of Power: War, Money and the English State 1688–1783*, pp. 101–5
8 Ehrman, *The Younger Pitt: The Years of Acclaim*. Nelson to Suckling 14.1.1784: Nicolas II, pp. 479–80
9 Nelson to Hughes January 1785, and copied to the Secretary to the Admiralty 18.1.1785: Nicolas I pp. 114–18
10 Rawson ed. *Nelson's Letters from the Leeward Islands*, pp. 23–40
11 Nelson to Suckling 25.9. and 14.11.1785; Nicolas I pp. 140–6
12 Nelson to Locker 5.3.1786; Nicolas I pp. 156–60
13 Nelson to Moutray 6.2.1785 and Nelson to Admiralty 17.2.1785; Nicolas I pp. 118–19, 121–3
14 Fanny's letters to him were burnt on the eve of the attack on Tenerife.
15 Nelson to Fanny 4.5.1786; Nicolas I p. 167. Vincent notes at p. 71 that this was still being used as a homily for young naval officers in 1954.
16 Nelson to Fanny 6.3.1787; Naish ed. *Nelson's Letters to His Wife and Other Documents, 1785–1831*, p. 50
17 William to Hood 9.2.1787: Ranft, ed. 'Prince William and Lieutenant Schomberg', in Lloyd, ed. *The Naval Miscellany: Vol. IV*. London, 1952 pp. 270–2

18 William to Nelson 3.12.1787 and William to Hood 26.12.1787 and
   5.1.1788; Ranft pp. 286–95
19 Howe to Hood 2.7.1787; Ranft p. 287
20 Rose recalled this meeting in conversation with Clarke or McArthur. See
   C&M (1840) I p. 150
21 Nelson to Clarence 10.12.1792; Nicolas I pp. 294–7
22 Ziegler, *King William IV*, pp. 37–95, for Prince William's relationship with
   Nelson and the Navy.
23 Clarence to Nelson 3.10.1796; Add. 34,904 f. 400
24 Nelson to William 2.6.1788; Nicolas I pp. 275–6
25 Nicolas I p. 288

CHAPTER III

1 Goodwin, pp. 118–31; Deane, *Nelson's Favourite: HMS Agamemnon at War.
   1781–1809*, pp. 75–130
2 Sherwig, *Guineas and Gunpowder*, p. 11
3 Sherwig, p. 25. Ehrman II p. 278
4 Ehrman II pp. 278–80
5 Nelson to Wife 15.3.1793; Naish pp. 74–5
6 Nelson to William Nelson 18.4.1793; Nicolas I p. 304.
7 Letters of 18, 20 and 25 May 1793; Nicolas I pp. 306–7. Naish pp. 80–1.
8 The Sea Journal, reproduced in Naish pp. 128–150, can be compared with the
   contemporary letters.
9 Nelson to Clarence 14.7.1793; Nicolas I pp. 311–15. Nelson still believed
   Clarence would be employed.
10 Nelson to Wife 15.7.1793; Naish pp. 84–5
11 Nelson to Wife 4.8.1793; Naish pp. 87–8
12 Nelson to Father 20.8.1793; Nicolas I pp. 319–20
13 Ehrman II p. 303
14 Nelson to Wife 7–10.9.1793, 14.10.1793 and Nelson to Suckling 14.9.1793;
   Naish pp. 92–4, Nicolas I p. 327
15 Nelson to Suckling 11.10.1793: Nicolas I pp. 331–2
16 Nelson to Wife 12.10.1793; Naish pp. 93–4
17 Sea Journal 22.10.1793; Naish pp. 138–9
18 Sea Journal 6 and 10.11.1793; Naish pp. 139–40
19 Elliot to Wife 16 and 17.12.1793 Minto, Countess ed. *The Life and Letters
   of Sir Gilbert Elliot, First Earl of Minto, 1751–1806*, II p. 199

CHAPTER IV

1 Rose, J. H. 'British Rule in Corsica' in Rose ed. *Pitt and Napoleon: Essays
   and Letters*. London, 1912. pp. 60–2.
2 Hood to Nelson 15 and 28.12.1793; Godfrey, J. H, ed. 'Corsica 1794' in
   Lloyd, C. ed. *The Naval Miscellany Volume IV*. Navy Records Society (henceforth NRS) London. 1952, pp. 364–5.

3 Nelson to Wife 16.1.1794; Naish pp. 99–100
4 Nelson to Locker 17.1.1794; Nicolas pp. 347–8. It is significant that letters to naval correspondents are altogether more analytical, reflecting the cerebral aspect of his work, while those to his family are narratives interspersed with reflections on thwarted ambition.
5 Nelson to Wife 30.1.1794; Naish pp. 101–2
6 Journal 6.2.1794; Naish pp. 144–5
7 Fortescue, J.W. *A History of the British Army*. Vol. IV, 1906 pp. 182–5. A severe critic of Hood, Fortescue provides a useful counter to the naval accounts. However, his bias is excessive, and largely self-defeating. His other target, Henry Dundas, is also now seen in a more favourable light.
8 Nelson to Wife 13.2. 1794; Naish pp. 102–3
9 Nelson to Wife 28.2.1794; Naish pp. 103–4
10 Hood, Nelson, Dundas and Elliot correspondence of 8–9.3.1794; see NRS, 371–3, Minto and Nicolas.
11 Minto II p. 247
12 D'Aubant to Henry Dundas 2.4.1794; NRS pp. 382–3
13 Moore Diary 21.3.1794. NRS; pp. 378–9. Nelson to Wife 22.3.1794; Naish pp. 106–7
14 Nelson to Hamilton 27.3.1794; Nicolas pp. 377–9
15 Hood to Nelson 20 and 21.4.1794; NRS pp. 387–8
16 Hood to Nelson 24–31.4.1794; NRS pp. 389–91
17 Nelson to Wife 1–4.5.1794; Naish pp. 109–111
18 Moore Diary 3.5.1794; NRS pp. 392–3
19 Hood to Nelson 5, 8,9, 11, 13 and 15.5.1794; NRS pp. 393–7
20 Moore Diary 15.5.1794; NRS pp. 397–8
21 Hood to Nelson 22.5.1794; NRS p. 399
22 Nelson to Locker, William Nelson and Wife 30.5.1794; Naish, pp. 112–13, Nicolas pp. 402–4
23 Nelson to Hood 23.6.1794; Nicolas I p. 413
24 Hood to Elliot 15.7.1794; Naish p. 172
25 Hood to Elliot 3.7.1794; Moore Diary 19.6.1794; NRS pp. 403–4
26 Nelson to Hood 3, 4, 6 and 7.7.1794; Nicolas pp. 417–24 Stuart to Nelson 4.7.1794; NRS p. 405
27 Nelson to Pollard 14.7.1794; Nicolas p. 436
28 Moore Diary 13.7.1794; NRS pp. 405–6
29 Nelson to Hood and Hood to Nelson 12.7.1794; Nicolas pp. 432–3
30 The precise nature of the injury was never determined. Pugh, *Nelson and his Surgeons*, p. 8
31 Stuart to H. Dundas 13.7.1794; NRS p. 406
32 Nelson to Hood 18 and 19.7.1794; NRS pp. 407–9. Fortescue p. 193
33 Hood to Nelson 19.7.1794; NRS p. 408. Nelson to Hood 20.7.1794; NRS p. 409
34 Hood to Nelson 20, 21 and 22.7.1794; NRS pp. 410–12
35 Elliot to Duke of Portland (Secretary of State for Home Affairs, now responsible for the island). 28.8.1794; NRS pp. 417–18

36 Nelson to Wife. 25.8.1794. Naish p. 121.
37 Nelson to Elliot 4.8.1794. Nelson to Hood 5, 8, 9 and 10.8.1794. Nelson to Agent of Transports at San Fiorenzo 6.8.1794; Nicolas I pp. 464–73
38 Nelson to Clarence 6–10.8.1794; Nicolas I pp. 474–6
39 Nelson to Wife 18 and 25.8.1794; Naish pp. 119–21
40 Rose, pp. 73–4

CHAPTER V

1 Nelson to Wife 1.9.1794; Naish pp. 121–2
2 Nelson to Wife 12.9.1794; Naish pp. 122–3
3 Nelson to Suckling 20.9.1794; Nicolas I p. 485
4 Nelson to Hood 23.9.1794; Nicolas I p. 486. Nelson to Wife 27.9.1794; Naish pp. 124–5. See Nelson to Suckling 20.9.1794; Nicolas I p. 486 for a more favourable view. A week was all it took to disabuse him of his optimism.
5 Nelson to Hood 2.10.1794 and Hood to Nelson 1.12.1794; Nicolas I pp. 487–8
6 Lambert, A. D. 'Admiral Lord Hotham, Command and Reputation in the Age of Nelson', in Lefevre, P. and Harding, R. eds. *Contemporaries of Nelson.* 2004
7 Nelson to Wife 10.10.1794 and continuation on 12.10; Naish pp. 125–6
8 Nelson to Wife 24.10.1794; Naish pp. 185–6
9 Nelson to Locker 10.10.1794; Nicolas I p. 490.
10 Nelson to Elliot 10.11.1794 and encl.; Nicolas I pp. 497–8
11 Nelson to Clarence 19.1.1795; Nicolas II pp. 1–2
12 Nelson to Clarence 11.1794; Nelson to Suckling 28.11.1794; Nicolas pp. 501–3
13 Nelson to Wife 12 and 28.11.1794; Naish pp. 187–9
14 Nelson to Wife 12.11.1794; Naish p. 187
15 Nelson to Wife 23.1.1795; Naish p. 193
16 Nelson to Wife 31.1.1795; Naish pp. 194–5. Pocock, T. *Horatio Nelson*, pp. 124–5. Vincent pp. 139–41.
17 Nelson to Wife 17.1.1795; Naish p. 192
18 Nelson to Wife 23.1.1795; Naish p. 193
19 Nelson to Wife 23–24.1.795; Naish p. 193
20 Nelson to Wife 31.1.1795; Naish pp. 194–5
21 Nelson to Wife 7.6.1795; Naish pp. 210–1
22 Nelson to Wife 25.2.1795; Naish p. 197
23 Nelson to Wife 2, 6 and 10.3.1795; Naish pp. 197–9
24 Nelson to Clarence 24.4.1795; Nicolas II p. 31
25 Nelson to Clarence 15.3.1795, Nelson to Locker 21.3.1795; Nicolas II pp. 19–22
26 Nelson to Suckling 22.3.1795; Nicolas II pp. 22–3. Nelson to Wife 23.3. and 28.3.1795; Naish pp. 201–3.
27 Nelson to Wife 1.4.1795; Naish pp. 203–5
28 Nelson to Locker 4.5.1795; Nicolas II pp. 34–6

29 Nelson to Elliot 12.4.1795; Naish pp. 405–6. Nelson to Elliot 16.4.1795 and Nelson to Clarence 16.4.1795; Nicolas II pp. 30–1

30 Nelson to Wife 7.5.1795; Naish p. 208

31 Nelson to Suckling 24.4.1795; Nicolas II p. 33. Nelson to Wife 28.4.1795; Naish pp. 207–8.

32 Nelson to Wife 22 and 29.5.1795; Naish pp. 209–10

33 Nelson to Wife 7.6.1795; Naish pp. 210–11. Nelson to Suckling 7.5.1795; Nelson to William Nelson 8.6.1795; Nicolas II pp. 40–2

34 Nelson to Wife 15.6.1795; Naish pp. 211–12

35 Nelson to Locker 18.6.1795; Nicolas II pp. 43–4

36 Nelson to Wife 1.7.1795; Naish p. 214

37 Syrett, D. and DiNardo, R. eds. *The Commissioned Sea Officers of the Royal Navy; 1660–1815*. London Navy Records Society, 1994, p. 6.

38 Nelson to Locker 8.7.1795, Nelson to Clarence 15.7.1795; Nicolas II pp. 49–52. Nelson to Wife 9–14.7.1795; Naish pp. 215–16

39 Nelson to Drake 18.7.1795; and Nelson to Hotham 22.7.1795; Nicolas II pp. 53–4, 57–9. Nelson to Wife 18.7.1795; Naish pp. 216–17

40 Nelson to Spencer 19.7.1795, Spencer to Hood 27.3.1795; Nicolas II pp. 56–7

41 Nelson to Wife 2.8.1795; Naish pp. 218–19

42 Nelson to Wife 24.7.1795; Naish pp. 217–18

43 Nelson to William Nelson 29.7.1795; Nicolas II pp. 63–4

44 Nelson to Drake 6.8. to Cockburn 8.8. and Elliot 13.8.1795; Nicolas II pp. 66–9

45 Nelson to Locker 19.8.1795; Nicolas II pp. 69–71

46 Nelson to Hotham 27 and 31.8.1795; Nicolas II pp. 73–7

47 Nelson to Wife 1, 15.9.1795, Hotham to Nelson 4.9.1795, Nelson to Hotham 20.9.1795; Naish p. 221–2, 236, 246–7. Nelson to De Vins 9 and 17.9.1795, to Drake 9 and 18.9.1795, to Hotham 17.9.1795; Nicolas II 79–86

48 Nelson to Wife 21.9.1795; Naish pp. 222–3. Nelson to Elliot 24.9.1795; Nicolas II pp. 87–9.

49 Nelson to Neapolitan Commander 1.10.1795; Nicolas II pp. 90–1

50 Nelson to Suckling 27.10.1795; Nicolas II pp. 92–3

51 Nelson to Wife 2.11.1795; Naish pp. 225–6

52 Nelson to Wife 13.11.1795; Naish pp. 227–8. Nelson to De Vins 7.11. to Drake 12.11. and to Admiralty 13.11.1795; Nicolas II pp. 95–7

53 Nelson 6.11.1795; Nicolas II p. 94

54 Nelson to Drake 27.11.1795. Nelson to Elliot 4.12.1795; Nicolas II pp. 108–9, 112–4. Nelson to Hyde Parker 2.12.1795; Naish pp. 251–2

55 Nelson to Wife 2.12.1795; Naish pp. 228–30

56 Nelson to Jervis 21.12.1795; Nicolas II pp. 120–1. Vado Bay Journal; Naish pp. 241–5

57 Nelson to Wife 18 &25.12.1795; Naish pp. 230–3

58 See Nelson's speech to the House of Lords on 30.10.1801, Nicolas IV p.520.

59 Hood, *The Admirals Hood* is the only full length treatment, although Hood

shares the book with his younger brother Alexander, Lord Bridport, and his cousins Alexander, and Samuel, one of the Nile captains. Hannay, ed. *Letters Written by Sir Samuel Hood (Viscount Hood) in 1781–2–3.* London Navy Records Society 1895 offers a valuable record of the Admiral when Nelson joined his school. Duffy, M., 'Samuel Hood, First Viscount Hood 1724–1816', in LeFevre, P. and Harding, R., *Precursors of Nelson; British Admirals of the Eighteenth Century,* London, 2000, pp. 249–78, is the latest treatment.
60 Crook, M. *Toulon in War and Revolution,* pp. 144–60
61 Rose, *Lord Hood and the Defence of Toulon.*
62 Duffy, p. 268
63 Duffy, p. 259
64 Nelson to William. Nelson 31.1.1783; Nicolas I p. 98

CHAPTER VI

1 Thorne, R. G. *History of Parliament 1790–1820. Members G–P,* pp. 305–6
2 Jervis to Spencer 18.7.1796; Corbett, J. (ed.), *The Spencer Papers* vol. II (henceforth Sp. II) p. 37
3 Jervis to Spencer 18.5.1796; Sp. II p. 23
4 Jervis to Spencer 29.12.1796; Sp. II p. 84
5 Nelson to Wife 14.12.1796; Naish pp. 310–11
6 Jervis to Spencer 29.7.1796; Sp. II p. 43
7 Jervis to Spencer 8.1796; Sp. II p. 48
8 Jervis to Spencer 11.11.1796; Sp. II p. 72
9 Jervis to Spencer 22.5.1797; Sp. II p. 403
10 Berckman, *Nelson's Dear Lord; A Portrait of St Vincent,* p. 196
11 See BL Add. 34, 918 f. 50 for an example.
12 Arthur, *The Remaking of the English Navy by Admiral St Vincent,* 1986 provides a useful treatment of the Earl's contribution.
13 For Cornwallis see Lambert in Lefevre and Harding.
14 *Minto II* pp. 278–81, 345–51
15 Nelson to Wife 23.8.1796; Naish pp. 301–2. This may explain the initially cold relationship between the two men in the spring of 1801.
16 Nelson to Wife 6 and 14.1.1796; Naish pp. 233–4
17 Nelson to Wife 20.1.796; Naish pp. 281–2
18 Jervis to Spencer 24.1.1796 *Spencer Papers* II pp. 10–12
19 Spencer to Nelson 15.1.1796; Naish pp. 333–4
20 Nelson to Wife 27.1.1796; Naish p. 282
21 Nelson to Wife 12.2.1796; Naish p. 283
22 Nelson to Wife 28.1.1796; Naish pp. 284–5
23 Nelson to Trevor 2.3.1796; to Locker 4.3.1796; to Elliot 10.3.1796; to Hamilton 11.3.1796; to Jervis 16.3.1796; Nicolas pp. 128–38. Nelson to Wife 11.3.1796; Naish pp. 285–6
24 Chandler, D. *The Campaigns of Napoleon,* pp. 41, 47
25 Ibid. p. 47

26 Sherwig, p. 76
27 Jervis to Spencer 28.3.1796; Sp. II p. 21
28 Nelson to Wife 24.4.1796; Naish pp. 290–1
29 Nelson to Wife 1 and 9.4.1796, Jervis to Elliot 5.4.1796; Naish pp. 287–8, 338–9. Nelson to Drake 6 and 11.4.1796; , to Jervis 8, 9 and 13.4.1796; Nicolas II pp. 142–52. Nelson to Spencer 11.4.1796; Nicolas VII p. xlvii.
30 Spencer to Nelson 26.5.1796; Naish p. 335
31 Nelson to Wife 19.4.1796; Naish p. 289
32 Nelson to Jervis 25.4.1796; Nicolas II pp. 161–2
33 Nelson to Jervis 26.4.1796; Nicolas II pp. 162–3
34 Nelson to Jervis 1, 8, 15, 18.5.1796; Nelson to Elliot 16.5.1796; Nicolas II pp. 164–73
35 Nelson to Jervis 14.5.1796; Nicolas VII p. lxix
36 Jervis to Nelson 11 and 22.5.1796; Naish pp. 336–7
37 Nelson to Jervis 23.5.1796; Nicolas II p. 174
38 Nelson to Wife 20 and 27.5.1796; Naish pp. 292–5
39 Cockburn was one of Hood's protégés, and Nelson's dispatch was carefully shaped to secure his place in Jervis's affections.
40 Nelson to Jervis 4.6.1796; Nicolas VII p. lxxix
41 Nelson to Colonel Graham 19.6.1796; Nicolas VII pp. lxxxiii–iv
42 Nelson to Jervis 20.6.1796; Nicolas VII p. lxxxv
43 Jervis to Nelson 1.6.1796; Nicolas II pp. 335–6. Nelson to Jervis 4 and 9.6.1796; Nicolas VII p. lxxix–lxxxii. Nelson to Wife 13.6.1796; Naish pp. 295–6
44 Nelson to Jervis 28.6.1796; Nicolas II pp. 194–5
45 Nelson to Wife 21.6.1796; Naish p. 296
46 Nelson to Jervis 23, 24 and 28.6.1796; Nicolas II pp. 189–95
47 Jervis to Nelson 29.6.1796; Brenton I pp. 176–7
48 Nelson to Elliot 2.7.1796; Nicolas II pp. 198–200. Elliot to Nelson 6.7.1796; Naish p. 341
49 Nelson to Neutral Consuls at Leghorn 7.7.1796; Nicolas II p. 206. Nelson to Wife 7.7.1796; Naish pp. 296–7
50 Nelson to Jervis 9 and 10.7.1796; Nicolas II pp. 207–9
51 Jervis to Nelson 13 and 14.7.1796, Jervis to Elliot 14.7.1796; Naish pp. 337–9
52 Elliot to Nelson 17.7.1796; Naish pp. 341–2
53 Nelson to Wife 21–3.7.1796; Naish pp. 297–8
54 Nelson to Clarence 20.7.1796; Nicolas II pp. 218–9
55 Nelson to Jervis 23.7.1796; Nicolas VII p. xlii
56 Jervis to Elliot 25.7.1796; Naish p. 339. Jervis to Spencer 18 and 27.7.1796; Spencer II pp. 37 and 42
57 Nelson to Elliot 5.8.1796; Elliot to Nelson 6.8.1796; Naish pp. 341–2. Nelson to Elliot 10 and 11.8.1796; Nicolas II pp. 238–40
58 Jervis to Nelson 31.7.1796; Brenton I pp. 192–3. Nelson to Jervis 15.8.1796; Nicolas VII p. xlix
59 Jervis to Spencer 11.8.1796; Spencer II pp. 46–7. Jervis to Elliot 12.8.1796;

Naish p. 339.
60 Nelson to Father 19.8.1796; Nicolas II pp. 244–5
61 Nelson to Elliot 25.8.1796; Nicolas II. pp. 253–5
62 Nelson to Clarence 19.8.1796; Nicolas II pp. 245–6
63 Elliot to Nelson 30.8.1796; Naish pp. 344–5
64 Nelson to Wife 10.9.1796; Naish p. 303
65 Nelson to William Wyndham 3.9.1796; Nicolas VII pp. cvii–cx. Nelson to Jervis 11, 14 and 19.9.1796; Nelson to Elliot 21.9.1796; Nicolas II pp. 262–74
66 Jervis to Spencer 27.9.1796 enclosing Nelson –Jervis 15.9.1796; Spencer II pp. 54–7
67 White, 1797: Nelson's Year of Destiny, pp. 16–17
68 Jervis to Spencer 15.9.1796; Spencer II pp. 52–4
69 Jervis to Nelson 25.9.1796; Naish p. 338
70 Jervis to Elliot 26.9.1796; Naish p. 340
71 Nelson to Jervis 26 and 28.9.1796; Nicolas II pp. 282–5
72 Nelson to Jervis 19.10.1796; Nicolas II pp. 291–4
73 Jervis to Nelson 13.10.1796; Naish p. 338
74 Rose, p. 77
75 Jervis to Elliot 17.10.1796; Naish p. 340
76 Nelson to Jervis 15 and 17.10.1796; Nicolas II pp. 288–9
77 Nelson to Wife 13 and 24.10.1796; Naish pp. 30–6
78 Jervis to Spencer 2.10.1796; Spencer II p. 58
79 Jervis to Spencer 23.10.1796; Spencer II pp. 61–4
80 Nelson to Locker 5.11.1796; Nicolas II pp. 298–9
81 Nelson to Collingwood 20.11.1796; Nelson Suckling 29.11.1796; Nicolas II pp. 304–7. Nelson to Wife 22.11.1796; Naish pp. 308–9
82 Nelson to Collingwood 1.12.1796; Nicolas II p. 307. Nelson to Wife 1, 9 and 12.12.1796; Naish pp. 309–10
83 Jervis to Nelson 10.12.1796; Nicolas II p. 311
84 Jervis to Elliot 10.12.1796; Brenton I pp. 272–4
85 Spencer to Jervis 16.12.1796 Spencer .II p. 78
86 Nelson to Jervis 20.12.1796; Nicolas II pp. 312–15
87 Nelson to Governor of Cartagena 24.12.1796; Nicolas II p. 317
88 Nelson to Jervis 24.12.1796; Nelson to Elliot 24.12.1796; Nelson to De Burgh 29 and 30.12.1796; Nicolas II pp. 317–24

CHAPTER VII

1 Nelson to Spencer 4 and 16.1.1797; Nicolas VII pp. cxxvii–iii
  This chapter draws extensively on Colin White's 1797: Nelson's Year of Destiny, 1998
2 Minto to Portland (Home Secretary) 24.1.1797; Minto II p. 371
3 Nelson to Wife 13.1.1797; Naish p. 312
4 Nelson to Jervis 25.1.1797; Nicolas VII p. cxxix
5 Nelson to Wife 27.1.1797; Naish pp. 312–13

6 Jervis to Spencer 16.2.1797; Nicolas II pp. 355–6

7 Quoted in Nelson to William Nelson 17.2.1797; Nicolas II pp. 351–2

8 Nelson to Locker 21.2.1797; Nicolas II pp. 353–5

9 Nelson received the letter on rejoining the fleet after Tenerife; Nelson to Parker 19.8.1797; Nicolas II p. 438. Parker was disgraced in 1800 for leaving his station in search of prize, and died in 1802.

10 Nelson to Wife 28.2.1797; Naish pp. 317–18

11 Jervis to Spencer 26.2.1796; 5.3.1797; 6.4.1797 and Spencer to Jervis 3.4.1797; Spencer II pp. 93–7; 379–85

12 Jervis to Spencer 5.3.1797; Spencer II p. 372

13 Nelson to Jervis 11.4.1797; to Saumarez 12.4.1797; Nicolas II pp. 376 and 381.

14 Robert Blake, Cromwell's leading 'General at Sea', destroyed a Spanish fleet at Tenerife in 1657.

15 Nelson to Jervis 12.4.1797; Nicolas II pp. 378–81

16 Nelson to Jervis 21.4.1797; Nicolas VII pp. cxxxii–iii

17 Nelson to Wife 27.5.1797; Naish pp. 324–5

18 Nelson to Mazzaredo and reply 30.5. and 1.6.1797; Nicolas II pp. 388–9

19 Nelson to Jervis 19.4.1797; Nicolas II pp. 378–81

20 Nelson to St Vincent 6, 7, 9, 10, 12 and 13.6.1797; Nicolas II pp. 392–7 and VII pp. cxxxix–cxli

21 Nelson to Wife 15, 29 and 30.6.1797; Naish pp. 325–8

22 St Vincent to Spencer 3.8.1797; Spencer II 413

23 Nelson to Jervis 27.7.1797; Nicolas II pp. 434–5

24 Nelson to Wife 5 and 16.8.1797; Naish pp. 332–3. Nelson to Jervis 16.8.1797 and reply of same day; Nicolas II pp. 435–6

25 St Vincent to Lady Nelson 16.8.1797; Naish p. 371. St Vincent to Admiralty 16.8.1797; Nicolas II pp. 434–5.

26 The section on Tenerife is drawn, unless otherwise noted, from the much richer account given in Colin White's magnificent *1797: Nelson's Year of Destiny*, pp. 89–133.

27 St Vincent to Spencer 16.8.1797; Spencer II 414

28 Walker: Abbott had already painted Hood and Bridport, among other naval sitters.

29 In an early letter he declares 'my mind has long been made up to such an event': Nelson to Wife 3.8.1797; Nicolas II p. 436

30 Correspondence October–December 1797; Nicolas II pp. 447–61

31 It appears that there were no current plans of this sort, although 25,000 men had been embarked over the summer. Desbrière *Projets* I pp. 264–6

32 Nelson would command several ex-Dutch ships in 1801.

33 Lord Grenville to Spencer 13.10.1797; Sp. II pp. 195–6

34 Tomlinson, B. 'The Battle Sanctified', in Duffy, M. and Morriss, R. *The Glorious First of June*. Exeter, 2001 pp. 165–6.

35 Pitt to Spencer 22.10.1797 Sp. II pp. 213–15

36 Coupland, R. ed. *The War Speeches of William Pitt the Younger*. Oxford, 1915 Speech of 10.11.1797 pp. 227–8. The republication of these rousing

calls to national unity in the next total war was not accidental.
37 Jordan, G. and Rogers, N. 'Admirals as Heroes; Patriotism and Liberty in Hanoverian England', *Journal of British Studies* 28 (1989), p. 213

CHAPTER VIII

1 Nelson received several trophies and rewards for this service from City companies, for whom the events of 1798 were a great relief. The Levant Company's silver cup was a particular favourite.
2 Baring, ed. *The Diary of William Windham, 1784–1811*, p. 382
3 Ibid. p. 389
4 Naish p. 381
5 Nelson to St Vincent 10.1.1798; Nicolas III p. 3
6 Spencer to Grenville 6.4.1798; Spencer II pp. 433–4
7 Nelson to Mrs Collingwood 12.3 and Nelson to Father 14.3.1798; Nicolas III p. 6
8 Nelson's will 21.3.1798; Naish pp. 405–6. Nelson to William Nelson 31.3.1798; Nicolas III pp. 7–8.
9 Spencer to St Vincent 30.3.1798; Spencer II p. 432
10 Nelson to Clarence 24.4.1798; Nicolas III p. 10
11 Nelson to Wife 1.5.1798; Naish p. 394–5
12 Spencer to St Vincent 29.4.1798; Spencer II pp. 437–9
13 Mackesy, *Statesmen at War; The Strategy of Overthrow 1798–1799*, pp. 3–5
14 Lavery, *Nelson and the Nile; The Naval War against Bonaparte 1798*, pp. 93–8. This excellent campaign study informs the operational and tactical discussions of this chapter. Battesti, *La Battaille d'Aboukir; Nelson contrarie la Stratégie de Napoleon* provides a compelling assessment of the campaign from the French perspective, stressing the strategic impact of the battle, denying France, and Bonaparte, the dream of escaping the limits of Europe for world empire.
15 Mackesy, pp. 16–41
16 Lavery, p. 101
17 St Vincent to Spencer 19.5.1798; Spencer II pp. 446–7
18 St Vincent to Nelson 21.5.1798; Nicolas III pp. 25–6
19 Lavery, pp. 7–24
20 Nelson to St Vincent 6.5.1797; Nicolas VII pp. cl–cli
21 Nelson to the captains of HMS *Orion, Alexander* and *Vanguard* 7.5.1798; Nelson to St Vincent 8.5.1798; Nicolas III pp. 13–15
22 Lavery, pp. 63–4
23 Nelson to St Vincent 17.5.1798; Nicolas III pp. 16–17
24 Lavery, pp. 117–19
25 Nelson Order 7.6.1798; Nicolas III p. 23
26 Berry, p. 49
27 Lavery, p. 122
28 Nelson to Hamilton and St Vincent 12 and 12–15.6.1798; Nicolas III pp. 28–30

29 Nelson to Hamilton 14.6.1798; Nicolas III p. 30

30 Nelson to Spencer 15.6.1798; Nicolas III p. 31. Naish p. 398

31 Nelson to Hamilton 17.6.1798; Nicolas III pp. 32–3

32 Nelson to Hamilton 18 and 20.6.1798; Nicolas III pp. 33–4

33 Naish pp. 407–9. Lavery pp. 127–8

34 St Vincent to Spencer 15.7.1798; Spencer II pp. 447–8

35 Nelson to St Vincent 12.7.1798; Nicolas III p. 41

36 Nelson to St Vincent 20.7.1798; Nicolas III p. 45. Nelson to Wife 20.7.1798; Naish p. 398

37 Nelson to Hamilton 20, 22. and 23.7.1798; Nicolas III pp. 42–7

38 Nelson to St Vincent 3.8.1798; Nicolas III pp. 58–61

39 Mornington to Grenville 18.11.1798; cited on Mackesy p. 43

40 Nelson to Spencer 9.8.1798; Nicolas III pp. 98–9

41 Nelson to Wife 11.8.1798; Naish p. 399

42 Nelson to Nepean 16.8.1798 and to St Vincent 19 and 26.8.1798; Nicolas III pp. 105–7

CHAPTER IX

1 Barry Unsworth's *Losing Nelson* confronts this issue with imagination. The scale of the debate should not disguise the poverty of hard evidence. The case against Nelson would not stand in a court of law, being wholly based on hearsay and innuendo.

2 Touchette, L-A. 'Sir William Hamilton's "Pantomime Mistress": Emma Hamilton and Her Attitudes.' In Hornsby, C. ed. *The Impact of Italy; The Grand Tour and Beyond*, London, 2000, pp. 123–46: an excellent illustrated account of her art.

3 Winifred Guerin's account in *Horatia Nelson*, Oxford, 1981, is the most hostile on this score.

4 Hamilton to Nelson 8.9.1798; Nicolas III pp. 71–2

5 Hamilton to Nelson 1.8.1798; Morrison, A. *The Hamilton and Nelson Papers. Volume II.* London 1894 privately printed pp. 15–17

6 Acton to Nelson 9.9.1798; Nicolas III p. 118. Nelson to Spencer 16.9.1799; Nicolas III pp. 126-7

7 Paret and Moran eds. *Carl von Clausewitz: Historical and Political Writings*, p. 246 as quoted in Gooch, J. 'The Politics of Strategy', *War in History* 4 (2003), p. 424

8 Rodger, *The War of the Second Coalition, 1798 to 1801: A Strategic Commentary* is the leading source for this analysis. It has been widely, and uncritically adopted.

9 Nelson to Father 25.9.1798; Nicolas III p. 131

10 Nelson to St Vincent 27.9.1798; Nicolas III p. 132

11 St Vincent to Nelson 27.9.1798; Nicolas III pp. 84–5

12 Admiralty to St Vincent 3.10.1798; Nicolas III pp. 143–4

13 Nelson to Captain Hood 13.9.1798; Nicolas III pp. 121–2

14 Nelson to St Vincent 30.9.1799; Nicolas III p. 138

15 Nelson to St Vincent 4.10.1798; Nicolas VII p. clxiv
16 Nelson to Pitt 4.10.1798; PRO 30/8/367 ff. 42-3
17 Nelson to St Vincent 4.10.1798; Nicolas VII clxiv
18 Nelson to Spencer 9.10.1798; Nicolas III pp. 146-7
19 Hamilton to Nelson 16.10.1798. Morrison II. pp. 23-4. Nelson to St Vincent
   22.10.1798; Nicolas III pp. 150-1
20 Testa, C. *The French in Malta 1798-1800*. Valletta 1997
21 Nelson to St Vincent 7.11.1798; Nicolas III p. 166
22 Mackesy, *Statesmen at War: The Strategy of Overthrow 1798-1799*. London
   pp. 54-6
23 Nelson to St Vincent 30-31.12.1798: Nicolas pp. 213-15
24 Nelson to Spencer 1.1.1799; Nicolas III pp. 217-18
25 Nelson to Pitt 4.10.1799; PRO 30/8/367 ff. 42-3
26 Nelson to Wife 17.1.1799; Naish pp. 480-1
27 Acton, H. *The Bourbons of Naples*. London 1956 pp. 314-334. While Acton
   dismisses the pro-Jacobin effusions of the Neapolitan historians, he goes on to
   mistake the role of Nelson and the Hamiltons on very limited evidence.
28 Nelson to General Sir Charles Stuart 7.1.1799; Nicolas III pp. 227-8
29 Acton, pp. 337-8.
30 Nelson to Howe 8.1.1799; Nicolas III pp. 230-1
31 Walker pp. 88-90
32 Nelson to St Vincent 17.1.1799: Nicolas VII p. clxx. Nelson to Minto
   19.1.1799: Nicolas III pp 235-690
33 Nelson to Ball 21.1.1799; Nicolas III pp. 236-8
34 Nelson to St Vincent 1.2.1799; Nicolas III p. 239
35 Nelson to Lady Parker 1.2.1799; Nicolas III pp. 248-9. Nelson to Davison
   2.2.1799; Nicolas VII p. clxxii
36 Nelson to St Vincent 1, 2 and 3.2.1799; Nelson to Ball 4.2.1799; Nelson to
   Acton 2.2.1799; Nelson to Niza 1.2.1799; Nicolas III pp. 249-56
37 Nelson to Commissioner Coffin at Port Mahon 5.2.1799; Nicolas III p. 258
38 Nelson to Spencer 17.2.1799; Nicolas VII p. clxxv. Nelson to Stuart
   16.2.1799; Nelson to Troubridge 18.2.1799; Nicolas III pp. 267-9
39 Nelson to Spencer 7.2.1799; Nicolas VII p. clxxii
40 Nelson to Ball 28.2.1799; Nicolas III pp. 272-3
41 Nelson to Ball 8.3.1799; Nicolas III pp. 286-7
42 Nelson to St Vincent 20.3.1799; Nicolas III pp. 297-9
43 Nelson to Oushakov 23.3.1799; Nicolas II p. 304
44 Nelson to St Vincent 20.3.1799; Nicolas III pp. 297-9
45 Lloyd, C. ed. *The Keith Papers II*. London, Navy Records Society 1950. pp.
   36-51
46 King to Ruffo 11.4.1799; Gutteridge, ed. *Nelson and the Neapolitan
   Jacobins*, pp. 38-41
47 King to Ruffo. 1.5.1799; Gutteridge p. 45
48 Nelson to Troubridge 30.3.1799; Nicolas III p. 310
49 Nelson to Ball 9.4.1799; Nicolas III p. 319
50 Nelson to Spencer 6.4.1799; Nicolas VII pp. clxxvii-iii

51 Hamilton to Charles Greville 8.4.1799; Morrison II pp. 40–1
52 Mackesy, p. 98 is a typical modern example.
53 Lord Keith to Sister 19.4.1799; Keith II p. 37. Typically this is a piece of second-hand reportage, based on an unknown source, by someone who had not met Nelson for a year.
54 Nelson to St Vincent 8.3.1799: Nicolas III pp. 285–6
55 Nelson to Ball 21.4.1799; Nicolas III pp. 332–3
56 Nelson to Troubridge 25.4. and to Stuart 28.4.1799; Nicolas III pp. 333–7
57 Nelson to St Vincent 9.5.1799; Nicolas VII clxxxi
58 De la Gravière, *Sketches of the Last Naval War.* London 1848, Vol. I pp. 224–31
59 Rodger, *The War of the Second Coalition 1798 to 1801; A Strategic Commentary* is widely cited, but repeats several important errors, and adds a few new ones. Rodger underrates the importance of Naples and Sicily, while over-valuing Minorca and Malta.
60 St Vincent to Nelson 6.5.1799; Gutteridge p. xxxvii
61 Nelson to various 12.5.1799; Nicolas III pp. 352–4
62 Nelson to St Vincent 28.5.1799; Nicolas III p. 367
63 Nelson to St Vincent 23.5.1799; Nicolas III pp. 364–5
64 Hallowell to Nelson 23.5.1799; in Beresford, Lord C. and Wilson, H. W. *Nelson and his Times* 1897 p. 123
65 Lambert, 'Cornwallis'
66 Nelson to Emma 22 and 24.5.1799; Nicolas VII p. clxxxiii
67 Nelson to Wife 24.5.1799; Naish p. 484
68 Nelson to Emma 19.5.1799; Nicolas III p. 362
69 Nelson to St Vincent 30.5.1799; Nicolas III pp. 368–9
70 Foote to Nelson 28.5.1799; Nicolas III p. 360
71 Nelson to Wife 5.6.1799; Naish p. 485
Nelson to St Vincent 5.6.1799; Nicolas III pp. 374–5
72 Nelson to St Vincent 6.6.1799; Nicolas VII p. clxxxiv.
73 Nelson to St Vincent 10 and 12.6.1799; St Vincent to Nelson 11.6.1799; Nicolas III pp. 377–9
74 Keith to Sister 30.3.1799; *Keith II* pp. 36–7. On the evidence of this letter Keith was a better judge of service politics than enemy intentions.
75 Collingwood reports that Keith was in sight of the enemy before he abandoned the chase to secure Minorca. Collingwood to Edward Collingwood 17.8.1799; Duffy, M. ed. *The Naval Miscellany VI.* Aldershot 2003 pp. 168–9
76 Keith to Nelson 6.6.1799; Nicolas III pp. 379–80
77 Nelson to Keith 16.6.1799, and to St Vincent 16.6. and to Wife 17.6.1799; Nicolas III pp. 379–81 and Naish pp. 485–6
78 Nelson to Hamilton 21.6.1799; Gutteridge p. 144
79 Nelson to Keith 27.6.1799; Gutteridge p. 264
80 Acton to Hamilton 19 and 20.6.1799; Nicolas III pp. 391–2. Nelson to Magra 20.6.1799; & to Hamilton 20.6.1799; Nicolas III pp. 382–3 and VII p. clxxxv.
81 Nelson to Keith 27.6.1799; Nicolas III pp. 390–2

82 Nelson to Duckworth 21.6.1799; Nicolas III p. 384
83 Nelson to Admiralty 27.6.1799; Nicolas III p. 389
84 Gutteridge p. xci
85 Pakenham, T. *The Year of Liberty* London 1969 p. 327
86 Nelson to Acton 29.6.1799; Gutteridge p. 279
87 Queen to Ruffo 17.5. and 19.6.1799; Gutteridge pp. 55 and 135. King to Ruffo 20.6.1799; Gutteridge p. 141
88 Nelson to Troubridge 26.6.1799; Nicolas III pp. 388–9
89 Acton to Nelson 30.6 and 2.7.1799; Croker MS, NMM CRK/17.
90 Acton p.409.
91 Nelson to Hood 4.7.1799; Nelson to Keith 13.7.1799; Nicolas III p. 400, 403–4
92 Nelson to Spencer 13.7.1799; Nicolas III pp. 406–7
93 Nelson to Keith 13.7.1799; Nicolas III pp. 407–8
94 Keith to Nelson 9.7.1799; Nelson to Keith and Admiralty 19.7.1799; Nicolas III pp. 414–16. Nelson to Spencer 19.7.1799; Nicolas VII pp. clxxxv–vi
95 Nelson to Sidney Smith 20 and 22.7.1799; Nicolas III pp. 416–18
96 Collingwood to Edward Colllingwood 17.8.1799; Owen in Duffy, *Naval Miscellany VI* pp. 168–9
97 Nelson to Duckworth 22.7.1799; Nicolas III pp. 418–9. Nelson to Spencer 23.7.1799; Nicolas VII p. clxxxvii.
98 Nelson to Admiralty; to Spencer; to Keith 1.8.1799; Nicolas III pp. 425–9
99 Nelson to Ball 14.8.1799; Nicolas III p. 440
100 Sermonetta, Duchess *The Locks of Norbury*. London 1940.pp. 151–201. The author/editor of the volume was a member of the Caracciolo family, and does not try to hide her bias. This problem is compounded by errors of fact. See pp. 166–70 for the Caracciolo story, and the family connection. Nelson to Lock 23.7.1799; to memorandum 24.7.1799. Nicolas III pp. 420–1. See also Nicolas IV pp. 101 and 129 for further correspondence on this issue. Russell, J. *Nelson and the Hamiltons.* 1969 pp. 88–90. Acton, pp. 337–9, 405–6, 413–14.
101 Acton, pp. 428–30.
102 Nelson to King Ferdinand 13.8.1799; to Father 15.8.1799; Nicolas III pp. 438–9, 441
103 Nelson to Duckworth 16.8. to Suvarov 16.8. and to Oushakov 18.8.1799; Nicolas III pp. 446–9
104 Nelson to Duckworth 20.8. to Troubridge/Martin 22.8.1799; Nicolas III pp. 453–9
105 Nelson to Ball 21.8.1799; Nicolas III pp. 456–7
106 Admiralty to Nelson 20.8.1799; Morrison II pp. 64–5
107 Nelson to Davison c.23.8.1799; Nicolas III pp. 460–1. Nelson to Wife 23.8.1799; Naish pp. 488–9
108 Nelson to Wife 23.8.1799; Naish p. 488. Nelson to Admiralty 24.8.1799; to Troubridge 31.8.1799; Nicolas III pp. 462, 469–70
109 Nelson to Minto 20.8.1799; Nicolas III p. 452

CHAPTER X

1 Admiralty to Nelson 20.8.1799; Spencer IV p. 30
2 Nelson to Admiralty 20–21.9.1799; Nicolas IV pp. 23–7
3 Nelson to Spencer 5.9.1799; Nicolas IV p. 3
4 Nelson to Davison 23.9.1799; Nicolas VII pp. cxci–ii
5 Nelson to Oushakoff 25.9.1799; to Spencer 26.9.1799; to Ball 27.9.1799; Nicolas III pp. 29–31
6 Nelson to Admiralty and Troubridge 1.10.1799; Nicolas IV pp. 34–5
7 Nelson to Troubridge and Admiralty 1.10.1799; to Acton, and Troubridge 2.10.1799; to Ball and Graham 3.10.1799; Nicolas IV pp. 34–42. Quotes from letters to Troubridge.
8 Nelson Standing Orders 10.11.1799; to Erskine 11.10.1799; to Duckworth 14.10.1799; Nicolas IV pp. 46–52. Nelson to Hamilton 11 and 13.10.1799; Morrison II pp. 71–2. Nelson to Admiralty 15.10.1799; Nicolas IV pp. 53–5
9 Nelson to Admiralty 3.11.1799; to Spencer 6.11.1799; Nicolas IV pp. 85–91
10 Nelson to Wife 7.11.1799; Naish pp. 491–2
11 Nelson to Admiralty 9.11.1799; Nicolas IV p. 94
12 Nelson to Victualling Board 14.11.1799; – Lock 15.11.1799; Nicolas IV pp. 100–1. Sermonetta has Lock's correspondence.
13 Nelson to Admiralty and Lock 4.12.1799; – Victualling Board 5.12.1799; Nicolas IV pp. 128–9
14 Nelson to Admiralty 11.11.1799; to Erskine 12.11.1799; to Wyndham 26.11.1799; Nicolas IV pp. 96–9, and 111. Testa. C. *The French in Malta* for these developments.
15 Nelson to Troubridge 25 and 28.11.1799; to Graham 25.11.1799; to Niza 15, 17 and 24.11.1799; Nicolas IV pp. 102–3, 107, 109–10, 119
16 Nelson to Niza 18.12.1799; Nicolas IV p. 144
17 Nelson to Admiralty 26.11.1799; Nicolas IV p. 110
18 Nelson to Duckworth 27.11.1799; Nicolas IV pp. 113–14
19 Nelson to Lord William Bentinck 22.11.1799; to Wyndham 2 and 13.12.1799; Nicolas IV pp. 106, 125–6, 135–6
20 Nelson to Troubridge and Blackwood 16.12.1799; Nicolas IV pp. 142–4
21 Nelson to Udney (Consul at Leghorn) 26.9.1799: Nicolas IV p.30
22 Nelson to dockyard officers, Port Mahon 14.12.1799: Nicolas IV pp. 138–9
23 Nelson to Troubridge 16.12.1799: Nicolas IV 142–3
24 Nelson to Lord Elgin (Minister to the Sublime Porte) 21.12.1799: Nicolas IV pp. 158–60
25 Nelson to Davison 19.12.1799: Nicolas VII p. cxciii
26 Nelson to Troubridge 22.12.1799; Nicolas IV pp. 155–6
27 Nelson to Graham 22.12.1799; to Admiralty and Spencer 23.12.1799; Nicolas IV pp. 158–60
28 Keith to Spencer 23.12.1799; Spencer IV p. 105
29 Troubridge to Nelson 1, 5, 7 and 8.1.1800; Nelson to Troubridge 29.12.1799, 1, 5 and 8.1.1800; Nelson to Graham 7.1.1800; Nicolas IV pp. 166–73
30 Nelson to Troubridge 14.1.1800; Nicolas IV pp. 176–7

31 Troubridge to Emma 14.1.1800; Morrison II pp. 79–80
32 Nelson to Keith 7.1.1800; Nicolas IV pp. 170–2; Nelson to Wife 9.1.1800; Naish pp. 493–4
33 Hamilton to Charles Greville 25.1.1800; Morrison II pp. 82–3
34 Nelson to Emma and Hamilton 3.2.1800; Nicolas IV pp. 185–6, Morrison II p. 84
35 Nelson to St Vincent 1 and 6.2.1800; Nicolas IV pp. 184–5
36 Keith to Spencer 9.2.1800; Spencer IV pp. 108–9
37 *Le Genereux* was rated by ther British as an 80-gun ship with 24-pounders on her main deck.
38 The battle ensign of *Le Genereux* has recently been re-discovered in the Norwich Museum. A vast tricolour, 60 feet long and 20 feet deep, it hung in St Andrew's Hall, close by Sir William Beechey's portrait and a Spanish admiral's sword, taken at Cape St Vincent.
39 Nelson to Keith 18.2.1800; to Maurice 20.2.1800; Nicolas IV pp. 188–90. Nelson to Hamilton 18 and 20.2.1800; Morrison pp. 86–7
40 Nelson to Maurice 27.2.1800; Nicolas VII pp. cxciii–iv
41 Keith to Nelson 24.2.1800; Nicolas III p. 191
42 Nelson to Keith 24.2.1800 [public and private letters]; Nicolas IV pp. 191–2
43 Nelson to Hamilton 25.2.1800; Morrison II p. 88
44 Hamilton to Minto 3.3.1800; Naish pp. 521–2. Ball to Emma 10.3.1800; Morrison II p. 90
45 Nelson to Admiral Goodall 11.3.1800; Nicolas IV pp. 204–6
46 Nelson to Spencer 10.3.1800; Phillips Collection, NMM 15
47 Pugh, *Nelson and his Surgeons*, p. 5
48 Nelson to Troubridge and Keith 20.3.1800; Nicolas IV pp. 206–8
49 *Guillaume Tell* was taken into the Royal Navy as HMS *Malta*, serving for the next fifteen years.
50 Berry to Nelson 30.3.1800; Nicolas IV p. 218
51 Ball to Emma 31.3.1800; Morrison II p. 97. Nelson to Berry 5.4.1800; Nicolas III pp. 219–20
52 Nelson to Spencer 8.4.1800; Nicolas IV pp. 224–5
53 Nelson –Blackwood 5.4.1800; Nicolas VII p. lxcv
54 Nelson to Admiralty 4.4.1800; Nicolas IV pp. 218–19
55 Nelson to Davison 9.5.1800; Nicolas IV p. 232
56 Nelson to Wife 20.6.1800; Naish p. 493
57 Ball to Emma 19 and 26.5.1800; Morrison II pp. 99–100
58 Spencer to Keith 25.4.1800, 9.5.1800; Naish p. 525
59 Spencer to Nelson 9.5.1800; Nicolas IV p. 242
60 Nelson to Spencer 20.6.1800; Nicolas VII p. cxcviii. The target of this Shakespearian flourish was, once again, Sidney Smith.
61 Nelson to Keith 12.5.1800; Nicolas IV p. 236
62 Ehrman, *Pitt III* pp. 360–5. Rodger, *Second Coalition* pp. 209–11.
63 Nelson to Berry 21.6.1800; to Commodore Saraiva, Portuguese Navy 25–6.6.1800; Nicolas IV 258–6–62.
64 Robbins-Landon, H., *Haydn; The Years of 'The Creation', 1796–1800*, pp.

327–8, 433, 557–65. Indeed Haydn later supplied her with piano accompaniments for the Nelson songs that she sang with the noted soprano Brigida Banti.
65 For example; Bougard, *The Little Sea Torch; or, True Guide for Coasting Pilots*. London 1801. Nelson was a subscriber to this English edition of a richly illustrated French volume with over a hundred views of key locations from England to the Barbary coast and through the Mediterranean.
66 Many years later the Duke of Wellington would be more discreet in setting aside his wife, and less constant in his subsequent amours.
67 Nelson to Admiralty 6.11.1800; Nicolas IV p. 267
68 Young to Keith 10.11.1800; Keith II p. 146
69 St Vincent to Spencer 30.11.1800; Spencer IV p. 21
70 Spencer to St Vincent 28.11.1800; Spencer IV pp. 273–4
71 Navy Board to Nelson 1.12.1800; Add. 34,934 f15
72 Baring, *Windham Diary* p. 434
73 *The Times* 11.11.1800
74 Walker, R. *The Nelson Portraits*. Portsmouth 1998 pp. 30–55
75 Wife to Nelson 6.5.1798; Naish p. 429
76 Czisnik, 'Nelson and the Nile: The Creation of Admiral Nelson's Public Image', 2002, contains a full overview of this process.
77 Colley, L., *Britons: Forging the Nation, 1707–1837*, 1992, is the key text on this period.
78 Robert Smirke's 1803 engraving of Nelson and his Nile captains.
79 Admiralty to Nelson 1.1.1801; BL Add. 34,934 f18
80 Czisnik, pp. 50–2.
81 Hilliard, G. S. ed. *Life, Letters and Journals of George Ticknor*, Boston, 1876, vol. I p. 63, cited in McNairn, A, *Behold the Hero: General Wolfe and the Arts in the Eighteenth Century*, Liverpool, 1997, p. 182
82 Walker, pp. 120–1.
83 Greig, J. ed. *The Farington Diary I*. London 1923 entry for 13.2.1801 at p. 300.
84 White 'The Wife's Tale' makes the break-up altogether more businesslike than previous accounts, and suggests a great deal more forethought on Nelson's part. This would be more like the man.

CHAPTER XI

1 Spencer to St Vincent 28.11.1800; Morriss, R. ed. *The Channel Fleet and the Blockade of Brest 1793–1801*, Aldershot, Navy Records Society, 2001, p. 590.
2 Feldbaek, O. *Denmark and the Armed Neutrality: 1800–1801* is the definitive study of this issue. His *The Battle of Copenhagen 1801* contains an excellent summary.
3 Le Donne, J. *The Russian Empire and the World 1700–1917: The Geopolitics of Expansion and Containment*, pp. 54–64, 302
4 Ehrman, *Pitt III*, p. 398; speech in House of Commons on 2.2.1801
5 Smith, E A. *Lord Grey, 1764–1845*, pp. 78–9
6 Coupland, ed. *The War Speeches of William Pitt the Younger*, pp. 288–301.

The appearance of this volume in 1915 only emphasises the extent to which that generation looked back to the French wars for inspiration.

7 Ehrman, J. *The Younger Pitt: Vol.III*, p. 411
8 Spencer to St Vincent 28.11.1800; Spencer IV pp. 273–4
9 St Vincent to Spencer 7.12.1800; Spencer IV pp. 274–5
10 Lord Whitworth (ex Amb.) to Spencer 18.12.1800; Spencer IV p. 275
11 Dundas to Spencer 3.1.1801 SP III pp. 287–8
12 Grenville to Carysfort 16.12.1800. Fortescue VI pp. 407–9
13 King's speech 31.12.1800; St Vincent I p. 51
14 Dundas to Admiralty Secretary Evan Nepean 9.1.1801; ADM 1/4168
15 St Vincent was keen to get rid of old followers of Hood, including Donnett and Young, from the Channel fleet. Morriss pp. 567, 578–9
16 Admiralty to Nelson 9.1.1801; Add. 34,934 f19
17 Spencer to St Vincent 26.1.1801; Spencer IV p. 279
18 See Lyon, D. *Sailing Navy List* pp. 250–1 for the six vessels purchased.
19 Parker to Spencer 11.1.1801; Spencer IV pp. 275–7
20 Thesiger to Spencer 16.1.1801; Spencer IV pp. 278–9
21 Nelson to Spencer 17.1.1801; Nicolas IV pp. 274–5
22 Admiralty to Nelson 17 and 18.1.1801; Add. 34,934 f25 and 34,923 f25
23 St Vincent to Spencer 23.1.1801; Spencer IV p. 264
24 St Vincent to Nelson 26.1.1801; Croker Collection, NMM 10
25 Nelson to Emma 25.1.1801; Morrison II pp. 108–9. Pettigrew printed many of these letters in the 1840s, but this quote, and much of the other interesting matter, was edited out.
26 Nelson to Emma 26 and 28.1.1801; Morrison pp. 1909–10, and Nicolas IV p. 279.
27 Nelson to Emma 14.2.1801; Morrison II pp. 114–15
28 Nelson to Emma 19 and 22.2.1801; Morrison II pp. 118–21
29 ADM 3/144N
30 Lord Grenville to Admiralty 2.2.1801; FO13/1
31 Nelson to Admiralty 2.2.1801; Nicolas IV p. 282
32 St Vincent to Nepean 9.2. Spencer IV p. 265
33 The Nelson–Troubridge Correspondence in CRK/14 and *Naval Miscellany I* is critical to this process, and the inner history of the campaign.
34 St Vincent to Simcoe 22.2.1801; St Vincent Papers I p. 82. Dundas to Admiralty 23.2.1801 and Dundas to Duke of York (Secret) 23.2.1801; ADM 1/4168. *The Cumloden Papers.*
35 Secretary of State to Admiralty 23.2.1801; ADM 1/4168
36 Admiralty to Nelson 26.2.1801; Add. 34,934 f. 32
37 Nelson to Emma 1, 4, 6 and 11.3.1801, ; to Wife 4.3.1801; Morrison II pp. 123–9
38 St Vincent to Nelson 8.3.1801; St Vincent I p. 84
39 Nelson to Troubridge 7 and 10.3.1801; Laughton, J.K. ed. *The Naval Miscellany I*, Navy Records Society 1901 pp. 415–18. St Vincent to Hyde Parker 11.3.1801; St Vincent I pp. 86–7
40 Nelson to Troubridge 11.3.1801; *Miscellany I* p. 419

41 Nelson to Troubridge 7.3.1801; *Miscellany I* pp. 414–15
42 Nelson to Troubridge 10 and 29.3.1801; *Miscellany I* pp. 417–18 and 424–5
43 Order of Battle 10.4.1801; Add. 34,918 f.16.
44 Dundas to Admiralty (Secret) 14.3.1801; ADM 1/4186
45 Admiralty to Hyde Parker (Secret) 15.3.1801; Add.34,934 f. 38
46 Nelson to Troubridge 16.3.1801; *Miscellany* I pp. 420–1
47 Vansittart to Hawkesbury 14.3.1801; Add. 31,233 f. 11–9
48 Vansittart to Hawkesbury 19.3.1801; Add. 31,233 f. 34
49 Hyde Parker's Journal 22.3.1801; ADM 50/65.
50 *Cumloden Papers* 23.3.1801. Hyde-Parker to Admiralty 23.3.1801; ADM 1/ 4 39 and 48
51 Nelson to Hyde– Parker 24.3.1801; Nicolas IV pp. 2956
52 Hyde Parker to Nelson 24.3.17801; CRK/8
53 *Cumloden Papers* 24.3.1801
54 Ibid. 26.3.1801
55 Domett to Nelson 26.3.1801; CRK/4
56 Nelson to Troubridge 29.3.1801; *Miscellany 1* pp. 424–5
57 Nelson to Emma 30.3.1801; Morrison II p. 132
58 Parker's Journal 31.3. and 1.4.1801 ADM 50/65
59 *Cumloden Papers* 31.3 and 1.4.1801
60 The key words in the Stewart quote are usually given as 'jug' and 'bale', but these make no sense. Allowances should be made for Nelson's accent and the noise of battle. Nelson to Berry 9.3.1801; Nicolas IV p. 292
61 Minto letter of 19.5.1801; Minto III p. 219
62 Nelson to Davison 4.4.1801; Nicolas VII p. ccv
63 Hamond to Captain Andrew Hamond 5.4.1801; Hamond Papers, Duke University
64 She became HMS *Nassau* and captured another Danish battleship in 1808
65 The main focus of literature on this campaign has been the Slagt por Reden, the battle for the roadstead. This has diverted attention from the wider aims of the campaign, and the impact this terrifying demonstration of power had on European opinion.
66 Nelson to Emma 6.4.1801; Morrison II p. 135. Nelson to St Vincent 9.4.1801; Nicolas IV p. 341
67 Nelson to Admiralty 9.4.1801; Nicolas IV pp. 339–41. Nelson to Troubridge 9.3.1801; *Miscellany I* p. 427
68 Nelson to Minto 9.4.1801; Nicolas IV p. 342
69 Balfour to Nelson 17.4.1801; CRK/2
70 St Vincent to Parker 5.4.1801; St Vincent I pp. 88–9
71 Parker to Admiralty 9.4.1801; ADM 1/ 4
72 Typically Bligh, who had fought like a lion, was so unsure of himself as to ask Nelson for a testimonial, which he was told was 'perfectly unnecessary'. Nelson to St Vincent 14.4.1801; Nicolas IV p. 343
73 Hobart to Admiralty 16.4.1801 Secret; ADM1/4187. Admiralty to Parker 17.4.1801 Secret; Add.34,934 f. 43
74 Spencer to Nelson 19.4.1801; CRK/10

75 St Vincent to Lord Mayor 15.4.1801 to Parker, Nelson 17.4.1801; St Vincent
   I pp. 89–91
76 Davison to Nelson 4.4.1801; CRK/3
77 St Vincent to Nelson 25.4.1801; St Vincent I p. 93. Nelson to Maurice
   15.4.1801; Nicolas IV p. 138
78 Admiralty to Nelson 21.4.1801; Add. 34,934 f. 57
79 St Vincent to Nelson 21.4.1801; St Vincent I pp. 92–3
80 St Vincent to King 21.4.11801; Aspinall, *George III 1798–1801*. p. 517
81 Parker to Admiralty 25.4.1801; ADM 1 /4 65. Parker to Nelson 23.4.1801;
   CRK/8
82 Nelson to Emma 20 and 23.4.1801; Morrison II pp. 139 and 142
83 Nelson to Davison 23.4.1801; Naish pp. 586–7. Nelson to Troubridge
   23.4.1801; *Miscellany I* p. 429
84 Nelson to Troubridge 28.4.1801; *Miscellany I* pp. 431–2
85 Nelson to Davison 22.4.1801; Nicolas VII pp. ccvii–ix. Parker to Admiralty
   30.4.1801; ADM 1/ 470. St Vincent to Nelson 1.5.1801; St Vincent I p. 94
86 Hyde Parker to Nelson 9.4.1801; CRK/8
87 St Vincent to Lord Hawkesbury (Foreign Secretary) 4.5.1801; St Vincent I
   pp. 94–5
88 Hobart to Admiralty 5.5.1801; ADM 1/4187. Admiralty to Nelson 6.5.1801
   (Secret); Add. 34,918 f. 86
89 St Vincent to Duckworth (C.in.C. West Indies) 15.5.1801; St Vincent to
   Hawkesbury 21.5.1801; St Vincent I pp. 96–7
90 Nelson to Admiralty, Davison, St Vincent, Addington 5.5.1801; Nelson to
   Admiralty 7.5.1801; Nicolas IV pp. 352–9. Nelson to Troubridge 7.5.1801;
   Miscellany I pp. 432–3. *Cumloden Papers.*
91 Nelson to Emma 5.5.1801; Morrison II p. 144
92 Nelson to Admiralty 5.5.1801; ADM 1/ 4 71 and 74
93 Nelson to Vansittart 12.5.1801; Nicolas IV p. 368
94 Nelson to St Vincent 16.5.1801; Nicolas IV p. 370. *Cumloden Papers.*
95 Garlike to Nelson 15.5.1801; FO 95/217
96 Nelson to St Vincent 16.5.1801; Nelson to Davison 12.5.1801; quote Nicolas
   IV pp. 370 and 373.
97 Nelson to Admiralty 17.5.1801; Nicolas IV 375.
98 St Vincent Standing Orders 25.4.1801; Add. 34,918 f. 52.
99 Nelson to Admiralty 22.5.1801; ADM 1/4 81–3 and 86. are typical.
100 Nelson to Lord Carysfort (Minister at Berlin) 19.5.1801; Nicolas IV p. 375.
   Dr Baird to Sick and Hurt Board 10.5.1801; Baird to Nelson 30.5.1801; Add.
   34,918 f59 and 65.
101 Nelson to Admiralty 23.5.1801; Nicolas IV p. 383
102 Nelson to Admiralty 23.5.1801; ADM 1/4 90, enclosing Fremantle to
   Nelson 23.5.1801; CRK/5
103 Nelson to St Vincent 22.5.1801; Nicolas IV pp. 379–80
104 Lambert, *The Crimean War: British Grand Strategy against Russia,*
   1853–1856, p. 74
105 Nelson to St Helen's 22.5.1801; Nelson to Admiralty 23.5.1801; Nicolas IV

pp. 380–3

106 Garlike to Hawkesbury (Secret) 24.5.1801; FO 95/217
107 Nelson to Count Pahlen 26.5.1801; Nicolas IV pp. 393–4
108 St Vincent to King 24.5.1801; Aspinall, *George III* pp. 542–3
109 St Vincent to King 30.5.1801; Aspinall, *George III* p. 545
110 St Vincent to Addington and Nelson 31.5.1801; St Vincent I pp. 100–1
111 Nepean to Nelson (Personal) 31.5.1801; Add. 34,918 f. 67
112 Hood to Nelson 1.6.1801: CRK/6
113 Admiralty to Nelson 31.5.1801; Add. 34,934 f. 98
114 Admiralty to Nelson 8.6.1801; Add 34,934 f. 112
115 Hobart to Admiralty 12.6.1801 (Secret); ADM 1/4187
116 Nelson to Admiralty St Vincent 12.6.1801; Nicolas IV pp. 411–12
117 Nelson to Ball 4.6.1801; Nicolas IV pp. 400–1
118 St Vincent to Nelson 3.6.1801; St Vincent 1 p. 103
119 Nelson to Admiralty 13.6.1801; Nicolas IV pp. 413–14. Nelson to Davison
      15.6.1801; Nicolas IV p. 416
120 St Helen's Hawkesbury 18.6.1801; FO 95/217.
121 Totty to Nelson 16.6.1801; CRK/12
122 Nelson to Admiralty 12.6.1801; ADM 1/4 108. Admiralty to Nelson
      26.6.1801; Add. 34, 934 f. 119
123 Admiral Pole's Journal 21.6.1801; ADM 50/43
124 Pole to Admiralty 26.6.1801; ADM 1/4 123. Pole Journal 26.6.1801; ADM
      50/43
125 Pole to Nelson 30.7.1801; CRK/10
126 Pole to Admiralty 9.8.1801; and endorsement of 10.9.1801; ADM 1/ 4
127 Nelson to Nepean 29.6.1801; ADM /4 127

CHAPTER XII

1 Gash, *Lord Liverpool*, pp. 41–2
2 Monaque, 'Latouche Tréville; the Admiral who defied Nelson'
3 St Vincent to King George III 24.7.1801; George III p. 582. Admiralty to
   Nelson 26.7.1801; Morrison II pp. 157–9. St Vincent to Admiral Lutwidge
   24.7.1801; St Vincent pp. 125–6. Lutwidge had been Nelson's captain on the
   Arctic expedition. Nelson Memorandum 25.7.1801; Nicolas IV pp. 425–8
4 White, 'The Public Oder Book', pp. 253–5 gives a full list.
5 Nelson to Admiralty 27 and 28.7.1801; to St Vincent 28.7.1801; Nicolas IV
   pp. 429–32
6 It had opened in 1796. Wilson, *The Old Telegraphs*, pp. 17–20
7 St Vincent to Nelson 29.7.1801; CRK/11. also St Vincent 1 pp. 127–8
8 Nelson to Admiralty 30.7.1801; to St Vincent 30 and 31.7.1801; Nicolas IV
   pp. 432–3. St Vincent to Nelson 31.7.1801; CRK/11 and St Vincent I pp.
   128–9
9 Nelson to Addington 31.7.1801; Nicolas IV p. 434
10 Ware, C. *The Bomb Vessel: Shore Bombardment in the Age of Sail*, pp. 54–8
11 Nelson to St Vincent 2.8.1801; Nicolas IV p. 434. St Vincent to Nelson

3.8.1801; CRK/11

12 Nelson to Lutwidge and Admiralty 3.8.1801; Nicolas IV pp. 435–8
13 Nelson to Admiralty 4.8.1801; to Addington (quote) 4.8.1801; Nicolas IV pp. 438–41
14 Nelson to Clarence 5.8.1801; Nicolas IV p. 441
15 Nelson to Admiralty; to Captains of the Sea Fencibles 6.8.1801; Nicolas IV pp. 443–5
16 Nelson to St Vincent 6.8.1801; Nicolas IV p. 445
17 St Vincent to Nelson 7 and 8.8.1801; St Vincent I pp. 131–3
18 Nelson to St Vincent 7.8.1801 and Nelson to Admiralty 10.8.1801; Nicolas IV pp. 446–7 and 451–2
19 Nelson to St Vincent 10.8.1801; Nicolas IV p. 449
20 Nelson to Emma 11.8.1801; Nicolas IV pp. 454–5
21 Nelson to Emma 4.8.1801; Morrison II p. 160
22 Wareham pp. 145–7.
23 Owen to Nelson 9.8.1801; Add. 34,918 ff. 123 and 125.
24 Nelson to Bedford 10.8.1801; Nicolas IV pp. 452–3
25 Troubridge to Nelson 13.8.1801; CRK/13
26 St Vincent to Nelson 10, 11 and 12.8.1801; St Vincent I pp. 133–6
27 Nelson to St Vincent 13.8.1801; Nicolas IV pp. 456–7
28 Nelson to Davison 13.8.1801; Nicolas IV pp. 458–9
29 Collingwood to Edward Collingwood 13.8.1801; Owen ed. *Miscellany VI* pp. 173–5
30 St Vincent to Nelson 14.8.1801; St Vincent I pp. 135–6
31 Nelson to Admiralty ; to St Vincent 16.8.1801; Nicolas IV pp. 464–7
32 St Vincent to King 17.8.1801; George III p. 594
33 Addington to Nelson 17.8.1801; CRK/1, St Vincent to Nelson 17.8.1801; St Vincent I pp. 136–7. Nelson to Squadron Captains 18.8.1801; Nicolas IV pp. 471–2.
34 Nelson to Emma 18.8.1801; Nicolas IV pp. 473–4
35 Hood to Cornwallis 31.8.1801; *Manuscripts of Cornwallis* p. 395
36 St Vincent to Nelson 18.8.1801; St Vincent I pp. 137–8. Addington to Nelson 19.8.1801; CRK/1
37 Nelson to Addington 21.8.1801; Nicolas IV pp. 474–6
38 Nelson to Admiralty 23.8.1801; Nicolas IVB pp. 476–7
39 Troubridge to Nelson 13.8.1801; CRK/13. Owen to Nelson 21.8.1801; CRK/9. Owen to Nelson 22.8.1801; Add. 34,918 f. 189. Nelson to Owen 23.8.1801; Nicolas IV p. 476.
40 Nelson to Lutwidge and St Vincent 24.8.1801. Nelson to Admiralty 25.8.1801; Nicolas IV pp. 477–80.
41 Nelson to Stewart 26.8.1801; *Cumloden Papers.*
42 St Vincent to Nelson 19 and 26.8.1801; St Vincent I pp. 138–40. Troubridge to Nelson 28.8.1801; CRK/13
43 Nelson to Davison 31.8.1801; Nicolas IV pp. 481–2
44 St Vincent to Countess of Malmesbury 20.8.1801; St Vincent I p. 209
45 Nepean to Nelson 28.8.1801; Add. 34,918 f. 200

46 Haslewood to Nelson 25.8., 31.8. and 2.9.1801; Add. 34,918 ff. 193, 210, 215

47 Nelson to Davison 18.12.1801; Nicolas IV p. 556

48 Troubridge to Nelson 20.9.1801; CRK/13

49 Troubridge to Nelson 9 and 12.9.1801; CRK/13

50 Nelson to Hercules Ross 12.9.1801; Nicolas IV pp. 487–8

51 Nelson to Davison 14.9.1801; Nicolas IV p. 489

52 Nelson to Admiralty 14.9.1801; to St Vincent 15.9.1801; Nicolas p. 487–90

53 St Vincent to Nelson 14, 21 and 22.9.1801; St Vincent I pp. 144–5

54 Nelson to Stewart 23.9.1801; *Cumloden Papers*

55 W. Owen to Nelson 26.9.1801; CRK/9. Nelson to Owen 1.10.1801; Nelson to Admiralty 3.10.1801; Nicolas IV pp. 500–2. Burrows, E. H. *Captain Owen of the African Survey, 1774–1857*, Rotterdam, 1979, pp. 31–2.

56 Nelson to St Vincent 29.9.1801; Nicolas IV pp. 499–500

57 St Vincent to Nelson 2 and 5. 10.1801; St Vincent I p. 146

58 Nelson to Lutwidge 3.10.1801; Nicolas IV pp. 503–4

59 Nelson to Admiralty 3 and 4.10.1801; Nicolas IV pp. 502–5

60 Nelson to St Vincent 4?.10.1801; Nicolas IV p. 505. George III to Addington 20.9.1801; Aspinall, *George III* p. 613.

61 Addington to Nelson 8.10.1801; Nelson to Davison 9.10.1801, to Addington and St Vincent 10.10.1801; Nicolas pp. 506–8. Nelson to Lutwidge 14.10.1801; Nicolas IV p. 511

62 Nelson to Admiralty 14 and 15.10.1801; Nicolas IV p. 511

63 St Vincent to Nelson 20 and 24.10.1801; St Vincent I pp. 147–8

64 Addington to Nelson 26.10.1801; Add. 34,918 f. 290.

65 Nicolas IV pp. 520–1

66 Nelson to St Vincent 29.9.1801; Nicolas IV pp. 499–500. Nelson to Lord Mayor, Addington, St Vincent 20.11.1801; Nicolas IV pp. 524–7

67 Nelson to St Vincent 21.11.1801; Nicolas IV p. 527

68 St Vincent to Addington 3.1.1802; ST VINCENT I pp. 105

69 Addington to Nelson 27.11.1801; Nicolas IV pp. 525–6

70 *Cumloden Papers*. Admiral of the Fleet Sir Graham Eden Hamond (1779–1862) commanded the *Blanche* in the battle. Hamond Papers; William R. Perkins Library, Duke University.

71 Nelson to Sir Brooke Boothby 1.5.1802; Nicolas IV pp. 12–13

72 Baird to Nelson 27.1.1803; CRK/1

73 Nelson to Suckling 15.4.1802; Nelson to Mrs Bolton 11.6 1802; Nicolas V pp. 10 and 15

74 Ball to Emma 30.4.1802; Morrison II p. 187

75 Diary entry 4.1.1810 at Bath; Bickley, F. ed. *The Diaries of Sylvester Douglas, Lord Glenbervie*, London, 1928, II, p. 50.

76 Guerin, *Horatia Nelson*, pp. 24–58 is very hostile and a powerful corrective to the usual gushing romantic nonsense.

77 Nelson to McArthur 23 and 28.4.1802; 7.5.1802; 11.6.1802; Nicolas V pp. 11–15.

78 Nelson to St Vincent 28.1.1803; endorsed by Nelson 25.2.1803; Nicolas V

pp. 40–1. Nelson gave up some of his own share to ensure that Stewart took the same proportion as a junior flag officer. Clearly he had impressed Nelson as much as Nelson had impressed him.

79 e.g. over Malta see; Ziegler, *Addington* pp. 120, 124. Nelson to Boothby 1.5.1802; Nicolas V pp. 12–13. Nelson to Addington 17.7.1802; Nicolas VII p. ccxii.

80 Nelson to Addington 31.1.1802; Nicolas V p. 3

81 Addington to Nelson 19.2.1802 and 30.5.1802; Morrison II pp. 185–6. and CRK/1. See Ziegler at pp. 139–40 for Addington's Episcopal appointments.

82 Nelson to Addington 23.2.1802, 25.3.1802; Nicolas V pp. 6 and 8–9

83 Nelson to Addington 30.6.1804; Ziegler p. 226

84 Nelson to Troubridge 17.2.1802; Nicolas V p. 5

85 Nelson to Sutton 15.1. and 6.2.1802. Nicolas V p. 2

86 Nelson to St Vincent 16.6.1802; Nicolas V p. 16

87 Ziegler, p. 101

88 Nelson to Boothby 1.5.1802; Nicolas V pp. 12–13

89 Stewart to Nelson 10.10.1802; Morrison II pp. 198–9. Nelson to Stewart 12.10.1802; Cumloden Papers

90 Nelson to Davison 11 and 14.9.1802; Nicolas V pp. 29–31

91 Minto II p. 258

92 Nelson to Addington 4.12.1802, covering his Memorandum on Malta; Nicolas V pp. 36–7. Ziegler p. 182

93 Minto 23.2.1803; Minto II pp. 273–4

94 Nelson to Addington 8.3.1803; Nicolas V pp. 47–9. Curiously Vincent misdates this letter to 1802, pp. 472–4

95 Ziegler, *Addington* p. 184, citing the original note

96 Nelson to Addington 23.4.1803; to Rose 15.5.1803; Nicolas V pp. 59–60, 65

97 Nelson to Murray 22.3.1803; Nelson to St Vincent 24.3.1803; Nelson to Berry 26.3.1803; Nicolas V pp. 50–1

98 Glenbervie I p. 338. Farington II p. 20. The busts were modelled by Whig artist Mrs Damer. Foreman, *Georgiana*, p. 47.

99 Ziegler, *Addington* p. 184.

CHAPTER XIII

1 Nelson to Davison; to St Vincent 6.5.1803; Nicolas V p. 63

2 Admiralty to Bickerton 1.2.1803; ADM 2/1360

3 Admiralty to Bickerton 7.3.1803; ADM 2/1360

4 Admiralty to Bickerton 7.5.1803; ADM 2/1360

5 Ziegler, pp. 197–8

6 Admiralty to Nelson 18.5.1803 Secret; ADM 2/1360. The next Admiralty letter was sent on 9.11.1803

7 Nelson to St Vincent 22.5. to Admiralty and Cornwallis 23.5.1805; Nicolas V pp. 71–5. Cornwallis to Nelson 25.5.1803; CRK /2

8 Nelson to Emma 20.5.1803; Morrison II p. 210–1. 23.5.1803; Nicolas V p. 73

9 Scott to Emma 3.6.1803; Nelson to Emma 10.6.1803 Morrison II pp. 212–13. See Nelson to Emma 4.6.1805: Pettigrew II p. 473 and compare with Monmouth EL167 to see how far Pettigrew removed the passion that distinguished this correspondence from that with Fanny.

10 Nelson to Acton 10.6.1803 Public and private letters; he also wrote on the same day to both the King and the Queen; Nicolas V pp. 81–5

11 Nelson to Acton 19.6.1803; Nicolas V p. 92

12 Ferdinand to Nelson 20.6.1803; CRK/3

13 Nelson to Jackson 10.6.1803; to Drummond c.11.6.1803; Nicoals V pp. 85–7

14 Nelson to Addington 4.6.1803; Nicolas V p. 79

15 Nelson to Hardy and Admiralty 1.7.1803; Nicolas V pp. 112–14

16 Lord Hobart to Nelson 23.8.1803; Nicolas V pp. 220–1

17 Nelson to Davison 27.7.1803; Nicolas V pp. 143–4

18 Nelson to St Vincent; to Moira 2.7.1803; Nicoals V pp. 114–15

19 Nelson to St Vincent 4.7.1803; Nicolas V pp. 116–17

20 Nelson to Captain Richardson HMS *Juno* 26.6.1803; Nicolas V p. 103

21 Nelson to Elliot; to Acton 25.6.1803; there were public and private letters to both men. Nicolas V pp. 95–101

22 Nelson to Villettes 26.6.1803; Nicolas V pp. 104–5

23 Nelson to Clarence 6 and 17.4.1803; Nicolas V pp. 57–9

24 Troubridge to Nelson 27.6.1803; CRK/13

25 Melville to Nelson various; CRK/8. Nelson to Henry Duncan 4.10.1804; Nicolas VI p. 216. Lord Duncan to Nelson 18.7.1803; CRK/4

26 St Vincent to Nelson various 1803–04; CRK/11. Admiral Sir Peter Parker to Nelson 20.8.1803; CRK/10

27 Layman to Nelson 27.6.1803; Add. 34,919 f.173

28 James Duff at Cadiz, Price at Cartagena and Hunter at Madrid all provided vital evidence while Spain remained neutral; CRK/4 /7 /10

29 Duff to Nelson 8.10.1803; CRK/7

30 Foresti to Nelson 2.7.1803; CRK/5. Hawkesbury to Nelson 8.7.1803; CRK/6

31 Noble to Nelson 4.7.1803; CRK/9

32 Wellesley to Nelson 9.11.1803; CRK/13

33 List of books June 1803; Add. 34,919 f. 180

34 Nelson to Davison 24.8.1803; Nicolas V p. 175.

35 Davison to Nelson various; CRK/2

36 Nelson to Emma 5 and 8.7.1803; Nicolas V pp. 117–20

37 Nelson to St Vincent 8 and 13 7.1803; to Villettes 9.7.1803; Nicolas V pp. 122–36

38 Nelson to Elliot 11.7.1803; Nicolas V pp. 129–30

39 Nelson to St Vincent 5.10.1803; Nicolas V p. 223

40 Nicolas prints a sample section for 25–31.10.1803; Nicolas V p. 273

41 Mahan, *Nelson*, 2nd edn. pp. 572–3

42 Nelson to Ball 16.9.1803; Nicolas V pp. 203–5

43 Nelson to Addington 16.7.1803; to St Vincent 21.7.1803; Nicolas V pp. 136–8

44 Drummond to Nelson 22.7.1803; CRK/4
45 This was his 'Guardian Angel', painted in Dresden by Schmitt for Hugh Elliot, then British Minister at the Saxon Court..
46 Gatty, *Recollections of the Life of the Reverend A J Scott DD Lord Nelson's Chaplain.*provides first-hand testimony, although more interested in the picturesque, and doubtless somewhat censored by contemporary views on the role of intelligence gathering, and Nelson's private affairs. Reprinted as *Nelson's Spy?* in 2003, a title reflecting modern taste.
47 Nelson to Ryves 2.11.1803; to Ball 7.11.1803; Nicolas V pp. 277-8 and 282-4. See Add. 34,919 for a range of Nelson's chart and intelligence papers, including Ryves' report.
48 Nelson to Admiralty 12.7.1803; Nicolas V pp. 133-4
49 Baird to Nelson 30.101803; CRK/1
50 Nelson to Moseley 11.3.1804; Nicolas V pp. 437-8
51 Crimmin, 'Letters and Documents relating to the Service of Nelson's Ships'
52 Nelson to Minto 11.1.1804; Nicolas V pp. 365-7
53 Mackesy, *War in the Mediterranean* p. 62
54 Nelson to Cornwallis 31.7.1803; *Manuscripts of Cornwallis* p. 399
55 Admiralty to Nelson 13.1.1804 (Secret); ADM 2/1362
56 Nelson memo. 28.4.1804 and Sailing Direction for Leghorn nd. Nicolas V pp. 519-21
57 Nelson to Sir William Bolton 3.5.1804; Nicolas VI pp. 2-3 is typical of his mastery of local detail.
58 Nelson Disposition of the Fleet 21.6.1804; Nicolas VI pp. 79-81
59 Nelson to Lord Melville 10.3.1805; Nicolas VI p. 353. This is the letter that inspired Nicolas to compile his edition. It concerns the unfortunate Captain Layman, who had lost two ships in quick succession, and been censured for the second loss, much to Nelson's dismay, as Layman was a very successful intelligence officer.
60 Nelson to Emma 2.10.1804; Morrison II pp. 240-1
61 Nelson to Berry 8.8.1804; Nicolas VI p. 146
62 Captain Capel to Nelson 20.11.1804; CRK/3
63 Nelson to Emma 12.8.1804; – Melville and to Elliot 15.8.1804; Nicolas VI pp. 152-7
64 Nelson to Elliot 7.10.1804; Nicolas VI pp. 221-2
65 Nelson to Ball 3.8.1804; Nicolas VI p. 131
66 Nelson to General Villettes (Malta); Nicolas VI pp. 189-90
67 Nelson to Ball 6.9.1804; Nicolas VI pp. 191-3
68 Nelson to Emma 23.11.1804; Nicolas VI p. 278
69 Nelson to Ball 15.12.1804 Nicolas VI pp. 285-6
70 Nelson to Davison 29.12.1804; Nicolas VI pp. 306-7
71 Orde to Admiralty 27.3.1805; Nicolas VI pp. 383-4. Orde was never again employed.
72 Hunter to Nelson 1804; CRK/7. Trigge to Nelson 27.10.1804; CRK/12
73 Admiralty to Orde 15.11.1804; ADM 2 /1362
74 Nelson to Admiralty 29.1.1805, 18.2.1805. Nelson to Ball 11.2.1805;

Nicolas VI pp. 332–4
75 Nelson to Admiralty 13.3.1705; Nicolas VI p. 357
76 Collingwood to Nelson 13.12.1804; CRK/3
77 Nelson to Collingwood 13.3.1805; Nicolas VI p. 35
78 Nelson to Lord Moira n.d.; Nicolas VI p. 310
79 Gillespie to Nelson 12.4.1805; CRK/6
80 Nelson to Admiral Lord Radstock 1.4.1805; Nicolas VI pp. 391–2

CHAPTER XIV

1 Desbrière, *Projets et tentatives de débarquement aux Iles Britanniques 1792–1805*, 5 vols. Paris 1900–2
2 Nelson to Emma 4.4.1805; Morrison II p. 256
3 Nelson to Ball 6.4.1805; Nicolas VI p. 399
4 This chapter is largely based on Julian Corbett's brilliant survey, *The Campaign of Trafalgar*, a text developed through his teaching on the Naval War Course. Aside from a few errors in footnotes, and the occasional heavy hint to his high-ranking pupils that they would face similar problems, and might profit from the example, it remains a compelling work.
5 The official correspondence for this period is very full, and reveals a clear and effective direction. ADM 1/4206; 2/149–150; 2/1363 (Secret) 2/923; 3/154 and War Office WO 1/282; 1/711
6 Nelson to Davison 7.5.1805; Nicolas VI p. 427
7 Nelson to Emma 16.5.1805; Nicolas VI pp. 441–2. Pettigrew prints other letters but badly edited. The originals are at Monmouth.
8 Waters, *The Art of Navigation in England in Elizabethan and Early Stuart Times*, pp. 262–3. Hakluyt's *Principal Navigations* was a compendium of Tudor and early Stuart sea knowledge. It must be presumed that Nelson owned a copy, and consulted it.
9 Nelson to Davison 12.6.1805; Nicolas VI pp. 453–4
10 Matra (Consul at Tetuan) to Nelson 17.7.1805; CRK/9. Matra had been to the Pacific with Cook.
11 Nelson to Davison 24.7.1805; Nicolas VI p. 494
12 Villeneuve to Decrès 13.8.1805; Corbett p. 257
13 Cornwallis to Nelson 1.8.1805; CRK/2 A few weeks later Cornwallis would bitterly regret that he had not called Nelson over, so that they could meet one last time.
14 Fremantle to Nelson 15.8.1805; CRK/6
15 Nelson to Rear Admiral Louis 15.8.1805; Nelson to Fremantle 16.8.1805; Nicolas VII pp. 4–5
16 Nelson to Admiralty 18.8.1805; Nicolas VII pp. 8–9. Rose to Nelson 20.8.1805; Add. 34,930 f. 167.
17 Clarence to Keats 22.8.1805; Keats MSS NMM KEA/3; Hood to Nelson 22.8.1805; Keats to Nelson 23.8.1805; Add. 34,930 ff.187–90
18 Nelson to Keats 24.8.1805; Nicolas VII pp. 15–16
19 Hood to Nelson 26.8.1805; Add. 34,930 f. 250

20 Rose to Nelson 26.8.1805; Add. 34,930 f. 251. Nelson to Sir Richard Neave, Chair of the West India Committee 27.8.1805; Nicolas VII pp. 17–18
21 Exeter to Nelson 25.8.1805; Add. 34,930 f. 235.
22 Minto II p. 368
23 Ehrman III pp. 789–90.
24 Barham to Pitt and enclosure 4.9.1805; Instructions for Lord Nelson 5.9.1805; Laughton ed. *The Barham Papers III*. London, Navy Records Society 1910 pp. 312–15.
25 Minto II p. 369
26 Admiralty to Collingwood 4.9.1805; ADM 1/1363. Hardy to Nelson 3.9.1805; Add,. 34,931 f30.
27 Marsden and McArthur 6.9.1805. Bligh and Saumarez 10.9.1806; Lord Mulgrave 12.9.1805. Add. 34,931 ff. 111–80. Dalrymple 31.8.1805 Add.34,930 f319.
28 Nelson to Davison 6.9.1805; to Collingwood 7.9.1805; Nicolas VII pp. 30–2
29 Lady Bessborough to Lord Granville Leveson Gower 12 & 13.9.1805: Countess Granville ed. *Lord Granville Leveson Gower, First Lord Granville: Private Correspondence 1781–1821*. London 1916 Vol. II pp.112-4. Lady Bessborough was Gower's mistress, and had his child.
30 Nelson to Emma 1.10.1805; Morrison II p. 267. He invited the young man to dine with him.
31 Sidmouth to Nelson 10.9.1805; Add. 34,931 f. 125
32 Ziegler, *Addington*, pp. 244–5.
33 Stanhope, *Life of Pitt*, IV p. 330.
34 John Wilson Croker Diary entry of 1.10.1834, minuting a conversation with Wellington on that day. Croker was a lifelong confidant of the Duke, and a key figure in the creation of the Nelson legend.
35 Col. McMahon to Nelson 11.9.1805; Morrison II p. 265

CHAPTER XV

1 Castlereagh to Nelson and Matra (Consul at Tangier) 14.9.1805; Add. 34,931 ff.192–3
2 Nelson to Matra 25.9.1805; Frost, A. *The Precarious Life of James Mario Matra*. Melbourne, 1995, pp. 137–8. .
3 Nelson to Emma 17.9.1805; Nicolas VII p. 40
4 See for example Nelson to Emma 20.9.1805; Morrison II p. 266
5 Collingwood to Admiralty 30.8.1805; Add. 34,930 f. 304.
6 Castlereagh to Nelson 27.10.1805; WO 1/282 f. 131.
7 Castlereagh to Nelson n.d. and Francis to Nelson 4.9.1805; Add. 34,930 f.247 and Add. 34,931 f. 689
8 Fremantle to Buckingham 30.9.1805; Buckingham, Duke of, *Courts and Cabinets of George III*, London, 1855, Vol. II, p. 446
9 Duff to Wife 1.10.1805; Nicolas VII p. 70
10 Edward Codrington *Orion* to Wife 4.9.1805; Bourchier, Lady *Memoir of Sir*

Edward Codrington, London, 1873, Vol. I, p. 47

11 Codrington 20.9.1805; Bourchier p. 49

12 Nelson to Emma 1.10.1805; Nicolas VII p. 60

13 Lempriere to Collingwood 24.9.1805; Bayntun to Nelson nd; Add. 34,931 ff. 207–8

14 Nelson to Acton 30.9.1805; Nicolas VII pp. 53–4

15 Young to Nelson nd. Add 34,931 f. 219

16 Nelson to Admiralty 2.10.1805; Nicolas VII pp. 62–4

17 Senhouse to Pellew 3.10.1805; Add. 34,931 f. 253

18 Blackwood to Nelson 10.10.1805; Add. 34,931 ff. 296–7
Nelson to Blackwood 14.10.1805; Nicolas VII pp. 121–2

19 Nelson to Elliot 9.10.1805; Monserrat MS. MON/III 54

20 Knight to Nelson 5.10.1805; Add.34,931 f. 266.

21 Nelson 10.10.1805; Nicolas VII 106

22 Nelson to Admiralty 10.10.1805; Nicolas VII pp. 98–9. Pocock, *Remember Nelson; The Life of Captain Sir William Hoste* for the career of this brilliant officer.

23 Blackwood to Nelson 15.10.1805; Add. 34,931 f330. This may the basis for the famous Nelson quote 'Here comes Berry, we are sure to have a battle now!' cited by Nicolas at VII p. 117.

24 Codrington 21.8.1805; Bourchier p. 46. Duff to Wife 10.10.1805; Nicolas VII p. 71

25 Admiralty to Nelson 21.9.1805; ADM 2/1363 (Secret) arrived 8.10.1805. Nelson to Admiralty 10.10.1805; Nicolas VII pp. 109–10

26 Corbett, *Trafalgar*, pp. 342–59. *Report of a Committee appointed by the Admiralty to consider the tactics employed at Trafalgar*, HMSO London. 1913.

27 Nelson Memorandum 9.10.1805; Nicolas VII 89–92, and Corbett pp. 447–9

28 Blackwood to Wife 23.10.1805; Nicolas VII p. 226

29 Nelson to Collingwood 9.10.1805; Nicolas VII p. 95

30 Nelson to Stewart 8.10.1805; *Cumloden Papers*

31 Blackwood to Nelson 19.10.1805; Nicolas VII pp. 130–1

32 Nelson to Collingwood 12.10.1805; Nicolas VII p. 115

33 Nelson to Emma 19 and 20.10.1805; Nelson to Horatia 19.10.1805; Nicolas VII pp. 132–3

34 Nelson Diary 21.10.1805; Nicolas VII p. 139

35 Both Blackwood, who knew him well, and Codrington, who did not, were struck by how profoundly the loss of his chief had affected the flag captain. They had missed, as have most others, the intense relationship between the two men, forged in war, and sustained through years spent working, living and relaxing together. He even cut up the one-armed admiral's meat. All great admirals needed a Hardy, an officer to provide the calm, efficient ship administration, exemplary seamanship and emotional support that relieved them of the daily routine, to concentrate on the business of command. When Nelson asked him why they got on so well Hardy explained that it was because he knew when to let Nelson take over as captain. J. Gore, *Nelson's Hardy and his Wife*, p. 18.

36 Blackwood to Harriet Blackwood 22.10.1805; Nicolas VII p. .225–7. Blackwood, like Codrington, considered that some of the ships at the rear of the line had not engaged at close range, as Nelson required, and were therefore derelict in their duty. Collingwood rejected such carping, after the loss of his friend, and the victory. I am indebted to Dr Michael Duffy for this observation.

37 Collingwood to Moutray 9.12.1805; Nicolas VII pp. 238–9. Collingwood to Cornwallis 26.10.1805; Cornwallis p. 412

38 Collingwood to Pasley 16.12.1805; Nicolas VII p. 241

CHAPTER XVI

1 Coleridge, S. T. *The Friend I*, pp. 574–5, from his wonderful essay on Alexander Ball. Holmes, R. *Coleridge, Darker Visions*, London, 1998, pp. 1–63 covers his period in Malta.

2 Barker, J. *Wordsworth: A Life*, pp. 337–40, 867. Published in 1807, the poem was composed between Trafalgar and the funeral. It was a Victorian favourite.

3 Pitt to Earl Nelson 9.11.1805; Stanhope, *Life of Pitt*, Vol. III, pp. 344–5

4 Guerin, *Horatia*, p. 298

5 Hawkesbury to King 10.11.1805; Aspinall, *George III* Vol. IV p. 364

6 Parissien, *George IV; The Grand Entertainment*, p. 27

7 Hawkesbury to Earl Nelson 12.12.1805; MON E218

8 Hood to Hawkesbury 6.1.1806; MON E387

9 Lady Bessborough to Granville Leveson Gower 9.1.1806; *Granville* II pp. 154–5

10 The King to London Corporation 21,11.1805; Prince of Wales to Davison 18.12.1805; Nicolas VII pp. 306–10

11 Sidmouth, 21.1.1806, at the opening of Parliament, House of Lords; Nicolas VII p. 312

12 Lady Londonderry to Castlereagh 15.11.1805; Nicolas VII p. 323

13 Greig, *Farington IV* p. 269–72

14 For Devis, West and the competition see Greig, *Farington IV* pp. 109n, 138, 150–9

15 Butlin, M. and Joll, E. *The Paintings of J. M. W. Turner*. Vol. I Text Yale 1977 p. 39

16 Wilton, *Painting and Poetry; Turner's Verse Book and his work of 1804–1812*, p. 48

17 Erdman, *Blake; Prophet Against Empire*, p 220.

18 Ibid. pp. 318–19

19 Ibid. p. 449.

20 Raine, *Blake and Tradition*, Vol. I p. 359; Raine, 'A New Mode of Printing' in Lucas, *William Blake*, 1998, p. 125.

21 Erdman, p. 449

22 Coleridge, *The Friend* pp. 551–2

23 Ibid. pp. 572–4

24 Earl Nelson to Col. MacMahan 13.2.1806; and reply of 15.2.1806; STW/8 NMM
25 Earl to Nelson Prince of Wales 16.2.1806; Earl Nelson Memorandum; Add. 34,992 ff. 105–8
26 McArthur to Earl Nelson 31.3.1806 and Earl Nelson to McArthur 4.4.1806; Add. 34,992 ff. 120–3.
27 Clarke to Earl Nelson 28.5.1806; Add. 34,992 f. 146
28 Clarke to Earl Nelson 5.1807 and nd; Add. 34,992 ff.174 and 280
29 *Morning Post* 3.9.1809. Cadell and Davies to McArthur 25.7.1809, and 17.12.1809; PHB/16. The publishers were later taken over by Messrs Longman.
30 Farington records that he was at work on this piece by March 1807. IV p. 100.
31 Cadell and Davies to McArthur 22.10.1812; PHB/16
32 McArthur to Cadell and Davies 11.1.1816
33 Storey, M. *Robert Southey: A Life*, pp. 210–21
34 'Lives of Nelson', *Quarterly Review*, February 1810, pp. 218–62., esp. pp. 220–4
35 Spencer Perceval (Prime Minister) to Charles Yorke (First Lord) 8.7.1811; YOY/14 NMM. Southey to Thomas Southey 28.8.1812; Curry, K. ed, *New Letters of Robert Southey I*, London, 1965, pp. 39–41
36 Fulford, T. 'Romanticising the Empire; The Naval Heroes of Southey, Coleridge, Austen and Marryat', pp. 171–4
37 Eastwood, D. 'Patriotism Personified; Robert Southey's *Life of Nelson* Reconsidered'
38 Southey to Mrs Southey 25.9.1813; Curry II pp. 74–5
39 But Emma did, and complained bitterly about his 'falsehoods' concerning Naples. Emma to James Perry 22.4.1814; Morrison II p. 369. In this she was telling the truth, although the other half of her letter about the newly published *Nelson Letters* is less honest.
40 Steffan and Pratt, *Byron's Don Juan; Volume II*, 1st canto, 4th verse, p. 23
41 MacCarthy, *Byron*, 2002, p. 505
42 MacCarthy, p. 158
43 Pocock, *Remember Nelson*, pp. 178–9
44 'Mad, Bad and Dangerous: The Cult of Lord Byron': exhibition at the National Portrait Gallery, January–February 2003
45 MacCarthy, p. 195
46 MacCarthy, pp. 85, 296, 349, 383
47 Bolger, W. and Share, B., *And Nelson on his Pillar, 1808–1966*.
48 Yarrington, A. *The Commemoration of the Hero; 1800–1864. Monuments to the British Victors of the Napoleonic Wars*, p. 131
49 Parker, H. *Herman Melville; A Biography Volume One 1819–1851*, p. 147. On a later visit Melville the celebrity saw many more sights – the gallery, paintings and preserved coat at Greenwich (p. 677), including the stump of the *Victory's* mast and the Nelson bust placed at Windsor Castle by William IV – and he even passed by the *Victory* (p. 687). In his wanderings around

London he must have seen the column and the sarcophagus in St. Paul's, reinforcing a heightened sense of meaning. Nelson occupied a prominent place in his imagination.

50 *The Norfolk Pillar.*
51 Captain Alexander Milne to Admiralty 16.9.1838; Milne Papers NMM. MLN/101/12. I am indebted to Professor John Beeler for this reference.
52 Ramage and Ramage, *Roman Art; Romulus to Constantine*, pp. 88–90
53 *The Mirror* 6.7.1839; Add. 38,678. Papers of E. H. Baily, who sculpted the statue
54 Salmon, 'The Impact of the Archaeology of Rome on British Architects and their Work *c.*1750–1840', esp. pp. 230–5
55 Crook and Port, *The King's Works VI* 1973, pp. 491–4
56 Taine, H. *Notes on England*, p. 9
57 Nicolas I, p. v
58 Ibid. p. xvii
59 Nicolas to Hood 29.8.184; HOO/29 NMM This file contains the Nicolas–Hood and McArthur correspondence.
60 Nicolas to Hood 10.5.1844; HOO/29. Nicolas Colonel Davison 17.12.1844; Eg. 2241 f. 5 makes the same point
61 Nicolas to Josiah French 12.6.1844; PHB/P/22
62 Storey, p. 323
63 Fenwick, *HMS Victory*, p. 346
64 Ibid. p. 348.
65 Weston, N. *Daniel Maclise: Irish Artist in Victorian London*. Dublin, 2001
66 *The Spectacular Career of Clarkson Stanfield 1793–1867: Seaman, Scene Painter, Royal Academician* [Stanfield] pp. 108–111, 17–18
67 Ibid. pp. 163–4
68 Edgerton, J. *Making and Meaning; Turner, The Fighting Temeraire*, p. 77
69 Stanfield, p. 20.
70 Russett, A. *George Chambers, 1803–1840*, pp. 125–7
71 Ibid. p. 126
72 Hardy had given the coat to Emma; she left it with Alderman Smith, who loaned her far more money than she ever repaid. It was bought from his widow. George Anson (the Prince's Treasurer) to Nicolas 28.6.1845. Nicolas VII pp. 351. The blood was John Scott's.
73 Stanfield p. 20
74 Rosenberg, *Carlyle and the Burden of History*, p. vii
75 Carlyle, 'Nelson', at p. 77
76 Ibid. pp. 89–91
77 Pettigrew, *Memoirs of the Life of Vice Admiral Lord Viscount Nelson*, I pp. ix–xiii.
78 Hume to Aberdeen correspondence 1853–54. Add. 43,200 ff. 224–257.
79 Nelson to Rev Gaskin 4.1.1801; SPCK Archive Website page 1, accessed 12.12.2002. Nelson helped to distribute Society tracts to the fleet, a policy that continued for much of the nineteenth century. Clarke, *A History of the SPCK* , p. 171

80 *Life of Horatio, Lord Viscount Nelson* abridged form, Southey, London SPCK, 1837. Naples is covered on pp. 116–18. Comparison with Southey shows that this contentious passage has been reproduced verbatim. The sanctity and eulogy are on pp. 214–15.

81 The two large pictures are considered disturbing by Westminster security staff. Weston p. 251.

82 Weston, p. 243.

83 Boase, p. 215.

84 Ibid. p. 218.

85 Quoted in Weston at p. 249.

CHAPTER XVII

1 Tennyson to Stead, 14.3.1885; in Lang and Shannon, *The Letters of Alfred, Lord Tennyson Volume III*, pp. 311–12. For Tennyson and defence in the early 1850s see Thompson, N. 'Immortal Wellington: literary tributes to the hero', in Woolgar, ed., *Wellington Studies III*, p. 265

2 Mackenzie, p. 181

3 League Pamphlet cited in Marder, *The Anatomy of British Sea Power: Naval Policy 1880–1905*, p. 52.

4 See Marder, pp. 44–61

5 Lambert, 'HMS *Foudroyant* and *Trincomalee*'

6 Foote, E J. *Vindication of his Conduct when Captain of HMS Seahorse etc. 1799*, London, 1807

7 For this issue see Lambert, *The Foundations of Naval History; John Knox Laughton, the Royal Navy and the Historical Profession*, pp. 173–193.

8 Davis, J A. 'The Neapolitan Revolution: 1799 to 1999; Between History and Myth'; the quote is by Croce, p. 350.

9 Ibid.

10 Samuel Rawson Gardiner, Editor of the *English Historical Review* from 1890 to 1902, Laughton's predecessor as Professor of Modern History at King's College, a close personal friend and intellectual supporter. Gardiner's new 'Scientific' German historical professionalism provided an authoritative stamp of approval for Laughton's self-devised 'scientific' historical methodology.

11 Schurman, *Julian S. Corbett 1854–1922*.

12 Marder, A.J. *From the Dreadnought to Scapa Flow. Vol. I 1904–1914*, p. 348.

13 Gordon, *The Rules of the Game: Jutland and British Naval Command* addresses this question, and shows how Nelson's legacy was frittered away.

14 William Graham-Greene (Secretary to the Admiralty) to John Laughton 18.12.1904; Lambert, A. ed., *Letters and Papers of Professor Sir John Knox Laughton1830–1915*. Aldershot, 2002 p. 228.

15 Beresford, *Memoirs*, pp. 513–14

16 Beresford and Wilson, *Nelson and his Times*

17 Beresford, pp. iii–vi.

18 In 1815 the new HMS *Nelson* was the biggest battleship afloat, and although

she saw no active service, she remained on the list for four decades, latterly as a steam powered ship. Finally the old ship went out to Australia as a school ship, but the greatest name ever to grace a warship was not re-used until the late 1870s. Even then it was improperly applied to a second rate ironclad, which briefly served in Australian waters in the 1880s.

19 Mackay, R. *Fisher of Kilverstone*, pp. 3, 88, 140, 180, 287–9, 365, 385.
20 The records of these donations can be found in ADM 169/47–926. I am indebted to Dr Quintin Colville for this reference.
21 Fisher to Arthur Balfour (ex Prime Minister) 23.10.1910; Mackay p. 428
22 Fisher to Churchill 26.10.1911, 30.12.1911 and 31.7.1914; Churchill, *Churchill. Companion Volume II*, Part II pp. 1299, 1366 and Part III p. 1965. He repeated the point to opposition leader Balfour on 31.7.1914; Gilbert, M. *Churchill Vol. III*, p. 16.
23 Fisher to Arnold White 25.2.1913; in Marder, ed. *Fear God and Dreadnought: The Correspondence of Admiral of the Fleet Lord Fisher of Kilverstone. Vol. II 1904–1914*, pp. 483–4.
24 Bold, *Greenwich*, p. 204. Roberts, *Eminent Churchillians*, pp. 292–4
25 Ramsden, J. *Man of the Century: Winston Churchill and his Legend since 1945*, p. 123. It was no surprise to find Bryant's account of the Napoleonic wars made very obvious links with Churchill's wartime leadership.
26 Ramsden, pp. 57–78. Churchill to G M Young 10.9.1939; Gilbert ed. *The Churchill War Papers I: The Admiralty*, pp. 69–71. Young was one of the historians who drafted much of the book for Churchill.
27 Speech of 23.2.1940; Gilbert p. 794
28 ADM 239/262 quoted in Levy, *The Royal Navy's Home Fleet in World War II*, p. 26
29 John Colville 10.8.1940 re destroyers; Speech of 20.8.1940; Broadcast of 11.9.1940. Gilbert II (1994) pp. 644, 691, 802.
30 Presented at a Club dinner of 3.10.1940; Gilbert II p. 846
31 Richards, J. *Films and British Identity; From Dickens to Dad's Army*, p. 87
32 Churchill to Korda 15.6.194 and 1.7.194. Memoirs of Oliver Harvey and Hastings Ismay 2.8.1941; Gilbert III pp. 807, 882 1027–8.
33 Alexander; Foreword 1942 Mahan, *Life of Nelson*
34 Mace, *Trafalgar Square*
35 Admiral Leach's father was captain of the battleship HMS *Prince of Wales* in 1941, when she engaged the German *Bismarck*, took Churchill to meet President Roosevelt and was sunk off Singapore. He was lost with his ship.
36 Thatcher, *The Downing Street Years*, p. 179
37 Thatcher, p. 235
38 Colley, *Britons*, pp. 8–9 provides a clear indictment of such attitudes.
39 Colley, p. 9
40 Hood to Nelson 26.8.1805; Add. 34,930 f 250. Hood admits passing a letter to Lord Aylesbury.
41 The prominent position given to Nelson was sustained in the 1999 edition of the Doctrine. *British Maritime Doctrine BR 1806*. London HMSO 1999
42 Collingwood to Admiral Sir Peter Parker 1.11.1805 and Collingwood to

Edward Collingwood 25.10.1805; Owen, C. H. H. ed. 'Letters from Collingwood, 1794–1809' in Duffy, M. ed. *The Naval Miscellany VI.* Aldershot Navy Records Society 2003, pp. 182-5

APPENDIX

1 Williams, H. M. *Sketches of the State of Manners and Opinions in the French Republic*, 2 vols. London 1801. I p. 206 and 222–3. Nelson's own copy, suitably annotated, is Add. 34,391

2 Nelson to Alexander Stephens 10.2.1802; Nicolas V p. 43

3 Charnock, *Life of Nelson*, p. vii.

4 Ibid. pp. 184–6

5 Joshua White's *Professional Life of Lord Nelson*, 2nd revised edn. pp. 144–5, calls Ruffo's armistice 'infamous' but misunderstands Nelson's actions. A second book by the same publisher appeared in 1813, to profit from the sales of Southey. The author was named as 'Richard Clarke'.

6 Harrison, *The Life of Horatio, Lord Viscount Nelson of the Nile*

7 Harrison, II pp. 104–5. Harrison invented the nonsense that 'Tyrolese riflemen' were in the French fighting-tops; II p. 499

8 Harrison II p. 99

9 Foote, E. *Vindication* 2nd edn, London 1810. This edition is the most useful, as it reproduces his correspondence with Clarke.

10 Clarke to Foote 20.4.1807; Foote pp. 40–1

11 Clarke to Foote 31.1.1809; Foote p. 43

12 Clarke and McArthur I have used the late 1830 three-volume edition, which is at least portable. II pp. 162 and 187

13 Both Gutteridge and Russell make this point.

14 Southey, R. *Life of Nelson*, 1922 edition ed. G. Callendar, p. xxviii

15 Ibid, p. 183

16 *Quarterly Review* 1814, p. 73. The entry was unsigned, but Shine uncovers the authors, p. 41.

17 Ibid. p. 77.

18 James, W. *The Naval History of Great Britain*. 4, later 6 vols. London 1822–4, 2nd edn 1826. See the introduction to the 2002 edn. for a discussion of James, his methods and motives.

19 James II pp. 274–80

20 Brenton, E. P. *The Naval History of Great Britain*. 2 vols. London 1837 vol. I p. 484.

21 Collier to Nicolas 16.5.1845; Nicolas III p. 522

22 Harcourt, Rev. L V. *Diaries and Correspondence of the Rt. Hon. George Rose*, London, 1860, Vol. I, pp. 215–39

23 Alison, A., *History of Europe* in 19 volumes, London 1833–42 and 1852–59

24 Gooch, G. P., *History and Historians in the Nineteenth Century*, London, 1913, p. 435. Acton, H. *The Bourbons of Naples*, London, 1956 provides a critical assessment of Colletta's position and conduct.

25 Dumas, A. *Le Corricolo*, Paris, 1983 edn., Chapter X pp. 110–25 comprises

a detailed discussion of the capitulation of the forts and the trial and execution of Caracciolo, which is entirely hostile to Nelson and Ferdinand.

26 Hemmings, *The King of Romance: A Portrait of Alexandre Dumas*, pp. 189, 197–8

27 White, A. J., *The Political Life of Cavour 1848–1861*, Oxford, 1930, p. 442

28 Mahan *Life*, 2nd edn. 1899, p. v and Chapters XI and XII. Comparing those chapters to the 1st edn. reveals just how much extra work had been required.

29 Published by the Navy Records Society.

30 Vincent is a distinguished exception here, pp. 325–33. His defence is realistic, well founded and robust.

31 Southey is the chief culprit, although more because of the literary success of his text that the sophistication of his argument. For his treatment of these events, and an effective demonstration of his many errors of fact and interpretation, see Callender's 1922 edition, at p. 166. The entire chapter on Naples repays close reading.

32 Herbert Butterfield's short book of this title, published in 1931, examines the mindset of this school with elegance and insight.

33 Southey, Callender edn., pp. 165–6

Index